Proceedings

13th TRON Project International Symposium / TEPS '96

Proceedings

13th TRON Project International Symposium / TEPS '96

December 4 – 7, 1996

Tokyo, Japan

Sponsored by

TRON Association

In cooperation with

IEEE Computer Society

IEEE Computer Society Press
Los Alamitos, California

Washington • Brussels • Tokyo

IEEE Computer Society Press
10662 Los Vaqueros Circle
P.O. Box 3014
Los Alamitos, CA 90720-1264

IEEE Computer Society Press Order Number PR07658
IEEE Catalog Number 96TB100080
ISBN 0-8186-7658-2 (paper)
ISBN 0-8186-7660-4 (microfiche)
ISSN 1063-6749

Additional copies may be ordered from:

IEEE Computer Society Press
Customer Service Center
10662 Los Vaqueros Circle
P.O. Box 3014
Los Alamitos, CA 90720-1264
Tel: +1-714-821-8380
Fax: +1-714-821-4641
Email: cs.books@computer.org

IEEE Service Center
445 Hoes Lane
P.O. Box 1331
Piscataway, NJ 08855-1331
Tel: +1-908-981-1393
Fax: +1-908-981-9667

IEEE Computer Society
13, Avenue de l'Aquilon
B-1200 Brussels
BELGIUM
Tel: +32-2-770-2198
Fax: +32-2-770-8505

IEEE Computer Society
Ooshima Building
2-19-1 Minami-Aoyama
Minato-ku, Tokyo 107
JAPAN
Tel: +81-3-3408-3118
Fax: +81-3-3408-3553

Editorial production by Regina Spencer Sipple
Cover design by Dr. Ken Sakamura
Printed in the United States of America by KNI, Inc.

The Institute of Electrical and Electronics Engineers, Inc.

Table of Contents

Message from the Chair of the TRON Association

Half a century has passed since the birth of a computer. In the beginning, the computer was literally a tool only for calculation. But it has evolved to an advanced tool capable of communicating and transferring information in due course. All of its capacity is dedicated to "human interface" functioning as a new kind of media. These changes were made possible thanks to the innovations in highly advanced electronics technologies including semiconductors, telecommunications and visual image processing. In the coming 21st century, we will realize a society of more advanced information and telecommunication, in which we can communicate anytime with anyone in the world much more easily.

The TRON project which started in 1984 promotes a standard operating system, whose goal is to realize a system capable of real time, multi task function and Japanese language based processing. This year marks the twelfth year since the beginning of the project. I have a feeling that our era has now begun to recognize that the project's original goal to build an open architectural/media oriented computer which can be used by anybody represents the core of computer technology after all, which everyone in the world agrees on.

This year, the Japanese Ministry of International Trade and Industry (MITI) has announced a plan to encourage a creative software industry to grow in Japan. The plan includes subsidy to a selected project to give full support to the promotion of fundamental improvement in the Japanese software industry as well as to the contribution to the international society. Among many proposals submitted to MITI regarding this project, "Research and Development on basic software for computer-augmented environments" was selected. The main goal of this proposal is to strengthen basic technology which realizes computer-augmented environments, using ITRON which has been the industry's standard operating system.

This project will certainly expand the assets of basic technologies and applied technologies that have been developed and accumulated in the last 10 years. In accordance with the expansion, it will become necessary to develop more advanced hardware and software that can cope with the need of the people in the world under the new multimedia network environment.

How wonderful it would be if we can bring about a society, in the coming 21st century, where "individual" and "the world" can communicate by face-to-face contact through the network. For this to happen, the ideas and concepts built around the TRON Project shall be continuously sent out to the world to be improved, to be developed into an actual products and the products to build a new relation between people and machine, which is the true fruition of this project.

I sincerely hope that this 13th TRON International Symposium will provide an exciting occasion in which people from all over the world, who share the common goal, can extensively exchange ideas and concepts.

Takashi Kitaoka
Chairman, TRON Association
President, Mitsubishi Electric Corporation

General Chair's Message

Recently the concept of mobile computing has become popular as a result of improved telecommunications infrastructure. This concept includes networking using the Internet and intranet as well as an increase in the use of mobile phones and PHSs (Personal Handyphone Systems).

In the world of mobile computing, we are witnessing the advent of a high-level information driven society in daily-life generated primarily through multimedia. This phenomena is becoming more clear with advancements in high-speed visual picture processing systems and high-speed network and wireless communication technologies.

This is exactly the world of a "computer which can be used everywhere at anytime through an open-architecture function" – something we have been advocating for the last twelve years built around TRON (The Real-time Operating System Nucleus).

TRON Project consists of sub-projects such as TRON Chip, ITRON (Industrial TRON), BTRON (Business TRON), and CTRON (Communication and Central TRON). The phase of development of the main components has been completed in sub-subject fields to realize "computers which can be used everywhere at anytime." Already the results of this development phase have been applied to actual products. Especially, regarding ITRON, from the beginning, it has been developed as an installed operating system for small-size computers. Therefore, it has been utilized actively for such products as network computers, Internet terminals, and information related consumer electronic products.

Right now, further technological developments of sub-projects are being conducted to cope with the era of truly advanced multimedia processing. In this number 13th TRON International Symposium, I take great pride in reporting the results of the TRON Project as well as having an opportunity for useful discussions with participants.

TRON Project will further activate its actions as a source of the most advanced technological information as in the past.

Takao Nakano
General Chair of the 13th TRON Project International Symposium
Director & General Manager, Mitsubishi Electric Corporation

Program Chair's Message

Welcome to the 13th TRON Project Symposium! TRON gets its name from "The Real-time Operating System Nucleus," as a project starting out from the conviction that real-time computing will become increasingly important in the future information society. Naturally there are many other important technologies, among them networking, semiconductors, and human interface. The reason for our special emphasis on real-time computing stems from a decisive difference between the present and future, namely, that our living environment will become filled with computers in huge numbers, which will have to operate in real time in order to be functional. Moreover, those systems will have to be usable by people of all kinds.

The TRON Project has been carrying out researches continually now for well over a decade, concentrating on the fundamental requirements for computer systems in an age when thousands of items around us are computerized. We have been studying such issues as dialog between computers and human beings, communication among computers, real-time protection of the living environment, and ways of safeguarding individuals from all kinds of harm.

Research and development focused on the computerizing of living environments is carried out mainly in the ITRON (Industrial TRON) subproject. The ITRON specifications for real-time embedded operating systems have been so successful that this is now the most widely used OS architecture in the field of civilian embedded systems. These specifications have been implemented in telephones, air conditioners, facsimiles, videos, car navigation systems and a host of other products. Lately their application has spread to the area of low-cost Internet terminals, the so-called network computer, thanks to the small footprint and real-time capability of the ITRON OS design.

Computers in the future, when they have made deep inroads into society, will have to be readily usable by all, which for one thing means by people of all languages. The BTRON (Business TRON) subproject is proceeding with research and development for incorporating multilingual processing technologies in computers, making possible efficient handling of large-scale character sets like those used in Japan, China, Korea and other countries. Many other R&D projects are being carried out that are essential for the future computer society, such as Enableware technologies, giving active assistance to the disabled through computers. Recently these technologies have been implemented in computers and are getting the benefit of feedback from the real world.

Once again a large number of papers have been submitted for this year's TRON Project Symposium. The best of these, as selected by a distinguished panel of reviewers, will be featured in technical sessions. There will also be a session devoted to recent progress in compact, lightweight TRON Project technologies for use in everyday life. Another technical session will take up the Digital Museum, an application project of great interest in which computerization is being pursued to new levels. Tutorial sessions are planned as well. It is my wish that again this year we can further deepen our discussions of computer technologies required in the future society, together with the many people who are kindly giving presentations and the other participants.

Along with the TRON Project Symposium, I hope you will take the time to enjoy the TRONSHOW '96 exhibition of future computer technologies, and the Enableware Symposium TEPS '96.

Ken Sakamura
The Leader, TRON Project
The University of Tokyo

Organizing Committee for the Thirteenth TRON Project International Symposium

Steering Committee

Chair: Ken Sakamura (University of Tokyo)
Vice-Chair: James J. Farrell, III (Motorola Inc.)

Symposium Committee

General Chair
Takao Nakano (Mitsubishi Electric Corp.)

Program Chair
Ken Sakamura (University of Tokyo)

Finance Chair
Hiroaki Takada (University of Tokyo)

Publicity Chair
Shosuke Mori (Fujitsu Ltd.)

Registration Chair
Eiji Tange (Oki Electric Industry Co., Ltd.)

Local Arrangement Chair
Hisashi Ohara (Nippon Telegraph and Telephone Corp.)

Publications Chair
Akira Matsui (Personal Media Corp.)

Program Committee

Chair: Ken Sakamura (University of Tokyo)
James J. Farrell, III (Motorola Inc.)
Noboru Koshizuka (University of Tokyo)
Kenji Kudou (Fujitsu Devices Inc.)
Akira Matsui (Personal Media Corp.)
Henry Neugass (independent consultant)
Toshikazu Ohkubo (NTT Software Corp.)
Toru Shimizu (Mitsubishi Electric Corp.)
Haruki Taguchi (Hitachi, Ltd.)
Hiroaki Takada (University of Tokyo)
Kiichiro Tamaru (Toshiba Corp.)
Eiji Tange (Oki Electric Industry Co., Ltd.)
Hank Wang (Sun Microsystems, Inc.)
Tetsuo Wasano (Advanced Telecommunications Research Inst. International)

CALL FOR PAPERS

(tentative)

The 14th TRON Project International Symposium

December, 1997
Tokyo, Japan

sponsored by: TRON Association

We are pleased to announce the 14th TRON Project International Symposium to be held in December, 1997, in Tokyo. The symposium will feature presentation of papers, poster sessions, panel discussions, tutorial sessions, and an exhibition (TRONSHOW'97).

Submission of Papers

Papers may be submitted on any TRON-related field, and should present the results of new research or development. Topic areas include, but are not limited to, those listed below.

- ITRON
- BTRON
- CTRON
- TRON-specification VLSI CPU
- TRON Human Machine Interface
- MTRON and HFDS (Highly Functionally Distributed Systems)
- Computer Augmented Environments
- Enableware (Assistive Technology)
- Multilingual Processing
- TRON Multimedia
- TRON-concept Intelligent Building
- TRON-concept Intelligent House
- TRON Consumer Electronics

Papers presented at the symposium should be full papers, in English, of between 4,000 and 12,000 words. Those wishing to submit papers should first send an abstract to the program chairman. Send abstracts by June 2, along with the title (provisional), authors' full names, affiliations, contact addresses, and telephone/fax numbers. E-mail addresses should be included if available.

You should then submit four copies of the full paper by June 16 to the program chairman. Notice as to whether the paper has been accepted for presentation will be sent by August 4. For papers that are accepted for presentation, camera-ready copy for publication is to be submitted by September 8.

Poster Sessions

Proposals for poster sessions should be sent by August 25. Send four copies of short notes to the program chairman. Papers not accepted as full papers can be accepted as poster session materials.

Panel Discussions

Proposals for panel discussions will be accepted until June 16.

Exhibition (TRONSHOW'97)

We are planning an exhibition of TRON-related products and publications. Contact the program chairman for detailed information.

Program Chairman

All submissions or inquiries should be directed to the following address:

International Symposium Steering Committee
Ken Sakamura, Chairman
TRON Association
Katsuta Bldg. 5F, 3-39, Mita 1 chome, Minato-ku,
Tokyo 108, Japan
Tel: +81-3-3454-3191
Fax: +81-3-3454-3224

IMPORTANT DATES (tentative)

June 2, 1997 .... Abstracts deadline
June 16, 1997 .... Full paper submission deadline
August 4, 1997 .... Notification of acceptance
August 25, 1997 .... Poster sessions deadline
September 8, 1997 .... Camera-ready copies deadline

Keynote Address

K. Sakamura

TRON and the Digital Museum

Ken Sakamura
The University of Tokyo
Tokyo, JAPAN 113

1. Introduction

TRON is a project aimed at realizing "computing everywhere" environments.[1] In the process of carrying out this project, we have come to realize the wide range of issues involved in bringing such an environment into being.

In the early stages of the TRON Project we initiated fundamental projects for solving such technological issues, as well as application projects for proving the technologies.[2] In one of the application projects we built an intelligent house, using it as a testbed for many of our concepts by means of live-in and other experiments. In another project we have designed an intelligent building, planned for actual construction.[3]

Through these projects we have demonstrated "computing everywhere" technologies for living spaces and working spaces. There are some objectives of the "computing everywhere" environment, though, that cannot readily be proven in applications of these kinds. One is to resolve the issues that arise when such an environment is used by the general public, on a temporary basis, as in a public facility. A second objective is study the "computing everywhere" environment used for conveying information.

While the first is easy to understand, the second needs some explanation. That's because the function of conveying information is normally considered as one of the usual functions of a computer. A "computing everywhere" environment, however, results from technologies for making computers unseen presences. Conveying information in such an environment requires that we dismantle the information-conveying functions that a computer normally has and rebuild them. An intelligent house, for example, is an environment for convenient, comfortable living;[4] its purpose is not to convey information. An intelligent building, even though the use of "visible computers" such as personal computers and workstations is assumed for the purpose of doing work in an office, the predominating purpose of the building functions, other than a few signboards, is to enable people to work in convenience and comfort. So we are now starting up a new application program, in which we are putting together a Digital Museum as an application having both the aspect of a public institution and that of information conveyance.

This paper gives an overview of the Digital Museum, while also looking at the directions now being taken in TRON Project research and development. One aim of this development is to resolve the technology issues that have come to light in the process of building the Digital Museum.

2. What is the Digital Museum?

2.1. From a "collection" to "museum" to "Digital Museum"

As of this year the University of Tokyo's collection of research materials has been transformed into the Tokyo University Digital Museum.

Since its inception, the main function of this institution has been to collect, organize and preserve materials used in scientific research at the university. Yet few people were aware of the existence, let alone the worth of this huge collection, said to total some 6 million items. It was therefore decided that instead of simply collecting, organizing and preserving this rich content, it should actively be made available to the public for use. The result was the establishment of a comprehensive "university museum," unlike anything that has existed up to now. It is not a typical university museum used for exhibitions of special collections, nor is it a specialized museum for certain fields, belonging to a particular faculty or research laboratory. Rather, as a repository of all the materials used throughout the University of Tokyo, it is a facility that will be used for comprehensive research into methods of making these materials available to the public.

The idea of starting a Digital Museum application project comes out of the realization that the objectives of the Tokyo University Digital Museum mesh with the goals of the TRON Project, as well as its need for application projects in new application fields. The Digital Museum is so called because it makes extensive use of computer technologies to organize the materials and to

0-8186-7658-2/96 $05.00 © 1996 IEEE

offer them to the public.

The spread of new computer technologies such as multimedia and the Internet is giving new importance to "content." In that sense the huge Tokyo University collection is a veritable treasure-trove of content. By using the latest computer technologies to put that content into digital form, our aim is to open new horizons for the functions of preserving, organizing and making available the materials held by the museum.

2.2. Concepts of the Digital Museum

In creating the Digital Museum, a key concept is that of "openness of knowledge," which is why we are making it an "open museum." This openness has three aspects, as explained below. Each of them can be seen as an aim of conventional museums as well, yet there have been numerous obstacles preventing these aims from being fulfilled adequately. The great significance of the Digital Museum is that it is able to clear each of these obstacles by means of the latest computer technology.

2.2.1. Open cases

The reason museums lock up exhibits in glass cases is not for the benefit of visitors, obviously, but to protect the items. Ideally visitors should be able to touch the exhibits with their own hands, the better to understand them. In the case of solid items such as pottery, they should be able to feel the shape; and to take out ancient writings and leaf through them at their own pace. It would be nice to try playing ancient instruments or striking an old temple bell to hear its sound. And researchers have a natural desire to measure different parts of materials and approach them in various other ways, which are not possible if they are locked away inside glass cases.

Unfortunately, the use of materials must be restricted to prevent them from being damaged, since they are bound to deteriorate over time. From a security standpoint as well, valuable materials need to be protected from the hands of the public.

In the Digital Museum we aim to satisfy both needs, that of preserving materials and that of making them readily available, by taking advantage of digital technologies.

2.2.2. Open to everyone

A traditional museum offers many barriers to the disabled, and especially those with sight disabilities. Since a museum exists to "put exhibits on view," it has very little information to offer the visually impaired.

Even the explanations accompanying exhibits often consist only of written words on panels. The more detailed these explanations are, the more frustrating they are for visually handicapped persons. If the explanations are written only in Japanese, this represents a barrier for people from other countries. If a handicap restricts a person's ability to hear or speak, such persons are prevented from asking questions and getting answers about the materials they see.

Barriers like these that tend to create a distance between certain people and the materials in a museum can also be overcome by digital technology, in a Digital Museum.

2.2.3. Open with respect to space and time

The scientific materials held by the University of Tokyo, said to number 6 million items in all, would require an enormous amount of space to put on display all at once, making this impossible under the present circumstances. Special exhibits built around a common theme can be held for limited periods; but once that time is past, the materials are no longer available for viewing. Moreover, such an exhibit cannot be seen by people who do not come to that place. For people who for some reason or other cannot be in that place at that time, this is yet another barrier.

In the Digital Museum concept, the materials held by the University of Tokyo can be seen from anywhere, at any time. Even after a special exhibition has ended, the exhibited materials can still be seen. Questions can be asked from any place, at any time. What's more, comprehensive exhibits can be put on in certain fields, combining the resources of other museums as well. The Digital Museum even solves the problem of not being able to show the same item in more than one place, as when one item is a key exhibit for more than one exhibition.

The aims of the Digital Museum, then, are to employ digital technology and networking technology to overcome the constraints of time and place.

2.3. Functions of the Digital Museum

Next let us look at the functions with which the Digital Museum must be equipped in order to realize the above concepts.

2.3.1. Digital archiving

The Digital Museum is first of all a museum for digital archiving of materials. Conventional paper-based materials and photographs deteriorate over time, causing information to be lost. By recording them in digital format, however, the information can be preserved intact almost permanently.

Even things like pottery or human bones can be preserved by three-dimensional digitizing using lasers, or by various sensors, as sets of data in various forms. One

Figure1: Information terminals in The Digital Museum.

vase, for example, can be captured not only as data for reproducing its appearance, such as three-dimensional digitized data, CAD data, or surface texture data, but also as X-ray CT data, or as data providing a chemical analysis of its glaze material. Additional forms of data would include everything from an explanation of its design to an analysis of how it was made. The Digital Museum can store this entire set of data in a database, complete with information linking the different kinds of data to each other.

Putting all these minute details into electronic form reduces the need for access to the original material, allowing a full effort to be put into preserving its condition and minimizing damage to the material over the long run.

2.3.2. Multimedia presentations

The Digital Museum is not just for looking with the eyes. Going beyond the bounds of conventional museums that put items "on view," it offers the materials as multimedia, for a wide range of senses including hearing and touch.

In the Digital Museum, information terminals will be located in various places, and the exhibit will change according to the viewer's flow of interest (see Figure 1). The language of presentations will change to meet each person's needs. Explanations will make use of multimedia, from video to audio. Visitors to the museum will carry wireless portable terminals, enabling them to tap into a network from which they can access information anywhere in the museum.

In addition to sight and sound, equipment for creating replicas will be introduced to allow tactile exhibits. In this way, the solid objects stored in a digital archive can be "taken out" in the form of replicas. So long as the replicas can be reproduced easily, visitors will be able to touch them freely without worrying about damaging the materials (see Figure 2). It will even be possible to make special types of replicas by processing the original data so

Figure 2: a plastic replica of a ancient vase.

as to change the scale, or emphasize certain features, as an aid to understanding.

Computer-augmented environment technology[5] will be put to use in the Digital Museum as well. For example, sensors and microchips deployed in the museum and embedded in replicas will make it possible for the exhibits themselves to answer questions, or to provide detailed explanations of the part of an exhibit that is the focus of a viewer's attention, or to turn a replica into a simulation of the real thing. For example, tapping on a plastic replica of a pottery vase will cause it to respond with the same sound as the original.

These uses of multimedia in museum exhibits will not only help ordinary visitors understand the exhibits, but will open the door to people with various kinds of disabilities that up to now have prevented them from enjoying the benefits of museums.

2.3.3. Virtual museum

The Digital Museum, besides putting on actual exhibits in the halls of the museum, will make extensive use of exhibits by network.

Using the Internet, people all over the world will be able to search for items from among the accumulated materials, retrieving them in an instant. Networking will enable the museum resources to be accessed simultaneously from many different places.

Moreover, when materials are put in electronic form, various related information will be compiled in a relational multimedia database, so that not only audio and video, but even three-dimensional data can be obtained over the network. This will also make it possible to measure distances on solid objects via the network.

Virtual exhibits like these will substantially raise the value of using the museum's materials, and will encourage research making use of the materials.

The technological innovation and infrastructure provision described above will make it possible to offer the public valuable and useful materials over computer networks. This is highly significant also from the standpoint of contributing to the world at large.

2.4. The basic system underlying the Digital Museum

In order to implement a Digital Museum with the kinds of functions outlined above, the Tokyo University Digital Museum has designed a basic system with the features described below. The next step will be to develop and install on this system software of various kinds, and to add new I/O devices as needed.

At the heart of the basic system is a server with a disk array, having a capacity of 0.5 Terabytes. For digital archiving, the museum materials must be stored in a form matched to the type of data, such as Photo-CD images, audio, and so on. An ATM network in the museum is capable of sending data at 155 Mbps. An education-on-demand system sends large-capacity video data (MPEG1-compressed) over this network from the server to terminals throughout the building, at high speed. In the exhibit halls, visitors can search for information freely on terminals with plasma displays equipped with touch panels. The conference hall and muse hall will have presentation systems making effective use of large-screen displays and sound equipment as well as various computers. All of these system will be centrally controlled by an AV environment control system, using touch panels for simple control of the audio-visual equipment, computers, and even the room environment.

Other systems to be introduced in the museum include a 2,048 x 2,048-pixel full-color high-resolution video display screen, a high-resolution scanner capable of full-color input at 6,000 dpi, a replica-making system, and a system for making and displaying 3D video images. In such ways multimedia technologies will be used to provide highly realistic exhibits.

It will further be possible to link up with the University of Tokyo UTNet2 network system, and through it to send multimedia information all over the world, fulfilling the desire of the Tokyo University Digital Museum to make the university truly open, and becoming an important interface with the world.

3. Problems with using existing technologies

At first we considered using the Internet and other existing technologies in the Digital Museum, partly because of the time constraints involved in starting operation by January 1997. In a number of ways, however, we discovered that today's technologies are not up to the task. Here we talk about the problems with these technologies.

3.1. Character codes

3.1.1. Digital archiving of character-based data

A major function of the Digital Museum is the digital archiving of character-based materials. Let us consider for a moment what is involved here.

Many of the expository writings and other character-based information in the collection will be preserved as text data only. On the other hand ancient writings, for example, will be archived first of all by capturing each page as a picture. That's because these works are studied not just for their content but also for the form of writing, right down to the density of the brush strokes.

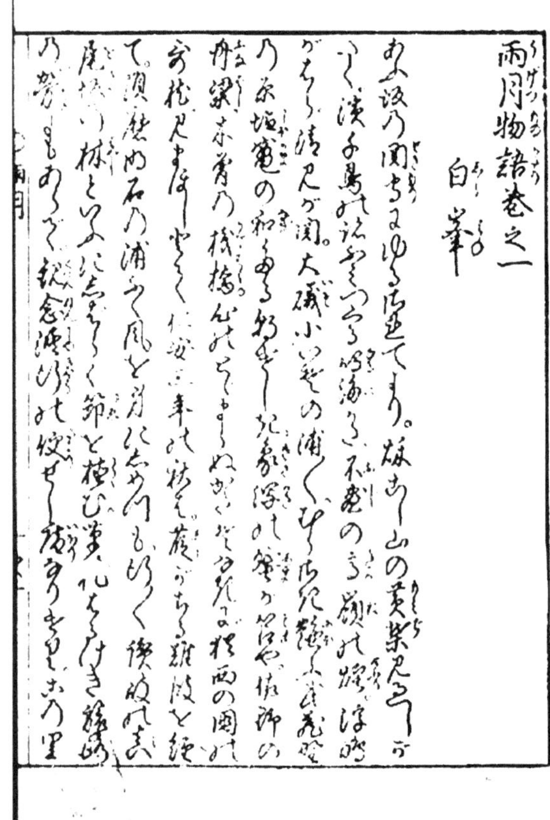

Figure 3: First page of "Ugetsu Monogatari".

Even so, it will be necessary to include text data along with the pages, preserving the data in a form that can readily be processed by computers. Otherwise it would be all but impossible to run a search for specific words and phrases in a collection of writings, for example, or to compile statistics on the author's use of language. Computer processing also allows the words to be read out audibly. And since graphical data typically takes several hundred times more bytes to store than text data, having documents only in graphical form would put an enormous load on network facilities in the case of virtual exhibits and the like. Text data is also easier to copy and quote in papers.

3.1.2. Characters that cannot be archived as text

The problem when archiving character-based documents as text files is whether all the characters are contained in the table of character codes used on the computer. The Japanese character codes widely used with computers today are all based on the JIS standards. These standards, however, are industrial standards created by the Ministry of International Trade and Industry (MITI), mainly with the purpose of rendering modern texts. Moreover, they were originally drawn up at a time when it was necessary to make the best use of limited resources, by narrowing down to the minimum required characters. Since that time computers have become able to handle a more abundant range of resources and nearly all computers support JIS Level 2, but even that amounts to only 6,355 characters. When we try to archive the first page of the literary work shown in Figure 3 with this set of characters, the result is as follows.

雨月物語巻之一
白峯

あふ坂の関守にゆるされてより。＝こし山の黄葉見過しがたく。濱千鳥の跡ふみつくる鳴海がた。不盡の高嶺の煙。浮嶋がはら。清見が関。大礒小いその浦＝。むらさき艶ふ武蔵野の原塩竈の和たる朝げしき。象＝の蜑が笘や。佐野の舟梁。木曽の桟橋。心のとゞまらぬかたぞなきに。猶西の国の哥枕見まほしとて。仁安三年の秋は。葭がちる難波を経て。須磨明石の浦ふく風を身にしめつも。行＝讃岐の真尾坂の林といふにしばらく＝を植む。草枕はるけき旅路の労にもあらで。観念修行の便せし庵なり
けり。この里…

The places shown as "＝" are characters that could not be displayed. Even though archiving is supposed to preserve literary works from the ravages of time, we end up with a moth-eaten document instead.

3.1.3. The need for a system with total encoding capability

We also have to think about what happens when a document from a digital archive is sent over a network to computers outside of Japan. If those computers do not support Japanese text, the characters will be interpreted based on character code tables for other languages and will be displayed as gibberish, as in the example in Figure 4.

âJåéï®åÍä™îVàÍ
îîıı

Ç†Ç"ç‚ÇÃä÷éÁÇ…Ç‰ÇÈÇ≥ÇÍÇƒÇÊÇËÅBÅ¨Ç±ÇµéRÇÃâ©óťå©âfl
ÇµÇ™ÇΩÇ≠ÅB‡_êÁíπÇÃê'Ç"Ç›Ç–Ç≠ÇÈñ–äCÇ™ÇΩÅBïs·∂ÇÃçÇó
‰ÇÃâåÅBïÇìàÇ™ÇÕÇÁÅBê¥å©Ç™ä÷ÅBëÂ‚Eè¨Ç¢Ç»ÇÃâYÅ¨ÅBÇ
fiÇÁÇ≥Ç´âêÇ"ïêë†ñÏÇÃå¥âñ‚}ÇÃòaÇΩÇÈí©Ç∞ÇµÇ´ÅBè¤Å¨ÇÃÂâÇ
™‚òÇ‚ÅBç≤ñÏÇÃèMó¿ÅBñÿë]ÇÃû†ã¥ÅBêSÇÃÇ∆ÅUÇ‹ÇÁÇÊ©ÇΩ
ÇºÇ»Ç´Ç…ÅBóPêºÇÃçëÇÃöFñçå©Ç‹ÇŸÇµÇ∆ÇƒÅBêmà¿éOîNÇÃè
HÇÕÅB‰Ç™ÇøÇÈìÔîgÇåoÇƒÅBê{ñÅñæêŒÇÃâYÇ"Ç≠ïóÇêgÇ
…ÇµÇflÇ–Ç‡ÅBçsÅ¨é]äÚÇÃê^î˜ç‚ÇÃóÇ∆Ç¢Ç"Ç…ÇµÇŒÇÁÇ≠Å¨Ç
êAÇfiÅBëêñçÇÕÇÈÇØÇ´óΣòHÇÃòJÇ…Ç‡Ç†ÇÁÇ≈ÅBäœîOèCçsÇ
Ãï÷ÇπÇµà¡Ç»ÇËÇØÇËÅBÇ±ÇÃó¢Åc

Figure 4: Example of miss interpreted Japanese character in the case of the literary work shown in Figure 3.

Similarly, a computer designed for Japanese may not be able to display properly an archived document in a different language.

3.1.4. Unicode or ISO10646-1

One solution that has been offered which is supposed to solve these problems is Unicode. This character code standard was created by Microsoft and other mainly U.S. computer makers with the aim of representing all the world's characters in one character code scheme, and it later became the base for the international standard known as ISO10646-1. As it turns out, however, Unicode suffers from the same problem as JIS, since it limits the number of characters that can be displayed for the sake of use with limited computer resources. For this reason it is not

Code in ISO10646-1	In Japanese	In Chinese
5742	坂	坂
6D44	海	海

Figure 5: Examples of transformed Japanese character in the case of the literary work shown in Figure 3.

adequate for digital archiving. In fact, many other problems have been pointed out with Unicode[6], which stem from the priority given to marketing needs. In other words, it was created out of a desire to develop for all the world's markets with just one character code set. In the case of the literary work shown in Figure 3, for example, which was not chosen particularly to find fault with Unicode, we immediate run into characters that are not supported in Unicode, such as "泻". And because Unicode adopts Han unification, lumping all Han-derived characters into one set, unique Japanese characters get transformed into their Chinese counterpoints as in Figure 5.

3.2. Use of Internet technologies

The Digital Museum is making use of Internet technologies to build an intranet consisting of a LAN in the museum, and the World Wide Web framework is used to offer the museum holdings to the rest of the world, through connection with UTNet2. The same protocols are thus used both for presentations in the museum and for provision on the Internet, allowing the same data to be used for both purposes. This is an advantage of the so-called intranet idea.

3.2.1. The need for a variety of data structures

For letting the world view the museum holdings, use of the Web is a natural choice in light of the ready availability of Web browser clients. The Web, however, which was designed mainly around text and computer display-level images, is not adequate for providing an environment in which people may conduct scholarly studies of the museum holdings, rather than simply reading explanations and looking at pictures.

For allowing objects to be viewed in three dimensions and rotated, by means of virtual reality, for the time being we are making full use of all the available plug-ins for Web browsers. We would like to do much more, however, as noted earlier when we described digital archiving. For example, there are many different types of data just for one vase. For now, we are making the data available by FTP, after the desired item is found using the Web browser, and are forced to depend on the applications provided by users in their own environment.

Ideally, however, it should be possible to handle these data as well in an integrated Web browser environment. Not only would that be easier for the user, but switching to FTP gets in the way of attempts to show the relationships between the data and the Web browser images. For example, with a vase the positional relation of X-ray CT data to CAD data needs to be clear, as does the relation of vase coloring to the data from a chemical analysis of its glaze material.

In other words, we need a framework for objectifying all these different types of data – of which the data types may well be endless – into one displayed item, and we further need a Web browser that can handle the entire process.

3.2.2. The need for expanded Web browser functions

A Web browser able to fill the kinds of needs described above should have a variety of functions that are necessary for use in museum research but that have yet to be implemented. Examples of such functions which have become clear in our work up to now include such basic ones as being able to measure the distance from one point to another on an object displayed three-dimensionally. Or, while viewing an object on the screen, it should be possible to position it and then zoom by any desired magnitude. It should also be possible to put virtual marks on an object and save them.

3.2.3. The need for a CSCW (Computer Supported Cooperative Work) environment

Another important requirement is to carry out this kind of work on a network, with a number of different scholars participating interactively.

In a museum, two or more researchers need to be able to examine materials together, taking out related materials as needed, and discussing freely with each other as they mark and measure the specimens. In order to realize a "virtual museum," we need an environment in which different researchers, sharing the same MUD (Multi-User Dungeon), can freely access the same materials, obtain a variety of highly precise data from them, and annotate or take measurements of them, then show the results to all the participants on their respective clients, all the while carrying on discussions in real time.

4. Current status of the Digital Museum systems

4.1. TRON Code

In order to resolve the above-noted character display issues, we have developed a TRON character code set, described in some detail in last year's keynote paper.[6] Below is an update on research in this area since the 1995 report.

4.1.1. Character database

What is special about the TRON code set is that, rather than simply specifying character codes in a single fixed code table, it uses a character database to achieve both the singularity of codes and diverse ways of expressing them.

In the TRON code set, text description and text expression are treated as two separate layers. By text description is meant the way the character codes represent text in text data, whereas text expression means the way the text description is expressed when the characters are actually printed or displayed.

In the case of ligature, for example, two characters that as text are no more than f and i can be expressed as either two characters or as fi ligature, depending on the situation. This is why it is important to separate these two concepts. A search for "fi" should also find instances of "fi" ligature and "f i".

The TRON code set therefore stores character data in the form of text descriptions, and converts these to text expressions at the time of printing or displaying based on information in a character database. This conversion function is performed not from a simple conversion table but as an extended function of the character database.

The attributes information stored in the character database includes character type, to distinguish characters as popular forms, abbreviated forms, ligature, etc., and links to the original character when a character is a variant form derived from another character. The database also contains kanji radicals, stroke counts, readings and other keys that can be used for searching in a large-scale character set; and it gives for each character the codes in other code sets that contain it. For Japanese kanji it also notes if a character belongs to a designated classification such as the essential characters to be learned in schools, general-use characters, and additions for proper names, etc. This makes it possible, for example, to limit a document at the time of text expression to the kanji studied through grade 3. Another advantage of introducing a database like this is that it makes it possible to store in the database the information necessary for deciding which characters are identical, which are different forms of the same character, which are differences in font design, and so on. These decisions can then be made use of in text expression. Much of this decision-making is sensory, and can be called "character sense," which is something that changes from one age to the next. Trying to codify this sensitivity into logical rules is bound to fail; the only real option is to enumerate all the relationships in a database.

This work of compiling a database of the changes in how each age perceives kanji is one more important part of the Digital Museum infrastructure. At the same time it can be seen as a major contribution to research on written language.

4.1.2. Todai Mincho

As a first step toward realizing the kind of multilingual environment described above, the TRON Project is going ahead with work related to kanji. For this enormous undertaking, we are creating fonts that can be used both for making a thoroughgoing collection of kanji and for creating a dictionary. Naturally all the characters already included in existing dictionaries like the Dai Kanwa Jiten and Kojien will be incorporated. In addition we have obtained the cooperation of printing companies in order to include characters used to print older works. Among these are numerous variant forms, original forms, and even mistaken characters; but they are characters that were actually used in publications and the like. A great many of these characters are not found in dictionaries, but with the help of the University of Tokyo Department of Literature we are compiling them in our collection.

We estimate that the total number of characters will come to somewhere between 80,000 and 100,000. Since most of these are not found in any computer, we are having to create an outline font for all of them and then a 48-dot font on that basis. This will be made generally available as a font set called Todai Mincho. Since the font set will include the entire collection of characters, it will ultimately make it possible for scholars to share ancient works over computer networks without having to worry about moth-eaten holes or greeked display. BTRON-specification computers will be able to take full advantage of this font set, but at present it may be difficult for other kinds of computer systems to handle the entire character set at once.

4.1.3. The TRON code set as a worldwide communication infrastructure

Character code problems are problems with the code sets generally used on the Internet, and are separate from Internet technologies themselves. So long as the MIME framework prescribed for the Internet is used, any new code set can be introduced. The problem is rather that there is no new code set to be used, which is where the TRON code set comes into the picture.

The text processing environment that we are seeking to develop for the Digital Museum is not merely for research into ancient writings. It is an infrastructure for all the characters in existence, of all ages and all places. By introducing the two layers of text description and text expression, and using a character database to bridge these two layers, it is possible to achieve both processing efficiency and the flexibility to accommodate the vagaries of human writing. Providing such an infrastructure will make the Internet a better environment for exchanging the diverse range of cultural knowledge, not just that of English.

4.2. Museum TAD

The information in the Digital Museum, as noted earlier, is of great variety, with one vase being described by shape data, texture data, X-ray CT data, a chemical analysis of its glaze material, explanations using figures, and so on. Moreover, all of these data are interrelated.

In the case of appearance and CT data, for example, three-dimensional mapping ought to be provided to show which part of the vase a given CT cross-section corresponds to. The same goes for graphical explanations. Music and other sounds, or a classic work being read aloud in the pronunciation of its time, need to be linked to time and to documents.

From this standpoint the need becomes apparent for cross-mapping the various information in the digital archive on a four-dimensional time-and-space continuum. In a database or in a special application it is possible to represent data to the user in a form that preserves these relationships, but there is a further need to send the data over a network in parts, with these relationships still intact. For this purpose we are studying a four-dimensional time-space mapping object data format, as an extension of the TAD specifications, which are the data exchange protocol adopted in the TRON Project. The type of information and mapping relations vary greatly depending on what is being described. The format will be given class definition and inheritance functions for flexible adaptation to these different needs, and it will be possible to define conversion functions for four-dimensional cross-mapping.

4.3. Flora specimens browser

The various requirements for expanded Web browser functions for a virtual museum, described earlier, were studied together under the topic of a specific application, and on that basis a flora specimens browser was developed. Among the holdings of the museum are specimens of each flora type. These are original specimens of each plant having a name. When a new plant is discovered, it can be compared to these type specimens to find out whether it is really a new variety. The conventional way of doing this involves first looking at black-and-white printed catalogs of these type specimens, and if it is found, finally checking it against the actual original specimen. Since the type specimens are very valuable, only specialists could be allowed access to them; and someone living far away was further disadvantaged. By digitally archiving these specimens, we are making them accessible to the whole world. Moreover, detailed data and related information are being added to the specimens, resulting in an illustrated catalog of flora that anyone can use. Looking at picture books of plants can be fun, but the popular ones do not provide enough data and often do not have the plant one is looking for. On the other hand, the flora catalogs used by specialists are not readily available or easy to use. An electronic flora, however, can serve both the needs of specialists and those of more general users. To this end, however, the proper browser functions are needed and a database must be compiled. First of all, for finding the plant one wants to see, searching must be possible by a variety of methods. The names of flora adopt a hierarchical classification, giving the class, order, family, genus, species, and variety. Besides the Latin name there are the various names in other languages (Japanese, etc.). To make searching easy it should be possible to search from any point in the hierarchy, while also being clear as to how that fits into the rest of the hierarchy and how to proceed from that point. The genus names, for example, will be sorted alphabetically; but the Japanese names are sorted according to the "aiueo" order adopted for Japanese, and the same goes for names in other languages. At each level the candidates are reordered accordingly. Another function is necessary for searching based on a plant's attributes, especially considering use by the general public. Users should be able to search according to the shape of leaves, the shape and color of flowers, seeds, fruits, plant shape, height, habitat and so on, narrowing down from the information that is known. The data in an electronic flora will have a rather complex structure and will include multimedia data. For this reason the database is designed as an object-oriented relational database.

Once the search has been narrowed down, pictures of plants are shown along with names and other related information. If there is a type specimen, a type specimen button appears for bringing up a table of specimens. Since a type specimen is intended for research use, a variety of tools are made available. These include tools for displaying a label of information noted when the sample was taken, and tools for zooming and scrolling pictures and for gamma correction (for making dark areas more visible, etc.), a ruler, protractor and rangefinder for measuring distance and angle, tool for calculating area, and pen and eraser for marking and making comments.

The above description indicates the variety of additional functions required in a browser for use with an electronic flora. A prototype of such a browser was developed for the MCUBE personal computer built around a TRON-specification microprocessor and running on a BTRON3-specification OS (see Figure 6).

The most important functions are those for enabling a variety of search methods and those for taking measurements of the specimens once they are found, especially those that are displayed in images. A remaining function we would like to implement is one that allows users to scan in pictures and use these as the basis for finding similar items, which would require an advanced image search facility.

4.4. Multi-User Virtual Environment System

The concept of "virtual space" is a useful metaphor when thinking about ways of enabling researchers who are not computer experts to take items out of a digital archive, and to aid them in working jointly with other researchers.

Figure 6: Flora specimens browser on a BTRON3-specification OS.

The CSCW goes beyond this by making it possible for multiple users to access the same virtual space at the same time.

In the MUD (Multi-User Dungeon) framework, each user has an alter ego in the virtual space. By controlling this other self in the virtual space, it is possible to pick up items located in the space, or to carry on dialogs with the alter egos of other users, and to make presentations.

A number of examples of this kind of virtual space, based on MUD[7,8,9], have appeared recently on the Internet. However, these are geared mainly to game playing and chat, and are not suitable for a CSCW environment for researchers in a virtual museum.

In order to realize a Multi-User Virtual Environment System for a virtual museum, it is important first of all to be able to create very large virtual spaces. The reason is that while game spaces can be designed any way one pleases to fit within the limitations of the system, the size of a virtual museum is governed by the needs of the museum holdings. Moreover, it should be possible to adopt a multi-server configuration and to link the virtual spaces provided by each of the servers, resulting in one big virtual space in which the participants can come and go freely.

If it is necessary to create a large virtual space with a multi-server configuration, it is also desirable to accommodate large numbers of users at one time. Also, whereas a MUD uses text or simple illustrations for background information, it would be far preferable to eliminate the need for guesswork or imagination by making use of three-dimensional rendering, so that participants can get a direct perception of the virtual space as an ordinary space from the viewpoint of their alter ego.

Presently we are developing a Large-Scale Multi-User Virtual Environment System for the Digital Museum, capable of simultaneous access by at least 1,000 users, and with practically unlimited capacity for updating or adding holdings.

The users of this virtual space, besides being able to take measurements and other actions for obtaining information, will be able to perform many other actions such as making a copy of a stored object and taking it with them.

Whenever the status of a museum holding or alter ego changes, the server sends an update message to the clients. When a client receives this message it redoes the rendering. In this case, necessary information is sent from important changes that are especially noteworthy, and very detailed priority control is carried out in the network and the rendering process. This feature of our system makes it possible for a wide range of users to take part in the virtual museum, even those with low-performance computers or users who access over narrow-bandwidth telephone lines.

There is a tendency for the introduction of new, convenient technologies to leave behind the "weak," as the GUI has excluded visually handicapped users. The gap between rich and poor should not be allowed to create a gap in access to knowledge. The TRON Project concept of "usable by everyone," which in the Digital Museum means "open to all," is here again a key policy.

4.5. Portable terminals and the μBTRON-specification OS

The spread of communications infrastructure such as the Internet and cellular phone systems has raised the demand for PDAs (Personal Digital Assistants) and other portable terminals, with the same ease of use as pocket calculators, and for mobile computing. Attempting to equip handheld computers with a full-fledged windowing system, however, runs into major obstacles in terms of hardware resources, battery capacity and the like. At the handheld computer level it is impractical to use Windows 95 or other PC windowing systems. Here the BTRON-specification OS, whose specifications were designed in the TRON Project, and even more so the μBTRON-specification OS specialized to PDA application, can be used to realize a highly advanced HMI on very limited hardware resources. In particular, the ability to run at a practical level without needing a high-performance CPU means the CPU clock speed can be kept low to minimize power consumption. This makes possible lightweight batteries and longer battery life. Personal Media Corporation has already developed a μBTRON-specification OS called "B-right", which has been implemented on Seiko Instruments Inc. PDA hardware to realize a system tentatively called BTRON-BrainPad, currently being tested.

B-right reportedly requires 6 MB of ROM and 4 MB of RAM, which is well within the range of feasibility for a PDA. BTRON-BrainPad in fact incorporates a low-power RISC CPU, 8 MB of ROM and 6 MB of RAM, as well as a PC Card interface, in a package only 170 x 100 x 20 mm, weighing approximately 300 g, making it fully capable of running the B-right, μBTRON-specification OS. The developers expect to achieve a battery life of 60 hours or more from two AA alkaline cells, resulting in a very practical and portable PDA. The combination of the B-right μBTRON-specification OS and BTRON-BrainPad shows it is possible to implement a practical windowing system even on a PDA with its limited hardware. On this basis a portable terminal is being developed for the Digital Museum by adding functions for position determination, with the idea of lending the terminals to visitors. They will then be able to call up explanations of exhibits in which they are interested, based on where they are at the time. In the case of large exhibits, the explanations can even be made to focus on different parts of the surface, or show pictures of the interior, for example. It will further be possible to provide visually handicapped users with voice explanations, and to read aloud the written explanations accompanying exhibits.

4.6. Voice interface

When people today look at unfamiliar writings from the past, unless they are specialists they do not know how the words would sound if read aloud. We are now studying a voice interface for providing interactive reading of written information. Naturally such a voice interface is important for giving access to the visually handicapped. When people get information aurally, they need more than simply a synthetic speech function. We have found that they need to be able to have a certain part repeated, to jump ahead to a related section, and perform other fine control over the reading process. Relying on an external speech synthesis device, or not having a multi-threading function, for example, can lead to such problems as not being able to find out in real time how far the reading has proceeded, or delays when trying to stop in mid-utterance.

For users of such a system – especially sight-impaired users who cannot tell the location in a passage by looking at the screen – the result is a system just as difficult to use as a text editor in which the cursor position cannot be controller precisely, with the cursor running ahead of where you want it to be.

Real-time control of the volume level and reading speed should also be possible even in the middle of a reading, which requires a speech synthesis architecture with a high level of real-time control.

If the output is in stereo sound the listener can obtain position information, distinguishing the location of the sounds in the sound field, which we found to have many advantages. This feature can be used, for example, to give location feedback when moving the cursor position, and to give a separate audible confirmation of the extent of selected text. Currently we are implementing a voice interface on a BTRON3-specification OS, with an architecture consisting of two main servers. One is a translate server, for converting text data into waveform data. The other is an audio output server, which generates the actual voice from the output mechanism based on the waveform data. Each of the servers is realized by means of monitor tasks and run tasks, with the text data and waveform data used by these tasks located in shared memory, through which they have interfaces with individual applications. A PC card with speech synthesis and speech recognition functions will be incorporated in the portable terminals described above, so that in combination with the voice interface a museum browser for the sake of visually handicapped users can be realized.

5. In conclusion

In many ways the Digital Museum applications are well suited for furthering research into the "computing everywhere" environment that is the subject of the TRON Project. In addition the realization of a Digital Museum is significant in its own right, producing results that we hope will be put to use in the growing number of university museums throughout Japan as well as in existing museums. Not only will this advance the incorporating of general "Enableware" functions in museums, but eventually, by networking the data in standardized Digital Museums it may become possible to realize a huge virtual museum.

It is my belief that the provision of the infrastructure described in this paper will make a major contribution to the world's cultures, scholarship, and industry.

References

[1] K. Sakamura, "Infrastructures for an Age of Computerized Environments," Proc. of the Tenth TRON Project Symposium, IEEE Computer Society Press, 1993, pp. 2-14.

[2] K. Sakamura, "TRON Application Project: Gearing Up for HFDS," Proc. of the Eighth TRON Project Symposium, IEEE Computer Society Press, 1991, pp. 2-14.

[3] K. Sakamura, "After a Decade of TRON, What Comes Next?," Proc. of the Eleventh TRON Project Symposium, IEEE Computer Society Press, 1994, pp. 2-16.

[4] K. Sakamura, "Human Interface with Computers in Everyday Life," Proc. of the Ninth TRON Project Symposium, IEEE Computer Society Press, 1992, pp. 2-12.

[5] Special Issue: Computer Augmented Evivironment: Back to the Real World, Comm. ACM, Vol.36, No.7, July 1993.

[6] K. Sakamura, "Multilingual Computing as a Global Communications Infrastructure," Proc. of the Twelfth TRON Project Symposium, IEEE Computer Society Press, 1995, pp. 2-14.

[7] Thomas A. Funkhouser, "Ring: A client-server

system for multi-user virtual environment," 1995 Symposium on Interactive 3D Graphics, ACM SIGGRAPH, 1995, pp. 85-92.

[8] Chris Greenhalgh and Steve Benford, "MASSIVE: a distributed virtual reality system incorporating spatial trading," Proc. of the International Conference on Distributed Computing Systems, 1995, pp. 27-34.

[9] Michael J. Zyda, David R. Pratt, and Paul T. Barham, "NPSNET: A multi-player 3D virtual environment over the internet," 1995 Symposium on Interactive 3D Graphics, ACM SIGGRAPH, 1995, pp. 463-469.

Project Updates

Current Status and Future Directions of the ITRON Subproject

Hiroaki Takada

Department of Information Science
School of Science, University of Tokyo
7–3–1, Hongo, Bunkyo-ku, Tokyo 113, Japan

Kiichiro Tamaru

Semiconductor Device Engineering Lab.
TOSHIBA Corporation
580–1, Horikawa-cho, Saiwai-ku, Kawasaki 210, Japan

Abstract

The ITRON Subproject is to define and promote a standard operating system specification for embedded systems. A series of ITRON real-time kernel specifications has been defined and published so far. Among them, the μITRON specifications, which are designed for small-scale embedded systems, have been implemented for a large number of microcontroller units (MCUs) and have been utilized in numerous applications. In this paper, we describe the current status and recent results of the ITRON Subproject, after reviewing the design principles and the history of the ITRON specifications. Then, we discuss the future directions of the subproject.

1 Introduction

Advances in microcomputer technologies have been expanding the application fields of embedded systems. What came into the world originally for industrial applications later expanded to communication equipment, office applications, and other business uses. More recently, the application areas of embedded systems have spread out to consumer applications including automotive systems, electronic musical instruments, TVs, VCRs, audio gear, cellular phones, airconditioners, and many more small-scale applications.

Because small-scale embedded systems tend to be manufactured in great quantities and be priced cheap, lowering the cost of the final product is usually considered more important than reducing development costs. Therefore, how to realize an application system with minimum hardware resources is the concern. Another feature of small-scale embedded systems is that once a product is put on sale, the embedded software is rarely modified. Therefore, the software development life cycle is very short.

In the field of small-scale embedded systems, it is common practice to use a single-chip microcontroller unit (MCU), integrating a processor core with ROM, RAM, general I/O devices, and application-specific peripheral modules. According to the World Semiconductor Trade Statistics (Table 1), nearly three billion MCUs were shipped in 1995, accounting about 90% of processor shipments. The MCU to MPU ratio is especially high in Japan, with MCU shipments in Japan accounting for around 40% of the world total, whereas MPU shipments are less than a tenth of the worldwide total.

Type		8-bit	16-bit	32-bit
Typical	ROM	48 KB	64 KB	96 KB
	RAM	0.5 KB	1 KB	2 KB
Large-Scale	ROM	64 KB	128 KB	128 KB
	RAM	2 KB	4 KB	4 KB

Table 2: Memory sizes of one-chip MCUs

Another point worth noting here is that the shipments of high-end (16-bit or greater) MCU are rapidly increasing. This is driven by highly computerized (or digitalized) embedded applications emerged very recently, such as digital audio components, digital TVs and VCRs, digital cameras, digital cellular phones, and PDAs (personal digital assistants), heating up the embedded system market. Even though high-end MCUs are adopted, these applications share the same features with other small-scale embedded systems, in that they are manufactured in great quantities with low cost and that lowering the cost of the final product is very important.

A particular problem in developing software for small-scale embedded systems is the limited hardware resources, which comes from the need for cost reduction. Memory size limits are especially severe, with a typical 16-bit one-chip MCU having around 64 KB of ROM and 1 KB of RAM. Even larger-scale chips have no more than 128 KB of ROM and 4 KB of RAM (Ta-

Kinds	Quantity (unit of million)		
	1993	1994	1995
8-bit MPU	63.6 (2.7%)	56.9 (2.0%)	48.2 (1.5%)
16-bit MPU	50.8 (2.1%)	44.5 (1.6%)	58.8 (1.8%)
32-bit or greater MPU	52.4 (2.2%)	68.8 (2.4%)	104.6 (3.2%)
4-bit MCU	1,036.3 (43.4%)	1,089.4 (38.5%)	1,066.0 (32.5%)
8-bit MCU	1,073.4 (45.0%)	1,372.7 (48.5%)	1,667.4 (50.9%)
16-bit or greater MCU	59.6 (2.5%)	119.8 (4.2%)	199.2 (6.1%)
DSP	51.6 (2.2%)	77.2 (2.7%)	134.2 (4.1%)
Total	2,387.6	2,829.3	3,278.4

Table 1: Shipment of MPU and MCU
(World Semiconductor Trade Statistics, worldwide, 1993 – 1995)

ble 2). Moreover, the requirement for high cost performance in an MCU-based system frequently makes the processor design be optimized to the application, resulting in a large number of different processor cores, which is among the obstacles to standardize software development process.

Even in this field of small-scale embedded systems, raising software productivity is an important issue. Use of C, C++, or other high-level programming languages is one solution; another approach is to use a real-time kernel like those implementing the μITRON specifications. Lately, this trend is accelerated, because of the ever increasing size and complexity of the embedded software and because the requirement to shorten the time to market is very keen.

2 Design Principles of the ITRON Specifications

The ITRON specifications are designed so that the following requirements on a standard operating system for embedded systems are satisfied [1, 2].

- Being able to derive maximum performance from hardware
  Given the severe hardware resource limitations of a typical MCU-based system, the ability to derive maximum performance from the available hardware is a prerequisite for real-time OS adoption.
- Helping to improve software productivity
  Especially important is standardization from a training standpoint, such as adopting consistent concepts and terminology, and standardizing design methods.
- Being uniformly applicable to various processor scales and types
  The hardware used in an embedded system is normally designed optimally for its application. The processor scale, moreover, may vary widely from 8-bit to 32-bit processors depending on the kind of equipment to be controlled.

In addition to the above requirements, another very important issue is whether the specifications are truly open. This means not only that the specification documents can be obtained, but also that everyone is free to implement and sell products based on those specifications.

Responding to the need for standardization described above, around ten years ago we began investigating on a standard real-time kernel specification for embedded systems [3], leading to the development and release of a series of ITRON specifications [4]. The first ITRON kernel specification was released in 1987 as ITRON1. Thereafter studies were carried out on a reduced-function specification called μITRON (Ver 2.0) for smaller-scale 8-bit and 16-bit MCUs, and on the ITRON2 specification for larger-scale systems with 32-bit MPUs. Both of them were released in 1989. The reason for centering these studies on a kernel specification is that in most deeply embedded systems, only the kernel functions are used.

The following design principles were established for the ITRON specifications, in order to satisfy the requirements [2].

- Avoid excessive hardware virtualization
- Allow for optimization to application
- Allow for optimization to hardware
- Emphasize ease of software engineer training
- Create a specification series and/or divide into levels
- Make available a full range of functions

A concept common to many of these design principles is that of loose standardization. This means setting uniform standards only to the extent that performance will not suffer, rather than trying to force

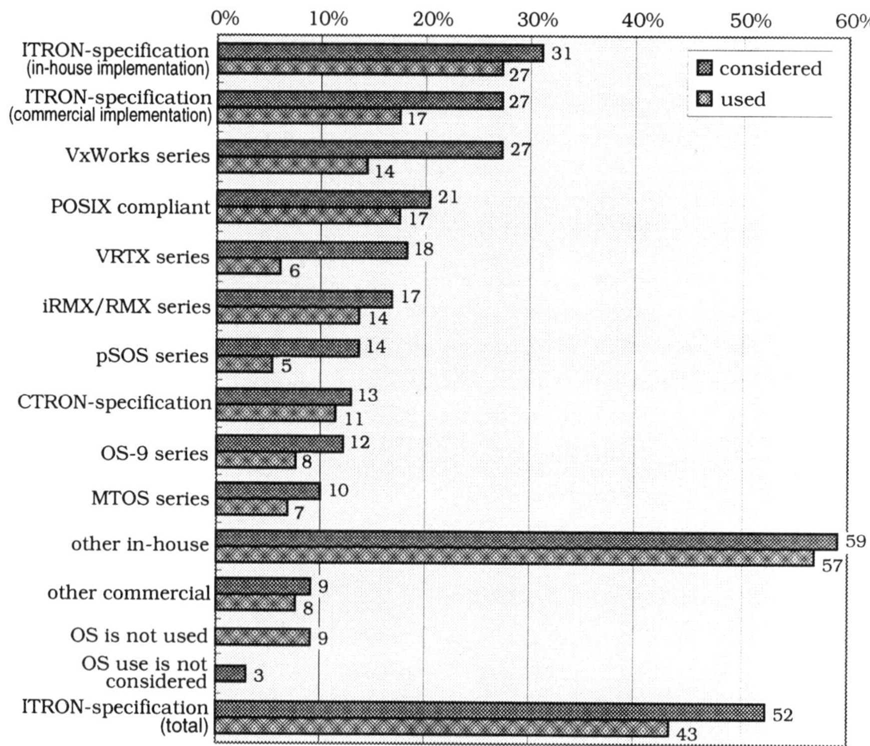

Figure 1: Real-time OSs used (or considered for use) in embedded systems (TRON Association survey, in Japan, 1995)

all systems into one rigid mold, and leaving room to decide matters dependent on the processor or application.

3 Current Status and Recent Results

3.1 The μITRON3.0 Specification

The μITRON3.0 specification [5, 6] is the newest version of the μITRON real-time kernel specification and was published in 1993. This revision was motivated by the fact that the μITRON specification (Ver 2.0) had been applied for some 32-bit processors, something we had not originally anticipated. Consequently, the μITRON3.0 specification is designed to be applicable to the wide range of processors in use today.

Another major purpose of the μITRON3.0 specification is to support embedded systems consisting of some MCUs interconnected on an intra-system network. Connection functions, with which tasks and other kernel objects on other nodes can be directly manipulated using ordinary system calls, are introduced to the μITRON3.0 specification. However, the embedded systems which was controlled with several MCUs tend to be realized with one MCU recently, because of the strong requirement for reducing the cost of the final product and because of the improved performance of microprocessors. As the result, no μITRON3.0-specification kernel supporting connection functions has been marketed so far, while there are some experimental implementations.

After the first release of the specification in 1993 (Ver 3.00), we have revised the specification twice in 1993 (Ver 3.01) and in 1994 (Ver 3.02). These revisions have resolved some ambiguities in the specification as well as correcting some errors remained in the first release. The most important one of the resolved ambiguities is the definition of the transient state of tasks which occurs while task dispatching is delayed. A section has been added to the specification to clarify this ambiguity.

3.2 Current Status of the ITRON Specifications

The ITRON specifications, especially the μITRON specifications, have been implemented on many different MCUs. In fact, it would not be going too far to say that μITRON-specification kernels have been developed for the 8-bit, 16-bit, and 32-bit MCUs of all

```
Ques-2131: Can sus_tsk be invoked from task portions?
                Function: suspend task [Level SN]
Answ-2131:      [a|b]
Ques-2132: Can sus_tsk be invoked from task-independent portions?
Answ-2132:      [a|b|c|d]

Cond-4031...Cond-4033: Answer only when 2131=[a] (when sus_tsk is supported).
Ques-4031: Is the nesting of the SUSPEND state supported?
        a. supported (the maximum nesting level is more than one) [Level X]
        b. not supported
Answ-4031:      [a|b]

Cond-4032: Answer only when 4031=[a].
Ques-4032: How to specify the maximum nesting level of the SUSPEND state?
        a. The maximum nesting level can be specified at the configuration.
        b. The maximum nesting level is fixed.
        z. others
Answ-4032:      [a|b|z]
Answ-4032z:     (* Describe, or answer the page or section number in the manual only
 when 4032=[z].)

Cond-4033: Answer only when 4031=[a].
Ques-4033: How many is the maximum nesting level of the SUSPEND state?
   * Notice
      - When 4032=[a], answer the upper bound of the maximum nesting level which can
 be specified at the configuration.
      - When 4032=[b], answer the maximum nesting level.
Answ-4033:      (* Describe, or answer the page or section number in the manual.)
```

Figure 2: Sample questionnaires in the compatibility checksheets

major Japanese semiconductor makers. Just counting the μITRON-specification products that have been registered officially with the TRON Association, there are around 30 implementations for more than 20 processors. In addition to them, the μITRON specification has been used in numerous developments exclusively for in-house systems. There are also a number of μITRON-specification kernels that have been made available as free software.

These ITRON-specification kernel implementations are widely applied for various application areas. According to the survey taken in Japan by the TRON Association in 1995, about 50% of the application developers are using ITRON-specification kernels (Figure 1). Now, we can say that the μITRON specification has become a de-fact industry standard in this field.

3.3 Compatibility Checksheets

A possible problem of loose standardization, which is one of the most important concepts in designing the ITRON specifications, is the difficulty in grasping the functions supported by a particular ITRON-specification kernel or the differences among kernels based on the specification. Incorporating levels in the specification is one of the methods to ease this difficulty.

As a more general approach to remedy this problem, we have prepared a set of checksheets for confirming the compatibility of real-time kernels implementing the μITRON3.0 specification (called the compatibility checksheets, in short). The checksheets are designed mainly for use in comparing different kernels implemented based on the μITRON3.0 specification, and for estimating the amount of work involved in porting applications from one μITRON3.0-specification kernel to another. In more precise, they make it easy to grasp the extent to which each kernel implements optional features of the μITRON3.0 specification, or in cases where the specification offers a choice, to determine which choice is taken.

The checksheets are designed to be machine-readable, so that the data can be converted readily to tables or graphs that tell the functions supported by each kernel at a glance. Figure 2 and Figure 3 illustrate some of the questionnaires in the checksheets and example answers to them, respectively.

The official version of the compatibility checksheets

```
Answ-2131:      [a]
Answ-2132:      [a]

Answ-4031:      [a]
Answ-4032:      [b]
Answ-4033:      2^31-1
```

Figure 3: Example answers to the checksheets

for the μITRON3.0 specification has been released in January 1996. Before the official release, a beta version was released in July 1995 for soliciting comments from the general public. The comments received were reflected in the official version. Since October 1996, when an μITRON3.0 implementation is registered with the TRON Association, the applicant is requested to provide the answers to the compatibility checksheets on the registered product, which are distributed to the users through the Internet.

4 Future Directions

4.1 Standardization of Software Components

As the software of embedded applications becomes larger and more complicated, application developers generally want to reuse more parts of software to shorten the development time (and the time to market) or to buy them as package software. Especially, the recent trends to replace hardware components with software modules increase the necessity of package software components for embedded systems. Typical examples include sound/voice processings such as voice synthesis and software-implemented data modem, image processings such as decompression of JPEG and MPEG data, and communication protocol handlings such as the TCP/IP protocols and application layer protocols on them. These software components are also called as *middleware* for embedded systems.

As many vendors are beginning to provide these software components, requirements to standardize their application interface are emerging [7]. In spite of the necessity, diverse requirements from different application areas have been the obstacle to the standardization in the embedded system field. Recent increase in software size and strong requirements to shorten the application development time make the standardization possible in some areas. Also, the concept of loose standardization will be very effective for this standardization. The ITRON Technical Committee has begun the effort for the standardization in late 1996.

4.2 Hard Real-Time Support

Hard real-time features are often required on the software modules that replace hardware components. Another necessity of hard real-time support is the increased complexity of the software of embedded systems even in the fields of consumer and other small-scale embedded applications.

The ITRON Technical Committee has also begun the activity to investigate on hard real-time support for the ITRON specifications in 1996. As the initial step of the investigation, the ITRON Hard Real-Time Support Study Group has stared in October 1996 to make the requirements clear.

4.3 Standardization of Development Environment Interface

Another important interface to be standardized is the operating system interface with software development environments, especially debugging environments. Though we have recognized this requirement since several years ago, the standardization is not easy due to the diverse software development environments of embedded systems. The ITRON Technical Committee is also planning to start the investigations on this issue.

4.4 Multiprocessor Support

Another future direction of the ITRON specifications is to support multiprocessor systems. The ITRON kernel specification extended to support shared-memory multiprocessors is called the ITRON-MP specification and will be very important when more than one processor cores can be integrated in a chip. Until now, we have proposed the basic concept of the ITRON-MP specification [8] and reported the results of some experimental implementations [9, 10].

4.5 Towards the Realization of HFDS

The last and most important goal of the ITRON specification and the TRON project is to support highly functionally distributed systems (HFDS) [11]. To this end, some difficult problems are necessary to be tackled [12]. The ITRON specifications will be integrated to the IMTRON, which supports various functions necessary for the realization of HFDS.

5 Conclusion

The μITRON-specification kernels are widely applied to various kind of embedded applications as a result of the development and promotional activities in the last ten years. Though μITRON is well-known in the field of embedded systems in Japan, it is not so famous in U.S. and other foreign countries. In 1995, the ITRON Technical Committee has started various activities to widen the use of the μITRON specifications; it has participated in the Embedded Systems Conference West, which is the world largest trade show in this field, twice in 1995 and in 1996, and has sponsored a seminar on the ITRON specifications in China (Beijing and Shanghai) in 1995. It usually takes a long time and requires a great deal of efforts to spread an operating system standard to the world. We plan to continue these activities in the future.

Acknowledgments

We would like to thank Dr. Ken Sakamura and the other members of the ITRON Technical Committee for their support and effort for the ITRON Subproject.

References

[1] H. Takada, K. Tamaru, K. Kudou, T. Shimizu, and H. Tsubota, "The present and future of the ITRON subproject – kernel specifications and their implementation –," *Journal of IPSJ*, vol. 35, pp. 903–909, Oct. 1994. (in Japanese).

[2] H. Takada and K. Sakamura, "μITRON for small-scale embedded systems," *IEEE Micro*, vol. 15, pp. 46–54, Dec. 1995.

[3] H. Monden, "Introduction to ITRON, the industry-oriented operating system," *IEEE Micro*, vol. 7, pp. 45–52, Apr. 1987.

[4] H. Takada and K. Sakamura, "Advances in the ITRON specifications – supporting multiprocessor and distributed systems," in *Proc. 9th TRON Project Symposium*, pp. 89–95, IEEE CS Press, 1992.

[5] K. Sakamura, ed., *μITRON 3.0 Standard Handbook.* Tokyo: Personal Media, 1993. (in Japanese).

[6] K. Sakamura, ed., *μITRON 3.0 Specification.* Tokyo: TRON Association, 1994. (can be obtained from "ftp://tron.um.u-tokyo.ac.jp/pub/TRON/ITRON/SPEC/mitron3.txt.Z").

[7] K. Tamaru, H. Takada, N. Ito, H. Takahashi, T. Kamada, and Y. Kasai, "Approaches to the standardization of middleware," *TRONWARE*, vol. 41, Oct. 1996. transcript of panel discussion (in Japanese).

[8] H. Takada and K. Sakamura, "ITRON-MP: An adaptive real-time kernel specification for shared-memory multiprocessor systems," *IEEE Micro*, vol. 11, pp. 24–27,78–85, Aug. 1991.

[9] H. Takada and K. Sakamura, "Inter- and intra-processor synchronizations in multiprocessor real-time kernel," in *Proc. 4th Int'l Workshop on Parallel and Distributed Real-Time Systems*, pp. 69–74, Apr. 1996.

[10] C.-D. Wang, H. Takada, and K. Sakamura, "Prioritized inter-processor synchronization in an ITRON-MP implementation," in *Proc. 13th TRON Project Int'l Symposium*, IEEE CS Press, Dec. 1996.

[11] K. Sakamura, "The objectives of the TRON project," in *TRON Project 1987*, pp. 3–16, Springer-Verlag, 1987.

[12] H. Takada and K. Sakamura, "Compact, low-cost, but real-time distributed computing for computer augmented environments," in *Proc. 5th IEEE CS Workshop on Future Trends of Distributed Computing Systems*, pp. 56–63, IEEE CS Press, Aug. 1995.

The ITRON Technical Committee provides regular information on the ITRON specifications via the Internet, including the latest English-language specifications and the ITRON Newsletter. The URL is "http://tron.um.u-tokyo.ac.jp/TRON/ITRON/".

The Current Status and Future of the BTRON and Human-Machine Interface Subprojects

KOSHIZUKA, Noboru
Graduate School of Humanities and Sociology
The University of Tokyo

ABSTRACT

This paper makes a brief overview of current status and the future of the BTRON subproject and the TRON Human-Machine Interface Subproject. Especially, it reports research and development results in these three years (from 1994 to 1996).

1. INTRODUCTION

In the TRON project, human-machine interface (HMI) is considered as very important technology. The TRON project contains two subprojects related to HMI: the BTRON subproject [5] and the TRON HMI subproject [3].

The former one incorporates with computer architecture for HMIs. BTRON corresponds to workstations, personal computer, and PDAs (Personal Digital Assistants), which become very popular today. In these year, the BTRON subproject has issued three versions of the BTRON specifications. They are called BTRON1 [9], 2 [10], and 3. Some companies participating the subproject have released products based on these specifications.

The latter one, the TRON HMI subproject, incorporates with HMIs of all kinds of electronic equipments embedded with micro computers. This subproject aims to solve the consistency problem of *'computer everywhere'* environment. This problem is just a prediction of the near future that we will surrounded with enormous electronic equipments, and that, if their operation methods differ from each other, people will be confused much and will not benefit from the equipments. To solve this problem, we are building an HMI specification applicable to all kinds of electronic equipment [15, 17]. Further, we are developing new design methodologies and implementation mechanism of HMIs based on the TRON HMI specification.

The rest of this paper reports current status of the two subprojects, the BTRON and TRON HMI subprojects, and describes their future direction.

2. THE BTRON SUBPROJECT

2.1 Overview

BTRON is just the computer architecture of personal computers or workstations in the TRON-concept computers. It provides several novel features as follows. First, it contains a hyper-text file system called the Real-Object/Virtual-Object system. Sakamura has noted the effectiveness of hyper-text for the storage of human intellect [6]. In some sense, the spread of the World Wide Web (WWW) system is proving this statement. Additionally, the BTRON subproject has been emphasizing the importance of multilingual processing environments [7, 16] and accessibility for the physically challenged [1]. The BTRON multilingual environment [7] and the BTRON Enableware specification [8] realize these visions. Recent discussion of the Unicode problem and the operations of accessibility guidelines convince us that our vision has been farsighted, and that the solution by BTRON is proved as right. From this discussion, we know that the vision and feature of BTRON are not old-fashioned yet, but still shining.

2.2 Expansion of the BTRON Family

BTRON1 specification is an OS interface for rather small personal computers with restricted hardware resources. The BTRON1 specification OS [9] is ported upon OADG specification personal computers (so-called IBM compatible machines). This has drastically extended the kinds of hardware upon which BTRON runs.

In 1992, BTRON2 specification [10], which is for high-end workstation with high performance CPU and rich hardware resources, has been released. A workstation has developed on the basis of the specification. Another feature of the workstation is that its CPU is also based on the TRON specification [11].

In these years, the BTRON3 specification has been developed, which is upper-compatible with the BTRON1 specification. However, its architecture is completely

0-8186-7658-2/96 $05.00

different from the one of BTRON1. BTRON3 is consists of a micro kernel based on μITRON 3.0 [14] and several managers, external kernel (Figure 2). A workstation based on the BTRON3 specification has also developed. Its CPU is also based on the TRON specification [11]: GMICRO/300 or GMICRO/500. Its kernel is implemented by using a micro kernel technology. It consists of an internal kernel, based on ItIs (ITron Implementation is Sakamura-lab), and some managers implemented as a task of the internal kernel. Today, the BTRON3 specification operating system is being ported upon another popular hardware.

Network environment has also been developed upon the BTRON3 workstation. Its physical layer is just the Ethernet, and its upper layers are based on the TCP/IP protocol stacks. Sakamura Lab. has built a WWW browser on the BTRON3 workstation, and now researching seamless and consistent integration between the Real Object/Virtual Object file system of the BTRON and hypertext information webs of the WWW (Figure 1).

Figure 1 World Wide Web Browser on the BTRON3 specification operating system.

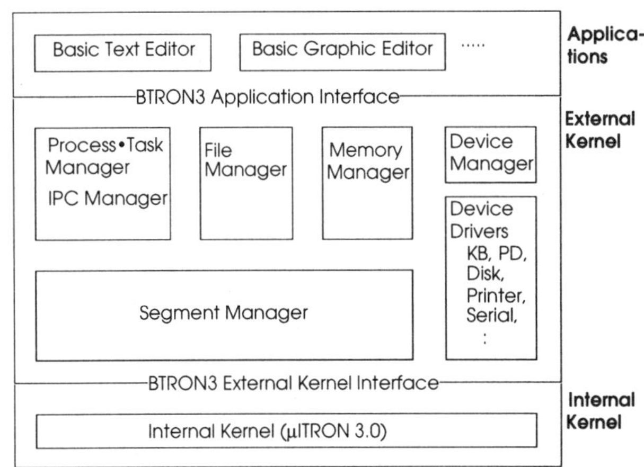

Figure 2 Kernel architecture of BTRON3

2.3 BTRON for PDA

The popularization of wireless communication such as cellular phones and PHSs is extending the possibility of the environment that one can access on-line information from *'anywhere'*. A small and portable terminal with the wireless communication functionality is a key technology of the environment. People always bring the terminal, read/write their e-mails, and retrieve information from remote databases by using the terminal.

The BTRON specification is a very light specification, that is, it requires a small amount of computer resources: memories, CPU power, and disk storage. So, its implementation can run on a low-end personal computer such as PDAs. The structure of BTRON is so modular that it is easy to tune the operating system for a particular hardware or application, for example, to add new modules or to detach unnecessary modules from the operating system.

2.4 Multilingual Processing

Multilingual processing is also a hot topic in the BTRON subproject in these years [7, 16]. With the spread of low-cost personal computers and Internet, a multilingual computing environment is much of interest. Our project has been tackling with this subject in pursuit of the ideal. The BTRON multilingual environment is featured by the following issues. 1) It is an entire text processing environment, including word-processing rules. 2) This environment is switched by language specifier codes. 3) It provides support at the system level. 4) It is language neutral. 5) It strives an ideal infrastructure.

In this year, as a first step toward the BTRON multilingual environment, we have developed a *provisional* multilingual computing environment [4], which is strongly needed by many BTRON users. The provisional multilingual environment is just an extension of the Japanese-language environment which is currently available existing BTRON-specific products. Its character code set is just one plane, that is 16 bit code length, and it contains characters equivalent with JIS X 0208, JIS X 0212, GB2312, KSC 5601, Braille, and other European character code sets (Figure 3). This environment has brought us a simple but useful multilingual system, which is featured by the mixture of Japanese Han-characters, Korean Han-characters, and Chinese Han-characters (Figure 4).

This environment is intermittent result of our multilingual research activity. Now, we are going forward to realize our ideal multilingual environment. In addition to this, we are developing the most powerful Japanese-language specific environment for the BTRON multilingual environment.

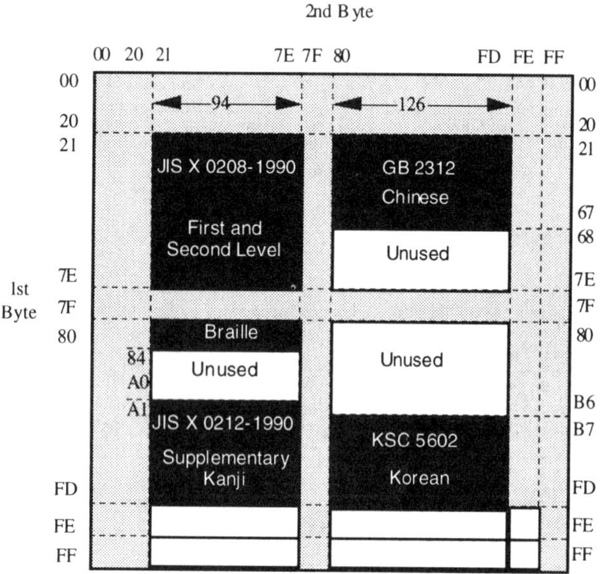

Figure 3 Character code map of the BTRON provisional multilingual environment.

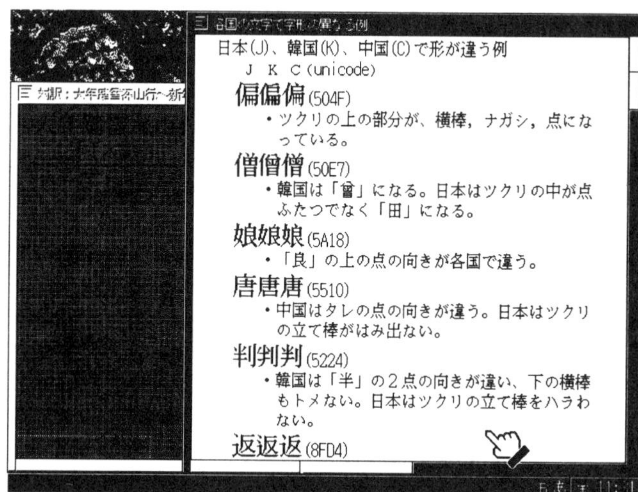

Figure 4 A Japanese explanation of the subtle differences in shape between Japanese, Korean, and Chinese Hanji. This document mixes all three languages.

2.5 Enableware

We have developed the BTRON Enableware specification [8] and implemented upon existing BTRON products. BTRON is the first personal computer in Japan which provides accessibility functionality as a standard. Most of the accessibility functions of the BTRON products were for motor impaired users. Functions for visually impaired users still remained unimplemented.

In these years, the Enableware group of the BTRON subproject has devoted their effort to the implementation of functions that support blind users. They are building a special text editor which interfaces with users only with sound. This editor adopts several new user interface technologies such as *announcer metaphor* for speech output interface, *whispering metaphor* for cut & paste operation interfaces, highly interactive audio control techniques, etc. Using these new technologies, we are trying to build the ultimate audio interface for text editors.

3. THE HUMAN MACHINE INTERFACE SUBPROJECT

3.1 Overview

The TRON HMI subproject has been initialized by the study of human-machine interfaces at the following three subprojects: TRON-concept computerized house research group, TRON-concept computerized building research group, and TRON computerized automobile research group

[3, 13]. The result of this research has been inherited by the TRON Electronic Equipment Human-Machine Interface Research Group, that was started in October 1990. In 1992, we have made TRON HMI specification of the version 1.00.00, on the basis of which we have held an HMI design competition. Then, we have received evaluation of the specification by designers participating the competition. After adoption of many comments from them, we have revised the specification and released a new version, ver. 1.10.00 [15].

We have two prominent advances of this subproject in these years: 1) constructing a new version of the HMI specification and 2) starting the research and development of an HMI design support tool.

3.2 Revision of the HMI Specification

We have revised the TRON HMI Specification and released the specification book of the ver. 2.00.00 [18] (Figure 5). Especially, the new version contains the following additional features:

Product liability:
Today, product liability is an important concept for consumer product development. Human-machine interface is not an exception. Our specification includes guidelines suggesting to get rid of causes which lead users to misoperation, and, furthermore, to assure safety even when users make wrong usage.

Normalization:
An important aim of the TRON HMI Guideline is to provide HMIs everyone can use. When electronic equipment has become playing important roles in the society, people who cannot use the equipment benefit nothing from it. This inequality of accessibility to the technology might brings a new social inequality. To prevent this problem, our specification contains many Enableware guidelines in standard and is trying to realize normalization of the accessibility to the electronic technologies.

Multimedia:
Consumer electronics are now adopting multimedia technologies in their HMIs. The typical one is the speech output interface. New version of our specification book contains several specifications guidelines for speech output interfaces. These can be applicable to telephone information systems and so on.

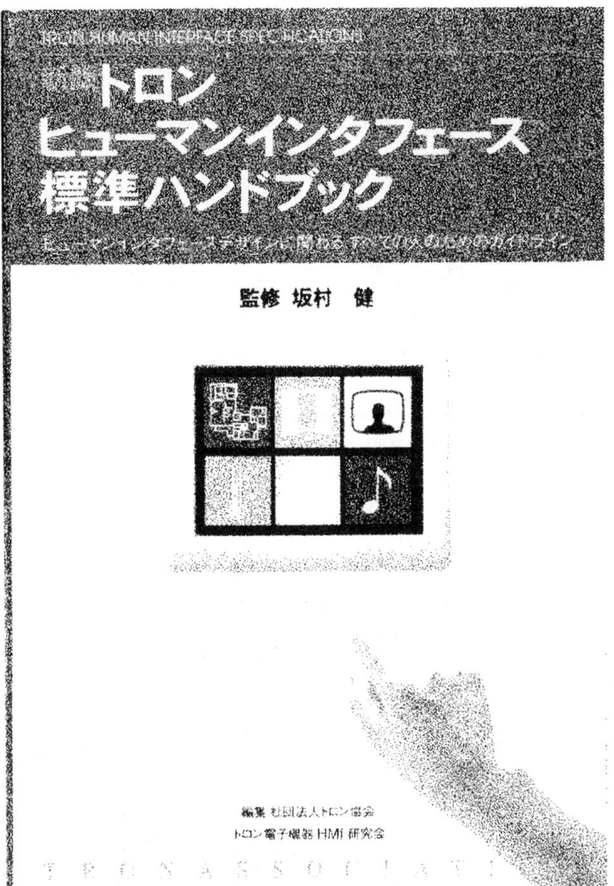

Figure 5 The TRON HMI specification book.

3.3 Human Machine Interface Builder

It is widely known that, to realize consistent HMIs, only an HMI guideline book is insufficient. This is because designing HMIs satisfying guidelines is a very difficult task. Designers often create invalid HMIs even after reading the guideline book. To make the guidelines effective, we are building a computer aided design tool which supports HMI designers to design HMIs satisfying the TRON HMI Guidelines (Figure 6). Main features of the tools are as follows:

Structured editor:
It contains an editor that automatically applies the TRON Design Guidelines. This tool is very effective to apply geometrical constraints to HMI designs. For example, a label must not be put above or right side of a part.

Guideline checker:

It contains a guideline checker which checks more complex rules/guidelines of HMIs. It works like a spell checker or grammar checker of word processors. It parses the whole layout of an HMI, checks invalidations of the TRON HMI Guideline rules, then outputs warning/error messages to the HMI designer.

On-line specification book:

The guidelines checker is tightly coupled with the on-line specification book. Error/warning messages of the checker are linked with the appropriate portion of the specification book. Designers can refer original specifications/guidelines by simply clicking a link embedded in the messages, and easily know what the invalidation is.

HMI database:

A database containing many HMI design examples is very important. An industrial designer may survey HMIs of conventional products to design HMIs compatible with conventional products. A novice designer may query some HMIs and imitate conventional designs for his/her design studies. Our tool provides an HMI database which contains many examples based on the TRON HMI Guidelines.

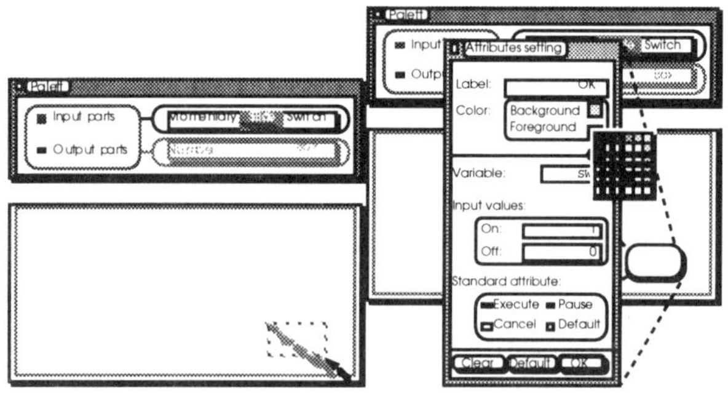

Figure 6 Sample screen shots of the Human-machine interface builder.

4. SUMMARY

In these years, both academic community and industrial community have noted the importance of the easy-to-use issue. However, most kinds of equipment around us are still difficult to use. The ultimate goal of the BTRON subproject and HMI subproject is to improve the quality of human-machine interfaces of equipment used in our daily life. This paper makes brief overview of important issues for an ideal human-machine interface.

ACKNOWLEDGMENT

We would like to appreciate the TRON Project leader, Professor Sakamura. We also acknowledge all the members of the BTRON technical committee, the TRON Electronic Equipment Human-Machine Interface research Group, TRON Enableware Working Group, and Sakamura laboratory.

REFERENCES

[1] Koshizuka, N, Uematsu, M., Kimura, N., and Sakamura, K.: Design and Implementation of the Enableware Specification — A Human-Machine Interface for Physically Challenged People. In *Proc. Ninth TRON Project Symposium* (1992), pp. 2-9. in Japanese.

[2] Koshizuka, N., and Sakamura, K.: Window Real-Objects: a Distributed Shared Memory for the Distributed Implementation of GUI Applications. In *Proc. ACM Symposium on User Interface Software and Technology* (Nov. 1993), pp. 237-247.

[3] Koshizuka, N., Mutoh, T., and Sakamura, K.: TRON Human-Machine Interface Specifications for Everyday Life. *Journal of Information Processing Society of Japan*, Vol. 35, No. 10 (Oct. 1994), pp. 934-939. in Japanese.

[4] Koshizuka, N.: A Multilingual Computing Environment for BTRON. TRON Project Journal, No. 44 (1996), TRON Association, pp. E24-26.

[5] Matsui, A.: The Current Status of the BTRON Subprojects and their Future. *Journal of Information Processing Society of Japan*, Vol. 35, No. 10 (Oct. 1994), Information Processing Society of Japan, pp. 910-917. in Japanese.

[6] Sakamura, K.: BTRON: The Business-oriented Operating System. *IEEE MICRO*, Vol. 7, No. 2 (Apr. 1987), pp. 53-65.

[7] Sakamura, K.: Multi-language Character Code Sets Handling in TAD. In TRON Project 19897 (1987), Springer-Verlag, pp. 97-111.

[8] Sakamura, K. ed: *Enableware Specification — Extracts from BTRON MMI External Specification.* TRON Association, 1988. in Japanese.

[9] Sakamura, K. ed: BTRON1 Specification Software Specification. TRON Association, 1989.

[10] Sakamura, K.: Design Policy of the Operating System Based on the BTRON2 Specification. In *TRON Project 1990* (1990), Springer-Verlag, pp. 103-118.

[11] Sakamura, K. ed.: *TRON Specification VLSI CPU Standard Handbook.* Personal Media Corporation, 1991. in Japanese.

[12] Sakamura, K. ed: *BTRON2 Kernel Standard Handbook.* Personal Media Corporation, 1992. in Japanese.

[13] Sakamura, K.: Human Interface with Computers in Everyday Life. In *Proc. Ninth TRON Project Symposium* (Dec. 1992), IEEE Computer Society Press, pp. 2-12.

[14] Sakamura, K. ed: *μITRON3.0 Standard Handbook.* Personal Media Corporation, 1993. in Japanese.

[15] Sakamura, K. ed: *TRON Human Interface Specifications for Computers in Everyday Life.* Personal Media Corporation, 1993. in Japanese.

[16] Sakamura, K.: Multilingual Computing as a Global Communication Infrastructure. In *Proc. 12th TRON Project Symposium* (Dec. 1995), IEEE Computer Society Press, pp. 2-14.

[17] Sakamura, K. ed: *TRON Human Interface Specifications.* Personal Media Corporation. 1996. in Japanese.

An Update on the CTRON Subproject

Tetsuo Wasano* and Toshikazu Ohkubo**

*ATR International Co. **NTT Software Co.

Abstract

This paper is reporting the current status of CTRON subproject in TRON projects. CTRON subproject has much vital activities. In section 2, we discribed all around the technical study items. In section 3, topics of implementation based on CTRON specification on many kinds of MPU are discribed. In section 4, promotion activeities of CTRON subproject around the world, espesially focused free software of CTRON kernel, are discribed. Finally, We describe the future study items of our subproject in section 5.

1. Introduction

This report covers the technical studies, product development and promotional work of the CTRON Technical Committee during fiscal year 1996.

2. Technical studies

2.1 Maintaining existing CTRON specifications

The existing CTRON specifications are mostly in the maintenance phase, as a result of which the working groups responsible for these specifications have been changed to specification maintenance groups, for dealing with inquiries from within or outside the subproject. Since the subproject members have completed prototype implementations of the specifications, there are few requests for specification changes, with most of the attention now focused on implementation performance issues, compatibility issues and the like.

2.2 Validation

The Basic OS document validation and function validation studies, for validating products that implement existing CTRON specifications, are mostly complete. Studies of document validation using checklists for the Extended OS programs, mostly covering file management, are likewise nearly complete, and attention is now turning to development of validation programs for Extended OS function validation. Compared to the Basic OS, the Extended OS programs encompass a much broader range of functions and are larger in scale, so that an important issue in these studies is how to enable this validation program development work to be carried out efficiently. Rather than developing each function separately, ways are being sought to generate these test programs from macro-descriptions based on the specifications. This methodology is now undergoing evaluation.

2.3 New study themes

Up to now, the CTRON interfaces have been tuned to get the maximum real-time response and performance from applications running individually on communications equipment. Studies are now moving ahead on new issues that will expand and optimize CTRON to true multimedia network services and distributed systems.

Telecommunications systems are an area where a lot of knowhow has accumulated on methods for managing distributed network resources efficiently, so they can be used economically and reliably by large numbers of users. However, a network also has a more advanced level of service resources, apart from the physical layer resources represented by telecommunications hardware. From the standpoint of network management, service management, and subscriber management, there are strong demands to enable the users, operators and managers of these service resources to control and manage them easily without having to be aware of how they are distributed.

In the field of information processing, the introduction of distributed systems has been taking place already, in the context of downsizing. In the case of network systems, however, as noted above, distributed systems have to be built while providing for both visible and

0-8186-7658-2/96 $05.00 © 1996 IEEE

invisible distribution; moreover, interfaces specific to communications systems will likely have to be provided for the sake of effective management and operation of network resources in multimedia communications.

The full-scale implementation of multimedia services will require that so-called continuous stream information, such as video, voice and music, be communicated or processed simultaneously, in synchronization with each other. As ATM technology is applied to wide area networks and LANs, greatly improving their carrying capacity, it will also be possible to allocate large numbers of communication paths at the same time for this stream information. Advanced multiprocessing meeting severe real-time response requirements will have to be realized for simultaneous control and management of these multiple communication paths.

The following specific study themes have been decided toward meeting these challenges. As the API studies proceed, some of the functions are also being incorporated in prototypes and studied in order to test and evaluate the effectiveness of the interfaces.

(1) Extending the functional and performance specifications for further improvement in real-time response performance, to enable multiple simultaneous operations on multimedia information.

(2) Expanding communication network functions geared to distributed control systems, so as to realize standard distributed platform interfaces as a basis for promoting multimedia service networks on a substantial scale.

(3) Making use of various agents in the network to realize a federation among multimedia network services provided on multiple servers, and defining an application model for implementing high value-added services on the network.

(4) Extending API validation technology to multimedia control interfaces.

2.4 Study of software quality evaluation criteria

The CTRON specifications define open OS interfaces, which anyone in the world is free to implement, including in the form of commercial products. Validation techniques are applied in order to evaluate the functional completeness of products implementing these open specifications.

For determining the optimum implementation conditions of software product application systems, evaluations must be carried out from such standpoints as software maintainability and portability, as well as from performance standpoints.

ISO/IEC 9126 (1992) presents guidelines on software quality evaluation criteria; and in accord with these guidelines, quantitative criteria were studied for rating a real-time microkernel in terms of functionality, reliability, usability, efficiency, maintainability, and portability, along with the evaluation methods. These criteria and methods were applied to the microkernel programming contest discussed below.

3. Product implementation

A large number of products implementing CTRON specifications have been shipped by vendors in Japan and elsewhere, and are today used in central office switches, PBXs, transmission control systems, message gateways and other key elements in networks. Other applications include the firmware kernels in control boards used in such equipment, and ISDN terminal control. Their uses thus range all the way from huge network systems to small embedded systems.

The CTRON concept of subsets was intended to allow systems to be configured and scaled optimally for a wide diversity of applications, and the actual ways in which CTRON-specification products are being used attest to the validity of this approach.

Table 1 shows current product development trends.

Table 1. Status of CTRON-specification Product Development

Vendor	Processor	OS elements provided					Application fields
		Kernel	I/O	File Mng	Comm. Control	Other	
A	I80X86	O				Device control	ISDN terminals
	Gmicro (100)	O				Device control	I/O device control
	(200)	O	O	O	O	Execution control, network management	Switching systems and transmission controllers
	(300)	O	O	O	O	Execution control, network management	ATM transmission controllers
	(500)	O	O	O	O	Switching control	Switching systems
	SPARC	O	O	O	O	Switching control	Switching systems
B	M680x0	O	O			Device control	ATM link control boards
	Gmicro (300)	O	O	O	O	Device control	Transmission controllers
	(500)	O	O	O	O	Switching control	Switching systems
	Proprietary	O				Device control	ATM line cards
C	I80X86	O	O			Terminal control	ISDN terminals
	M680x0	O	O			Multiplexing control	Multimedia multiplexers
D	M680x0	O	O			Video control	Embedded video processing equipment
E	I80X86	O	O	O		Switching control	Process control, packet switches
	M680x0	O	O	O	O	Switching control, device control	Mobile communications equipment, multiplexers
F	MIPS-R4400	O	O	O	O	UNIX	Switching systems and add-in units
	Proprietary	O	O	O	O	Device control	
G	M680x0	O	O	O	O	UNIX	ATM routers, cross-connect transmission control equipment, switching systems, PBX, transmission equipment
	PA	O	O	O	O	Switching control	
	Gmicro	O	O	O	O		

Vendor	Processor	OS elements provided					Application fields
		Kernel	I/O	File Mng	Comm. Control	Other	
H	M680x0	O	O	O	O	Switching control	ATM-PBX
	I80X86	O	O	O	O	UNIX	Software development workstations
I	M680x0	O	O		O	Device control	Embedded control systems
J	MIPS-R4400	O	O	O	O	Execution control, FTP, network management	TMR-architecture fault-tolerant systems; message gateway

4. Promotional activities

4.1 Seminars

As indicated above, products implementing CTRON-specification interfaces are being used in numerous information and communication processing systems, and especially in telecommunications equipment. The effort still goes on, however, to make the world more aware of this architecture and to win support on an international basis. To these ends, CTRON promotional materials are presented at TRON Association exhibits in trade fairs around the world. In addition, the CTRON Technical Committee holds seminars explaining the technology in depth.

Recently in China, CTRON technical seminars were held in Beijing and Shanghai. Co-sponsored by the China National Computer Software & Technology Service Corporation (CS&S), China's largest software house, these seminars were attended by more than 150 persons, mainly engineers, drawing an enthusiastic response in both cities. Although small-scale real-time systems are being developed in China and provided for equipment control use, examples of which were given in presentations by the Chinese hosts, application to large-scale telecommunications systems as aimed for in CTRON is practically unknown. Accordingly, the Chinese expressed a strong interest in working with the TRON Association to promote CTRON in that country.

4.2 Micro-C contest

As a way of promoting the CTRON subproject and microkernel technology in general, a programming contest was held in which contestants were asked to develop prototype programs implementing the micro-C specifications, the smallest subset of the CTRON specifications. The entries were evaluated based on the earlier-noted criteria for real-time microkernels, with awards given to those that met these criteria while also demonstrating good performance. The winning entries are being made available as free software via the Internet.

5. Directions for the future

The new study themes noted in section 2 are being approached by broad-based studies on leading-edge technologies, both inside and outside the CTRON Technical Committee. These studies are being accelerated toward the realization of a software platform architecture, geared to advanced multimedia network services that would be difficult or impossible to implement with any of today's general-purpose OSs.

Meanwhile, the CTRON Technical Committee is cooperating with other forums and consortia studying common architectures for global multimedia services and communication networks, including DAVIC, the ATM Forum, and the TINA Consortium. The aim of these activities is to expand the CTRON specifications while achieving connectivity and interoperability with new and existing systems providing multimedia services.

Some of the kernel functions are also being prototyped and tested to demonstrate the feasibility of new advanced interfaces.

At the same time, efforts are being stepped up to promote the CTRON specifications, both in their present form and as new extensions are made, so as to win acceptance and new allies on a worldwide scale.

Reference

[1] T.Ohkubo et al." Quality Criteria for Realtime Microkernel Products", RTSCA'96 Undersubmitting

[2] Original CTRON Specification Series. Ohmsha.

[3] ISO/IEC 9126 1992

[4] K. Yamamoto et al., "A CTRON Kernel Benchmark Program," Proc. of 9th TRON Project Symposium (IEEE Computer Press, 1992), pp. 185-193.

[5] T.Ohkubo,"A multimedia Operating System - Requirment and Study Issues," Proc. of 12th TRON Project Symposium [IEEE Computer Press 1995]

[6] T. Ohkubo et al., "Status and outlook of the CTRON Subproject," Information Processing, Vol. 35, No. 10 (1994), pp. 918-925. [in Japanese]

[7] I. Takenaka et al., "The CTRON Interface Validation System," TRON Project 1989 (Springer-Verlag, 1989).

[8] H. Kurosawa et al., "An Evaluation Method of Kernel Products Based on CTRON," TRON Project 1990 (Springer-Verlag, 1990).

[9] T. Ohkubo et al., "Normalization Method for Comparing Telecommunication OS Performance," '94 7th JC-CNSS (Gongjoo, Korea, 1994), pp. 313-318.

A Development Model for Disabled User Support Functions in the TRON Project: The Work of the TRON Enableware Research Group

Toshihisa Muto
TRON Enableware Research Group
Personal Media Corporation
MY Building,1-7-7 Hiratsuka, Shinagawa-ku, Tokyo, 142 Japan
tm@personal-media.co.jp

Abstract

The free market alone does not guarantee an ample supply of software with support functions for physically challenged computer users. In the TRON Project the TRON Enableware Research Group has been established as a university-centered volunteer organization. The work of this group includes drawing up software specifications for functions supporting disabled users, developing prototypes, and providing the results free of charge to software companies. These companies then develop software products based on these results and offer them on the market. By adopting this development model, it has been possible to supply the market with close to ideal support functions without depending on the whims of specific corporations.

1. Introduction

If computers are a valuable tool for people in general, they mean even more to the disabled. To many of us they may do no more than enable us to turn out better-looking documents, whereas for someone who cannot grasp a pen, a computer can be the only means for putting words into writing. Personal computers have opened up numerous possibilities for the handicapped.

Today's personal computers, unfortunately, seldom provide adequate functions supporting use by the disabled, particularly when it comes to the OS and other software. The reason can be seen as having less to do with technology than with the approach taken by software companies to developing such functions, and the model on which that development is based.

This paper begins by describing the approach taken in the TRON Project to developing support functions for the disabled. Next, it examines problems with the existing development model used by software companies. Then it goes on to discuss the distinctive model adopted in the TRON Project for developing functions that support disabled users. Finally, it reports on the actual development arrangement and its results to date.

2. The TRON Project Approach to Developing Support Functions for the Disabled

The appearance of the personal computer has opened up numerous possibilities for the disabled. In many cases, however, personal computers on the market cannot be used by the disabled without modifications. Even if the necessary functions can be provided by software, that software is typically developed on a volunteer basis and must be added separately. Besides, that development often cannot be done based on available information about the operating system but must rely on reverse engineering or similar means. Then when the OS is upgraded, the software is no longer usable. The cumulative results of all the efforts put in by third-party vendors to develop support functions for the disabled do not match the amount of that effort. A more efficient development approach is surely required.

In the TRON Project, the Enableware[1] concept was proposed at an early stage to deal with these issues. The need was emphasized for incorporating standard functions in the OS itself for the sake of disabled users, and this was put into practice in the BTRON specifications. The OS was given functions for adapting the computer to the user's physical conditions and features of the use

[1] "Enableware" is the overall term used in the TRON Project for assistive/adaptive technology. Computer and electronics equipment technology is used to "enable" the disabled.

0-8186-7658-2/96 $05.00

environment. The basic policy adopted for Enableware is that by making possible a wide range of adjustment, computers can be made accessible to a wide range of users.[1] In other words, the Enableware approach to the needs of the disabled is to provide the necessary functions in software to the extent possible, and in particular as standard operating system functions. Where that is not possible, standard equipment interfaces are defined for attaching the special hardware needed. As a result, general applications designed to run on BTRON will automatically be able to make use of Enableware functions.

This approach does require a certain initial cost. Once the initial development expenditure is made, however, the resulting technology will be widely applicable in the emerging advanced computer society, for quick return on the investment. This is the basic thinking behind Enableware.

3. TRON Project Development Model for Disabled User Support Functions

3.1 The situation with existing personal computer OSs

Most of the personal computer OS makers today are starting to become aware of the needs of disabled users. Support functions for the disabled are found in many of the latest OSs on the market. Yet, there are numerous problems with respect to ease of use even in the case of ordinary users, let alone those with disabilities. Before a product is brought out, the needs and views of the handicapped or experts in disabilities need to be taken into full account, and field tests carried out repeatedly, even more so than for ordinary users. Whether or not this development effort is made, however, depends primarily on the software companies; the small market represented by the disabled has practically no clout in the highly competitive software market.

That's why even functions that should preferably be offered by OS makers are instead dependent on third-party software developers. Compared to software companies in general, those third-party developers who specialize in products for the disabled can be expected to tailor their products more precisely to the needs of the disabled, and to carry out extensive field tests. This approach, however, is quite distant from the TRON Project ideal of incorporating as many of these functions as possible as basic OS functions, spreading the cost more evenly so the burden on the disabled will be lighter.

Recently OS makers have been equipping their products with graphical user interface (GUI) functions and employing multimedia technologies. Since this trend is designed to broaden the appeal of these products to ordinary users, it is likely to continue growing. At the same time, however, these same companies have not come up with solutions to such problems as the inability of blind users to operate a GUI-based OS. Ideally, they should be developing ways of making multimedia a tool for adapting computers to a multiplicity of users, allowing disabled users to supplement one medium with another as needed. The existing market model and development model, however, present serious obstacles to adopting the technical development approach that will make this possible.

3.2 The TRON Project approach

TRON-specification products are the result of a development model different from the conventional one. The direct results of the TRON Project itself are only specifications, not actual products. Moreover, this project is a joint effort by industry and academia, with the University of Tokyo playing a leadership role, so the specifications are drawn up based on high ideals and are offered to the public. Although industry cooperates greatly in the project, it is by no means dependent on the circumstances of one corporation or another. The results of the project are provided to the public domain, for use by anyone without charge.

In return for being able to use the TRON specifications freely, corporations are asked to include the Enableware specifications in their development. In this way users gain the benefit of products with built-in support functions even for the severely disabled. Corporations who implement the specifications contribute to society by assisting the disabled. The development model adopted in the TRON Project thus ends up benefiting both the end users and corporations.

4. The TRON Enableware Research Group

As noted above, in developing functions for disabled users, working closely with end users is even more important than in the case of ordinary product development. To this end the TRON Project formed the TRON Enableware Research Group as a non-profit, volunteer organization (chaired by Ken Sakamura, TRON Project Leader). The main purpose of this group is to study and draw up specifications reflecting the needs of the disabled.

The group is made up of specialists working on the front lines of computer use by the disabled. The final decision on Enableware specifications is made under the leadership of the University of Tokyo, but the ideas of

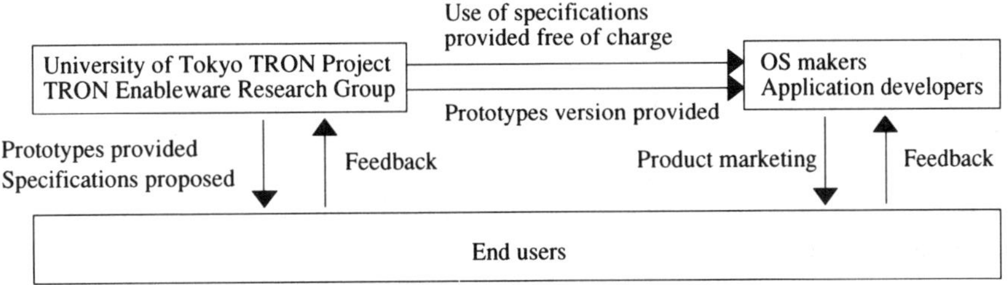

Figure

these specialists are fully taken into account. The members of this group include specialists with the following organizations: national public research institutions for the disabled, organizations developing work opportunities for the disabled, research centers in manufacturing companies, schools for the blind, special schools for the handicapped, and university research institutes studying assistive technologies. Also includes as members are end users with disabilities, and non-disabled end users interested in assistive technologies.

4.1 R&D organization

The organization devoted to TRON Enableware research and development is shown in the figure. The University of Tokyo, with the cooperation of the TRON Enableware Research Group, draws up the specifications and offers them to the public free of charge. Since the group includes members of research laboratories in manufacturing companies, the specifications reflect the current technology levels. The University of Tokyo develops prototypes based on the specifications, and field tests are carried out by organizations within the group or by the University itself. The results of field tests are fed back into the specifications and prototypes. At an appropriate stage, the prototype source code is provided to OS makers and application developers. These companies continue to refine the results further, through additional field testing, as they incorporate them in actual products for the market. Subsequent feedback from a wider range of users is used to upgrade the products in later versions.

4.2 Accomplishments to date and current activities

The TRON Enableware Research Group was formed in 1987, the third year after the start of the TRON Project. The first Enableware-related symposium, TEPS (TRON Electronic Prosthetics Symposium) '88, was held the following year. At that time the first edition of the Enableware specifications was made public, covering mainly functions for users with upper limb disabilities. A prototype edition of the specifications was announced in 1990, and the first product implementing the specifications was brought out in April 1992. At the symposiums held throughout this period, numerous proposals and ideas for improvements were made in response to the original specifications, contributing greatly to the final product.

Next attention was turned to the special needs of the visually handicapped, led by the University of Tokyo, with research and development carried out on character input functions, audio and Braille display output functions, text editing functions for the blind, and other functions. To date these specifications have been made public in a number of different prototype versions.[2]

In addition, the Enableware Research Group continues to hold symposiums once a year and two annual regular meetings, to announce R&D results and carry on discussions. Lately the themes taken up at these meetings have broadened beyond technology itself to include a wider look at the involvement of the disabled with computer technology, and even the position of the disabled in society. Through these activities we are helping to educate the public on the importance of using computer technology to assist the disabled.

5. Conclusions

Groups that deliberate issues relating to computer use by the disabled regularly make their needs known to manufacturers, at least indirectly. Moreover, user groups for specific types of products for the disabled often lobby manufacturers directly for improvements of one kind or another. What is special about the TRON Project is the central role of the project itself in actively seeking out the views of users, and its system for incorporating them in

An Enableware Chronology

1984	TRON Project started
Oct. 1986	Section 508 on Electronic Equipment Accessibility is added to U.S. Rehabilitation Act.
Oct. 1987	U.S. Secretary of Education and Government Procurement Office complete electronic equipment accessibility guidelines for implementing Section 508.
Dec. 1987	TRON HandyWare Group (present TRON Enableware Research Group) is started.
July 1988	JEIDA (Japan Electronic Industry Development Association) begins survey to prepare for drafting of Japanese information equipment accessibility guidelines, as requested by Machinery and Information Industries Bureau in Japan's Ministry of International Trade and Industry (MITI).
July 1988	First TRON Enableware Symposium (TEPS '88) is held, where Ver. 1 of the TRON Enableware specifications is announced.
Oct. 1988	U.S. Government Procurement Office presents electronic equipment accessibility guidelines (implementing Section 508) for disabled employees.
Dec. 1989	MITI's Machinery and Information Industries Bureau releases draft version of information equipment accessibility guidelines.
Dec. 1989	U.S. Congress passes Americans with Disabilities Act (ADA).
Mar. 1990	TRON Enableware Symposium (TEPS '90) features first release of TRON Enableware prototype for users with upper limb disabilities.
June 1990	MITI's Machinery and Information Industries Bureau releases final version of information equipment accessibility guidelines.
July 1990	U.S. President Bush signs ADA, enacting it officially.
Sept. 1991	BTRON-specification OS 1B goes on sale.
Apr. 1992	Enhancements to the Enableware prototype issued in March 1990 are implemented in the new version of the 1B OS.
Dec. 1992	TRON Enableware Symposium (TEPS '92) is held, featuring presentations and displays on Enableware functions for the visually handicapped.[2]
Mar. 1995	New version of 1B incorporates enhanced Enableware functions.

specifications and products. Moreover, these activities are not directed at individual products but are aimed at the operating system at the heart of computer technology. In this way, functions supporting the disabled can be incorporated more efficiently in the OS.

Countries all over the world frame their welfare policies from the standpoint that these issues cannot be resolved by free market mechanisms alone. The taxes and voluntary efforts by citizens are considered necessary for assisting the elderly and disabled. This is not just a matter of the weak helping the strong; it can also be seen as an investment in ones own future. Included in these issues is the supply of support functions for the disabled as described in this paper. That is, the principles of free competition alone are not enough to guarantee that software companies, who face severe competition, will provide an adequate supply of functions for supporting computer use by the disabled. The development model adopted by the TRON Project and put into practice through the TRON Enableware Research Group is offered as one solution to this problem.

References

[1] K. Sakamura. Enableware: Adaptive Technologies for Disabled People on the TRON Architecture. *Proceedings of the Tenth TRON Project Symposium* (Dec. 1993), IEEE Computer Society Press, pp. 166-168.

[2] N. Koshizuka, M. Uematsu, N. Kimura, and K. Sakamura. Design and Implementation of the Enableware Specification -- A Human-Machine Interface for Physically Challenged People. *Proceedings of the Ninth TRON Project Symposium* (Dec. 1992), IEEE Computer Society Press, pp. 23-39.

Technical Session I

ITRON and CTRON

OS Validation Programming Language: CVAL

Susumu Minami
NTT Software Corporation
209 Yamashita-cho Naka-ku Yokohama-shi
Kanagawa 231 Japan
minami@jts.ntts.co.jp

Ichizo Kogiku
Network Service System Laboratories,NTT
3-9-11 Midori-cho Musashino-shi,Tokyo 180
Japan
kogiku@nttiros.nslab.ntt.jp

Akiko Fukuya
Hitachi Software Engineering Co.,Ltd
Kurume Research Center Bldg.,2432-3
Aikawa-machi Kurume-shi Fukuoka 830, Japan
fukuya@pic.hitachi-sk.co.jp

Hideyuki Matsuda
Fujitsu Limited
Nakahara Bldg.,12-5 Simokodanaka
2-chome Nakahara-ku,Kawasaki 211,Japan
hmatsuda@csd.ts.fujitsu.co.jp

Abstract

Standardizing application program interfaces (API) is one aspect of assuring program portability, but it is likewise important to establish a means of checking products for conformance to the API.

This paper proposes an operating system (OS) validation programming language CVAL and describes how CVAL can be used to make an OS validation program. The proposed method was used for actual validation program development. Part of the same development was then carried out using the C language, and a comparison was made of the development scale and time involved. The results show that using CVAL for OS validation program development achieves at least twice the productivity as the existing approach using C.

1. Introduction

The rapid pace of change in today's world has increased the demands for developing computer systems in a short time and at low cost, while maintaining the necessary quality level. One way of meeting this need is to build systems using existing parts, selecting the optimum components for each system from the available pool, in order to reduce the amount of new development needed. When systems are build from components made by multiple vendors, however, problems arise with the portability of existing software resources and the need for programmer retraining. An important part of the solution to such problems is a standard application program interface (API). Additionally, a means is necessary for confirming the compliance of products with these interface standards, so as to assure software portability. This is what is called validation. Already there are standard specifications for programming languages including COBOL, C, FORTRAN, Pascal, and the database language SQL. Validation testing for these is carried out by NIST in the United States as well as by European and Japanese bodies. Validation testing facilities and standards are also under consideration in standards organizations.[1]

There are three main types of operating systems (OS), for time sharing systems (TSS), personal computers, and real-time systems. The Open Group, as is widely known, makes available standards and product validation for UNIX[1]-based TSS-oriented OSs. In the TRON (The Realtime Operating System Nucleus) Project, standard interfaces have been published for CTRON (Communication and Central TRON), designed as a real-time OS for the range of nodes making up a communications network; and a validation service is in place for products implementing these interfaces.[2][3]

So far, though, the CTRON function validation has been limited to Basic OS programs, with only a static document-based validation provided for Extended OS programs. The latter have a much broader range of functions than the Basic OS, so that if the same programming methods as were used to develop the Basic OS validation program were applied to the Extended OS, the cost would be prohibitive.

[1]UNIX is a registered trade mark in the United States and other countries, licensed exclusively through X/Open Company Limited.

0-8186-7658-2/96 $05.00 © 1996 IEEE

This paper reports on a new approach to lowering that cost. It makes use of a programming language developed specifically for writing validation programs, called CVAL (CTRON Validation Language).

In section 2 we discuss the CTRON interface configuration and existing validation systems. Section 3 looks at the requirements for a new Extended OS validation system, and measures for meeting these needs. Section 4 describes CVAL based on the concepts outlined in section 3, and a validation system using CVAL. Section 5 presents an evaluation of the productivity gains when CVAL is used to develop a validation system, comparing it with existing approaches. The evaluation focuses on the differences in validation program development steps, and presents data on development scale and person-hours.

2. CTRON interface configuration and validation systems

2.1. CTRON configuration

A layered configuration is adopted for CTRON, consisting of a Basic OS layer directly interfacing with hardware, and an Extended OS layer above it.

This configuration is illustrated in Figure 1 and outlined below.

(1) Basic OS

The Basic OS presents a logical computer interface to the Extended OS and application program layers above it, hiding architecture differences in processor and I/O device hardware. The Basic OS Kernel interfaces correspond to processor resources, and the I/O Control interfaces are provided for I/O device functions.

(2) Extended OS

The Extended OS provides the following six kinds of interfaces considered to be common requirements of application programs.

- Data storage control interfaces for files and databases
- Execution control managing program execution

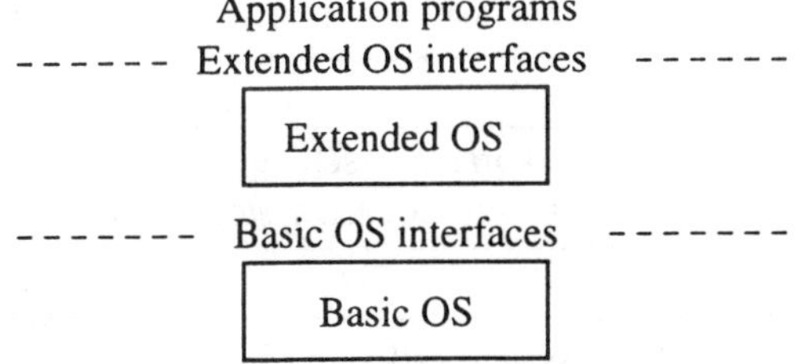

Figure 1. CTRON interface configuration

- Communication control for communication protocol processing
- Human interface control for processing commands and messages
- Speech path control for switching system applications
- Operation, administration and maintenance management for device management and notification of system operation status

2.2. CTRON validation

There are two types of CTRON validation testing.

(1) Function validation

The aim of this testing is to determine whether the software conforms to CTRON interface specifications when it is running on its intended hardware. The validation program suite is run on the OS to see if the response meets the specifications.

(2) Document validation

Document validation is aimed at finding whether a product implements functions not in the specifications. For this purpose checksheets are compared with the product manuals to find functions that are lacking or superfluous.

The validation suite developed to date are shown in table1.

Table 1 . Validation suite data

Basic OS	• Validation Program suite, report output tools, etc.: 110 Ks • Validation checksheets: approx. 1,000 sheets
Extended OS	• Validation checksheets: approx. 2,500 sheets*

*All checksheets except OSI transaction processing in Communication Control.

Our studies were undertaken in order to develop a validation program suite for the Extended OS, which is still unfinished business.

3. Extended OS validation system development principles

3.1. Requirements for an extended OS validation system

Let us look first of all at how much programming would be involved in developing validation programs for the Extended OS using the same approach as for the Basic OS.

The actual validation program development scale for the Basic OS is shown below.

System calls	Test items	Program scale
164	1,322	97.1 Ks

From the above results, the program scale per test item is 73 steps. Now we shall estimate the Extended OS validation program scale assuming the same programming method is used as that for the Basic OS. Here we assume 88 steps per test item, since the Extended OS involves more complex configuration setting.

System calls	Test items	Program scale
432	5,303	466 Ks

This estimate indicates that the development scale for Extended OS validation programs is five times that of the Basic OS, making it necessary to find ways of improving productivity.

3.2. Measures for increasing productivity

The need for precision in validation testing precludes any reduction in the number of test items. The emphasis must instead fall on eliminating waste from the program development and reducing the development scale.Possibilities here include the following.

- Looking for similar processing patterns and using common routines for these.
- Simplifying high-frequency processing.
- Simplifying or eliminating incidental functions that are not part of the testing process itself.

(1) Creating common validation program routines

The flow of validation program processing is shown in Figure 2. Since there is a consistent pattern here, it might be possible to create common routines for much of this processing. We discovered, however, that not much advantage can be gained from this approach, due to the differences in parameter values and system calls used for different test items.

(2) Making system calls easier to write

The frequency of system call issuing in validation programs is extremely high, so one effective way of improving validation program productivity would be to make this programming task easier. Possibilities here include the following.

(i) The programming related to one system call in the Basic OS validation program, written in C language, is structured as in Figure 3. Here the data declaration, parameter setting and system call invocation are required for each system call. Of these, the data declaration and parameter setting parts include similar coding repeated many times, suggesting a possible area for simplification.

(ii) Rather than writing the data declaration and parameter setting as part of each system call invocation, these can be treated by binding them at the time the system call is invoked. This enables the data declaration and parameter setting coding to be reused.

(3) Adopting an interpreter approch

Each validation program is small, with an average of 100 steps; but the number of programs in the validation suite is several thousand. Debugging can be made more efficient by adopting an interpreter approach, eliminating the need for compiling and linking.

Step 1: Issue environment preparation system calls.
Step 2: Issue system call to be tested.
Step 3: Check system call output information.
Step 4: Issue system call for checking state change and other results.
Step 5: Issue garbage processing system calls.
*1: Steps 2 and 3 vary depending on the nature of the test item.
*2: Steps 1, 4, and 5 often vary as to the type and number of system calls issued, or are unnecessary, depending on the nature of the test item.

Figure 2. Validation program processing flow

Data type declaration (common to validation program, declared only once)
Data declaration (must be declared for each data used with parameters)
Parameter setting (must be set for each system call)
System call invocation

Figure 3. Coding for one system call (Basic OS validation program)

(4) Employing interactive mode

The validation programs incorporate exception handling including the following functions, in order to handle cases where the tested product does not pass a test or where there is a bug in the validation program itself.

- A function for gathering information to be used in cause analysis.
- A function for restoring the environment so the next validation program can run.

These kinds of exception handling do not affect the contents or accuracy of the testing. Moreover, the processing is unnecessary if no error occurs while the validation program is running.

By introducing interactive processing, which can handle error situations more flexibly, exception processing can be greatly simplified. When an error occurs, switching from batch processing to interactive processing allows the necessary diagnostic system calls to be issued interactively.

We provided the following two interactive processing modes.

- Manual entry mode: CVAL statements are entered directly.
- Menu select mode: This feature is provided for vendors who are not familiar with CVAL. System calls are selected from a menu list, with parameter referencing and updating performed simply by responding to the on-screen prompts.

In order to implement the above measures, we developed the CVAL OS validation programming language and processing system.

4. Extended OS validation system

4.1. Configuration of the extended OS validation system

The configuration of the Extended OS validation system is shown in Figure 4, and its components are explained below.

(1) Validation programs
Programs written in CVAL, coding the testing procedures.

(2) CVAL interpreter
A program that interprets and executes the CVAL code. It is provided to the user (a vendor testing a product for validation) both as C language source and as an executable program.

(3) Test results file
A file containing the test results.

(4) Report output tool
A tool that collects and edits the test results files and test item management files, then creates a test report.

(5) Execution control
Used to issue CVAL interpreter.

(6) Standard C language libraries
Libraries used by the CVAL interpreter.

(7) CTRON Basic OS
A kernel subset used by the CVAL interpreter.

4.2. Outline of CVAL specifications

CVAL is a language for writing validation programs. Its specifications resemble C, although it has more limited functions and is simpler than C. CVAL has the following functions.

(1) System call issuing
In order to simplify the procedure for issuing system calls, functions are provided for defining system calls and system call parameter patterns. Once a system call has been defined, it can be called by designating the system call name and parameter pattern number.

(2) Data referencing and updating
Parameter definitions of system call, and definitions of data controlling the execution of validation programs, can be written in a simpler form than in C. The defined data can then be referenced and updated using code equivalent to a C language expression.

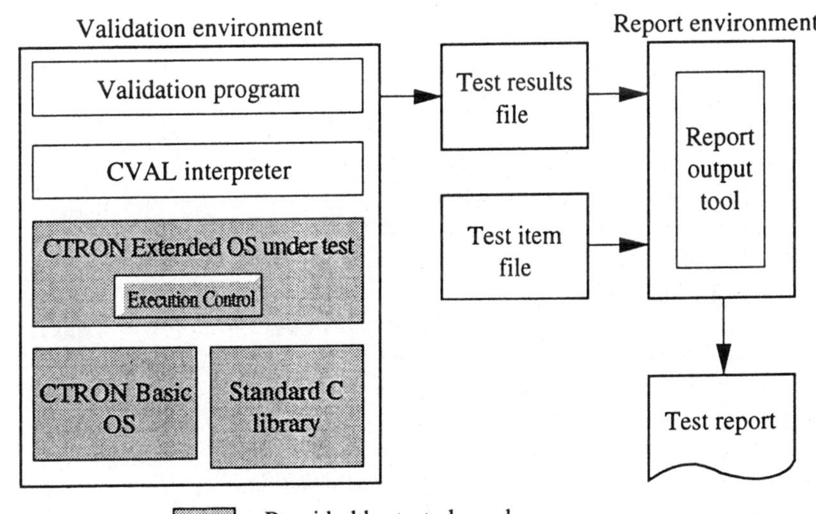

Figure 4. Extended OS validation system configuration and role

(3) Execution sequence control

The received message synchronization of system calls that use external synchronization can be controled, and validation program can be temporarily suspended. CVAL also makes it easy to change the flow of processing according to the system call result, using if and while statements.

(4) Resource definition

Special definition statements are provided for defining external synchronization message boxes and for memory allocation by the kernel.

(5) Macros

There is no function equivalent to the C language function definition, but a set sequence of processing can be defined as a macro. Once a macro is defined, it can be called from anywhere, any number of times. In addition, macros can be registered for processing when a specific message is received or when a specific exception occurs.

(6) Operation modes

The operation mode of the CVAL interpreter can be designated, including batch execution of the CVAL files or interactive execution by the operator.

A list of CVAL control statements is given in the Appendix.

5. Evaluation of the extended OS validation system

5.1. Qualitative evaluation

The steps required for developing a Basic OS validation program are shown in Figure 5. The number of steps for developing an Extended OS validation program does not differ from this, but three of the steps differ in content, as described below.

(1) Coding (Step 22)

(i) The Extended OS validation program is written in CVAL. The use of CVAL makes the data declaration in Figure 3 unnecessary because parameter areas are automatically ensured when parameters are set, so the amount of coding is less than with C. Parameter setting is also easier.

(ii) Exception handling in the Extended OS validation program is greatly simplified, since the program changes to interactive mode when an error occurs.

(2) Compiling and linking (Step 242)

CVAL is an interpreted language, making advance compiling and linking unnecessary. A syntax check like that performed by a compiler takes place when the program is run, but the syntax itself is simpler than C, so syntax errors are infrequent.

Another advantage is that the source code can be executed even in uncompleted state, enabling the program to be trial-run as it is being written.

(3) Confirming results (Step 245)

The Basic OS validation system does not have an intera ctive mode; instead, results are output to a printer after batch execution and checked. The interactive mode introduced for the Extended OS validation system enables detailed checking of any problems that arise during execution, for fast problem solving.

Step 1: Determine test items.
Step 2: Repeat the following for each test item.
  Step 21: Perform detail design.
  Step 22: Perform coding (C language).
  Step 23: Make program check list.
  Step 24: Test.
    Step 241: Check code.
    Step 242: Compile and link.
    Step 243: Create machine test data.
    Step 244: Run on workstation.
    Step 245: Confirm results.
  Step 25: Go to Step 2.

Figure 5. Basic OS validation program development steps

5.2. Quantitative evaluation

5.2.1. Benefits of CVAL use

In order to evaluate the advantages of our approach quantitatively, we used C language to develop similar program functions as some of the Extended OS validation programs developed with CVAL. We then compared the two approaches in terms of productivity (development scale and person-months).

(1) Evaluation conditions

(i) Validation programs having equivalent functions to those of the programs developed using CVAL were programmed in C, over the following range.

- System call developed:GET_NOD_INFORMATION (Get node information function in General File Management)
- Test items: 28
- Validation programs: 18 (The validation programs for ten of the items are common to other validation programs, so these were not included in the development scale.)

(ii) The steps of determining test items, detail design, and making program check lists are the same whether CVAL or C is used, since the validation programs have the same specifications.

(iii) Coding and testing (code checking and Unix workstation test) were carried out separately using CVAL and using C. (The workstation environment for testing the C language program was the same as that used for the Basic OS validation system.)

The work of preparing a test environment (sys tem call simulator, etc.) for the validation programs was not included in the comparison or evaluation. Also, no actual validation testing has yet been car ried out on an Extended OS product.

(2) Evaluation results

The development scale and time required for the program development are shown in Table 2.

(3) Analysis of the development scale

Using CVAL reduces the program scale by around 25% compared to C. In this development we simplified validation program exception handling for C in the same way as when CVAL was used. The main reductions in program scale with CVAL therefore came from eliminating the need for data declarations and from the simplified parameter setting.

(4) Analysis of the time required

Looking just at the coding and testing steps, which are development language-dependent, a major reduction of 44% is achieved. This is the result of the reduced development scale and the simpler testing thanks to the use of an interpreter. However, the language- independent steps for test item determination, detail design, and program check list (PCL) preparation take up a large part of the overall development process; so the overall reduction in time is only 25%.

5.2.2. Benefit of simplifying exception handling

When an error occurs while a validation program is running, the system switches to interactive mode. This approach greatly simplifies the exception handling by the validation program. To measure the benefit in terms of reduced development scale, we did a comparative analysis of exception handling in a Basic OS validation program and Extended OS validation program.

The flow of exception handling in a Basic OS validation program is shown in Figure 6. The figure shows the overall approach, but on an actual validation program the flow is not necessarily the same. The error recovery processing differs depending on where the error occurred, and the error level likewise varies with the location of the error.

The exception handling flow for an Extended OS validation program is shown in Figure 7. Essentially this processing is the same regardless of the error location.

Samples were taken of previously developed Basic OS validation programs to see what benefits are derived from substituting the Extended OS validation program exception handling for those parts of the Basic OS validation programs. The results are shown in Table 3. They differ from one sample to another; but for the Kernel the reduction is approximately 20%, whereas for I/O Control there was very little difference. This result can be explained by the small number of system calls in I/O Control, and the already simple exception handling, which in almost all cases involves issuing two system calls, TERMINATE_DEVICE and DELETE_DEVICE, for error recovery.

The Extended OS has a large number of system calls and many different recovery patterns, so it can be assumed that exception handling on the order of that for the Kernel is required. On this basis we assume that simplifying the exception handling reduces the development scale by 20%.

Table 2. Development scale and time required

	Scale (Ks)	Time (person-months)						
		Deciding test items	Detail design	Coding	PCL *1	Testing	Total	*2
(1) CVAL	0.9	0.26	0.48	0.27	0.10	0.37	1.48	0.64
(2) C	1.2	(0.26)	(0.48)	0.49	(0.10)	0.65	1.98	1.14
(1) ÷(2)	0.75	1	1	0.55	1	0.57	0.75	0.56

*1 PCL: program check list

*2 Values for language-dependent work (coding +testing) only.

*3 Figures in ( ) are those derived from development using CVAL.

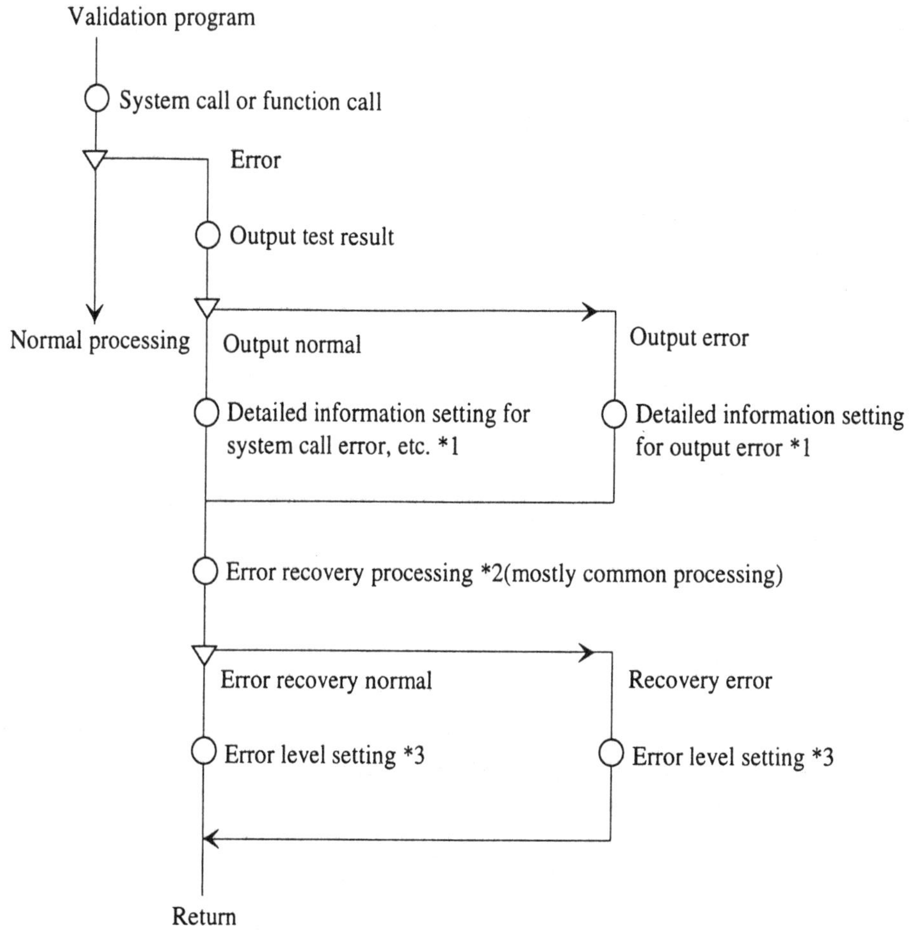

*1 Information setting for locating the error (differs depending on where the error occurred).
*2 Restoring the test environment so the next validation program can run (differs depending on where the error occurred).
*3 Information as to whether it is possible to continue with subsequent test items.

Figure 6. Exception handling in the Basic OS validation system

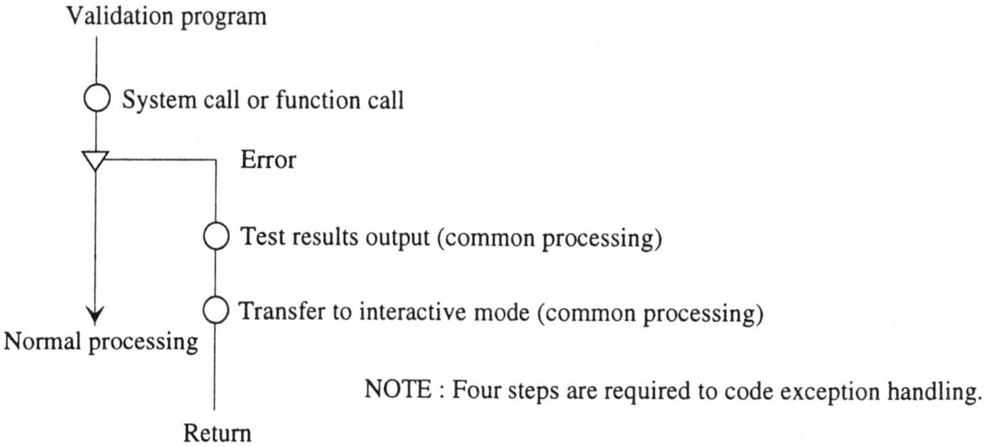

Figure 7. Exception handling in the Extended OS validation system

Table 3. Analysis of exception handling

Sample		Validation program steps [s]	Exception handling steps [s]	Exception handling occurrences	Reduction in exception handling steps [s]	Reduction rate for exception handling
1	Kernel	92	38	6	14	15%
2		271	132	13	80	30%
3		111	46	5	26	23%
4		121	36	4	20	17%
5	I/O Control	59	19	4	3	5%
6		74	22	5	2	3%

Note 1: (Reduction in exception handling steps) = (Basic OS validation program steps for exception handling) - (Extended OS validation program steps for exception handling).
Note 2: (Extended OS validation program steps for exception handling) = (Exception handling occurrences) × 4 steps.

5.2.3. Overall benefit of CVAL introduction

Extended OS validation program coding was done using CVAL, in addition to which exception handling was greatly simplified. The benefits of these two measures in reduced devel opment scale according to 5.2.1 and 5.2.2 above were assumed to be 25% and 20%, for a total of 45%.

To show the extent of this reduction, Table 4 gives the average scale of the Extended OS validation programs written in CVAL for this study, and the average scale of validation programs if they were to be written in C language (without simplifying exception handling), as estimated from the Basic OS development results.

Table 4. Average Extended OS validation program size

Item compared	Scale [steps]	Size ratio to (2).
(1) When written in CVAL	33	0.38
(2) Estimate if written under the same conditions as Basic OS validation program	88	1

The statistics for (1) in Table 4 are the average size for 208 test items for General File Management. According to these results, the Extended OS validation program scale is reduced by 62%. Since the number of samples in 5.2.1 and 5.2.2 is small, we can assume that using CVAL instead of C for Extended OS validation programs will re duce the development scale by approximately half, or 250 Ks. Developing the CVAL interpreter involves only 14 Ks of C language, so the benefits of CVAL are significant.

Only limited development of Extended OS validation programs has been carried out to data, offering little opportunity for reusing system call parameter patterns. As the extent of development increases, however, this is one more area where productivity gains can be looked for.

6. Conclusion

In this paper the authors have described the features and functions of CVAL, a programming language at a higher level than C, for the purpose of simplifying the development of OS validation programs. We have further proposed methods of writing OS validation programs with CVAL and presented evaluation results.

A particular advantage of CVAL is that, based on an analysis of existing OS validation programs, it eliminates the need for data declarations of system call parameter which appear repeatedly with similar coding, as well as simplifying parameter value setting. In addition it is an interpreted language, for more efficient debugging, since the size of each validation program is small but the number of programs is in the thousands.

Another measure taken was to change to interactive mode whenever an error occurs, greatly simplifying the coding for exception handling. This could be done because the individual exception handling routines in existing OS validation programs have no effect on test accuracy, and are not used unless an error occurs.

The above approaches were shown to reduce the development scale by at least half compared to writing the same programs in C.

Of the six kinds of Extended OS interfaces, so far CVAL has been used to develop validation programs for part of Data Storage Control. The applicability of CVAL will continue to be evaluated as additional programs are developed using it. We also plan to evaluate the extent to which system call parameter patterns can be reused, and the resulting improvement in productivity, given the increase in number of validation programs needed for the Extended OS.

One more issue taken up is the transfer from batch processing to interactive mode when an error occurs while the OS validation program is running. Error cause analysis is performed in interactive mode either by entering CVAL statements directly or by selecting Extended OS system calls and the like from menus. Based on Extended OS validation program debug experience, effective analytical methods will be drawn up and reflected in operation manuals or menus.

Acknowledgments

The authors are grateful to the OS Validation Working Group members in the TRON Association for their work on the CTRON Extended OS validation system, and to the CTRON Technical Committee members for their encouragement and valuable advice given during the course of these studies.

References

[1] IEEE Standard for Information Technology-Test Methods for Measuring Conformance to POSIX, IEEE Std 1003.3 (1991).

[2] TRON Association (Ed.), Original CTRON Specification Series. (Ohmsha, Tokyo:1989)

[3] Takenaka,I. and Oda,H.:CTRON Interface Validation System, Proceedings of TRON Symposium, pp. 171-181, Tokyo (1989)

Appendix A. CVAL control statements

(1) Execution control statements

(a) SYSCALL	Issue system call
(b) RECEIVE	Receive message
(c) WAITSK	Wait task
(d) PAUSE	Pause
(e) MCALL	Call macro

(2) Sequence control statements

(a) while	Loop
(b) break	Leave loop
(c) continue	Continue loop
(d) if	Decision

(3) Resource definition statements

(a) sysdef	Define system call
(b) msgdef	Define message
(c) exmdef	Define exception handler
(d) mbxdef	Define message box
(e) mpldef	Define message pool
(f) alcdef	Define ALC area

(4) Data operation statements

(a) print	List variable contents
(b) print_time	Show time stamp

(5) Macro definition statements

(a) MACRO	Start macro definition
(b) ENDMACRO	End macro definition

(6) Mode switching statement

(a) include	Input file (batch processing)
(b) user_input	Interactive mode (manual entry)
(c) TALK	Interactive mode (menu selection)

(7) Other

(a) help	Invoke online help
(b) quit	Return to beginning
(c) exit	Stop executing control statements
(d) #	Comment

Appendix B. CVAL coding sample

System calls and the values of common data are defined in a common file. The following coding sample doesn't include the file.

[CVAL Coding sample]

```
# GET_NODE_INFORMATION:15 Validation(ba0315)
MACRO ba0315;
# Setup Environment
   # CRE_DIR
   strcpy(directory_path_name, ev_dir);
   strcat(directory_path_name, EVDIR0);
   access_permission = EL3 {EVACSDALL, EVACSDALL,
                            EVACSDALL};
```

```
    SYSCALL CRE_DIR;
    if ($$ != 0) {
        ev_rt = R_NR;
        evtput( R_RESULT, ev_id, R_NR, ev_msg, EVSFMSG1, "CRE_DIR");
                MCALL evmerr;
                return;
        }
# Target Systemcall
    strcpy(path_name, directory_path_name);
    inf_id = 6;
    node_information = 0;

    SYSCALL GET_NOD;
# Check Result
    #  Check error class,error reason
    work_i1 = $$;
    work_i2 = offset(return_code,0);
    if ((work_i1 != 0) || (work_i2 != 0)) {
        ev_rt = R_NG;
        evtput( R_RESULT, ev_id, R_NG, ev_msg, EVSFMSG2, 0, 0,
                work_i2, work_i1);
        MCALL evmerr;
        return;
    }
    #  Check Output_information
    if (node_information != 1) {
        ev_rt = R_NG;
        evtput( R_RESULT, ev_id, R_NG, ev_msg, EVSFMSG3,
                "node_type", 1, node_information);
        MCALL evmerr;
        return;
    }
    #  Validation GOOD
    ev_rt = R_OK;
    evtput( R_RESULT, ev_id, R_OK, ev_msg, NULLP);
# Recover Environment
    # DEL_DIR
    SYSCALL DEL_DIR;
    if ($$ != 0) {
        evtdspf( ev_msg, EVSFMSG200, "DEL_DIR");
        MCALL evmerr;
        return;
    }
ENDMACRO;
#*************** Copyright (C) 1996 by TRON Association
```

Prioritized Inter-processor Synchronization in an ITRON-MP Implementation

Cai-Dong Wang†, Hiroaki Takada†, and Ken Sakamura‡

† Department of Information Science,
School of Science, University of Tokyo
7-3-1, Hongo, Bunkyo-ku, Tokyo 113, Japan

‡ The University Museum,
University of Tokyo
7-3-1, Hongo, Bunkyo-ku, Tokyo 113, Japan

Abstract

When a real-time kernel is implemented for shared-memory multiprocessors, there exists a requirement that a higher priority task should execute system calls faster. For this requirement, the inter-processor synchronization primitive, i.e. spin locks, should be prioritized. However, simple priority-ordered spin locks can cause uncontrolled priority inversions when they are used for nested spin locks. This paper points out the problem of uncontrolled priority inversions in the context of spin locks. In order to solve this problem while achieving fast response to external interrupts, we propose priority inheritance spin lock with preemption, which is a spin lock algorithm enhanced with a priority inheritance scheme and a preemption scheme. Real-time kernels with and without the proposed algorithm are implemented and their performance is measured.

1 Introduction

As the application areas of real-time systems expand, requirements for large-scale and high-performance real-time systems are increasing. In many application areas of high performance real-time systems, a large number of external devices such as sensors, actuators, and network controllers are connected to a system and the system must respond to the external events from the devices with predefined and short latency. Adopting function-distributed (or asymmetric) multiprocessors in which each device is handled by a fixed processor is a promising approach to satisfying this requirement (Figure 1).

We have investigated on the ITRON-MP specification, which is an extension of the ITRON kernel specifications to support (mainly function-distributed) shared-memory multiprocessors, and its implementation methods for these several years [1, 2, 3]. In this paper, we describe an implementation of ITRON-MP

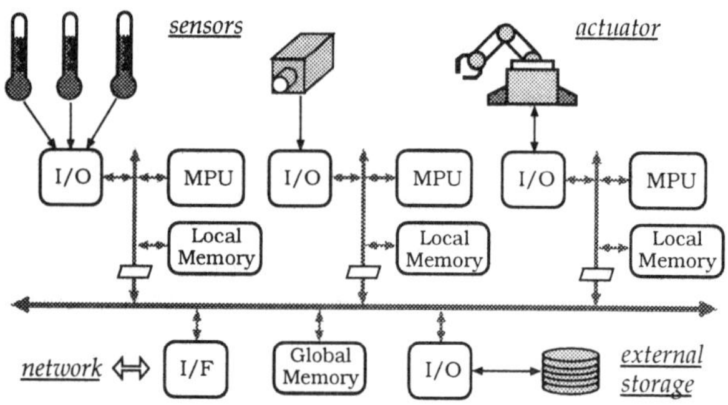

Figure 1: An Example of Function-Distributed Multiprocessor

in which task priorities are reflected to inter-processor synchronization.

With the ITRON-MP specification, tasks and other kernel objects are classified into some classes with different characteristics. Among them, a task belonging to a local class, the most basic class in ITRON-MP, is executed only on its host processor and can operate on kernel objects on other processors in the system. When a local task on a processor operates on an object on another processor, the operation should be realized by directly accessing the remote memory on which the control block of the object[1] is located [2, 4]. Consequently, some mutual exclusion mechanism among processors is necessary for the access control of the control blocks. In implementing a real-time kernel, because the execution time of each primitive operation is very short, spin locks are usually used for this exclusive control.

When some tasks on different processors try to operate on an object, these operations are necessary to be serialized. In a multiprocessor system, the order

[1] The control block of a kernel object is the memory area in which the state and other information of the object are managed.

0-8186-7658-2/96 $05.00 © 1996 IEEE

in which operations are serialized is one of the most significant factors on the execution times of the operations. Depending on the design methodology of a real-time system, there are two kind of (exclusive) requirements on the execution times of operations. The first requirement is that the worst-case execution time of each operation should be bounded. Needless to say, a shorter upper bound is preferable. The second requirement is that the time that a higher priority task executes an operation should be shorter. In other words, when two tasks on different processors try to operate on an object at the same time, the higher priority one of them executes the operation first.

This paper discusses an implementation method of the ITRON-MP specification that satisfy the second requirement. In order to give precedence to the operation by a higher priority task, inter-processor synchronization should be prioritized. In other words, a higher priority task should enter a critical section in precedence over a lower priority one. An implementation method satisfying the first requirement has been discussed in [5] and [6].

This paper is organized as follows. In Section 2, the basic real-time kernel model of ITRON-MP and its implementation approach are described. The granularity of lock units is discussed in detail, and it is shown that two lock units are necessary to be acquired in some system calls. In Section 3, the problem of uncontrolled priority inversions are pointed out, and the priority inheritance scheme is introduced. A preemption scheme is also introduced in order to achieve fast interrupt response. As the result, an algorithm of priority inheritance spin lock with preemption is presented. Section 4 presents the performance measurements of the real-time kernels with and without the proposed method.

In this paper, we assume that atomic read-modify-write operations on a single word (or aligned contiguous words) of shared memory such as test_and_set, fetch_and_store (swap), and compare_and_swap, are supported with hardware. Some existing priority-ordered spin locks are discussed on the same assumption [7, 8].

2 An Implementation Approach of ITRON-MP

In this section, the basic real-time kernel model of ITRON-MP is presented and its implementation approach is discussed, especially on the granularity of lock units.

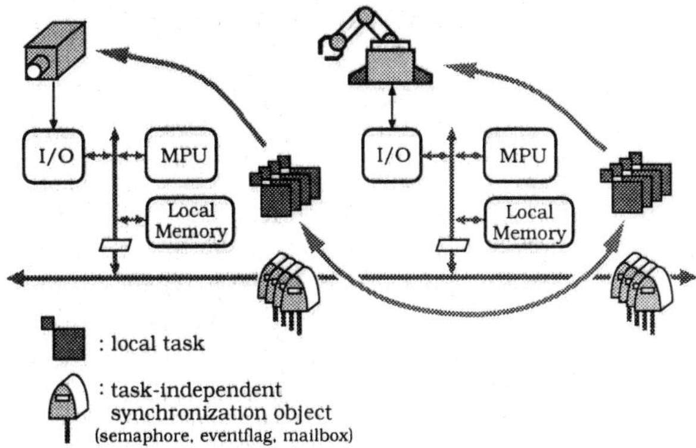

Figure 2: Basic Kernel Model

2.1 Basic Kernel Model of ITRON-MP

In function-distributed multiprocessors, because each external device is handled by a fixed processor, the task that handles the device should be bound to the processor. In the basic kernel model of ITRON-MP, each task has its host processor on which it is executed and is called a *local task* of the processor. Each task can synchronize and communicate with tasks on other processors through the same interface with tasks on the same processor. In other words, a task can operate on any task in the system with the same set of system calls. A ready queue is prepared for each processor in which all the local tasks that are ready to execute are included in the descending order of their priorities. Each task-independent synchronization and communication object (called simply as synchronization objects in this paper), such as a semaphore, an eventflag, and a mailbox, also has its host processor and can be accessed from any task in the system (Figure 2).

With the ITRON-MP specification, tasks and synchronization objects are classified into some classes with different characteristics. In this paper, we focus on the implementation issues of the basic kernel model of ITRON-MP.

2.2 Granularity of Lock Units

When a task operates on a kernel object on another processor, the task should directly access the control block of the object located on the local memory of the processor. This implementation approach is called the direct access method and is appropriate for implementing a real-time kernel on function-distributed shared-memory multiprocessors [2, 4]. The ITRON-MP specification is designed so that it can be implemented with this method.

With the direct access method, spin locks are necessary for the access control of shared data structures in the kernel, such as the task control blocks (TCBs), the control blocks of synchronization objects, and the ready queues. Here, the granularity of lock units of kernel data structures is a difficult issue. In general, using fine-grained lock units reduces lock contention and therefore improves concurrency. Conversely, using coarse-grained lock units reduces lock acquisition and deadlock avoidance overhead. For real-time kernels, making lock units so small that many locks are necessary to be acquired in nested structure in some operations is not appropriate, because the execution time of each critical section is very short in real-time kernels and the lock acquisition overhead is relatively large.

In order to determine an appropriate granularity of lock units, we have examined a real-time kernel implementation for single processors based on the μITRON3.0 specification [9]. The access pattern on kernel data structures of each level S system call of μITRON3.0 is analyzed, and which data structures should be entered in the same lock unit is investigated.

The simplest method to avoid nested locks is to enter all kernel data structures in a single lock unit. With this method, only one kernel service can be executed at the same time. Therefore, the execution throughput of kernel services cannot scale well. It is also reported that the computational power of a processor is not sufficient to execute all the kernel services, when kernel services are heavily used [10]. We have premised that kernel data structures on different processors, at least, should be placed in different lock units.

Under this premise, at least two locks are necessary to be acquired at the same time. In concrete, when a task begins waiting for a synchronization object, it first accesses the control block of the synchronization object and then accesses the TCB of itself. When the task and the synchronization object are located on different processors, their control blocks are placed in different lock units. A similar situation also occurs when a task operates on a synchronization object and wakes up another task that is located on a different processor from the synchronization object.

As the results of the investigations, we have concluded that the TCBs and the ready queue on a processor should be included in a lock unit (called a task lock) and that the control blocks of synchronization objects on the processor should be included in another lock unit (called an object lock). With this granularity of lock units, at most two lock units, a task lock and an

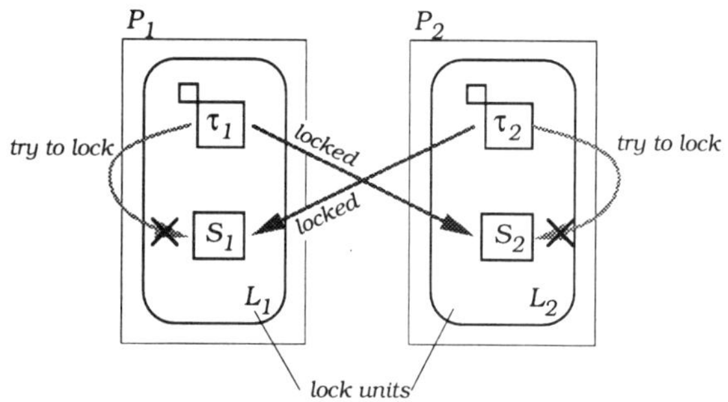

Figure 3: An Example of Deadlock

object lock, are necessary to be acquired at the same time. In order to avoid deadlocks, when both locks are necessary to be acquired, the object lock should be acquired first.

The essential reason for separating these two kind of locks is to reduce the possibility of deadlocks. If the TCBs and the control blocks of synchronization objects on a processor were guarded with a single lock, two parallel invocations of operations on synchronization objects, which are very frequent situation, could cause a deadlock. For example, suppose the case that a task τ_1 begins waiting for a semaphore S_2 and another task τ_2 begins waiting for another semaphore S_1. Suppose also that τ_1 and S_1 are located on the same processor and thus guarded with the same lock L_1, and that τ_2 and S_2 are located on another processor and guarded with L_2 (Figure 3). In this case, τ_1 locks L_2 then L_1 and τ_2 locks L_1 then L_2. Obviously, a deadlock can result.

Even though the proposed granularity of lock units is adopted, a deadlock detection and re-execution mechanism must be adopted in implementing special operations on a task (`rel_wai`, `chg_pri`, and `ter_tsk`), because a task accesses a TCB and then accesses the control block of a synchronization object in these system calls. Though it is very difficult to bound the maximum execution times of these system calls, the problem is not so serious because these system calls are used only in special cases.

3 Priority Inheritance Spin Locks for ITRON-MP

In order to satisfy the requirement that the execution time of an operation by a higher priority task should be shorter, a priority-ordered spin lock is necessary to be used for realizing mutual exclusion among processors. If a priority-ordered spin lock algorithm is simply used for nested spin locks, however, uncontrolled

```
acquire_lock(L2);
// critical section.
release_lock(L2);
```

routine (a)

```
acquire_lock(L1);
acquire_lock(L2);
// critical section.
release_lock(L2);
release_lock(L1);
```

routine (b)

Figure 4: Example of Nested Spin Locks

priority inversions can occur.

In this section, after illustrating the problem of uncontrolled priority inversions, we show that incorporating the basic priority inheritance scheme into priority-ordered spin locks can solve the problem. Then, we present an algorithm of priority inheritance spin lock with preemption that is used for the implementation of ITRON-MP. How the algorithm is used in the implementation of a typical system call of ITRON-MP is also presented in this section.

3.1 Uncontrolled Priority Inversion Problem in Nested Spin Locks

Priority inversion in the context of spin locks is the phenomenon that a higher priority processor is forced to wait for the execution of a lower priority processor. In our implementation of ITRON-MP, the priority of a processor is equal to the priority of the task that the processor is executing. Because priority inversion cannot be avoided unless a higher priority processor can steal the lock held by a lower priority one, how to minimize its duration is a concern. When the maximum duration of a priority inversion cannot be determined, it is called uncontrolled.

When priority-ordered spin locks are simply used for nested spin locks, uncontrolled priority inversions can occur. A typical case is described as follows.

Example 1 (uncontrolled priority inversion)
We assume that P_1, P_2, P_3, and P_4 are processors arranged in descending order of priority with P_1 having the highest priority. Note that the priority of each processor is the priority of the task executed on the processor. We also assume that these processors repeatedly execute one of the two routines presented in Figure 4. Suppose the case that when P_1 begins executing routine (b) and tries to acquire a lock L_1, P_4 is holding L_1 and is waiting for another lock L_2 in routine (b). If P_2 and P_3 repeatedly execute routine (a) in this situation, P_2 and P_3 can acquire L_2 alternately and P_4 must wait for L_2 all the while. Because P_1 must also wait for the executions of P_2 and P_3, this duration is a priority inversion. Obviously, the maximum duration of this priority inversion cannot be determined.

3.2 Priority Inheritance Spin Locks

In order to solve the problem of uncontrolled priority inversions, we have introduced the basic priority inheritance scheme to spin locks [11]. The fundamental concept of priority inheritance scheme is that when a processor makes some higher priority processors wait, its priority should be raised to the level of the highest priority processor among the waiting ones. In other words, the processor inherits the priority of the highest priority processor blocked by it. Also, priority inheritance must be transitive. For example, when P_2 should inherit the priority of P_1 and P_3 should inherit that of P_2, P_3 should inherit the priority of P_1.

With the basic priority inheritance scheme, wihch is the naive realization of this concept, the uncontrolled priority inversion problem illustrated in Example 1 can be solved as follows. When P_1 tries to acquire L_1 and begins waiting for it, P_4, which is holding L_1, inherits the priority of P_1 because P_1 is forced to wait by P_4. Because the inherited priority is higher than those of P_2 and P_3, P_4 can acquire L_2 with precedence over P_2 and P_3. As the result, P_1 need not wait for the alternate executions of routine (a) by P_2 and P_3, and the maximum duration of the priority inversion can be bounded.

In general, when a processor releases one of the locks, its priority is necessary to be re-calculated. Specifically, its priority is changed to the highest one of its original priority and the priorities of the processors that are waiting for the locks held by the former one. Also, when a processor waiting for a lock ceases the waiting, the priority of the processor that is holding the lock should be re-calculated. In this study, these re-calculations are omitted because the omission does not affect the worst-case behavior of each processor and because it has only a limited effect on the average performace. It is not difficult (but quite complex) to add the re-calculation routine to our implementation.

3.3 Spin Lock with Preemption for Improving Interrupt Response

Fast interrupt response and predictable interprocessor synchronization are two important requirements for multiprocessor real-time kernels. In order to satisfy both of the requirements at the same time, a spin lock algorithm is required to support a preemption scheme for the following reason [12].

In order to achieve fast response to external interrupts, interrupt services should not be inhibited while a processor is waiting for a lock. This is because the maximum number of critical sections that a lower priority task must wait for is very large or even unbounded. On the other hand, in order to realize predictable inter-processor synchronization, interrupt services should be inhibited once the processor acquires the lock for the following reason. In order to predict the time until a processor acquires a lock, the maximum duration that each processor holds the lock must be bounded. When multiple devices are connected to a processor, interrupt requests from them are usually asynchronous and the maximum time to service all of them becomes very long or even unbounded. Therefore, interrupt service times should not be included in the time duration that a processor holds a lock.

In summary, interrupt services must not be inhibited while a processor waits for a lock and must be kept inhibited once it acquires the lock. In order to realize this behavior, the processor repeatedly probes interrupt requests while it is waiting for a lock. When interrupt requests are detected, it must inform other processors that it is servicing interrupt requests by modifying some shared variable. The processor trying to release the lock checks if the succeeding processor is servicing interrupts. If the succeeding one is found to be servicing interrupts, its turn to acquire the lock is canceled, and the lock is passed to the next processor in line.

In order to achieve fast interrupt response with our kernel implementation, this extension (supporting preemption) should be incorporated in a priority inheritance spin lock algorithm. In [13, 11], we have proposed two priority inheritance spin locks; one of them is base on the Markatos' priority-ordered spin lock algorithm [7] and the other is based on the PR-lock algorithm [8]. Because the former algorithm is difficult to extend with the preemption scheme, we have adopted the latter algorithm as the base method.

3.4 Priority Inheritance Spin Lock Algorithm with Preemption

A typical usage of the priority inheritance spin lock algorithm with preemption is illustrated in Figure 5. In this pseudo-code, the keyword *shared* indicates that only one instance of the variable is allocated and shared in the system. Other variables are allocated for each processor.

The *acquire_first_lock* function acquires the lock *L1* and returns true when it succeeds in acquiring the lock. If an interrupt request is detected while waiting for the lock, the function returns false. Note that the function changes the value of *me1* to the

```
    // globally shared variables.
    shared var L1, L2: Lock;

    // local variables (allocated for each processor).
    var my_prio: integer;
    var me1, me2: NodePtr;

    me1 := NULL;
    me2 := NULL;
retry:
    disable_interrupts;
    my_prio := priority of the task;
    if ¬acquire_first_lock(&L1, me1) then
        enable_interrupts;
        goto retry
    end;
    //
    // critical section (first part).
    //
    if ¬acquire_second_lock(me1, &L2, me2) then
        release_lock(&L1, me1);
        enable_interrupts;
        goto retry
    end;
    //
    // critical section (second part).
    //
    release_lock(&L2, me2);
    release_lock(&L1, me1);
    enable_interrupts;
```

Figure 5: Usage of Priority Inheritance Spin Locks with Preemption

pointer to the queue node used for the lock acquisition. The *acquire_second_lock* function is similar to *acquire_first_lock*, but is used for acquire the inner lock *L2*. The first argument of *acquire_second_lock* indicates the queue node used to acquire the outer lock *L1*, which is necessary to inherit the priority of a higher priority processor that is waiting for *L1*.

The most important point is that when the processor detects interrupt request while waiting for the inner lock, it *releases the outer lock*, services the interrupt request (by enabling interrupts), and re-executes the critical region from the beginning.

Pseudo-code of the priority inheritance spin lock algorithm with preemption based on the PR-lock (denoted as PR-lock/PI/Prempt in this paper) is presented in Figure 11 – 13. In these figures, *CAS* is the abbreviation of compare_and_swap, which is a Boolean function with three parameters. It first reads the shared variable addressed by the first parameter and compares its contents with the second parameter. If they are equal, the function writes the third parameter to the variable atomically and returns true. Otherwise, it returns false. The binary operators *and*

and *or* are assumed to be the conditional-and and conditional-or operations, respectively. We also assume that a larger value represents a higher priority.

In this algorithm, the A-B-A problem [14] and the problem that the queue node designated by a pointer may be reused for another purpose are avoided by preparing many node area (the *my_locknode* array) and suppressing their quick reuse. *get_next_locknode* is the function to obtain the next queue node to be used from the *my_locknode* array, and *release_locknode* is to return an unused node to the array.

In the algorithm, one bit (usually the least significant bit) in the *next* filed of the *Node* structure is used for indicating that the node is dequeued. The *MARK*, *UNMARK*, and *MARKED* functions are to set, reset, and check this bit, respectively.

We omit the *acquire_first_lock* function from the figures. This is becuase the only difference between *acquire_first_lock* and *acquire_second_lock* is that the former function does not have the code to inherit priority from *me1*, and because *acquire_first_lock* can be easily reconstructed from *acquire_second_lock*.

For detailed explanation on the priority inheritance spin lock based on the PR-lock, please refer to [13]. Refer to [12] or [15] for the details of the preemption scheme.

3.5 Implementation of a Typical System Call

Each system call of ITRON-MP is implemented with the spin lock algorithm presented in the previous section. The implementation of a typical system call `sig_sem` (signal semaphore) is discribed below.

Figure 6 presents the pseudo-code for the `sig_sem` system call. After checking some statically detectable errors, such as the invalid object ID number error (`E_ID`) and the object access violation error (`E_OACV`), the processor acquires the object lock guarding the control block of the designated semaphore. After it succeeds in acquiring the object lock, the processor executes one of the four routines depending on the current state of the semaphore. In case that some tasks are waiting on the semaphore, the processor acquires the task lock guarding the control block of the first one of the waiting tasks. When an interrupt service is requested while waiting for the task lock, the processor releases the object lock and re-executes the critical region. Note that no shared variable is modified until the processor succeeds in acquiring the task lock or until the processor judges that the task lock is not necessary.

```
system call sig_sem(semid: ID): ER;
  var ercd: ER;
  var lock1, lock2: LockPtr;
  var me1, me2: NodePtr;
begin
  check static errors and return if detected;
  get the control block of the semaphore semid;
  lock1 := the lock guarding the semaphore control block;
  me1 := NULL;
  me2 := NULL;
retry:
  disable_interrupts;
  my_prio := priority of the task;
  if ¬acquire_first_lock(lock1, me1) then
    enable_interrupts;
    goto retry
  end;
  if the semaphore has not been created then
    ercd := E_NOEXS
  elseif some tasks are waiting for the semaphore then
    get the control block of the first task of them;
    lock2 := the lock guarding the task control block;
    if ¬acquire_second_lock(me1, lock2, me2) then
      release_lock(lock1, me1);
      enable_interrupts;
      goto retry
    end;
    release the task from wait state;
    release_lock(lock2, me2);
    ercd := E_OK
  elseif the current semaphore count is the max then
    ercd := E_QOVR
  else
    increment the semaphore count;
    ercd := E_OK
  end;
  release_lock(lock1, me1);
  enable_interrupts;
  return ercd
end
```

Figure 6: Pseudo-code for the `sig_sem` System Call

4 Performance Evaluation

In this section, the effectiveness of the proposed implementation method is examined through performance measurement. Their performance is compared with the simple priority-ordered spin lock with preemption (denoted as PR-lock/Preempt) and the priority inheritance spin lock without preemption (denoted as PR-lock/PI).

4.1 Evaluation Environment

A shared-bus multiprocessor system without coherent cache is used for the evaluation. The shared bus is based on the VMEbus specification, and each processor node consists of a GMICRO/200 microprocessor, which is rated approximately at 10 MIPS, and 1 MB

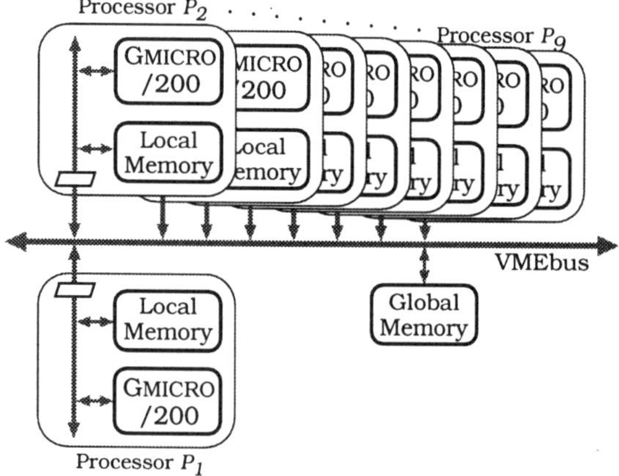

Figure 7: Evaluation Environment

of local memory. The local memory can be accessed from other processors through the shared bus. No coherent cache is equipped. All the program code and the data area for each processor are placed on the local memory of the processor. Global shared variables are placed on the local memory of the master processor, which does not execute spin locks (Figure 7).

Because the VMEbus has only four pairs of bus request/grant lines, processors are classified into four groups by the bus request line they use. The round-robin arbitration scheme is adopted among groups and the static priority scheme is applied among processors belonging to a same group.

4.2 Evaluation Method

We have measured the execution times of system calls and the interrupt response times using a synthetic workload illustrated in Figure 8.

The workload is determined so that the worst situations can easily occur. A task τ_1 on processor P_1 repeatedly invokes the `wai_sem` system call that acquires the semaphore S_1 on P_1 and the `sig_sem` system call that releases S_1. These system calls require at most two locks at once. On each of the other processors, only one task is executed. The task τ_2 on processor P_2 and the task τ_n on processor P_n execute the same routine with τ_1, i.e. they acquire and release S_1 repeatedly. The task τ_i on another processor repeatedly invokes the `sus_tsk` system call that suspends the execution of task $\tau_{1,i}$ on P_1 and the `rsm_tsk` system call that resumes its execution. In these system calls, only one lock is necessary to be acquired.

τ_1 and τ_2 have the same priority that is higher than the other tasks in the system. The task τ_3 on processor P_3 is assigned the next highest priority, τ_4 is assigned the next one, and τ_n is assigned the lowest priority. $\tau_{1,i}$ has lower priorities than τ_1 and is executed only when τ_1 is waiting for the semaphore S_1.

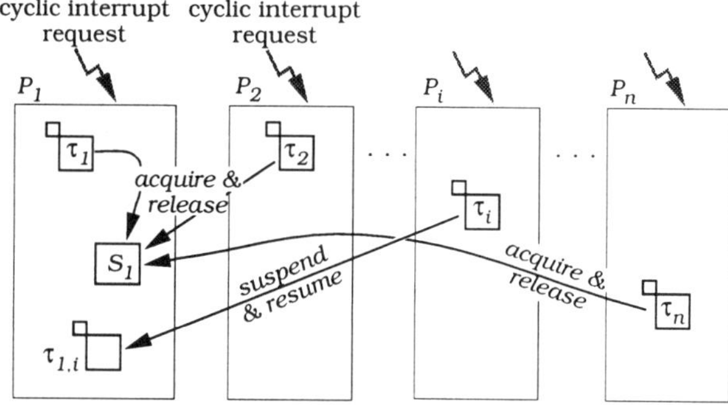

Figure 8: The Measurement Workload

During the measurement, periodic interrupt requests are also raised on each processor, and the interrupt response times are measured within the interrupt handler. The interrupt period is around 2 ms and is varied in 0 – 4% for each processor in order that the interrupts are not synchronized on each processor. Other external interrupt requests are inhibited during the measurement.[2]

In real-time systems, because the worst-case behavior of the system has primary importance, the effectiveness of the algorithms should be evaluated with their maximum execution times. Because maximum execution times cannot be obtained through experiments due to unavoidable non-determinism in multiprocessor systems, however, a p-reliable time, the time within which a processor finishes execution with probability p, is adopted as the performance metric instead of a maximum execution time [6]. In this section, we show the evaluation results when p is 0.99 (i.e. 99%) or 0.999 (i.e. 99.9%).

4.3 Evaluation Result

Under the workload described in the previous section, the execution times of the `sig_sem` system call by τ_2, one of the highest priority task in the system, and the interrupt response times on P_2 are measured. The execution times of the system call when an interrupt request is serviced during its execution are not recorded.

Figure 9 presents the 99.9%-reliable execution times of the `sig_sem` system call by τ_2, when no interrupt request is serviced during the execution. The number of contending processors (including P_1) is changed from two (one interfering task) to nine (eight

[2]The inter-processor interrupts should not be inhibited.

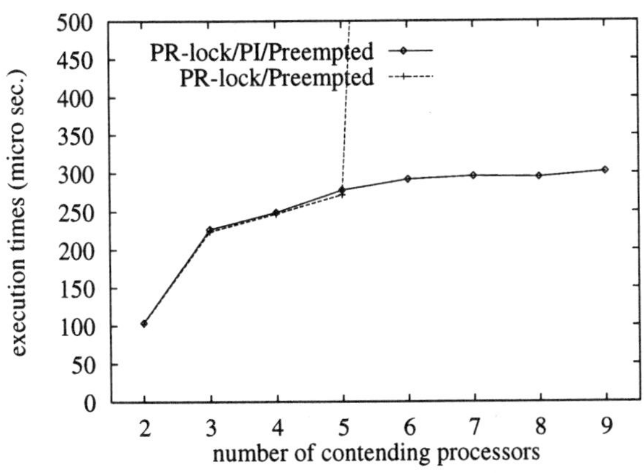

Figure 9: 99.9%-Reliable Execution Times of `sig_sem`

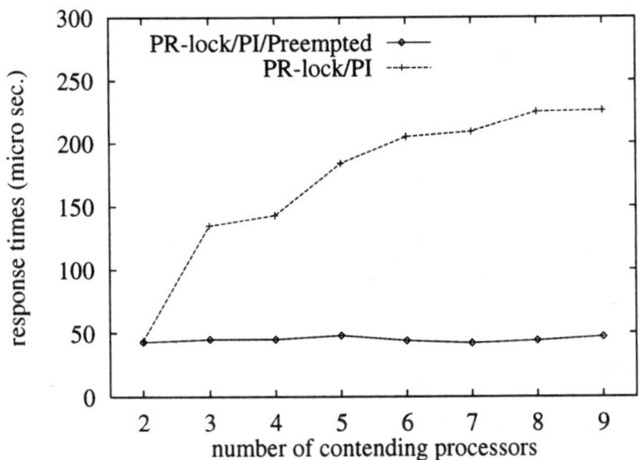

Figure 10: 99%-Reliable Interrupt Response Times

interfering tasks). With PR-lock/Preempt, the 99.9%-reliable execution times diverge when the number of processor is more than five due to uncontrolled priority inversions. When the number of processor is less than or equal to five, uncontrolled priority inversions do not occur and PR-lock/Preempt has a bit better performance than PR-lock/PI/Preempt.

Figure 10 presents the 99%-reliable execution times of the interrupt response on P_2 under the same condition. With PR-lock/PI (i.e. without the preemption scheme), the interrupt response becomes worse as the number of contending processor increases.

From these results, the proposed method (PR-lock/PI/Preempt) has the required properties, while other methods cannot satisfy the two important requirements at the same time. More investigations are necessary to confirm the effectiveness of the priority inheritance scheme in real environments.

5 Conclusion

For real-time kernels for shared-memory multiprocessors, there are two kind of (exclusive) requirements on the underlying inter-processor synchronization mechanism: bounded synchronization and prioritized synchronization. This paper discusses an implemenation of real-time kernel meeting the latter requirement and the underlying inter-processor synchronization mechanisms appropriate for it.

Though some priority-ordered spin locks have been proposed for the requirement, a simple use of them can cause uncontrolled priority inversions when they are used for nested spin locks. We incorporate the basic priority inheritance scheme to spin locks to solve this problem. The preemption scheme is also necessary to be introduced to spin locks for fast interrupt response. We extend the PR-lock algorithm, one of the priority-ordered spin locks, with the two schemes and present an algorithm of priority inheritance spin lock with preemption.

A real-time kernel based on the ITRON-MP specification is implemented with the proposed algorithm and its performance is compared with the real-time kernels without these schemes. As the result, the effectiveness of the proposed method is confirmed under the workload which causes the worst situations very easily. More investigations are necessary to clarify the effectiveness of the priority inheritance scheme in real environments.

References

[1] H. Takada and K. Sakamura, "ITRON-MP: An adaptive real-time kernel specification for shared-memory multiprocessor systems," *IEEE Micro*, vol. 11, pp. 24–27,78–85, Aug. 1991.

[2] H. Takada and K. Sakamura, "Implementation of inter-processor synchronization/communication and design issues of ITRON-MP," in *Proc. 8th TRON Project Symposium*, pp. 44–56, IEEE CS Press, Nov. 1991.

[3] H. Takada and K. Sakamura, "Advances in the ITRON specifications – supporting multiprocessor and distributed systems," in *Proc. 9th TRON Project Symposium*, pp. 89–95, IEEE CS Press, 1992.

[4] H. Takada and K. Sakamura, "Towards a scalable real-time kernel for function-distributed multiprocessors," in *Proc. 20th IFAC/IFIP Workshop on Real Time Programming*, Nov. 1995.

[5] H. Takada and K. Sakamura, "Inter- and intra-processor synchronizations in multiprocessor real-time kernel," in *Proc. 4th Int'l Workshop on Parallel and Distributed Real-Time Systems*, pp. 69–74, Apr. 1996.

[6] H. Takada, *Studies on Scalable Real-Time Kernels for Function-Distributed Multiprocessors*. PhD thesis, School of Science, University of Tokyo, 1996.

[7] E. P. Markatos, "Multiprocessor synchronization primitives with priorities," in *Proc. 8th IEEE Workshop on Real-Time Operating Systems and Software*, May 1991.

[8] T. Johnson and K. Harathi, "A prioritized multiprocessor spin lock," Tech. Rep. TR-93-005, Department of Computer Science, University of Florida, 1993.

[9] K. Sakamura, ed., *μITRON 3.0 Specification*. Tokyo: TRON Association, 1994. (can be obtained from "ftp://tron.um.u-tokyo.ac.jp/pub/TRON/ITRON/SPEC/mitron3.txt.Z").

[10] M. Joh, Y. Igarashi, and T. Ozeki, "CTRON-specification kernel implementation for a tightly coupled multiprocessor system," in *Proc. 8th TRON Project Symposium*, pp. 118–129, IEEE CS Press, 1991.

[11] C.-D. Wang, H. Takada, and K. Sakamura, "Priority inheritance spin locks for multiprocessor real-time systems," in *Proc. Int'l Symposium on Parallel Architectures, Algorithms, and Networks*, pp. 70–76, IEEE CS Press, June 1996.

[12] H. Takada and K. Sakamura, "Predictable spin lock algorithms with preemption," in *Proc. Real-Time Operating Systems and Software*, pp. 2–6, May 1994.

[13] C.-D. Wang, H. Takada, and K. Sakamura, "Performance evaluation of priority inheritance spin locks," in *IEICE Technical Report (RTP'96)*, vol. 95, no. 603, pp. 47–54, IEICE, Mar. 1996. (in Japanese).

[14] S. Prakash, Y.-H. Lee, and T. Johnson, "A non-blocking algorithm for shared queues using compare-and-swap," in *Proc. 1991 Int'l Conference on Parallel Processing*, pp. II-68–II-75, 1991.

[15] H. Takada and K. Sakamura, "Queueing spin lock algorithms with preemption," *Trans. IEICE (D-I)*, vol. J78-D-I, pp. 661–669, Aug. 1995. (in Japanese).

```
type Node = record
  next: pointer to Node;
  locked: (Released, Locked, Preempted, Removing);
  prio: integer
end;

type Lock = record
  top: pointer to Node
end;

type NodePtr = pointer to Node;
type LockPtr = pointer to Lock;

var my_locknode[NUM_LOCKNODE]: Node;
// locked field of each element of my_locknode
// should be initialized to Released.
var next_locknode: integer;
// next_locknode should be initialized to 0.

// mark the flag indicating that the node is
// dequeued and return the pointer to the next node.
function mark(node: NodePtr): NodePtr;
  var succ: NodePtr;
begin
  repeat
    succ := node→next
  until CAS(&(node→next), succ, MARK(succ));
  return succ
end;

// make the lock holder inherit my priority.
procedure inherit(lock: LockPtr, me: NodePtr);
  var head: NodePtr;
  var prio: integer;
begin
  repeat
    head := lock→top;
    if head = me then break end;
    prio := head→prio
  until prio ≥ my_prio
          or CAS(&(head→prio), prio, my_prio)
end;

// release the lock.
procedure release_lock(lock: LockPtr, me: NodePtr);
  var succ, pred : NodePtr;
begin
  succ := mark(me);
  lock→top := succ;
  while succ ≠ NULL then
    if CAS(&(succ→locked), Locked, Released) then
      break
    end;
    if CAS(&(succ→locked), Preempted, Removing) then
      pred := succ;
      succ := mark(pred);
      lock→top := succ;
      pred→locked := Released
    end
  end
end;
```

Figure 11: PR-lock/PI/Preempt Algorithm (1)

```
// acquire the inner lock.
function acquire_second_lock(me1: NodePtr,
        lock: Lockptr, var me: NodePtr): Boolean;
  var me2, pred, succ, succ1, next: NodePtr;
  var prio: integer;
begin
  if me ≠ NULL and me→locked = Preempted then
    if CAS(&(me→locked), Preempted, Locked) then
      goto spin;
    end
  end;
  me := get_next_locknode();
  me→prio := my_prio;
again1:
  // insert me to the waiting queue.
  pred := lock→top;
  while pred = NULL do
    me→next := NULL;
    if CAS(&(lock→top), NULL, me) then
      return TRUE
    end;
    pred := lock→top;
  end;
  // inherit priority from me1.
  prio := me1→prio;
  if prio > my_prio then
    my_prio := prio;
    me→prio := prio
  end;
  // insert me to the waiting queue (cont.)
  me→locked := Locked;
  while (TRUE) do
    succ1 := pred→next;
    succ := UNMARK(succ1);
    if succ ≠ NULL and succ→prio ≥ my_prio then
      pred := succ
    elseif MARKED(succ1) then
      me→locked := Released;
      goto again1
    else
      me→next := succ;
      if CAS(&(pred→next), succ, me) then
        break;
      end
    end
  end;
  // make the lock holder inherit my priority.
  inherit(lock, me);
spin:
  // spin loop
  until me→locked = Released do
    if interrupt_requested then
      if CAS(me→locked, Locked, Preempted) then
        return FALSE
      else
        goto spin
      end
    end;
```

Figure 12: PR-lock/PI/Preempt Algorithm (2)

```
      prio := me1→prio;
      if prio > my_prio then
        // inherit priority from me1.
        my_prio := prio;
        me→prio := prio;
        me2 := get_next_locknode();
        me2→prio := my_prio;
        me2→locked := Locked;
      again2:
        // insert me2 to the waiting queue.
        pred := lock→top;
        if pred = me then
          me2→locked := Released;
          release_locknode(me2);
          inherit(lock, me);
          goto spin
        end;
        while (TRUE) do
          succ1 := pred→next;
          succ := UNMARK(succ1);
          if succ = me then
            me2→locked := Released;
            release_locknode(me2);
            inherit(lock, me);
            goto spin
          end;
          if succ→prio ≥ my_prio then
            pred := succ
          elseif MARKED(succ1) then
            goto again2
          else
            me2→next := succ;
            if CAS(&(pred→next), succ, me2) then
              break
            end
          end
        end;
        // make the lock holder inherit my priority.
        inherit(lock, me2);
      again3:
        // remove me from the waiting queue.
        pred := me2;
        while (TRUE) do
          succ1 := pred→next;
          succ := UNMARK(succ1);
          if succ ≠ me then
            pred := succ
          else
            next := mark(me);
            if CAS(&pred→next, me, next) then
              me→locked := Released;
              me := me2;
              goto spin
            else
              me→next := next;
              goto again3
  end end end end end;
  return TRUE
end;
```

Figure 13: PR-lock/PI/Preempt Algorithm (3)

Technical Session II

Digital Museum

A Design and Evaluation of the Multi-User Virtual Environment Server System for the Digital Museum

Tomonori Usaka
Graduate School of Science,
The University of Tokyo
7-3-1, Hongo, Bunkyo-Ku, Tokyo 113, Japan
usaka@um.u-tokyo.ac.jp

Ken Sakamura
The University Museum,
The University of Tokyo
7-3-1, Hongo, Bunkyo-Ku, Tokyo 113, Japan
sakamura@um.u-tokyo.ac.jp

Abstract

The Digital Museum is one of the applications of the Multi-User Virtual Environment System. In the Digital Museum, objects in the Digital Museum are displayed as multimedia data stored in the Digital Museum Server System, and users can visit the Digital Museum by connecting user interface programs to the Digital Museum Server System via a network. Many users can explore the Digital Museum simultaneously, and then they can interact with other users or objects in the Digital Museum.

In this study, a prototype for the Digital Museum System is developed. To manage many users and large scaled virtual environment, this system is constructed as a multi server system connected with a fast network. The number of update messages received by each clients and servers are dependent on the density of users in the virtual environment but independent of the number of servers, so the size of the virtual environment can be enlarged as the number of servers increases without increasing the update messages processed by clients and servers.

1. Introduction

The Digital Museum is one of the applications of the Multi-User Virtual Environment and constructed as a server-client system. When a user wants to visit the Digital Museum, the user runs an interaction interface program as a client connected to the Digital Museum Server System via a network, and a *persona* object of the user is created in the Digital Museum. The interface program receives description of the virtual environment and objects surrounding the persona object, then it renders images of the Digital Museum from the viewpoint of the persona. The user can explore the Digital Museum by controlling its persona. By exploring the Digital Museum, the user can preview any objects, and then the user can see more information of the object that the user is interested in as multimedia data. In addition, the user is allowed to interact with the objects in the Digital Museum; for example, the user can create copies of the objects and carry them, can push buttons on the objects then see its reactions.

Multi-user interaction in the Digital Museum is supported as follows. If a state of some object is updated, the server system sends update messages to clients, then each client renders new images of the Digital Museum. So users can recognize the object's behavior. Because the persona is one of the objects in the Digital Museum, users can see the motion of other users. Moreover, interactions between personae are also provided. By this mechanism, the communication between users such as conversation, presentation, and so forth are enabled.

We are proposing to make the Digital Museum a world wide opened museum, so the Digital Museum System is required to manage many users simultaneously, at least 1,000 users at the same time. In addition, the Digital Museum has a vast multimedia data collection and the data are always updated and increasing. So the Digital Museum must be a very large scaled virtual environment. Moreover, a low cost clients and a low bandwidth network between clients and server system are expected (we suppose that use 28,800 bps modem is used for this network.)

Currently, there are many multi-user virtual environment systems, however, they are not well to the Digital Museum System. LambdaMOO[5] is a text based multi-user dungeon (MUD) system and users explore in the virtual environment by connecting client programs to the server, however, this is a single server system

0-8186-7658-2/96 $05.00 © 1996 IEEE

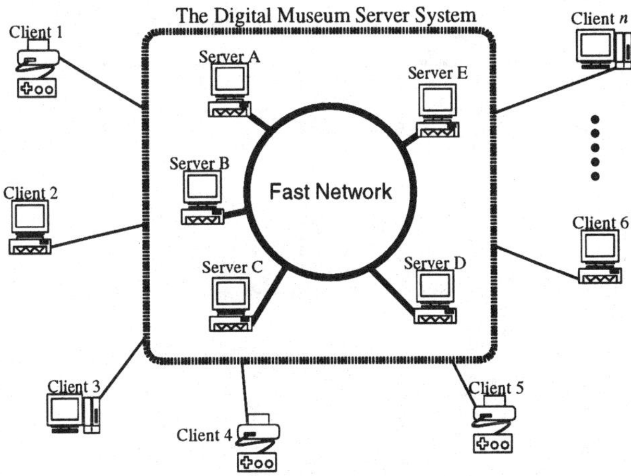

Figure 1. The Digital Museum System

so it is impossible to manage too many users. Reality Built For Two[1], VEOS[3], and MR Toolkit[9] are multi-user virtual environment systems. These systems adopt peer to peer communication to notify update messages, so if N users are in the virtual environment simultaneously, the total number of update messages will be $O(N^2)$ and do not scale to many simultaneous users before the network gets saturated. SIMNET[4], NPSNET[8], and VERN[2] are using broadcast messages instead of peer to peer messages and the number of messages are reduced $O(N)$, however, there are still too many messages for low cost clients and a low bandwidth network. RING[6] and MASSIVE[7] do not distribute update messages to all clients. In these systems, all object in the virtual environment have its interactive area and the destinations of update messages are determined by server system according to the interactive area. By this mechanism, these systems can manage a large number of users, however, the clients of both systems are required to store full data of the virtual environment, so they do not satisfy the requirements for the Digital Museum System.

In this study, a prototype for the Digital Museum System is developed. This system is constructed as a multi server system and the servers are connected via a fast network (see figure 1). A visual interaction between users is implemented because user tracking is required to provide visual interaction and it is one of the most frequently occurred interaction, i.e., by tracking other user's position, the user can see their motion. By restricting the interactive area, the number of update messages sent to each client is extremely reduced. In addition, the Digital Museum is divided into sub-environments in order to manage a large virtual environment and many users. Each sub-environment is managed by each server, however, the Digital Museum is still one large multi-user virtual environment from the view of users because seamless interactions are provided in this system. By this mechanism, the size of the virtual environment can be enlarged by connecting new servers to the system without increasing the messages processed by clients and servers.

2. Overview of the Digital Museum

2.1. Rooms and Objects

The Digital Museum consists of many *rooms* and *objects*. In the current implementation, a room is a rectangular area. All objects are placed in some room. The position of the object is described by the room where it is in and its coordinates in the room. As described in the introduction, a persona of the user is one of the objects. When a client program is connected to the Digital Museum, a new persona object is created in some room, then users can explore in the Digital Museum by updating the position of its persona object.

The rooms are connected to other rooms by *gates*. The gate is a rectangular area which belongs to a room, and a user can move to the neighboring room through the gate. The gate has a description that shows a room where the gate is connected to and offset values applied to the coordinates of objects or the room when a user sees them. See figure 2 and 3. In figure 2, user X is in room A and user Y is in room B, and the positions of each user are described by coordinates in the rooms, i.e., user X is standing at $(100, 250)$ in room A, and user Y is at $(200, 300)$ in room B. Gate C connects room A to room B and offset values is $(400, -100)$. The offset value is applied to the coordinates of room B and user Y when user X sees them, then these rooms are renders as figure 3 from the view of user A. The offset values are also applied when an object moves through the gate in order to adjust the coordinates of the object for the new room.

Because the connections between rooms are topological, it is possible to connect rooms in the Digital Museum so as to be impossible in the real world. This is one of magic in the Digital Museum.

2.2. Interactive Area in the Digital Museum

The Digital Museum is a very large scaled virtual environment and used by many users simultaneously, however, almost of all real-time interactions occur in very small area, i.e., in the same or the neighboring rooms, due to the occlusion of walls. Especially visual

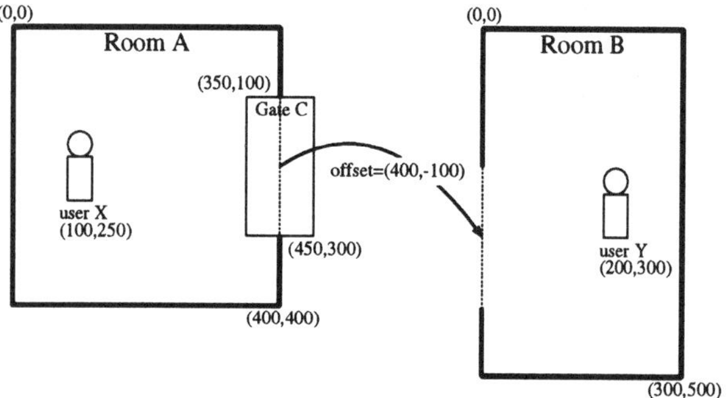

Figure 2. Rooms, objects and a gate in the Digital Museum

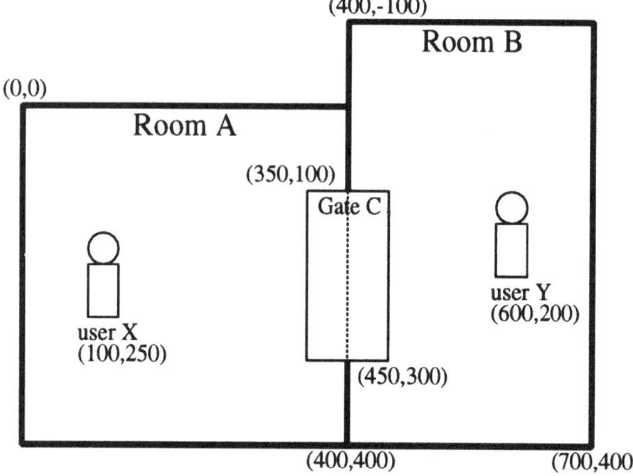

Figure 3. The offset values are applied to the room B and user Y

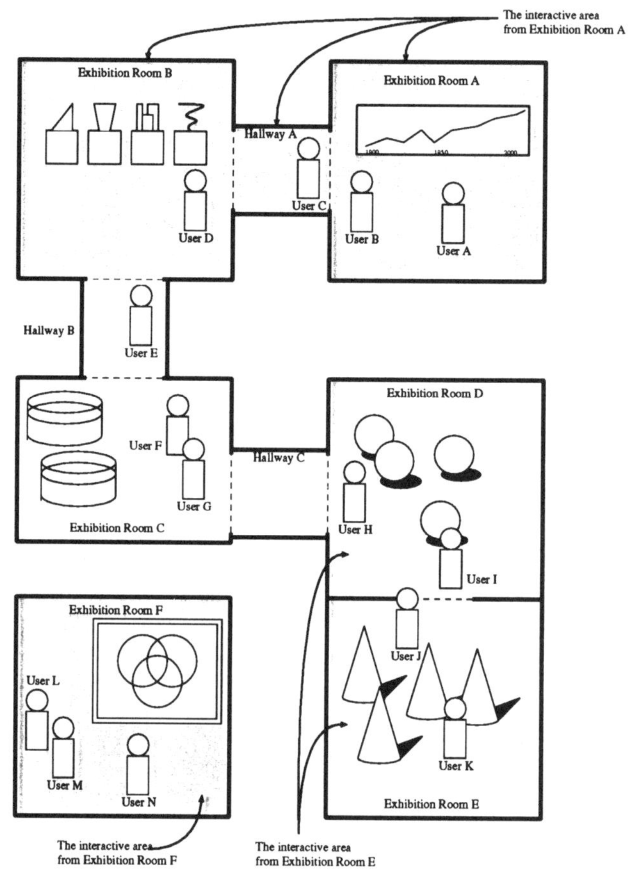

Figure 4. The interactive area of the Digital Museum

interactions never occur between rooms in the distance. This small area in which users and object can interact with each other is called an *interactive area.* The idea of interactive area is useful to reduce the number of update messages because it is not necessary for the server system to send update messages to all clients, but to the clients which control persona objects in the interactive area when a state of an object is updated.

In the Digital Museum, an interactive area is defined for each room and it is described as a set of rooms, i.e., users in the room can interact with other users or objects in rooms included in the interactive area of the room.

Figure 4 shows an example of the interactive area. In this figure, the Digital Museum has nine rooms, i.e., six exhibition rooms and three hallways. The interactive area of the exhibition room A includes exhibition room A, exhibition room B and hallway A, so users in room A can interact with users and objects in these rooms. As the same, users in the exhibition room E can interact with users and objects in the exhibition room D and exhibition room E. On the other hand, users in exhibition room A cannot interact with users in exhibition room E because they are not in their interactive area due to the occlusion of walls.

3. The System Design of the Digital Museum

3.1. Sub-environments and Servers

In order to manage a very large scaled virtual environment, the Digital Museum Server is constructed as a multi server system. The servers are connected with each other by a fast network. The virtual environment of the Digital Museum is divided into several sub-environments and each server manages one sub-environment. An interaction between users and objects in the same sub-environment is managed by the server that manages the sub-environment.

Although the Digital Museum is divided into sub-environments, it is still one large virtual environment because seamless interactions between sub-environments are provided to users. The word *seamless interaction* means that a user can obtain any information in the Digital Museum regardless of where the user is standing, the user can explore the Digital Museum across the sub-environments with no special operation, and the user can interact with other users or objects even if they are not in the same sub-environments as long as they are in the interactive area of the user.

In order to support seamless interactions, communication between servers is required when an interaction between different sub-environments occurs. However, most of the real-time interactions will occur in the same sub-environment due to the interactive area and they are processed without server-server communication. So the number of messages between servers can be reduced, and this is available to support many users. See figure 5. In this figure, the virtual environment shown in figure 4 is divided into three sub-environments. If a user in exhibition room C changes its position, the server A must communicate with server B because exhibition room D managed by server B is in the interactive area of room C. If a user moves in exhibition room A, the server-server communication is not required because all rooms in the interactive area of room A is managed by server A. In the case of figure 5, there are 14 users in the virtual environment, however, server-server communication is required by only four users, i.e., user F, user G, user H and user I.

In order to reduce server-server communication efficiently, it is necessary to divide the Digital Museum so as to reduce the number of rooms connected to rooms belonging to other sub-environments. For example, suppose that the Digital Museum consists of six floors and each floor is connected by a few stairs. In this situation, it is good decision to apply a floor to a sub-environment because interaction between different sub-environments occurs only if some users are on the stairs, otherwise all interaction is invoked in the same sub-environment.

One more advantage of the multi server system is that the Digital Museum can easily be expanded when new multimedia data are collected. In this case, new sub-environments for new collections managed by new servers are constructed, then they are connected to the Digital Museum by connecting rooms by gates. Once the new sub-environments are connected to the Digital Museum, users can explore in them as the same as the original virtual environment.

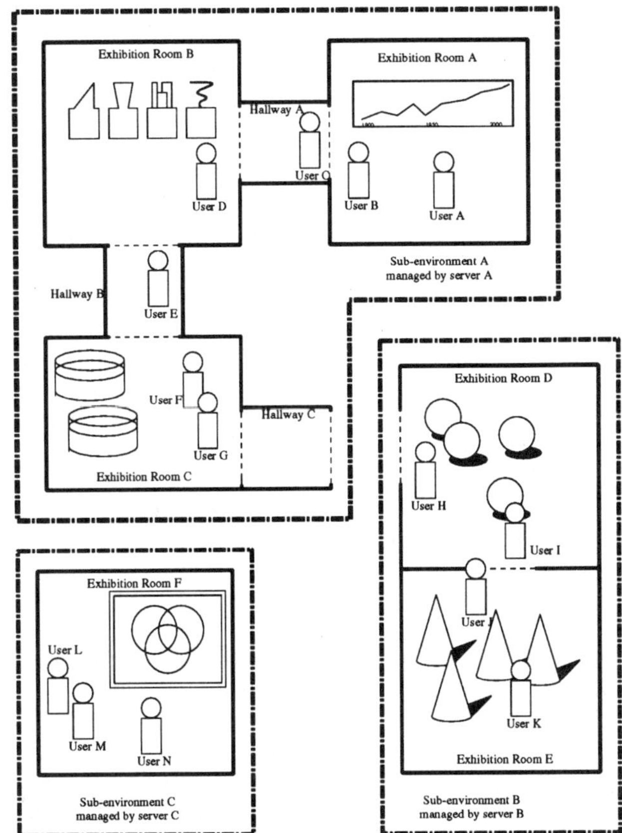

Figure 5. The virtual environment divided into three sub-environments

3.2. Communication between Clients and Server System

In the Digital Museum, the server system manages all descriptions of the virtual environment such as the size of rooms, positions of users and other objects, and various multimedia data for exhibition. In order to render images of the virtual environment, a client program manages a partial copy of description of the virtual environment (see figure 6). If the user moves then new rooms and objects appear in the user's interactive area, the client sends request message to the server and then receives description of them from the server. The descriptions of rooms and objects out of the interactive area are destroyed. When a user moves, the client program updates the position of the user. In this case, the client must send update messages to the server system and other clients, then an appropriate update is applied to the description of the virtual environment

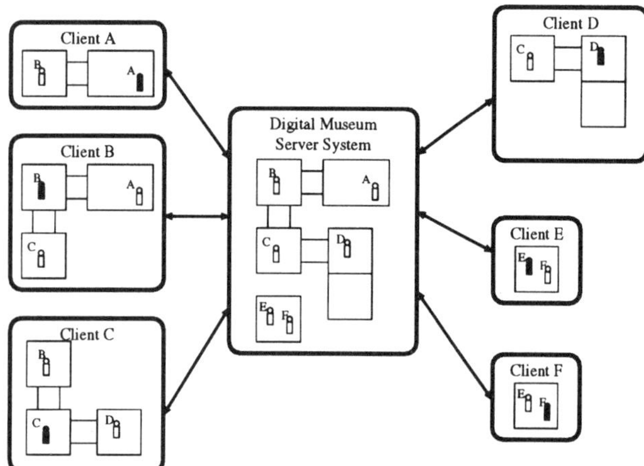

Figure 6. Each client manages a partial copy of description of the virtual environment

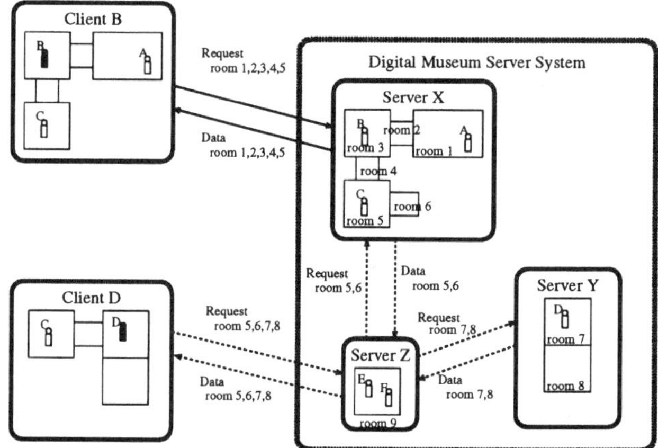

Figure 7. Flow of messages transfering description of the virtual environment

managed by server and every copy of the description of the virtual environment managed by clients.

Currently, this system supports two types of messages for communication between clients and server system. One is a message type for user tracking. They are periodically sent from clients and distributed to other clients in the interactive area. The other is a message type transferring virtual environment description such as sizes of rooms and positions of gates. By this message, clients request the server system to send some data, then the servers send them back to the client.

When a client program joins the Digital Museum, it is connected to some server in the server system. The clients do not send messages directly to other clients and servers, instead send them to the server where it is connected at first, then the server determines their destinations. If the destination of the message is a client that is connected directly to the server, the server forwards the message to the client. Otherwise, the server forwards it to other server where the destination is directly connected.

Figure 7 shows flow of messages transferring description of the virtual environment. Suppose that client B requires the descriptions of rooms 1—5. It is connected directly to server X, so the request messages are sent to server X. In this case, server X has all requested data, so it sends them back to the client A directly. On the other hand, client D is connected to server Z, however, all requested data are managed by other servers. So server Z forwards the request messages to server X and server Y. When server X and server Y receive the request messages, they must send data to client D, however, client D is not connected directroy to them. So they forward messages to server Z and server Z send these messages to client D.

The servers can process messages before propagating them to the destinations, culling, augmenting, or altering them. In addition, the servers can send auxiliary messages helpful for future processing. For example, clients update position of its persona object and send update messages. These messages are distributed in the interactive area, however, distant users need less information than neighboring users, so the server can cull messages for distant users.

3.3. User Tracking

It is required for client programs to determine positions of other users standing in its interactive area in order to provide visual interactions between users. In addition, the servers also need to chase users in their sub-environment because the destinations of update messages are determined by servers. The Digital Museum System employs *dead-reckoning* for user tracking in order to reduce update messages.

In the Digital Museum System, all objects excluding persona objects in some sub-environment are stored in the server managing the sub-environment, and each persona object is stored in the client of its user. The status of these objects such as positions and velocity can be updated directly by the servers and clients where they are stored, and these objects are called *live* objects in dead-reckoning technique. The persona objects in servers and objects in a client excluding its live object are called *ghost* objects. The server creates new ghost objects of the persona objects when they enter the server's sub-environment and the client creates new

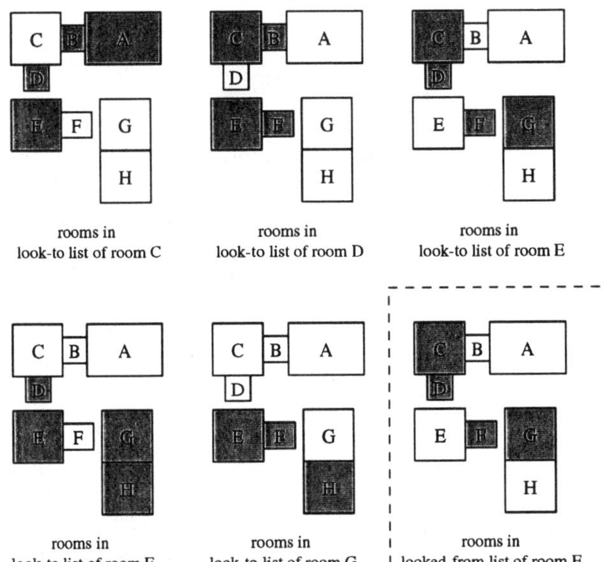

Figure 8. Look-to list and looked-from list of each room

ghost objects when new objects appear in its user's interactive area. The ghost objects are removed when they leave the sub-environment or the interactive area.

The position of the ghost object is updated according to the update messages from the manager of its live object. The update messages are sent from the manager of the live object when the velocity of the live object is changed and consists of such as the position and the velocity of the live object. Once the update message is received, the position of the ghost object can be calculated from the position and the velocity that is described in the last update message. This object's position calculation based on a last-known velocity is called dead-reckoning.

In the Digital Museum, update messages are also required when an object moves across the boundary between rooms because the object might be out of the interactive areas of other users. When the server receives this type of update message, it sends auxiliary messages called *remove ghost* message to the other clients in order to remove the ghost objects of the user's persona object. It is also required to send messages to create new ghost objects, i.e.,*entry new ghost* message, if the user enters the interactive areas of other users, however, they are substituted by usual update messages, i.e., if an update message for an unknown ghost object is received, it is a request to create a new ghost object.

To determine the destinations of update and auxiliary messages, each room has description that determines links to the rooms included in the interactive area of the room, and its reverse links. The former is called *look-to* list and the latter is called *looked-from* list. The update messages are distributed to the clients managing live persona objects in the rooms included in *looked-from* list of the room where the user is in. If the user moves to the other room, *remove ghost* messages are distributed to the clients managing live persona objects in the rooms included in the *looked-from* list of the old room and not included in the *looked-from* list of the new room. However, the server does not always know both lists because the Digital Museum is divided into sub-environments, e.g., if the old room and the new room are not in the same sub-environment, the server knows only one side. So the destinations of *remove ghost* messages are determined as flows. At first, the server managing the old room picks up the rooms included in the *looked-from* list of the old room. Then check if the new room is included in the *look-to* list of these rooms. If the room is not managed by the server, it sends request message to the server managing the room in order to leave this process to this server.

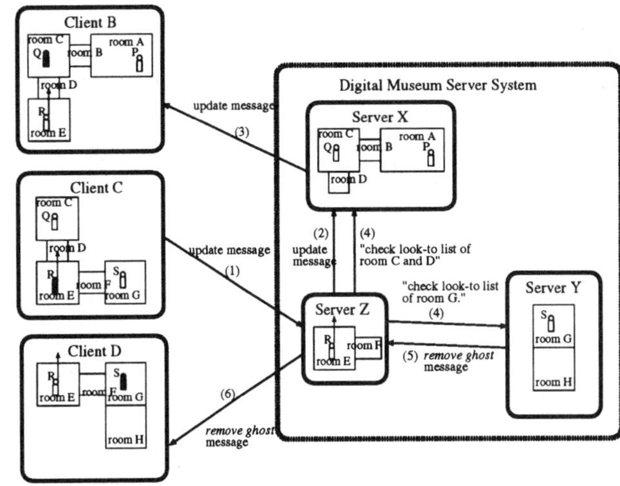

Figure 9. Flow of update and auxiliary messages

In order to distribute update and auxiliary messages to the clients managing live persona objects in the room managed by other server, the server sends request message to other server managing the room. This message includes contents of the update or the auxiliary message and ID number of the room. Then the server that received the request message distributes messages to the clients managing live persona objects in the room. See fgure 8 and 9. Suppose that user R in figure 9 moves to room D from room E. In this case, client C sends update message to server Z where the client is directly connected. Then the update message is forwarded to server X where room D is managed. Server X distributes update messages to clients managing live persona objects in the rooms included in *looked-from* list of room D, i.e., room B, C, D, E and F. Then server Z managing room E picks up the rooms included in the *looked-from* list of room E in order to send remove ghost messages. In this example, room C, D, E, F and G are included in the *looked-from* list of room E. Then server Z checks if room D is included in the *look-to* list of these rooms, however, room C, D and G are managed by other servers. So server Z sends request messages to server X and Y where these rooms are managed. In this case, *look-to list* of room G does not include room D, so server Y sends *remove ghost* message to client D that is in room G. Client D is not directly connected to server Y, so this message is forwarded to server Z then sent to client D.

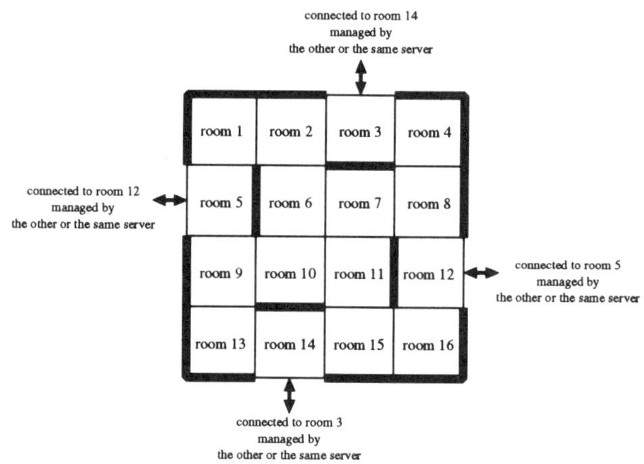

Figure 10. Connection of rooms in a server

4. Implementation

In the current implementation, the prototype system is implemented on Sun SparcStation and the server and the client programs employ Light Weight Process library. TCP/IP is employed for message passing.

Each server has a server ID. When servers send messages to the other server, the destination is described by server ID. Before start accepting client connection, all servers are connected. At first, one server is started. If the second server is connected, both the first server and the second server receive the hostname, port number, and server ID of the others. In order to connect a new server to the server system, the server sends a message including its hostname, port number, and server ID to some server already running. Then a list of running servers including hostnames, port numbers, and server IDs is received. The new server is appended to the server list. Then the new server sends connection requests to other running servers. By this process, servers are connected as a complete graph.

After all servers are connected, clients can send connection request to the server system. When a new client is connected, a server applies a new client ID and send it to the client. The destination of a message for a client is described by a pair of server ID and client ID.

In the current implementation, the persona object and its ghost object consist of the following parameter; user ID, room ID where the persona object is in, the coordinates in the room (x, y), moving speed, direction of the persona object ($0°$—$359°$), and rotation speed. The velocity of the persona object is calculated from moving speed and its direction. The coordinates of the persona object are updated periodically by applying the velocity to the coordinates and the rotation speed to the direction. The user generally controls its persona object by updating its moving speed and rotation speed.

The update message includes user ID, new room ID, old room ID, coordinates, moving speed, direction, and rotation speed. The new room ID field is as the same as the room ID of the persona object. The old room ID is equal to the new room ID if the user does not change the room, otherwise the old room ID shows that from which room the user comes. The size of an update message is 48 bytes in the current implementation.

5. Experimental Result

In these experiments, each server manages a sub-environment consists of 16 rooms. Each room is connected to the other rooms with two or three gates as shown in figure 10. The visual interactive area of the user is restricted in the same room that the user is in and its neighboring rooms connected by gates. The experiments are run with 1, 2, 4, 6 and 8 servers and sub-environment connections for each experiments are shown in figure 11.

Various numbers of clients are connected to each server so as to characterize the scalability of the system. During these experiments, the starting positions of user objects are randomly decided, then each client updates its user object's rotation speed randomly once every 2.5 seconds on average and invokes update messages. The table 1 shows an average client↔server message processing rates. In this table, Client↔Server Output is the number of messages sent from a single

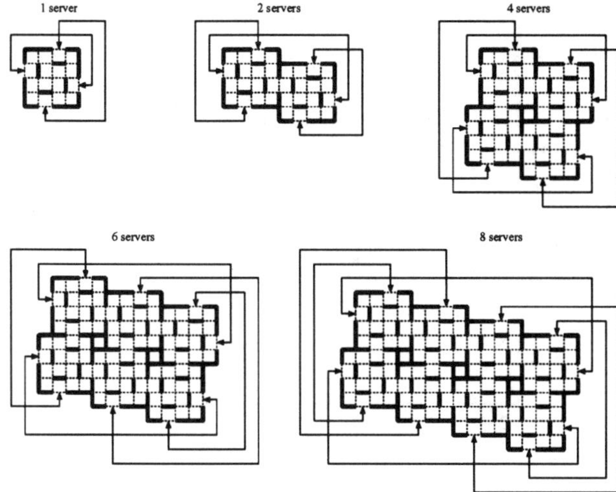

Figure 11. Sub-environments connection for each number of servers

client. Client↔Server Input is the number of messages received by a single client and it is also shown in figure 12. In this figure, points representing the same number of servers are connected by lines.

As shown in figure 12, the rate of messages received by a single client is proportional to the number of clients per server. Because each server manages fixed number of rooms and each client manages one user object, it means also the rate is proportional to the density of objects in the virtual environment. This is because the visual interactive area is a relatively constant sized region regardless of the whole size of the virtual environment. The number of servers does not affect the number of server-client messages. This means that the Digital Museum can be enlarged as the number of servers increases without increasing the update messages processed by the client. See row 10 of table 1. In this experiment, the density of user object is 1.5 users per room because there are 96 users and 64 rooms in the virtual environment. Users in room 1, 4, 13 and 15 can see three rooms and users in other rooms can see four rooms, so a user can see $(3 \times 4 + 4 \times 12)/16 = 3.75$ rooms. A user can see $3.75 \times 1.5 - 1 = 4.625$ users in average (the user cannot see itself). This is only about 4.8% of the 96 users and the number of update messages is the same.

The average number of messages sent to a single client is $1.92x + 0.52$ when the density of users is x users per room. If the client and the server system are connected via 9,600 bps network, the server can send $9600/8/48 = 25$ messages per second to the client (because the size of update messages is 48 bytes). So

Table 1. Average client↔server message processing rates

# servers	# clients per server	# users	Client↔Server	
			output	input
8	16	128	0.7	2.4
8	12	96	0.6	1.8
8	8	64	0.5	1.3
8	6	48	0.6	1.0
8	4	32	0.7	0.9
8	3	24	0.8	1.0
6	16	96	0.7	2.4
6	8	48	0.7	1.7
6	4	24	0.7	1.1
4	24	96	0.7	3.1
4	16	64	0.7	2.5
4	8	32	0.7	1.9
4	6	24	0.6	1.0
4	4	16	0.7	1.1
2	32	64	0.5	4.0
2	24	48	0.5	2.9
2	16	32	0.6	2.1
2	12	24	0.7	1.9
2	8	16	0.6	1.3
1	48	48	0.7	6.3
1	32	32	0.5	4.8
1	24	24	0.5	3.5
1	16	16	0.6	2.7
1	8	8	0.6	1.7

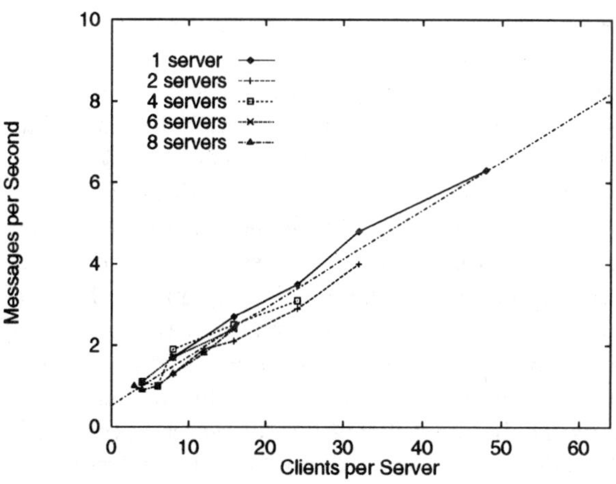

Figure 12. The average rate of client↔server messages sent to a single client

Table 2. Average server↔server message processing rates

# clients per server	# servers	# users	Server↔Server output	Server↔Server input
32	2	64	84.3	69.8
24	4	96	69.5	69.1
24	2	48	41.2	35.6
16	8	128	42.8	40.9
16	6	96	38.5	43.8
16	4	64	38.6	37.9
16	2	32	32.7	24.6
12	8	96	33.2	24.5
12	2	24	14.4	23.3
8	8	64	18.3	17.2
8	6	48	18.1	20.5
8	4	32	16.1	16.8
8	2	16	10.3	7.3
6	8	48	8.8	9.8
6	4	24	6.1	8.8
4	8	32	6.1	6.1
4	6	24	5.3	6.2
4	4	16	3.8	5.9
3	8	24	3.4	4.7

this system can accept $(25 - 0.52)/1.92 = 12.75$ users per rooms and 47 users in the interactive area of each user.

An average server↔server message processing rates are shown in table 2 and the average rate of server↔server messages received by a single server is plotted in figure 13. As shown in section 3.2, an update message sent from a client is received by a server, then the server forwards it to other servers where the destination clients are directly connected. So the average number of server↔server messages processed by a single server is $O(MN)$ where M is the number of clients connected to a single server and N is the density of users. However, because M is bounded by the server's computing power and N is bounded by the bandwidth of networks between clients and the server system, MN is bounded by a constant number. In addition, the number of servers does not appear in this formula, so this multi-user virtual environment server system can be enlarged by connecting new servers to the system without increasing the number of server↔server messages processed by each server.

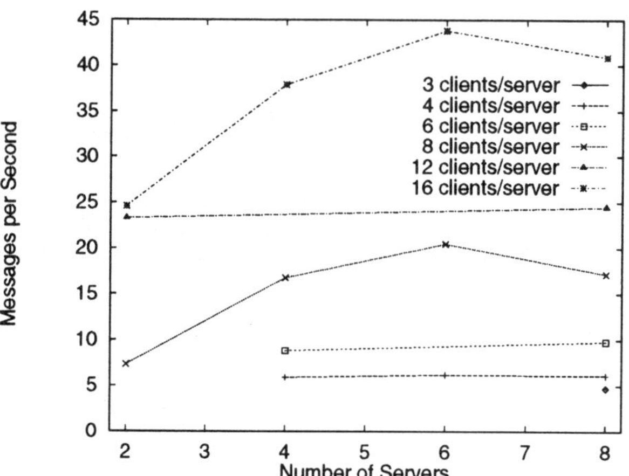

Figure 13. The average rate of server↔server messages received by a single server

6. Conclusion

In this paper, a prototype of multi-user interaction system for the Digital Museum is designed and an evaluation of the system is shown.

The virtual environment consists of many rooms and users can explore in the environment. A room is connected to other rooms by gates each of which describes a neighboring room and its relative coordinates. Because the rooms are connected to each other topologically, connection that is impossible in the 3D environment is also allowed.

The system uses a client-server design. The servers manage the environment by dividing it into sub-environments. Each server manages a single sub-environment that consists of many rooms and objects. The client provides an interface program to users. The interface program renders images of the environment from the user's viewpoint, and the user can control its user object by the interface program. If a state of the virtual environment is updated, the interface programs redraw the images.

The interaction is managed by servers; a client sends update messages to a server, and the server processed it, calculates its distributions by referring the information of room connection, then forwards it to clients that are in the interactive area. By restricting the interactive area, the number of update messages sent to each client is extremely reduced. The number of update messages received by a single client is dependent on the density of the user in the environment but independent of the number of servers managing the environment. In addition, the number of servers is not affect to the server↔server message rate. These characteristics show that the virtual environment can be enlarged as the number of servers increases without increasing the update messages processed by clients and servers.

References

[1] C. Blanchard, S. Burgess, Y. Harvill, J. Lanier, A. Lasko, M. Oberman, and M. Teitel. Reality Build for Two: A virtual reality tool. In *ACM SIGGRAPH Special Issue on 1990 Symposium on Interactive 3D Graphics*, pages 35–36, 1990.

[2] B. Blau, C. E. Hughes, J. M. Moshell, and C. Lisle. Networked virtual environments. In *ACM SIGGRAPH Special Issue on 1992 Symposium on Interactive 3D Graphics*, pages 157–160, 1992.

[3] W. Bricken and G. Coco. The VEOS project. Technical report, Human Interface Technology Laboratory, University of Washington, 1993.

[4] J. Calvin, A. Dickens, B. Gaines, P. Metzger, D. Miller, and D. Owen. The SIMNET virtual world architecture. In *Proceedings of the IEEE Virtual Reality Annual International Symposium*, pages 450–455, September 1993.

[5] P. Curtis. Mudding: Social phenomena in text-based virtual realities, 1992. ftp://parcftp.xerox.com/pub/MOO/papers/DIAC92.TXT.

[6] T. A. Funkhouser. RING: A client-server system for multi-user virtual environments. In *1995 Symposium on Interactive 3D Graphics*, pages 85–92. ACM SIGGRAPH, April 1995.

[7] C. Greenhalgh and S. Benford. MASSIVE: a distributed virtual reality system incorporating spatial trading. In *Proceedings of the 15th International Coference on Distributed Computing Systems*, pages 27–34, 1995.

[8] M. R. Macedonia, D. P. Brutzman, M. J. Zyda, D. R. Pratt, and P. T. Barham. NPSNET: A multi-player 3D virtual environment over the internet. In *1995 Symposium on Interactive 3D Graphics*, pages 93–94. ACM SIGGRAPH, April 1995.

[9] C. Shaw and M. Green. The MR Toolkit press package and experiment. In *Proceedings of IEEE Virtual Reality Annual International Symposium*, pages 463–469, September 1993.

Real-Time Browser for the Digital Museum Available with Low-Cost Terminals and Low-Bandwidth Networks

Shunsuke Yura
Graduate School of Science,
The University of Tokyo
7-3-1, Hongo, Bunkyo-Ku, Tokyo 113, Japan
yura@um.u-tokyo.ac.jp

Ken Sakamura
The University Museum,
The University of Tokyo
7-3-1, Hongo, Bunkyo-Ku, Tokyo 113, Japan
sakamura@um.u-tokyo.ac.jp

Abstract

We describe a real-time browser for the digital museum. It acts as a user interface to the multi-user virtual interaction environment that the digital museum provides as a browsing space of materials in the museum with multimedia data. The digital museum is available with low-cost terminals and through low-bandwidth networks such as telephone circuits, however, these factors influence to the real-time display of the view, a fundamental function in the browser. This function provides a view of the user player, the agent of the user in the virtual environment, in real time and enables the user to act in the virtual environment. Our browser divides available drawing power and network bandwidth to objects with giving high priority to the objects that are important for the view. As a result, our browser can provide a proper view to the user in real time even with low-cost terminals and low-bandwidth networks.

1 Introduction

The digital museum is a virtual museum constructed on the computer network and manages many academic materials and results of related researches as multimedia data. It provides a multi-user virtual interaction environment shared by many users as a browsing environment of multimedia data. Users can explore the virtual environment and appreciate exhibition materials by controlling their own agents called *players* simultaneously. Moreover, they can see and discuss with other players in real time because the virtual space is shared.

Since the digital museum manages a mass of data, it consists of a *server* that manages all sorts of data and *browsers* that work as user interfaces. The browsers are connected to the server through computer networks. They provide views of players and conversations of other players to users and execute user commands for controlling players in real time.

Since the digital museum is open to various people, it must be available with low-cost terminals and through low-bandwidth networks such as widely spread telephone circuits. These requirements influence a real-time display of the player's view, a main function of the browser. The terminals may not be able to display all objects in the player's view in real time because of their performance limitation. In addition, they may not be able to download all data of the visible objects before displaying a view because of the limitation of the network bandwidth. To solve these problems, our browser determines priority for the objects and divides the drawing power of the terminal and the network bandwidth to them based on their priority. As a result, it can provide a proper real-time view to the user.

The next section describes system organization of the digital museum. Section 3 describes problems in the real-time view more precisely and our approach. Then we examine effectiveness of our approach with a prototype browser in section 4.

2 System Organization

2.1 Virtual Environment

The digital museum provides a multi-user virtual interaction environment as a browsing space (figure 1). The virtual space consists of space units called *rooms* and *paths* connecting them each other. All things exist in the virtual space are called *objects*. Each object belongs to some room and has the coordinates in it. Objects can be divided into *player objects* and *exhibi-*

0-8186-7658-2/96 $05.00

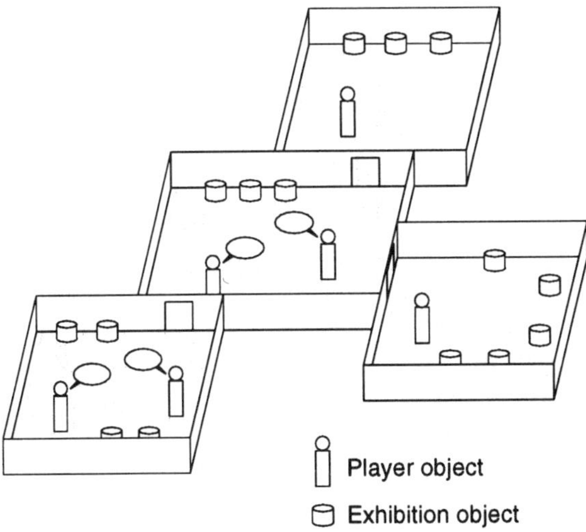

Figure 1. Multi-user virtual interaction environment

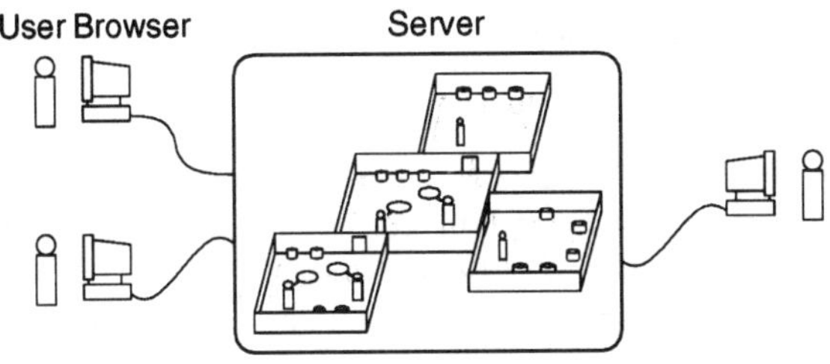

Figure 2. Server client architecture

tion objects. The player object is an agent of the user in the virtual environment. The user is provided a view of the player object, in other words, appearances of objects visible to the player object in real time. He can explore the virtual space by controlling his player object with the view of it. Since the space is shared by all users, the player object can see other player objects and talk with them if they are in the specified interaction scope. The virtual environment has more merits than real museums. He can acquire various information of exhibition objects with multimedia data by accessing them. Several types of magic are also available. For example, he can search interested exhibitions and jump to rooms where they exist or make copies of the exhibition objects and carry them.

2.2 Server-Client Architecture

The digital museum has server-client architecture (figure 2). The clients (browsers) are connected to the server through computer networks. The digital museum is assumed to be available when the lines connecting the browsers with the server have low bandwidth such as telephone circuits. The low-cost terminals are also assumed to be available as the platforms that the browser programs are running on.

The server manages all data related to the museum and has following functions:

- It maintains states of all elements in the virtual environment and provides renewal information of them to related browsers to maintain coherency. For example, it maintains location information of all objects, especially moving objects such as player objects, and provides location renewal information to related browsers.
- It enables real-time conversations in the virtual space. When some player object speaks, player objects in its interaction scope can hear the speech. To enable this it receives speech data from the browser and distributes them to related browsers.

The browsers are user interfaces to the virtual environment and execute the following operations:

- Display a view of the player objects in real time. To display the view they request necessary data to the server and manage data transmitted from it.
- Accept commands to control player objects such as movement and conversation from users and execute them. Since states of the player objects may be changed, they may also transmit some data to the server.
- Provide conversation of other players in the interaction scope in real time.

Since the server is needed to manage enormous data and many browsers connect to the server simultaneously, it may consist of several servers. However, they exchange data in real time and act as a single virtual server to the browsers.

When the user visits the digital museum through telephone circuits, the browser program establishes a connection to the digital museum server with possessing one telephone circuit. In this case, whole bandwidth of the telephone circuit is available and the network bandwidth is constant. Moreover, the latency of the telephone circuit is not so big. Therefore, the digital museum assumes that the low-bandwidth network has two properties: constant bandwidth and small latency.

2.3 Data Types

The virtual environment consists of three fundamental data types: *object data type*, *room data type*, and *model data type*. Object data and Room data define basic structures of objects and rooms respectively. The logical structure of the virtual environment, in other words, connection relationships between rooms and inclusion relationships between rooms and objects, can be determined from the object data and the room data. The digital museum assumes all rooms and objects to have cube figures. The fundamental physical structure can also be determined from the object data and the room data because object data have their own cube sizes and room data have their own cube sizes and coordinates of objects belongs to them.

Although the digital museum treats all rooms and objects as cube figures, they may not be seen as cubes. Model data types define appearance of rooms and objects. It spends time to transmit appearance data because they may have large size. In the digital museum users can start browsing at once with low-bandwidth networks because the fundamental physical structure of the virtual space can be determined without model data. Objects without model data are seen as cubes until the browsers download the model data from the server.

3 Real-Time Display of the View

3.1 Problems and Our Approach

The real-time display of the view is a main function of the browser. It displays a view of the player object in real time to enable the user to control the player object and act in the virtual environment in real time. In other words, it is needed to refresh the view with keeping particular *frame rate*. If the frame rate is not regular, the user feels unnatural [6].

To display a view it downloads model data of visible objects, executes several calculations such as coordinate transformations, and renders them on the screen of the terminal. The low-bandwidth network influences the data download speed and the low-cost terminal limits the calculation performance and the rendering performance. Therefore, it may not be able to display an accurate view in the specified frame time with the low-cost terminal and the low-bandwidth network in the following cases:

- There are too many objects in the view or descriptions of the objects are too detailed for the terminal to draw all model data of them accurately in the specified frame time because of its own performance limitation.

- The browser cannot download all model data required to create a view from the server until displaying the view because of the bandwidth limitation of the network.

It can provide a view without model data as described in the previous section, however, the user cannot recognize objects without model data because they are drawn as cubes. Therefore it is needed to draw objects with model data even if it cannot display all of them accurately.

To solve the problem, we determine *priority* of all visible objects and divides the available drawing power of the terminal and the available network bandwidth to them based on their priority. Priority of the object is determined depending on its importance for the user's view. This approach downloads necessary data in high priority and can display the user's view with keeping frame rate. The model data are needed to have the following properties to make this approach be more effective:

- They must be able to be drawn with multiple costs. If each drawing cost of them is unique, only the objects with priority higher than some threshold are drawn and the others are not drawn in the view.

- They must be able to be drawn although not all of their model data are ready. If they do not have this property, only the objects of which the model data are finished downloading are drawn.

For the former property we use the multiple LODs (levels of detail) technique [2]. In this technique, objects can be drawn with multiple resolutions. Lower resolution needs less time for computing and rendering. We also introduce the progressive technique to the model data type for the latter property. This technique can display an outline of the object roughly and increase its resolution gradually with downloading of its model data. The interlace GIF [5] and the progressive JPEG [7] use the technique and commonly used in such as WWW (World Wide Web) because of its effectiveness.

Our system currently limits the model data type to the bitmap image data. Our progressive algorithm extends the algorithm used by the interlace GIF to be more generally. The bitmap image data also supports the multiple LODs because it can be drawn naturally with multiple resolutions.

3.2 Priority Determination

Priority of the object is determined on the basis of its importance for the user. The importance means a degree of contribution to the view of the user player. Divisions of the drawing power and the network bandwidth are both depending on the priority, however, it has different means in the division of drawing power and in the division of network bandwidth. In the case of the drawing power, the priority has an effect in the same frame as it determined. In the case of the network bandwidth, however, the priority has an effect in later frames because download of data needs some time. Therefore, the degree of potential contribution must be also considered to determine the network priority. We determine the display priority and the network priority from the following factors:

- Distance between the user player and the target object

  Since we assume that the user approaches objects which he is interested in, we give high priority to objects near the user player. This factor is natural as the display priority. Near objects are drawn in detail and far objects vaguely. The factor is not so natural as the network priority because he may go away from the objects until their model data reach the terminal from the server. But we also apply the distance factor to the network priority because it is effective when the user player standing still or looking around at the same position. We represent the distance factor $Distance(O)$ for the object O as follows where $d(O, U)$ represents a distance between O and the user player U:

  $$Distance(O) = \frac{1}{\log d(O, U)}$$

  The log function is used to attenuate the distance factor.

- Visibility of the target object

  The visibility factor is different in the display priority and in the network priority. We assign zero display priority to invisible objects because they do not need to be drawn on the screen. The visibility factor of the display priority $Visibility_{disp}(O)$ for the object O is represented as follows:

  $$Visibility_{disp}(O) = \begin{cases} 1 & visible \\ 0 & invisible \end{cases}$$

  We assign high network priority v_1 to visible objects to increase quality of them quickly. We also assign some network priority v_2 to invisible objects. If they are assigned zero network priority, the quality of the view may decrease drastically when the user player turning around because model data of objects coming in sight are not ready at all. The visibility factor of the network priority $Visibility_{net}(O)$ is represented as follows:

  $$Visibility_{net}(O) = \begin{cases} v_1 & visible \\ v_2 & invisible \quad (v_1 > v_2) \end{cases}$$

From these factors the display priority $Priority_{disp}$ and the network priority $Priority_{net}$ for the object O can be represented as follows:

$$\begin{aligned} Priority_{disp}(O) &= Distance(O) \cdot Visibility_{disp}(O) \\ Priority_{net}(O) &= Distance(O) \cdot Visibility_{net}(O) \end{aligned}$$

3.3 Display Management

Display management part divides a drawing power of the terminal to visible objects depending on their display priority described above. The available drawing power is determined from the performance of the terminal and the frame rate.

The division of the drawing power means determination of LODs of visible objects. There are several approaches to determine LODs such as static approach [1, 8, 9, 4] and reactive approach [9], however, only predictive approach [3] can maintain the frame rate uniformly. The predictive approach estimates drawing costs of objects and determines their LODs so that total estimated costs do not exceed the target frame time. We apply this approach to our system where cube data and bitmap image data are mixed while [3] assumes that all model data are represented by polygons. Bitmap image data are represented with multiple LODs. The number of LODs of the bitmap image data is its number of lines of its rectangle drawn on the screen. When the object with image model data occupies n lines on the screen, its vertical resolution is n if it is assigned the highest LOD. If it is assigned the lowest LOD, its vertical resolution is 1 and it is drawn as a vertical stripe. Cube data are represented with two LODs: the accurate cube and the rectangle that has same size on the screen as the cube.

Since the predictive approach needs a function to estimate a drawing cost, we defined estimate functions for cube and bitmap image. The functions are needed to have little costs for calculation rather than accuracy because calculations of estimate values are executed in each frame on the terminal. Therefore, we use a following simple function for the object O where $L(O)$

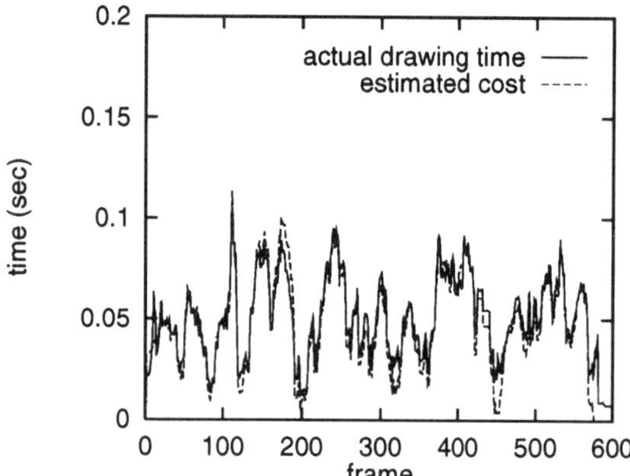

Figure 3. Comparison of estimated cost and actual rendering time of bitmap image

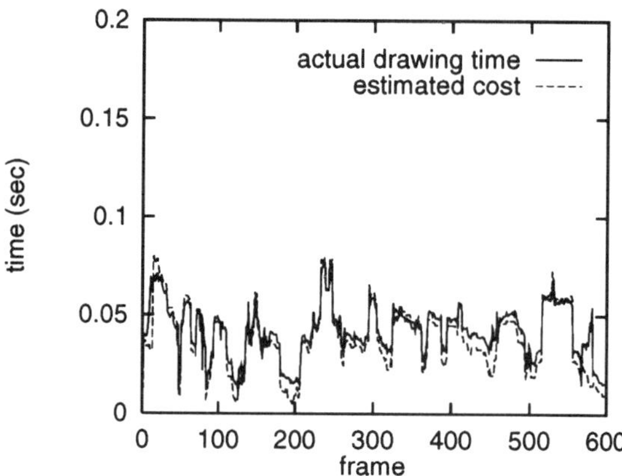

Figure 4. Comparison of estimated cost and actual rendering time of cube

represents a LOD of O and ranges between 0 and 1 and $NPixel(O)$ the number of pixels of the rectangle equals to the range O occupies on the screen:

for object O_i with image model

$$Cost(O_i) = c_{i_1} + c_{i_2} \cdot L(O_i) + c_{i_3} \cdot NPixel(O_i) + c_{i_4} \cdot NPixel(O_i) \cdot L(O_i)$$

for object O_c with cube model

$$Cost(O_c) = c_{c_1} + c_{c_2} \cdot L(O_c) + c_{c_3} \cdot NPixel(O_c) + c_{c_4} \cdot NPixel(O_c) \cdot L(O_c)$$

This function assumes that the drawing cost is in proportion to the size on the screen and in proportion to the LOD. The parameters (c_{i_1}, c_{i_2}, c_{i_3}, c_{i_4}, c_{c_1}, c_{c_2}, c_{c_3}, c_{c_4}) are determined from the computing power and the rendering power of the terminal.

The image data with LOD $L(O)$ is drawn with a following vertical resolution where $NLine(O)$ is its number of lines on the screen:

$$int(LOD(O) \cdot (NLine(O) - 1)) + 1$$

The cube data with LOD $L(O)$ is drawn as accurate cube or rectangle depending on $L(O)$ and specific threshold. If $L(O)$ is higher than the threshold it is drawn as accurate cube or else as rectangle. Figure 3 and figure 4 show comparisons between estimated costs and actual drawing time of the image data and of the cube data respectively when all objects are drawn with the highest LOD.

We divide available drawing cost, in other words, the target frame time, to the objects depending on their display priority. The equation (1) represents that the LOD of the object O is in proportion to its display priority. The parameter L in the equation (1) is determined so that the total of estimated costs equals to the target frame time $FrameTime$ (equation (2)). The equation (3) represents a calculated value of L.

$$L(O) = L \cdot Priority_{disp}(O) \quad (1)$$

$$\sum_O Cost(O) = FrameTime \quad (2)$$

$$\begin{aligned} L &= \frac{FrameTime - (\sum_{O_i} C_{i_1}(O_i) + \sum_{O_c} C_{c_1}(O_c))}{\sum_{O_i} C_{i_2}(O_i) + \sum_{O_c} C_{c_2}(O_c)} \\ C_{i_1}(O_i) &= c_{i_1} + c_{i_3} \cdot NPixel(O_i) \\ C_{i_2}(O_i) &= (c_{i_2} + c_{i_4} \cdot NPixel(O_i)) \cdot Priority_{disp}(O_i) \\ C_{c_1}(O_c) &= c_{c_1} + c_{c_3} \cdot NPixel(O_c) \\ C_{c_2}(O_c) &= (c_{c_2} + c_{c_4} \cdot NPixel(O_c)) \cdot Priority_{disp}(O_c) \end{aligned} \quad (3)$$

O_i and O_c in the equation (3) represent the object with image model data and with cube model data respectively. The equation (3) represents that L has a big value and the objects are assigned high LODs when the target frame time is long. Therefore, the view is drawn in detail when the target frame time is long. We specify two levels of the frame rate depending on the behavior of the user player. When the user player moves, we apply high frame rate to provide a smooth view to him. When he stands still, low frame rate are applied to provide a detailed view to him.

3.4 Network Management

Network management part divides a network bandwidth to objects depending on their network priority. Since the network bandwidth can be represented by available data size per specific time unit, the division of the network bandwidth means to allocate data sizes for transmission to the objects. Therefore, we are needed to determine a relation between the network priority and the network data size. In addition, we consider only the bitmap image model data because the cube data need much smaller network bandwidth then the image data. Our policy for determining network data sizes is to make the degree of accessing to the required data size be in proportion to the network priority. In this policy the network data size $Size_{net}(O)$ for object O is determined as follows:

$$
\begin{aligned}
&Size_{net}(O) = \\
&\quad S \cdot (Size_{req}(O) - Size_{cur}(O)) \\
&\quad \cdot Priority_{net}(O)
\end{aligned}
\tag{4}
$$

$Size_{req}(O)$ represents a *required data size* for the object O and $Size_{cur}(O)$ represents a current size of downloaded model data for the object O.

The equation (4) determines the network data size for each object. However, the network data size must be assigned to model data rather than objects because there may be objects that share same model data. Therefore, we determine the network data size $Size_{net}(M)$ for model data M from the maximum value of the network data sizes of the objects that share the model data M (equation (5)):

$$
\begin{aligned}
&Size_{net}(M) = \\
&\quad S \cdot max\{(Size_{req}(O) - Size_{cur}(M)) \\
&\quad \cdot Priority_{net}(O) : Model(O) = M\}
\end{aligned}
\tag{5}
$$

$Size_{cur}(M)$ represents a current size of downloaded data for the model data M. S is determined so that the total size of allocated network data equals to the network bandwidth $BandWidth$ (equation (6)).

$$\sum_{M} Size_{net}(M) = BandWidth \tag{6}$$

Now we must determine how to calculate the required data size $Size_{req}(O)$ for the object O. A policy to regard the required data size of the object as the full data size of its model data ($Size_{req}(O) = Size_{max}(Model(O))$) can be considered. However, the data size sufficient for the view is usually less than the full data size. Therefore, this policy allocates excess network data size to the model data that already have sufficient data size and cannot allocate so large network data size to the model data that do not have sufficient data size. As a result, the model data with insufficient data size cannot reach the sufficient data size rapidly. In addition, this policy requires large cache size for managing model data because all model data require full data size to be downloaded. Smaller required cache size is desirable since the storage size of the low-cost terminal is limited. We defined the required data size as a sufficient data size for the view. The maximum possible resolution of the object can be calculated from its coordinate, the coordinate of the user player, and the range of his view in the case of the bitmap image. We can calculate a sufficient data size of the image data from its maximum possible resolution because the bitmap image model data is a progressive data type. The sufficient data sizes do not change when the user player stays at the same position or looks around because the distances between the user player and the objects do not change. When the user player moves, the sufficient data sizes are recalculated.

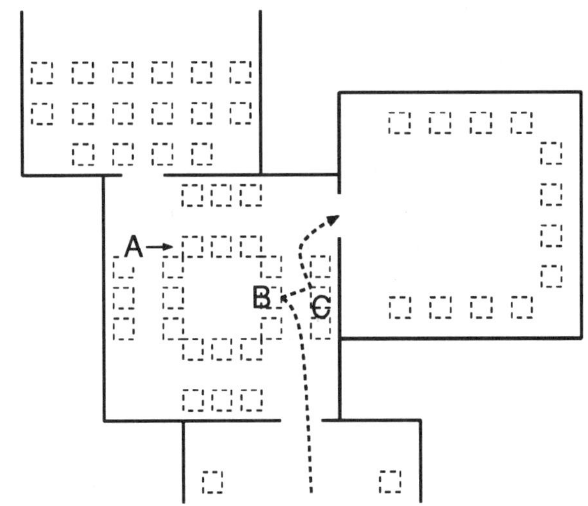

Figure 5. Sample virtual space

4 Experiment

We implemented a prototype system of the browser to examine the proposed methods. We also prepare a test server that provides a sample data of the virtual space (figure 5) to the browser. The test platform for the browser program is a laptop PC with the Intel 50MHz 486DX2 processor and 20MB memory. It displays a view on the X Window System. The browser terminal is connected to the server machine through

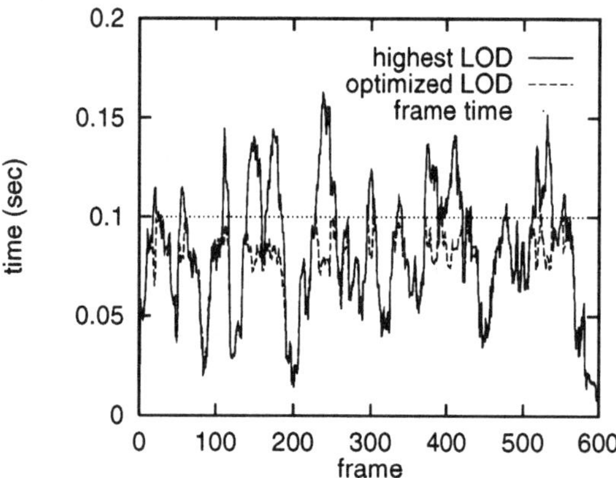

Figure 6. Plots of actual drawing times

the Ethernet, however, the server program emulates a low-bandwidth network. In the test we allocated 32Kbps bandwidth for downloading model data that is a half bandwidth of ISDN networks. For the priority determination, two parameters (v_1 and v_2) must be specified. We assigned 2 to v_1 and 1 to v_2.

4.1 Experiment of the Display Management

To examine whether the display management part of the browser can maintain regular frame rate, we compared the following two algorithms:

- Highest LODs: All visible objects are drawn with the highest LOD.
- Optimized LODs: Visible objects are drawn with their LODs calculated by the display management part.

We specified the frame time $FrameTime$ to 0.1 second (10 frames per second). The display management part needs parameters which represent the computing power and the rendering power of the terminal to estimate drawing costs. We implemented simple benchmark programs and calculated the parameters as follows (μ sec):

$$c_{i_1} = 1300, \quad c_{i_2} = 0, \quad c_{i_3} = 0.4, \quad c_{i_4} = 0.34$$
$$c_{p_1} = 500, \quad c_{p_2} = 800, \quad c_{p_3} = 0.06, \quad c_{p_4} = 0.04$$

In the optimized LODs, the LODs of the objects are determined from the equation (1). In the highest LODs, the LODs of all objects are set to 1. To show only effectiveness of the display management we draw the view after all model data are downloaded in this experiment.

We controlled the user player to go round with looking around in the center room of the sample virtual space and collected actual drawing times for all frames. Figure 6 shows plots of the drawing times for these algorithms. In the case of the highest LOD algorithm the drawing time sometimes exceeds the frame time and causes unregular frame rate. The optimized LOD algorithm can prevent peeks of the drawing time from exceeding the frame time seriously. Since sleep times are padded to the frames of which the drawing times are under frame time, our algorithm can maintain regular frame rate. In theory the peek times equal to the frame time, however, they are really less than it because the algorithm assigns continuous LOD values to the objects but they are truncated to discrete values. Views from the point A in the center room with the highest LODs and with optimized LODs are shown in figure 7-(1). Figure 7-(2) is enlargement copies of the figure 7-(1). In the optimized view faraway cubes are drawn as rectangles and faraway images roughly.

4.2 Experiment of the Network Management

To examine effectiveness of our network management approach we compared the followings:

- Uniform: All model data of the objects are allocated same network bandwidth.
- Optimized: Model data are allocated the network bandwidth based on our approach.

As described above, we specified the available network bandwidth to 32Kbps and the frame rate to 10 frames per second. Therefore, the available network bandwidth per frame $BandWidth$ is 400 bytes per frame. In the optimized approach, the network data sizes are determined from the equation (5). In the uniform approach, the network data sizes for all model data are equally set to $BandWidth/N$ where N is the number of models. All objects are drawn with the highest LODs in this experiment to show effectiveness of our network management without influence of the display management behavior.

We controlled the player object on the route shown in the figure 5: enter the center room, go to the point B and appreciate the exhibition objects for some time, turn around and approach the point C and wait for some time, and exit. We recorded four snapshots of the view in the route: at the point B, at the point B after waiting, at the point C, and at the point C after waiting. They are shown in figure 8-(1), figure 8-(2), figure 9-(1), and figure 9-(2) respectively with comparing the two approaches. Figure 8-(2) and figure 9-(2) show that our optimized approach can display interested objects with gaining their resolution quickly. In the uniform approach, details of the interested objects do not be drawn in a long time and the user feels irritation. Figure 9-(1) also shows that our approach can draw objects with some resolution when the user player turning around.

5 Conclusion

We have described a real-time browser for the digital museum and a real-time view of the player object that is one of its main functions. Our approach in the real-time display of the view divides the drawing power of the terminal and the network bandwidth to the objects based on their importance in the view. Experiments show that our browser can display a proper view with keeping uniform frame rate with low-cost terminals and through low-bandwidth networks. In the future we want to extend our browser to support more several data types that can be considered available in the digital museum.

References

[1] E. H. Blake. A metric for computing adaptive detail in animated scenes using object-oriented programming. In G. Marechal, editor, *Eurographics '87*, pages 295–307. North-Holland, Aug. 1987.

[2] J. H. Clark. Hierarchical geometric model for visible surface algorithms. *Communication of the ACM*, 19(10):547–554, Oct. 1976.

[3] T. A. Funkhouser and C. H.Séquin. Adaptive display algorithm for interactive frame rates during visualization of complex virtual environments. In *Computer Graphics (SIGGRAPH'93 Proceedings)*, pages 247–254, 1993.

[4] T. A. Funkhouser, C. H. Séquin, and S. J. Teller. Management of large amounts of data in interactive building walkthroughs. In *ACM SIGGRAPH Special Issue on 1992 Symposium on Interactive 3D Graphics*, pages 11–20, 1992.

[5] C. Incorporated. Cover sheet for the gif89a specification, June 1993. Available from `http://hyperarchive.lcs.mit.edu /HyperArchive/Archive/dev/info /gif-format-gif89a.txt`.

[6] F. P. B. Jr. Walkthrough — A dynamic graphics system for simulating virtual buildings. In F. Crow and S. M. Pizer, editors, *Proceedings of 1986 Workshop on Interactive 3D Graphics*, pages 9–21, Oct. 1986.

[7] T. Lane. Jpegimage compression: Frequently asked questions. Available from `http://www.cis.ohio-state.edu /hypertext/faq/usenet/jpeg-faq/top.html`.

[8] J. Rossignac and P. Borrel. Multi-resolution 3D approximation for rendering complex scenes. In *Second Conference on Geometric Modelling in Computer Graphics*, pages 453–465, June 1993. Genova, Italy.

[9] B. J. Schachter, editor. *Computer Image Generation*. John Wiley and Sons, 1983.

Optimized LODs

Highest LODs

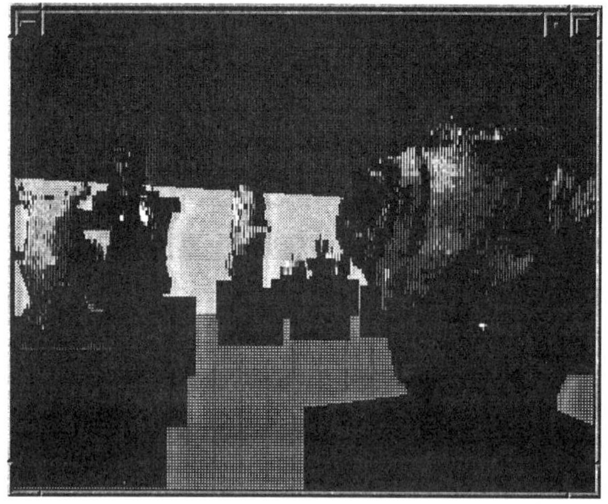

(1) Normal Size

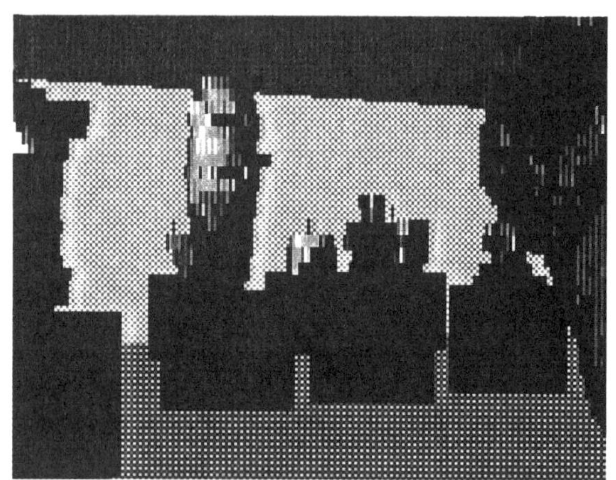

(2) Enlarged

Figure 7. Views from the point A

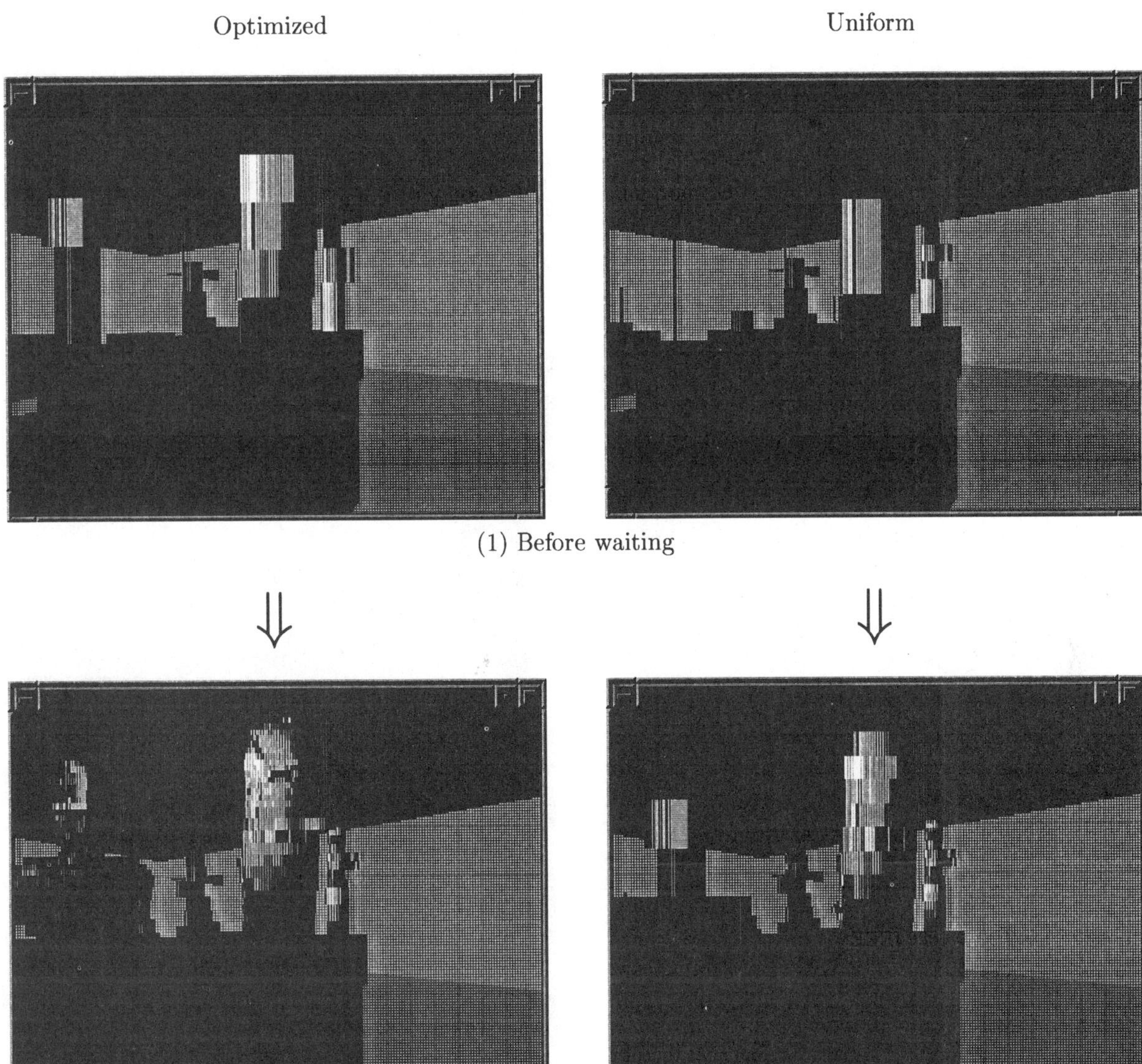

(1) Before waiting

(2) After waiting

Figure 8. Views at the point B

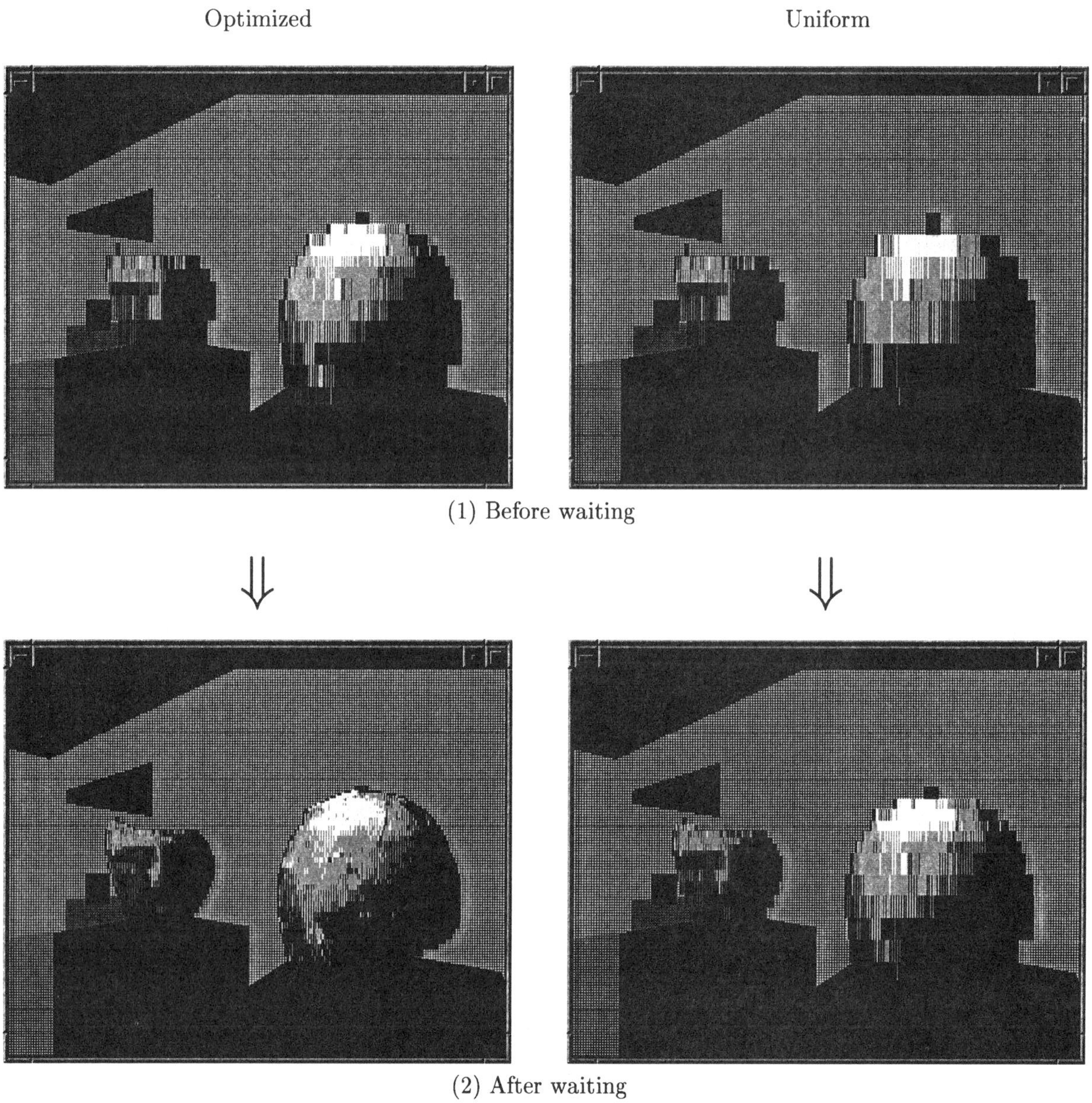

Optimized

Uniform

(1) Before waiting

⇓ ⇓

(2) After waiting

Figure 9. Views at the point C

Technical Session III

BTRON

The B-right: A μBTRON-specification OS for PDA with an Affordable Window System

Akira Matsui and Yoshio Kato
Personal Media Corporation
MY Building,1-7-7 Hiratsuka, Shinagawa-ku, Tokyo, 142 Japan
matsui@personal-media.co.jp

Abstract

The emergence of telecommunications infrastructure such as the Internet and cellular phones has heightened demands for so-called personal digital assistants (PDAs), with the same ease of use as pocket calculators, and for mobile computing. Attempting to equip handheld computers with a full-fledged windowing system, however, runs into major obstacles in terms of hardware resources, battery capacity and the like. At the handheld computer level it is impractical to use Windows 95 or other PC windowing systems.

In this respect the BTRON-specification OS, whose specifications were designed in the TRON Project, has the advantage of running on a low-end CPU and limited hardware resources, making it well suited for PDA and mobile computing uses. In particular, the ability to run at a practical level without needing a high-performance CPU means the CPU clock speed can be kept low to minimize power consumption. This makes possible lightweight batteries and longer battery life.

We have developed a μBTRON-specification OS, modifying the BTRON specifications for PDA use. Evaluations of the OS, called B-right, have shown that it can be used to implement a practical windowing system on a PDA with its many hardware limitations. The results of our work to date are reported here.

1. Introduction

Attempts to implement a windowing system on computers in the personal digital assistant (PDA) class or on mobile computers run up against severe obstacles owing to the limited hardware resources provided by such computers, and their small battery capacity. Workstations and personal computers have a range of general-purpose windowing systems to choose from, including the Unix-oriented X-window, OpenWindow, Windows NT, and Windows 95. All of these, however, require a powerful CPU, a large amount of system memory and ample secondary storage capacity, making it impractical to implement them on a PDA or mobile computer.

The BTRON-specification OS, whose specifications were designed in the TRON Project, is better suited to use with a PDA or mobile computer because of its ability to run on low-end CPUs and its modest hardware requirements. In particular, the ability to run at a practical level without needing a high-performance CPU means the CPU clock speed can be kept low to minimize power consumption. This in turn makes possible lightweight batteries and longer battery life. What's more, a modified version of the original BTRON specifications has been designed recently, called μBTRON and geared especially to use on PDA-class computers. Like the BTRON-specification OS, the μBTRON-specification OS boasts real-time multitasking, built-in hypertext functionality making use of the real/virtual object model, multilingual computing and many more highly innovative features, meeting all the requirements of an OS for 21st-century personal computers and PDAs.[1][2][3]

We have developed a μBTRON-specification OS called B-right, and implemented this OS on the PDA hardware called BTRON-BrainPad (tentative name) produced by Seiko Instruments Inc., demonstrating that a practical windowing system can be built on a PDA with its many hardware resource limitations and small battery capacity.[7] This paper first gives a general explanation of the μBTRON-specification OS B-right. Next it discusses the specific methods used to implement the HMI and power management functions of B-right. Finally, it presents an evaluation of B-right at its current stage of development.

0-8186-7658-2/96 $05.00

2. Overview of the μBTRON-specification OS B-right

2.1 Hardware assumed for B-right

The μBTRON specifications are a modified version of the BTRON specifications, optimizing the functions to run on the hardware resources typically provided by a PDA or other small portable computer. The specific changes to the original BTRON specifications are in the HMI specifications, to enable operations on equipment with a small display and no keyboard, and in the OS specifications underlying the HMI. In addition, new functions were added for power management. The μBTRON-specification OS B-right was implemented assuming the following hardware environment.

Pointing device and menu button

A pressure-sensitive electronic pen or a touch panel may be used as the B-right pointing device. This means that in addition to the two-button electronic pen or mouse assumed in the BTRON specifications, a single-button pointing device may also be used. In this case, preferably a menu button or similar switch will be built into the PDA itself, but this is not mandatory; the OS will run without a menu button as well. If a pressure-sensitive pen or touch panel is provided, there will be no physical switch equivalent to the tip of the electronic pen that comes with the TRON-specification keyboard; instead, the OS must be able to handle information as to whether pen or finger contact is made with the display surface. In this case, the BTRON-specification HMI is realized by regarding the action of contacting the display with a pen or finger in the same way as the action of pressing the main button.

To the B-right OS, it makes no difference whether the electronic pen tablet is integrated with the display or not. In other words, the B-right OS can be used on hardware in which the tablet is integrated with the display, as well as on hardware in which they are separate.

Keyboard

The B-right OS can be implemented on a computer

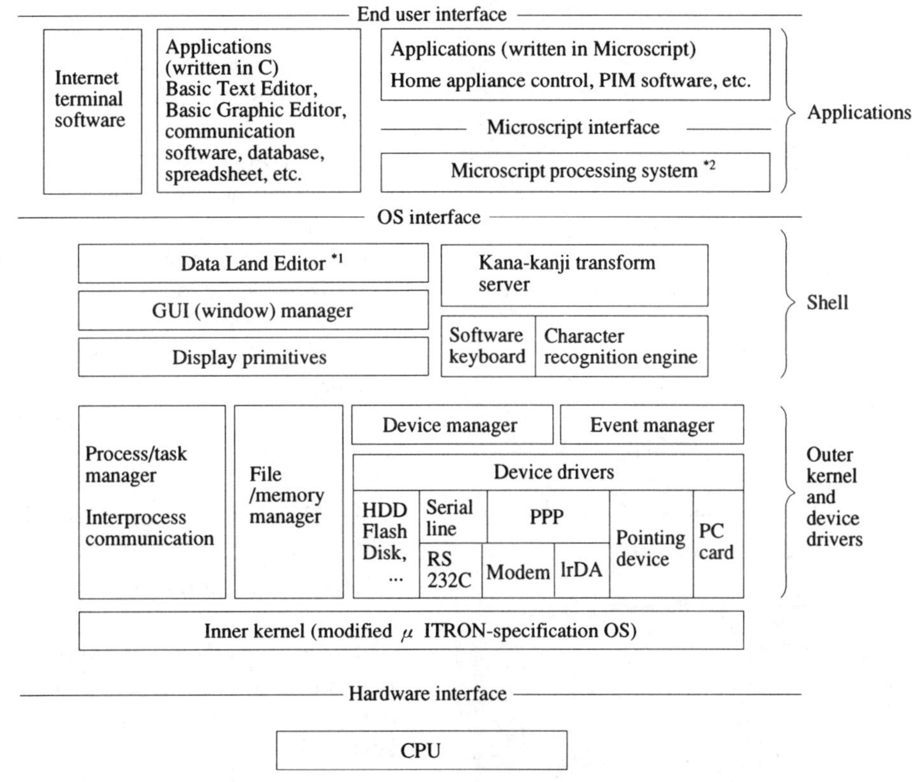

Figure 1. Overall configuration of the B-right OS

without a physical keyboard attached to it. In such cases, key input is made by pointing at the key tops of a software keyboard (keyboard emulator) on the screen with a pointing device. It is also possible to use handwritten character recognition and send the results to the application as key input.

Display

The B-right OS was designed to be usable with small displays, for implementation on highly portable PDAs. The specific screen resolutions supported are as low as 640 x 200 or 320 x 240 dots, and the screen image is designed accordingly. Furthermore, the HMI can be used with both color and monochrome displays.

2.2 Internal structure of B-right

The μBTRON-specification OS B-right adopts a microkernel internal structure, aimed at real-time response and ease of maintenance and extension. The OS consists of three layers called the inner kernel, outer kernel, and shell, with a subset of the μITRON3.0 specification (plus some additional functions) used as the inner kernel (see Figure 1). The inner kernel manages basis resources, such as tasks and memory, used by the outer kernel and higher layers and by device drivers. The outer kernel layer manages the files, devices, processes, events and other resources and functions used by μBTRON applications. The shell layer manages GUI (graphical user interface) related functions such as graphics, the windowing system, and kana-kanji conversion. The functions of the outer kernel and shell are implemented as independent managers based on the object of their operations. The managers consist of task groups running under the inner kernel. For example, page out and page in processing (if the CPU supports virtual memory), and the processing for file management as a whole, are realized as separate tasks. Device drivers likewise consist of task groups running on the inner kernel. By implementing some of the OS functions and device drivers not in the kernel but as tasks, the OS is given a modular structure for improved maintenance and ease of extension. Moreover, interrupts can readily be accepted even while the OS (outer kernel or shell) is executing, for better response.[5][6]

Another advantage of the microkernel approach and resulting OS modularization is that functions can be allocated in smaller units between ROM and RAM as needed. A PDA uses a low-cost mass-produced mask ROM, so it is necessary to incorporate as much of the OS and application object code in ROM as possible. Even so, minor specification changes and upgrades after the mask ROM is produced are unavoidable. To meet the need for such changes, the B-right OS provides the functionality for patching the ROM-encapsulated program in individual module units (functional units such as task management or synchronization and communication), causing a switchover to a program in RAM.

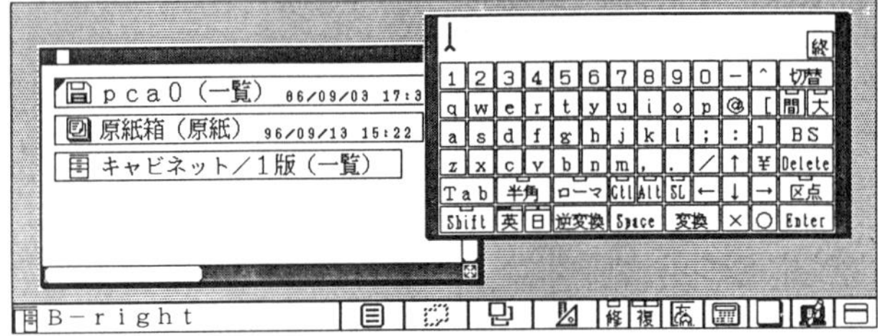

(a) Alphanumerics

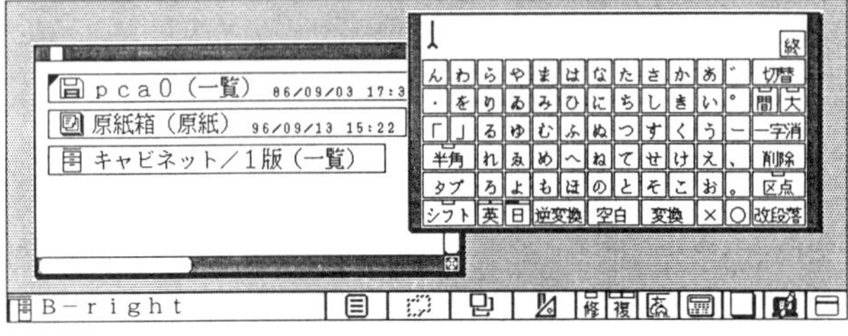

(b) Japanese

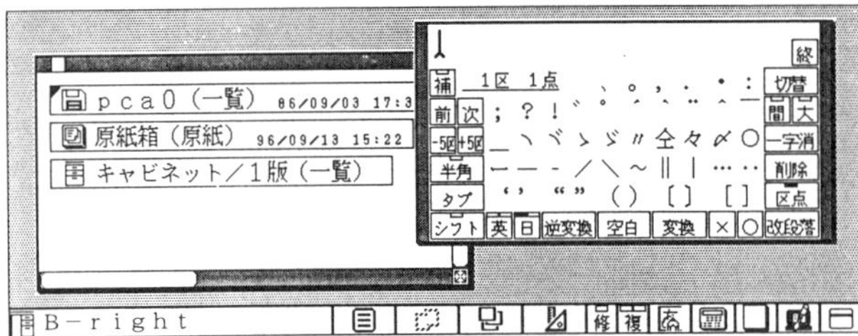

(c) Special Characters

Figure 2. Software keyboard and input modes

3. HMI Modifications for PDA Use

3.1 Keyboard emulator

The μBTRON-specification OS is designed for implementation on small portable computers, which in many cases lack a physical keyboard. A software keyboard function it therefore provided as a means of key input. The software keyboard is a screen-based keyboard emulator, using a pointing device to press keys displayed on the screen, with these actions being translated into key input by software. The keyboard display changes to allow input of alphanumerics, Japanese, and so on, as shown in Figure 2.

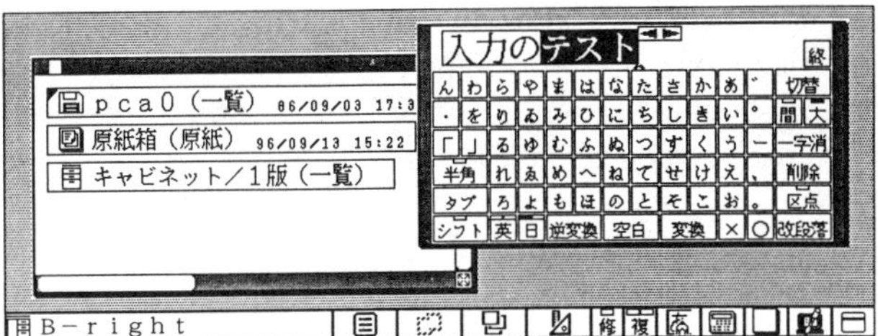

Figure 3. Kana-kanji conversion in the software keyboard window

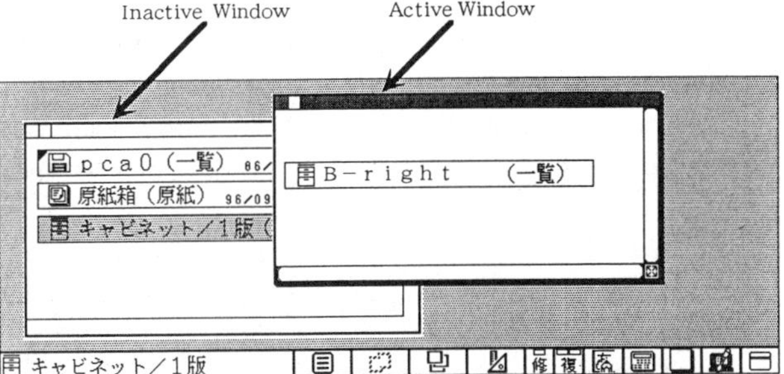

Figure 4. Active and inactive windows

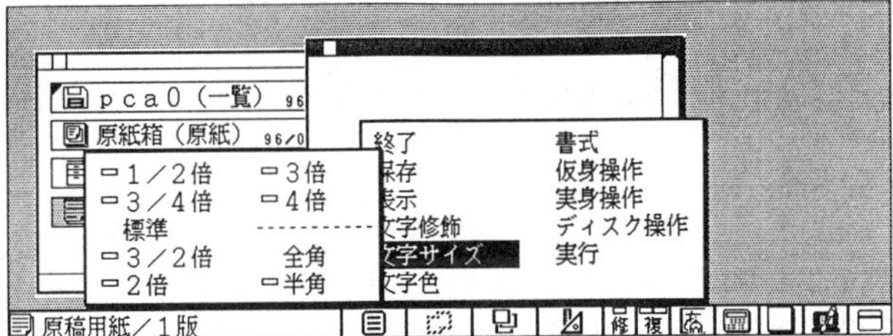

Figure 5. Multi-column menus

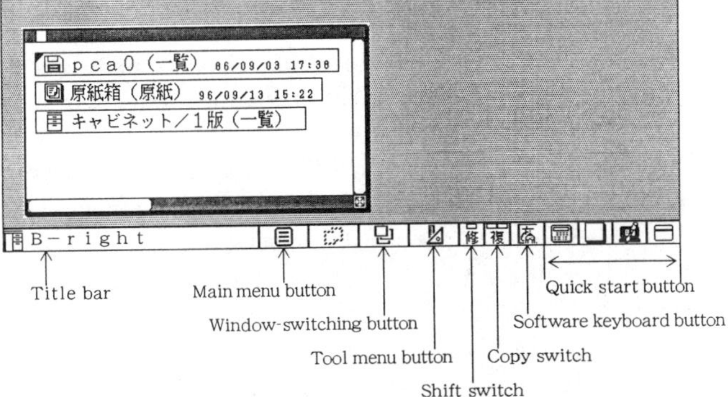

Figure 6. System message panel

The BTRON-specification kana-kanji conversion function is designed to minimize eye movement by the user. To this end the candidate characters are displayed inline, that is, at the same place as characters are input (e.g., at the caret position in the Basic Text Editor). When a software keyboard is used, however, the user is forced to look at the software keyboard window, away from the application. For this reason, it is easier on users to have the kana-kanji conversion also displayed in the software keyboard window, which is the approach adopted here.

Also, since both key input and kana-kanji conversion take place in the software keyboard window, it must be possible to use the pointing device for selecting conversion candidates, shifting the focus within a phrase, and so on. The specification adopted is shown in Figure 3.

3.2 Windows and menus

Because of the small screen size on most PDA-type products, the HMI must be designed to make efficient use of the available area. The original BTRON specifications for the screen and window display are already simple, but in the μBTRON specifications the screen as a whole is redesigned to allow the necessary operations to take place even in a screen size of 640 x 200 or 320 x 240 dots.

The specific changes are as follows. First of all, the title bar at the top of a window was narrowed to increase the window space in the vertical direction. In its place, the pictograms that are displayed on the title bar in a BTRON-specification window and their corresponding real object names are displayed at the left side of the system message panel on the bottom of the screen.

The method of distinguishing whether a window is active (the top window, able to accept input) or inactive is the same as that in the BTRON specifications, by differences in the frame pattern and shading. This is shown in Figure 4. The pictograms and real object names are not shown for inactive windows.

In order to allow long menus to be viewed even in small screens, a function is provided for extending menus to multiple columns. In the BTRON specifications, there is no function for displaying menus in multiple columns; instead, if a menu has too many items to be displayed at once, it is viewed by scrolling up or down as needed. This kind of scrolling, however, is hard to use on a touch panel; so the μBTRON specifications adopt multi-column menus rather than scrolling, as shown in Figure 5. This function applies both to main menus and submenus.

Further, in order to decrease the number of menus, the "Window" and "Tools" system menus in the BTRON specifications are directly accessible in the system message panel at the bottom of the μBTRON-specification screen, and are not included in the common system menus. The system message panel also has a software switch that acts like the menu button when single-button pointing devices are used.

3.3 System message panel

The μBTRON specifications provide various PD-operated software switches on the screen to allow for implementation of the windowing system on hardware without a keyboard or a PD menu button. These switches are located on the right side of the system message panel (Figure 6).

The switches on the system message panel are, from left to right, quick start buttons, window-switching button, software keyboard button, main menu button, "Tools" menu button, control button, and copy switch. On the left side of the system message panel are located the pictogram for the active window (called the application pictogram) and its title. The functions of each button and switch are as follows.

Quick start buttons

The quick start buttons are used to call up tool functions with a simple operation. Pictograms representing each of the tool functions (tool pictograms) are arranged in a row, and the corresponding tool can be started just by clicking on the pictogram. If the tool represented by the clicked pictogram is already started, clicking on the pictogram makes the window of that tool active.

The number of tool pictograms that can be displayed as quick start buttons is limited by the system message panel size, which means only a certain number of tools can be started by quick start buttons. The specification thereforerestricts the quick start buttons to frequently used tools having an important function in system management, such a those for keeping track of battery status or changing the contrast of the liquid crystal panel display. The remaining tools are started from the tool menu described later.

Window-switching button

A window-switching button function is provided for changing the active window. Clicking on this button brings up a menu listing all the displayed windows. Designating a window on this menu makes that window active. In the BTRON specifications, the system menus include a "Window" menu which plays a similar function; but in the μBTRON specifications this function is realized by an independent button.

Another way to make a window active is by clicking on any part of it, as long as some part of the window is visible. Here the BTRON and μBTRON specifications are the same. The need for the window-switching button arises when a window is hidden completely under other windows.

The μBTRON specifications assume a small display size, so that if several windows are open at once, it is fairly likely one or more will be obscured completely. The window-switching button offers a convenient way to switch to a window even if it is not visible.

Software keyboard button

The purpose of the software keyboard button is to display the software keyboard window. The high frequency with which the software keyboard is likely to be used is the reason for having a dedicated button for this feature.

Main menu button

The main menu button is provided for displaying and selecting the main menu list. Clicking on this button brings up the main menu list and enables menu selection. This function is necessary when a single-button pointing device is used. The "Tools" menu and "Window" menu found in the BTRON-specification GUI are replaced in the μBTRON specifications by the tool menu button and window-switching button, and are therefore not included in the main menu list.

Tool menu button

The tool menu button is provided for displaying a tools menu and selecting from it. Clicking on this button brings up the tools menu and enables tool selection.

Shift switch

The shift switch is used to toggle the "shift key pressed" status on and off. It is intended for products without a physical keyboard. Initially it is off (shift key not pressed); clicking it once changes to "shift key pressed" status, and clicking it once again toggles back to "not pressed" status. While the shift key pressed status is on, other key or button operations are modified by whatever action is specified for "shift+" operations. For example, a pointing device select operation is regarded as a shift-select operation.

In both the BTRON and μBTRON specifications, a shift-select operation either adds an object (text, drawing, virtual object, etc.) to the already selected objects or, if it is already selected, deselects it. This operation is performed by pressing the pointing device on an object while the shift key is pressed, or while the shift switch is on. A simple pointing device press not modified by the shift key (or while the shift switch is toggled off) means a new selection (previously selected objects do not remain selected).

Copy switch

When a selected object is dragged using the pointing device, the copy switch state determines whether the object is moved or copied.

In the BTRON specifications, the pointing device menu button is used to select copy or move. In the μBTRON specifications, however, the availability of a pointing device menu button cannot be assumed, so this copy switch is provided.

The copy switch has three states, off, temporary shift, and simple lock. The initial state is off, in which case a drag operation moves the object. Clicking the switch once changes it to temporary shift state, so that the next drag operation is a copy operation, after which the switch goes back to off state. Double-clicking on the switch locks it in the on state (simple lock state), so that all drag operations thereafter will be copy operations, until the lock is released by clicking or double-clicking on the copy switch again.

The names "temporary shift" and "simple lock" are the same as those used for similar functions in the BTRON Enableware specifications.

4. Implementing the μBTRON-specification OS B-right

Described below are the approaches taken in implementing the PDA-oriented HMI functions in B-right discussed in the previous section, and then the power management functions for longer battery life.

4.1 Implementing the software keyboard

The software keyboard must be capable of use by the applications running on the PDA for text input. This means that at a stage closer to hardware than the application, a pointing device operation must be translated to a key event and provided as such to the application. This functionality was realized by implementing the software keyboard using a μBTRON-specification front-end process and the top window function.

A μBTRON front-end process is able to usurp an event before the active process (the process in control of the active window) gets it and perform some kind of preprocessing on the event. The software keyboard makes use of this feature to convert pointing device-related events such as button down events (EV_BUTDWN) to keyboard events such as key down (EV_KEYDWN), before passing the event to the application. This is

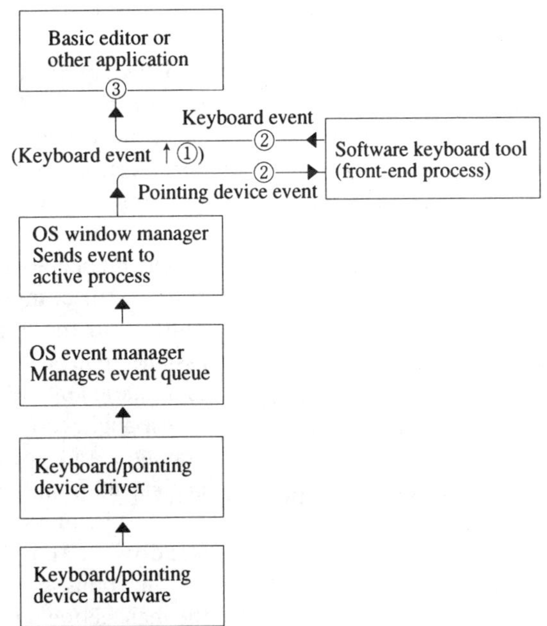

Figure 7. Event flow when the software keyboard tool is used

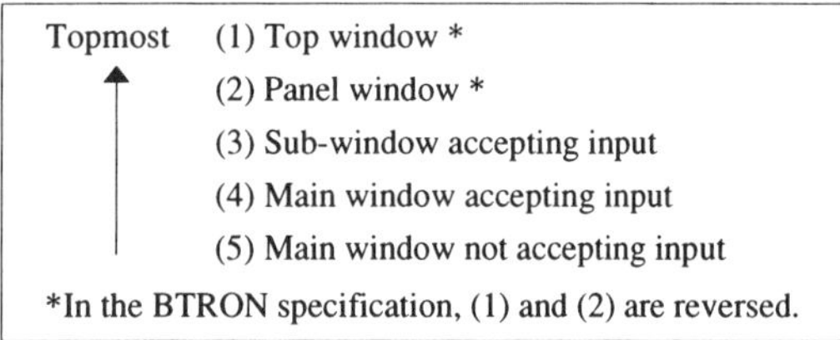

Figure 8. Relative window position in the μBTRON-specification OS

illustrated in Figure 7.

When a front-end process like the software keyboard has a window, it uses the μBTRON-specification top window. The top window is located on top of the active window (the top-most window, in which input is made), and is used for supplementing the active window operations. Interactive operations by the user are always sent to the active window via the top window.

The front-end process and top window functions can be used also with the BTRON specifications. In the case of the BTRON specifications, however, the top window is displayed one layer down from the panel window, which would be a problem when trying to enter text in the panel from the software keyboard.[1][4] To solve this problem, the μBTRON specifications call for displaying the top window on top of the panel window (Figure 8). This raises the possibility that top window movement and redrawing of the panel display will take place even while the panel is showing, so changes were made in the panel manager and other related modules.

When text input is made by handwritten character recognition, the software for character recognition (character recognition engine) is to be incorporated in the software keyboard tool. When kana-kanji conversion takes place in the software keyboard window, or when handwritten character recognition is performed, character codes for the resulting kanji-mixed text output are passed to the application. This approach means the application can perform its processing without having to be aware of how the character codes were input, whether from a physical keyboard, software keyboard, or by handwritten character recognition.

4.2 Functions added to the shell

The μBTRON specifications change the way the system message panel is used from that in the BTRON specifications, in order to allow for single-button pointing device use and to make more efficient use of the small screen size on a PDA. Preferably, however, the application programs that run on the PDA should not have to be dependent on the screen size or pointing device hardware specifications (i.e., they should be able to run on a BTRON-specification OS or a μBTRON-specification OS without distinction). For this reason the HMI changes describe above are absorbed on the OS side to the extent possible. To this end the following specific modifications were made in adapting the BTRON-specification shell to the μBTRON-specification shell.

Application pictogram processing

In the window manager as modified for the μBTRON specifications, when the system detects a pointing device press, it looks at the position code; and if it is on an application pictogram, it notifies the application that the active window pictogram has been pressed.

When an application detects that the press position is on the pictogram, it makes a double-click decision; if it determines a double-click, it performs Exit processing; if a press, it starts drag-move processing (this is unchanged from the BTRON specification).

In the μBTRON specifications, a window cannot be moved by dragging its application pictogram in the system message panel. To move a window the window frame, not a pictogram, must be dragged. For this reason the window manager of μBTRON specification OS was modified so that a drag-move is not accepted if the position code indicates a pictogram.

Quick start button and software keyboard button processing

In the window manager as modified in the μBTRON specifications, a function has been added so that when a pointing device press event is detected on a quickstart button or the software keyboard button, this is translated to a menu operation simulation key event (EV_KEYDWN event with command key and special character) and notified to the application. The special characters are assigned one each to the software keyboard tool and to the tools started by the quick start buttons.

An application receiving such an event calls the menu manager and goes to menu select processing (this is unchanged from the BTRON specification).

At the same time a function has been added to the window manager as modified in the μBTRON specifications, so that when a special character is received, the manager determines the tool application corresponding to that special key and returns to the application the tool menu number having the same tool name.

The application can then start the tool application corresponding to the menu item number returned by the menu manager.

Window-switching button, main menu button, and tool menu button processing

A function was added so that when the μBTRON-specification window manager detects a pointing device press event on these buttons, it translates this to an event representing a main menu button press (EV_MENU) and notifies the application.

An application receiving such an event calls the menu manager and goes to menu select processing (this is unchanged from the BTRON specification).

Another function was added so that when the μBTRON-specification window manager is called by an application as above, it determines based on the pointing device press position whether it is the window-switching button, main menu button, or tool menu button, then displays the corresponding menu items and goes to menu select processing.

Shift switch and copy switch processing

A function was added to the window manager as modified in the μBTRON specifications for detecting pointing device click and double-click actions on the shift switch and copy switch, and for changing the switch state accordingly.

When the window manager passes an event to an application while the shift switch is in on state, it notifies the application that the left shift key is pressed (ES_LSHFT). If the copy switch is in temporary shift or simple lock state when the window manager passes an event to an application, it includes the information that the command key is pressed (ES_CMD).

When the window manager receives notice from an application that a copy operation is complete, it releases the temporary shift state of the copy switch. The application change required as a result is noted below.

Other changes to the shell

A change was made so that title bar drawing will not take place while the μBTRON-specification window manager is drawing a window. Another change was made to the menu manager to allow multi-column menus when a menu is too long to fit on the screen vertically.

Application changes

The above changes to the shell for the μBTRON specifications were made so as to minimize the modifications required in existing BTRON-specification OS applications. However, in the case of the timing for releasing the temporary shift state of the copy switch after a copy operation is complete, only the application actually performing the copy operation is able to make this decision. For this reason, existing applications need to be changed, by adding a process for notifying the window manager when a drag-move or drag-copy operation is complete. The notification method makes use of a previously unused application event (EV_APPL4).

If an application modified in this way is run on a BTRON-specification OS which does not support the copy switch (using a physical menu button on the pointing device instead), there is no problem since the window manager can simply ignore the notice. Accordingly, the addition of the copy switch function does not prevent an application from being developed for common use on both a BTRON and μBTRON-specification environment.

4.3 Implementing power management functions

PDAs use power management functions of various kinds to prolong battery life. Some of these functions are realized in hardware; but in some cases measures are needed at the OS, device driver, application or other levels. The μBTRON-specification OS implements the power management functions described below.

In the μBTRON specifications the term SUSPEND is used to mean going from normal operating state to power off state while keeping information necessary for resuming normal execution. This kind of power off state is called SUSPEND state. Going from power off state to power on state is called RESUME. The SUSPEND factors supported in the μBTRON-specification OS are: power switch operation, battery cover unlock, low battery, and auto power off during idle states. RESUME factors include: power switch operation, timer elapse, and incoming telephone signal via serial line or PC card modem.[7]

4.3.1 Auto power off monitoring

When there is no operation for a set period of time, the power is turned off automatically to save power. This function is called auto power off. In the μBTRON specifications, a system call for notifying of the last event that occurred (las_evt) is added so user operations can be monitored efficiently. The function of this system call is to return the elapsed time since an event of the type designated in a parameter last occurred (see Figure 9).

In the μBTRON-specification OS B-right, a system daemon performs auto power off processing using las_evt. The system daemon, after a temporary wait state, uses las_evt to find out when the last event occurred. If the result of las_evt shows that there has been no user operation-caused event for a certain time period, auto power off processing is performed. If, on the other hand, a user operation-caused event has occurred (the user has performed some operation on the machine), auto power off processing is not performed, but the cycle of entering wait state and issuing las_evt is repeated.

[System call name]

las_evt Get time from last event

[Parameters]

W	t_mask	EventMask	Covered event type designation

[Returned parameters]

WERR	time	Time from Last Event	Elapsed time since last event

[C language interface]

WERR time = las_evt (W t_mask) ;

[Explanation]

The elapsed time (in ms) is returned since the last occurrence of the event type designated by t_mask.

If EM_BUTDWN or EM_BUTUP is designated as t_mask, pointer movement and menu button operations are also treated as event occurrences. If EM_KEYDWN or EM_KEYUP is designated, meta key state changes are also treated as event occurrences.

If EM_NULL is designated as t_mask, the reference time for measuring elapsed time is reset; that is, the last occurrence of all event types is set to the present time.

Figure 9. Specification for las_evt

4.3.2 Additional device driver functions

Whenever there is a device access request in the μBTRON-specification OS from an application or file manager, etc., device manager in the OS outer kernel calls a device driver. Device drivers run as independent tasks on the inner kernel, processing commands issued by device manager like those in Figure 10.

Of the commands in Figure 10, those provided for realizing the μBTRON-specification OS power management functions are DC_SUSPEND and DC_RESUME. When the system goes to SUSPEND state, device manager in the OS outer kernel sends a DC_SUSPEND command to any device drivers processing at the time. When the system processing resumes, device manager sends a DC_RESUME command to the same device drivers that received the DC_SUSPEND command. The processing to be performed by device drivers in response to these two commands is as follows.

Ordinary commands (commands processed in order)	DC_OPEN	Start device use
	DC_CLOSE	End device use
	DC_CLOSEALL	End device use and eject media
	DC_READ	Read data
	DC_WRITE	Write data
Special commands (command requests accepted even while another command is processing*)	DC_ABORT	Abort current processing
	DC_SUSPEND	SUSPEND processing
	DC_RESUME	RESUME processing
	DC_CARDEVENT	PC card event

*DC_RESUME does not fit this definition, but is included here because of its relation to DC_SUSPEND.

Figure 10. Commands issued to device drivers by device manager

Processing for DC_SUSPEND

(1) If there is a command currently processing, it either waits until the command processing is completed or else suspends or aborts the processing. Here "suspend" means the processing in the device driver is temporarily halted, to be continued after a RESUME; "abort" means the same processing as with DC_ABORT. In the case of an "abort," an error is returned to the application or other requester, so generally the requester will retry the device access after a RESUME.

The choice of waiting until processing is completed, suspending, or aborting is dependent on the device driver implementation. If, however, there is the possibility of a long wait period, it will be necessary to choose to suspend or abort instead. This is to make sure highly urgent SUSPEND factors such as low battery are handled promptly. "Abort" is to be avoided if possible, since it can have a major impact on applications.

(2) No further commands can be accepted other than DC_RESUME.

(3) Hardware suspend processing is performed as necessary.

Processing for DC_RESUME

(1) Hardware resume processing is performed as necessary.

(2) Ordinary command receipt is resumed.

Having the μBTRON-specification OS B-right and device drivers support DC_SUSPEND and DC_RESUME commands makes it possible to implement SUSPEND and RESUME functions matched to the nature of each device.

4.3.3 SUSPEND notice to applications

The processing for SUSPEND and RESUME is, as a rule, confined to hardware, device drivers and the OS, and does not affect applications. That is, even if an application is suspended and later, when power is turned back on, resumes processing, all the processing necessary for these changes is performed by hardware, device drivers and the OS, so there is no processing required of applications. From the application's standpoint, processing is at a standstill during SUSPEND state, and upon resuming the only change is that the clock has suddenly advanced. Ordinarily this clock change does not cause any problems, and it is not necessary to notify the application that processing has been suspended.

If, however, the use environment of the product has changed after the RESUME, there may be cases where the application must deal with this change. A couple of examples are given below.

When an application uses a modem or LAN for communication, the line may be disconnected by a SUSPEND and have to be reconnected after a RESUME (or, the connection destination may have to be confirmed).

In an application that is used by entering a password, it may be necessary to reenter the password after a RESUME, to allow for cases where the user changed during the SUSPEND interval.

The μBTRON specifications have a function for notifying an application of SUSPEND and RESUME states in order to handle cases like the above. This notification, however, does not take place to all processes and applications, but only those requesting it. The SUSPEND notification function is specified as follows, and is implemented using the earlier described system daemon.

(1) Registering a SUSPEND notification request

When an application requires SUSPEND or RESUME notification, it sends a message to the system daemon registering that request. To get the process ID of the system daemon, a global name management function is used. The registration can be canceled by sending the system daemon a message to that effect.

(2) Making a SUSPEND notification to applications

When a SUSPEND factor occurs and the system is about to be suspended, a message is sent to the applications registered with the system daemon as per (1), notifying them of the transition to SUSPEND state.

An application receiving a SUSPEND notification message performs the necessary processing, then must send the system daemon a response message indicating that the processing is complete. The system daemon delays the SUSPEND processing for the system as a whole until responses have been received to all SUSPEND notification messages. This function is provided to make it possible to guarantee that all the necessary application processing for a SUSPEND is completed. Care must be taken in implementation so that the response is not delayed too long in the case of low battery or other urgent SUSPEND factors.

(3) Making a RESUME notification to applications

Immediately after the system resumes, a message notifying of the RESUME is sent to applications that require it, as registered in the system daemon per (1) above. There is no need for the application to respond to a RESUME notice.

4.3.4 Reducing power consumption in idle state

The μBTRON-specification OS B-right has a function for making use of the power-saving mode supported in hardware, in order to minimize power consumption also when the product is running. Specifically, when there are no tasks to be executed of those managed by the inner kernel (no tasks in RUN or READY state), the system switches to the low-power mode provided in hardware (a low-power mode supported by the CPU, or a mode in which the CPU clock frequency is lowered).

The transition to low-power mode and return from that mode are handled in an inner kernel dispatcher. The specific algorithm for this is shown in Figure 11. For this function to work effectively, applications and the OS must not perform regular polling (busy loop) processing. That is, whenever there is a wait for some kind of state change in a process or task making up the OS outer kernel, shell, and applications, the prescribed wait state (WAIT or SUSPEND state of μITRON-specification) must be used. In order to satisfy this condition, the implementation method of the event loop processing of the shell, the "flickering frame" (used to indicate selected status) and blinking caret display program, the parts manager, and some applications has been modified from those of BTRON specification OS.

5. Evaluation

The μBTRON-specification OS B-right has been implemented on the BTRON-BrainPad (tentative name) PDA of Seiko Instruments Inc., with parts of the system already operable. Evaluations are currently being made of

```
[Processing by the inner kernel dispatcher]
   Saving the previous task context;
   while ( there is no RUN or READY task) {
      disable interrupts;
      go to low-power mode;
      /* Save power in low-power mode while waiting for interrupt */
      while (there is no interrupt request from peripheral devices or timer)
              {}
      /* interrupt is raised */
      return to normal mode;
      enable interrupts;
      /* This timing is used to run an interrupt handler for the above interrupt, then return from the interrupt. */
      /* Depending on the system call issued in the interrupt handler, some tasks may go to RUN or READY state. */
   }
   Return to the context of the next task to be executed;
```

Figure 11. Low-power mode processing by the B-right inner kernel dispatcher

the system's power consumption and battery life, although final figures are not yet available since the BTRON-BrainPad hardware and B-right OS have not yet been fully tuned. One thing that is apparent, however, is that the BTRON-BrainPad PDA powered by two AA batteries runs for far longer than the two or three hours of a typical lithium ion battery-powered PC/AT-compatible notebook PC running on Windows 95. We are aiming for a battery life of 60 hours or more by further tuning of the hardware and OS.[7]

Next we turn to the memory requirements of the μBTRON-specification OS B-right. Here again, final results will have to wait until tuning is completed; but as with battery life, by taking into account factors dependent on hardware, battery performance and other aspects besides the OS, it should be possible to arrive at figures with fairly high certainty.

First, from the object code of each B-right module we can calculate theoretical values for the ROM size (object code part) and RAM size (data part), as shown in Table 1. Next, the memory used for starting up the system and displaying the initial window was measured and found to be 3,632 KB. This figure is practically the same as the 3662 KB given as the sum of ROM and RAM size for the total of 1 through 5 in Table 1, verifying the accuracy of the theoretical values in Table 1.

Of this amount, the RAM needed for applications like the Basic Text Editor and Basic Graphic Editor varies with the data handled. The figures in Table 1 are for the necessary RAM when there is null data to be edited, so the required RAM size will increase based on the data to be handled. When multiple windows for these applications are open, however, the object code is shared, so the increase in required RAM is only for data. The memory requirements for other applications such as the communication software and Microscript are still being evaluated, but are not likely to deviate significantly from the memory requirements of the Basic Text Editor and Basic Graphic Editor.

In addition to the amounts in Table 1, considering for additional applications, it is estimated that the minimum memory requirement for the μBTRON-specification OS B-right is ROM 6 MB + RAM 2 MB, and in practical use ROM 6MB + RAM 4 MB is required. With this amount of memory it is possible to open at least ten application windows and operate the product in normal situations. This amount of ROM also makes it possible to locate all the applications and fonts, etc., in ROM, while storing user data in a flash disk or other secondary storage medium. On the other hand, if there is enough secondary storage to hold the application object code and fonts, the ROM size can be reduced.

The CPU used in the BTRON-BrainPad PDA is an NEC V810, which is a RISC chip, so the object code size is larger than that of a CISC-type CPU. It is quite possible that use of a different CPU would lower the memory requirement (mainly ROM) further. Additional memory reduction is possible by tuning the functions to specific uses and eliminating unnecessary functions (such as kana-kanji conversion).

Table 1. Memory requirements of the μBTRON-specification OS B-right

No.	Module name	Required ROM	Required RAM
1.	Boot/diagnose	52KB	(72KB (*1))
2.	Inner kernel	52KB	32KB
3.	Outer kernel (*2)	798KB	198KB
4.	Shell (*3)	1194KB	286KB
5.	Fonts (*4)	1050KB	_
Total of 1 to 5 (system started and displaying the initial window)		3146KB	516KB
6.	Character recognition engine	500KB	40KB
7.	Basic Text Editor	220KB	44KB (*6)
8.	Basic Graphic Editor	264KB	40KB (*6)
9.	Utilities (*5)	328KB	104KB
Total of 1 to 9 (running various applications)		4458KB (*7)	744KB (*7)

*1: After the OS is started, this RAM can be used for other purposes and is therefore not included in the total.

*2: The outer kernel includes the process/task manager, file/memory manager, device manager, event manager, and also device drivers for flash disk, serial line, pointing device, and PC card.

*3: The shell includes display primitives, GUI manager, kana-kanji transform server and dictionary, software keyboard tool, and data land editor. The character recognition engine is put under 6 by itself.

*4: Fonts include 16-dot JIS levels 1 and 2 and supplementary kanji, 12-dot JIS level 1, and 24-dot JIS levels 1 and 2. The B-right OS is also capable of handing fonts for displaying Chinese and Korean, but these fonts are not included in the size calculation here.

*5: Includes clock, MS-DOS file conversion, formatter, LCD brightness control, etc.

*6: Varies with the amount of text or graphic data to be edited. The value given here is the minimum. When two or more instances of the same application are run (for example, when multiple Basic Text Editor windows are open and editing separate documents), the object code is shared, so only the RAM requirement increases, not ROM.

*7: Some applications (Microscript, communication software, spreadsheet, database) are not included here.

6. Conclusions

PDAs and other handheld computers are assuming an important new role as new telecommunications infrastructure is put in place, with the rise of services like the Internet and portable telephone networks. The functions required of today's PDAs, however, are infinite in their variety, including email exchange, editing and management, Web browsing, document creation with pictures, database management, scheduling and much more, all of which require an advanced operation interface. Implementing such functionality in a non-OS environment would be next to impossible and would make it difficult to add new applications later. At the same time, a PC OS such as Windows 95, requiring a powerful CPU and abundant hardware resources, is not suited for use in a PDA or mobile computer. In order to implement a general-purpose, practical windowing system on a PDA with its limited hardware resources and battery capacity, a compact, high-performance OS is needed, and one that can easily be tuned and incorporated in ROM.

We have modified the BTRON specifications for PDA use, developing the μBTRON-specification OS B-right to meet the above requirements. The B-right memory requirements of ROM 6 MB + RAM 4 MB are well within the range of feasibility in a PDA hardware environment. We have shown that the B-right OS makes it possible to realize a practical windowing system on a PDA, with its many hardware limitations.

The B-right OS was developed with the aim of implementing it on a PDA and running general applications, but another effective use is for realizing a GUI HMI on embedded control equipment. The software in embedded control systems must meet real-time multitasking performance requirements; and the B-right OS shines in this area. Real-time performance and multitasking, after all, are features of the TRON Project as a whole, of which the μBTRON specifications are a part. In the case of embedded control and other uses where the system is dedicated to a specific application, the memory requirements can be reduced further by eliminating unnecessary modules.

Note

This paper discusses the OS development in progress. The final product version may be different from the system discussed here.

Acknowledgments

The authors wish to thank Dr. Ken Sakamura of Tokyo University for his guidance throughout the course of this study. Our appreciation goes also to Seiko Instruments Inc. for their assistance in implementing B-right on hardware.

References

[1] K. Sakamura, ed. *"BTRON1 Specification Software Specification,"* TRON Association (1989).
[2] K. Sakamura, "BTRON: An Overview," *TRON Project 1987*, Springer-Verlag (1987), pp. 75-82.
[3] K. Sakamura, "BTRON: The Business-oriented Operating System," *IEEE Micro*, Vol. 7, No. 2 (April 1987), pp. 53-65.
[4] K. Sakamura, ed., *"BTRON1 Programming Standard Handbook,"* Personal Media Corporation (1992). [in Japanese]
[5] K. Sakamura, "BTRON3 Specification Nears Release," *TRON Project Bimonthly*, No. 31 (February 1994), p. E-16.
[6] A. Matsui, "Implementing a BTRON3-specification Operating System," *TRON Project Bimonthly*, No. 39 (June 1995), p. E-15.
[7] H. Watanabe, N. Sasaki, K. Tanigawa, Y. Kanamori, "Development of the BTRON-BrainPad," in *this issue.*

Development of the BTRON-BrainPad

H. Watanabe, N. Sasaki, K. Tanigawa, Y. Kanamori
Seiko Instruments Inc., Information Systems Division
1-1, Akanehama 1-chome, Narashino-shi, Chiba 275

Abstract

In the last few years, software tools such as electronic mail and World Wide Web browsers have greatly increased productivity. And, especially in the last year, the demand to take these tools out of the office through small, lightweight hand-held devices called Personal Digital Assistants (PDAs) has been especially fervent. Manufacturers have had to scramble to supply this demand, but have run into problems with size, weight, batteries, and operating systems.

In order to solve these problems, the BTRON operating system was singled out because it operates on very few resources, which makes it perfect for use in PDAs. And, through the addition of power management functions, SII was able to create the BTRON-Brain Pad, the world's first PDA to run on the BTRON OS with long-life, small batteries for light-weight portability. This paper introduces the technical specifications of the BTRON-BrainPad, as well as how power management functions were added to the newest BTRON OS, BTRON3, to enable the realization of this small-sized, light-weight, and easy to use PDA.

1. Introduction

SII has been producing PDAs and other hand-held devices for corporations for about 10 years, but it is not until recently that corporations have pushed to make information available to their workers in an attempt to respond to the sudden changes in the environment brought about by the explosively popular Internet. This move toward interconnectivity has forced SII to revolutionize the PDA as well. Up until now, PDAs were mainly stand-alone devices, but in today's environment, they too must be equipped with the ability to connect to a network.

In order to satisfy all of these needs, the CPU must process more information on less power, which has become increasingly difficult on the same CPU architecture as in the past. Also, having to respond to the intricate tasks required by today's software and networks has made it evident that the single task OS was no longer adequate, and that future PDAs must contain a multi-task OS equipped with a Graphical User Interface (GUI). Therefore, we developed the BTRON-BrainPad to be small, light-weight, and powerful.

We thought about using Microsoft Windows® as the OS, but the hard disk, RAM, and CPU requirements would need too large a battery and make the overall device too heavy. Thus, we needed an OS that would be perfect for a device small enough to fit in a coat pocket. BTRON was the perfect OS for our PDA.

Once we decided on the OS, we asked Personal Media Co., Ltd. to develop a port of the BTRON OS. They made some PDA specific alterations to their version of the BTRON3 operating system, 3B, and called it "B-right". We then added our experience in PDA power management, and successfully ported the Bware to the BTRON-BrainPad.

In this paper we will explain the corporate environment for which the BTRON-BrainPad was developed, the reason the BTRON OS was selected, and the specifications of the BTRON-BrainPad. Throughout the paper we will also discuss how we combined the hardware and software to create a small, light-weight device and how we were able to assemble the hardware and OS to realize a battery with a longer life span.

2. PDA Demand

2.1 Corporate Environment

Systematizing white collar work to increase efficiency is very difficult because it has no fixed form and fluctuates from day to day. In order to increase efficiency, the white collar worker must have information always ready at his fingertips so he can accomplish his important tasks of deciding the specifications of a product or meeting customers, but, until now, it was not readily available. The age of selling a product on price alone has given way to having to quickly and accurately judge the tastes of customers and provide new products or services to fit those tastes. In this environment, information systems able to provide quick access to customer and product information have become especially important.

SFA (Sales Force Automation) has attracted the attention of companies, especially sales departments, as a means to increase productivity. Recently, the trend in these departments has been to restructure business activity and employ the latest information technology to increase sales and customer satisfaction [1]. It is imperative to for all sections to store, manage, and have quick access to all of the information about a company's clientele in order to raise customer satisfaction in today's business environment. Thus, a systematized flow of information and the ability to access it at anytime becomes increasingly important to SFA.

Furthermore, information management is not limited to only sales departments, but the administration of meeting rooms, projects, orders, schedules, and documents also needs quick informational input and retrieval methods as well. Up until now, these system s have been based on a client/server type of system; however, because both the server and client must be programmed to fit the specific needs of the enterprise, this type of system can be very costly.

The advent of the Internet has revolutionized all of this. Now, armed with electronic mail and WWW browsers, corporations can very easily manage the flow of information regardless of the type of platform used. In this new environment of connectivity, only the server needs to be updated with the latest information, the rest is left up to the browser on the client side, which has immensely increased productivity. The Internet has also solved the need for costly software updates, as any type of browser can easily retrieve the most essential information from the server.

The better the environment in a company the greater the gap between productivity as soon as the worker takes one step outside the company. Therefore, it is only natural for the worker to want to take that environment with him wherever he goes. This is especially true for those in the sales department.

Recently many people have begun lugging around a notebook computer to satisfy this desire to carry the office environment wherever they go, but a notebook is bulky and heavy and cannot be taken everywhere. For these people, the choice is a light-weight, portable, take anywhere PDA.

2.2 PDA Specifications for Business Use

This section takes a look at what kinds of functions are being demanded of PDAs. These demands include the following:

Network (Internet) Connectability
Usefulness
Easy Programmability
Small, light-weight
Long Battery Life Expectancy
Inexpensive

Network connectability is not just being able to use e-mail and simple communications applications, but to truly be able to connect to the office LAN both inside and outside the office that is desired.

Usefulness must be examined from various angles. First, we need to consider that, unlike a desktop computer, the PDA is not physically connected to the network, which is no problem when inside the office because several gateways exist and do not carry any additional costs. However, it is a different story when outside. The number of ways to access the network is limited to public, cellular or PHS telephones and is expensive. In the case of public and PHS phones, the number and points of access are limited. In other words, even if a PDA is network capable, it is still not connected most of the time. Thus, it can be said that the PDA is a terminal for accessing important personal and company data targeted at the individual. The PDA must be ready for use any time and anywhere. It must be able to store vital information even when not connected to a network. Although the network computer has been in the news recently, the PDA needs to have ample memory and programming to be useful all of the time.

To be easy to use, the PDA must react quickly to operations. It must be ready to use as soon as it is turned on. This is the difficult part on the limited resources of a PDA, but it must be accomplished.

The PDA must also be easy to program because the needs of each company and/or individual are different. However, creating a program from scratch requires time and money, therefore, the operating system must allow for very easy programming to reduce costs.

As the PDA becomes more of an indispensable tool for the individual to work on precious information, the more the owner becomes reliant on the PDA, and the more reliant the success of the PDA becomes on the life of the battery. Therefore, the battery has to work for a reasonable time after it is replaced and it must be readily available to the public.

The battery plays an important role in the design of the

case and portability of the unit. It is not only the size of the battery that determines the size of the case, but the size of the battery in respect with the rest of the circuitry. There is always a demand for smaller and smaller devices to run on less and less power. Thus, a smaller battery with a larger capacity is desired for the overall success of a PDA.

The BTRON-BrainPad was developed to run on two AA alkaline dry cell batteries for 44 hours, which is the same as the present BrainPad, with a CPU that is 10 times faster. This means, if used for 2 hours a day, the new BTRON-BrainPad can run for an entire month.

As far as cost is concerned, a PDA must be priced in a range that is affordable for everyone.

2.3 Conditions for a PDA OS

The operating system of the PDA must meet the following criteria:

Networking
Multi-Tasking
HMI (Human Machine Interface)
Simple Application Development
Needs Few Resources
Ability to Execute from ROM
Easy to Use, Multi-Language Processing
A Power Management System able to run on Several Different PDAs

Multi-tasking, networking and simple application development are the same as what is desired from the entire PDA, and are therefore omitted here.

Next on the list of requirements, HMI functionality, is extremely important for PDAs because in order to be accepted by the market the PDA must be require very few steps to operate in order to be useful to the user. This is a rule of thumb for applications, but it is also important for the operating system.

RAM, hard disk space, and CPU performance are all limited on a PDA, and increasing only consumes more battery power, leading to larger batteries and more weight when the aim is decrease weight and battery consumption. The way around this is to put everything in ROM. By putting everything in mask ROM, it is possible to save money because of the relatively low cost of flash ROM. It also save on RAM because it puts up from a disk image in the flash ROM, which allows the manufacture of a cheaper PDA.

Being able to communicate and process the language of the country in which it is used is another important requirement of a PDA in order to enhance ease of use.

In regards to power management, the ability to reduce the amount of power used by shifting power to where it is needed, when it is needed, and reducing it in areas where it is not, is a major function of the OS. With superior power management, it is possible to reduce the load on the batteries and, therefore, reduce the size of the battery, which in turn reduces the overall size and weight of the PDA.

Also, since batteries are less stable than electricity from an outlet and it is easier for users to make a mistake, the risk of losing data is much higher. The OS must be equipped with the ability to handle any type of situation in order for the PDA to be a success.

3. BTRON-BrainPad Specifications

3.1 OS

The BTRON operating system contains most of the features described in section 2.3. Since the BTRON was originally developed to run on an 80286 CPU and boot from a floppy disk, it requires very few resources to operate. Furthermore, the BTRON OS has an HMI function, it can handle several different languages, and it is a multi-tasking OS [2]. The small size of the OS means it can be stored in ROM, and, thus, easily updated if necessary.

Although there are three different forms of the BTRON OS (BTRON1, BTRON2, BTRON3), we chose 3B, which is based on the specifications of BTRON3, for the BTRON-BrainPad because of its application interface, application development based on micro-scripts, and 32 bit CPU [3][4][5][6][7]. The BTRON-BrainPad script is compatible with 1B microscript of the 3B and BTRON 1 specified OS. Therefore, if you heed the size and black and white display of the BTRON-BrainPad when creating software in BTRON, it will run as is on the BTRON-BrainPad. The fact that the program can be tested on 1B and 3B instead of having to test it on the BTRON-BrainPad every time, also allows for efficient program development. Programs can also be transferred from the computer through a PC-Card or serial interface. However, as the 3B was originally developed for a workstation using a TRON specified chip, we (SII and Personal Media Corporation) ported only those features that we felt were perfect for a PDA and then added other features such as communications and the following power management tools:

- Powering down of the CPU when it is not needed.
- SUSPEND/RESUME Routines
- SUSPEND/RESUME In-process Notification
- Auto-power Off

(Please see chapter 5 for a more detailed explanation, including key words.)

3.2 Communications

The BTRON-BrainPad uses TCP/IP to connect to company LANs and the Internet. Furthermore, we developed and installed exclusive WWW browser and electronic mail software for easy access anywhere. The WWW browser supports HTML 2.0 and part of 3.0 and automatically compresses image data to fit into the small screen of a PDA so the whole page can be seen without having to scroll to the side. It also supports FTP for easy data transfers to and from the server. The e-mail program supports POP, SMTP and MIME, and works as part of the browser. It can send and receive BTRON files through a file attachment function, as well exchange TAD files with other BTRON users. It is also equipped with the ability to play u-law PCM data and Voice-mail.

The 3B came equipped with TCP/IP because it was originally developed to run on a workstation with a TRON specified chip. Since ethernet was created for workstations and desktop computers to connect directly to the network, we had to create another method of connection for the PDA. Figure 1 shows a configuration of the system that the BTRON-BrainPad uses to connect to the LAN. Inside the office, it can connect via an IrLAN or through a PHS telephone and PC-Card and PHS base device. Outside the office, it connect via a cellular phone and PC-Card modem or through a PHS card and PHS telephone. These access methods make it possible to access the Internet and Intranet through the WWW browser, FTP function, and e-mail anytime and anywhere. Also, if the server is a 3B workstation, then it is possible to exchange TAD data allowing the user to download and view maps through the graphic editor, and to load and execute microscripts, thus expanding his/her world outside the office.

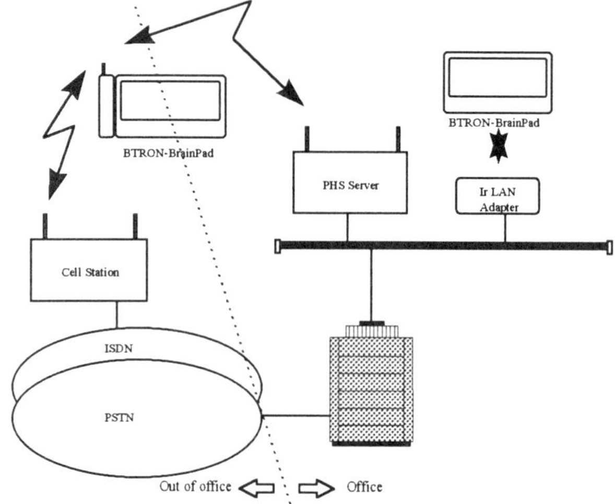

Figure 1 Connecting to a Network

3.3 Specifications

Table 1 shows the specifications of the BTRON-BrainPad. The BTRON-BrainPad, in order to realize low energy consumption and precise power control, needed a low voltage, low frequency CPU. Therefore, we chose the V810 RISC because it consumes very little energy. In fact, the V810 only consumes about 10 mW per MIPS and runs at clock speed of 32 KHz [8].

The OS, Japanese fonts, and a dictionary is stored in mask ROM. By storing everything in the mask ROM, we were able to reduce the amount of DRAM and lower costs as well as save space.

Table 1 Specifications

Component		Specification
CPU		V810 (9MHz / 18MHz)
Memory	Main Memory ROM	DRAM 4Mbyte 8Mbyte
Disk	Flash ROM	4 or 8 MByte
Display		640 x 240 4-level Black and white LCD
Tablet		Pressure Sensitive Pen Input Virtual Keyboard, Handwriting Recognition
Sound		PCM (μ-side) ADPCM (G.721)
Infrared Communications		IrDA 1.1 115 kbps, 1 Mbps。
PC-Card		JEIDA VS4.2 Based Can connect with PHS-Card
Power Supply	Main Backup	2 Alkaline Drycell Batteries 1 Flat Lithium Battery
Dimensions		170 x 100 x 20
Weight		Approx. 300 g

Figure 2 shows a block diagram of the BTRON-BrainPad.

Although it is a PDA, the configuration of the circuitry is similar to a PC. In order to save space on the limited board area of the PDA, all of the peripheral circuits with the exception of the PC-Card have been placed in one gate array. The gate array has a total of 256 pins arranged in BGA (Ball Grid Array) because the 40 mm x 40 mm area required by the 0.5 mm pitch between pins of the QFP (Quad Flat Package) would have been too big.

We were able to create a small, light-weight device by accomplishing the following:

- Placing all of the controller circuitry except the PC-Card controller on one gate array.
- Use of the BGA to place a large number of pins in small package.
- Selection of an OS that needed very few resources.

- Execution of the OS from ROM to decrease the amount of RAM and flash disks.
- Reduction of battery size by adding power management tools to the OS.
- Creation of a smaller but stronger case with stiffer materials.

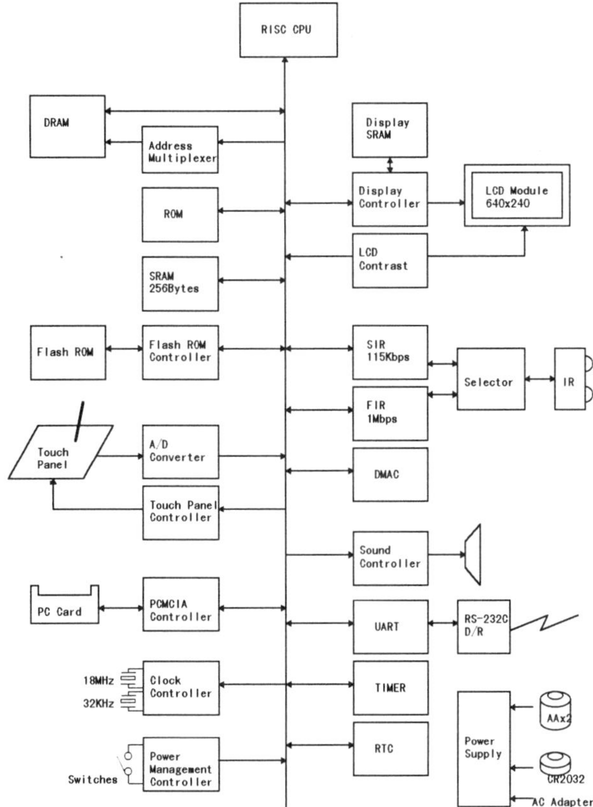

Figure 2 Block Diagram

4. Power Management

4.1 Power ON / OFF

Most desktop computers have a power switch to turn the power on and off. PDAs and Notebook computers, on the other hand, use a different method in order to shorten the length of time they are operating and to protect data. This is called RESUME mode in the BTRON1 specified OS [9].

Definition of Power ON/OFF

Even when the BTRON-BrainPad is OFF, power is still being supplied to the circuitry and the data in the registers of the CPU, DRAM, and the peripheral circuitry is retained. Table 2 shows the state at power ON and OFF. It is possible to judge by the appearance of both whether or not an LCD is on.

This paper uses "Power OFF" and "SUSPEND mode" to describe the state where power is still being supplied to certain circuits; and, "SUSPEND routine" to describe the shift from "Power ON" mode to "Power OFF".

Table 2 States at "Power ON/OFF"

Power ON/OFF	LCD	CPU	Memory	PC card	Analog Circuit
Power ON	ON	ON	ON	ON	ON
Power OFF	OFF	ON	ON	ON/OFF *1	OFF

ON represents that power is supplied.
OFF represents that power is not supplied.
*1- Software selectable.

SUSPEND and RESUME

The shift from "Power ON" to "Power OFF" is called the "SUSPEND routine"; and the shift from "Power OFF" to "Power ON" is called the "RESUME routine". The SUSPEND routine and RESUME routine are usually executed by some kind of event. The following events on the BTRON-BrainPad trigger the SUSPEND routine:

Power switch
PC Card Switch - Unlock
Battery Lid Switch - Unlock
BLDL (Battery Low Detect - Low) Detection
Automatic Power OFF

If the power switch is pushed in "Power ON" mode, the BTRON-BrainPad goes into "Power OFF" mode because the switch is a momentary switch.

The PC Card Switch protects the system from crashes or loss of data if the user mistakenly ejects the PC Card during access. If the system detects that the PC Card Switch is unlocked, it immediately stops all processing and enters SUSPEND mode. All recovery processing is executed during the RESUME routine. The reason recovery is not executed in SUSPEND mode is because there is usually very little time between when an unlock is detected and the card is ejected. This type of processing must be done by the PC Card driver.

As soon as the Battery Lid Switch detects that the batteries are ready to be changed or that the battery lid is open, it quickly shifts to "Power OFF" mode.

BLDL detects that the electrical voltage of the main battery has reached minimum operating voltage and puts the BrainPad in "Power OFF" mode. The power management system also has a BLDH (Battery Low Detect - High) function that activates just before BLDL to warn the user that the battery is getting low.

Auto-Power Off puts the BrainPad into SUSPEND mode when the BrainPad is not used for a certain period of time.

The CPU gives the highest interrupt priority to every

event from a power management tool except for Auto-Power Off.

The following events on the BTRON-BrainPad trigger the RESUME routine:

Power switch
Alarm Clock
Serial Ring Signal
PC Card RI# Signal

Pushing the power switch in the "Power OFF" state triggers the RESUME routine and puts the BTRON-BrainPad into "Power ON" mode.

When the internal clock reaches the time set by the user, the ALARM signal is sent and the RESUME routine is triggered.

Ring occurs when a ring signal is detected from the serial port.

The RI# signal from the PC Card is similar to the Ring signal and is used by a communications PC Card. However, the system must be set to supply voltage to the PC Card even in the "Power OFF" state.

4.2 Power Management Modes

Figure 3 shows the power management modes of the BTRON-BrainPad.

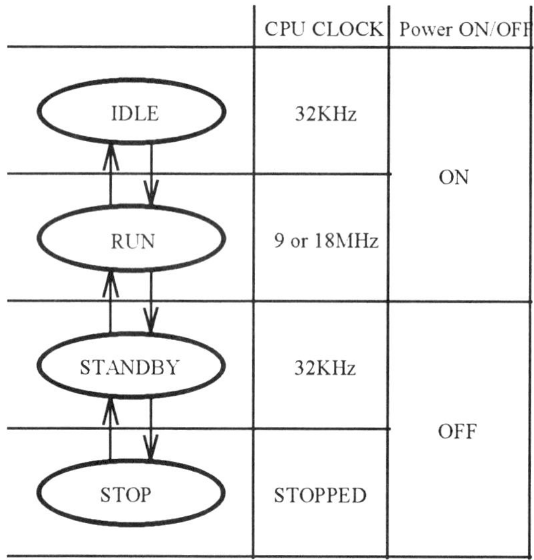

Figure 3 Power Management Modes

RUN is the state in which the CPU conducts processing at a clock speed of 9 MHz or 18 MHz. When there is no task, the CPU enters the IDLE state, in which the clock speed drops to 32 KHz to save energy.

In STOP mode, which is the "Power OFF" state, the CPU is stopped, and the RTC and DRAM conduct self-refresh. STANDBY mode is the process mode for the SUSPEND and RESUME routines, and the CPU operates at 32 KHz. RUN and IDLE occur in "Power ON" mode, and STOP and STANDBY in "Power OFF" mode.

4.3 IDLE

The IDLE routine was developed to save power because a PDA is often left ON when, for example, the user wants to look at the display and think or has just looked up an address and is dialing the phone while looking at the display, and an the CPU seldom operates at 100% IDLE saves power by lowering the clock speed of the CPU at times when full power is not needed, and also cutting power to parts of the PDA that do not need it.

Figure 4 is a flow chart of the IDLE routine.

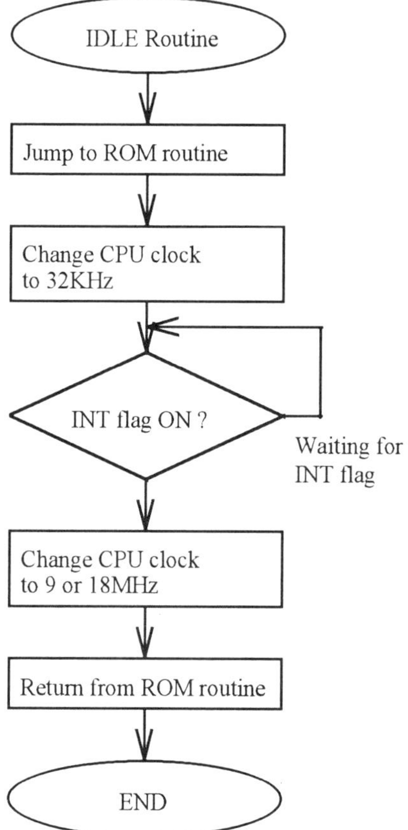

Figure 4 IDLE Routine

The OS calls up the IDLE routine, which lowers the clock speed of the CPU to 32 KHz, when there is no task to process. In previous PDA models, the IDLE routine completely stopped the CPU; however, in order to increase the functions of the CPU to monitor operations and power, the IDLE routine in the BTRON-BrainPad simply lowers the clock speed.

All processing is switched to ROM because it is not possible to access DRAM at 32 KHz. Because the BTRON-BrainPad is also equipped with SRAM, it is also possible to shift applications to SRAM for processing.

The IDLE routine is exited when there is an interrupt such as PEN DOWN, serial communications, or an OS timer. However, in order to avoid any reckless process from a forced switch to DRAM, the IDLE power management tool is programmed to inspect the flag of the interrupt and decide how to exit the IDLE routine. The clock speed of the CPU is switched by hardware because it has to be done quickly. It takes about 3 clock cycles of either 9 MHz or 18 MHz to change the clock.

The voltage at the battery is reduced to approximately mW with the display on in IDLE mode because power is only used for the operation of the OS interval timer and when it moves to RUN mode to process an interrupt. As the PDA uses about mW in normal operation, this is a major reduction.

4.4 SUSPEND

When the user pushes the power switch or BLDL detects a reduction in battery voltage, all processing is stopped and the SUSPEND routine is activated to shift to "Power OFF" mode. A SUSPEND routine that stops all other processing in the little time there is from when an event such as BLDL, Battery Lid Switch - Unlock, or PC Card Switch - Unlock triggers the SUSPEND routine until the PDA shifts to "Power OFF" mode is the most desired. But, there is also a need to finish serial processing such as flash ROM and PC Card access. Therefore, the SUSPEND routine must shift to "Power OFF" after completing all other processing because cutting off and reinitiating processing may not be able to be accomplished in 1 block.

SUSPEND needs to handle every device differently. We installed the SUSPEND and RESUME routines in the BTRON OS so that they could handle every device according to its corresponding driver. Figure 5 shows how the BTRON OS manages and interfaces with each driver. The device manager sends a request through a rendezvous with the device driver. A normal request is OPEN, CLOSE, READ, or WRITE and a special request is ABORT, SUSPEND, or RESUME. When the driver receives a SUSPEND request it stops all processing, and goes into "Power OFF" mode to save power as the need arises. Similar to a flash ROM driver, it finishes waits to finish the minimum unit of processing before stopping if it is in the middle of processing when a SUSPEND request is received. It does not return a rpl_rdv command until it is waiting for processing to finish. During this time, the OS waits to enter STANDBY mode.

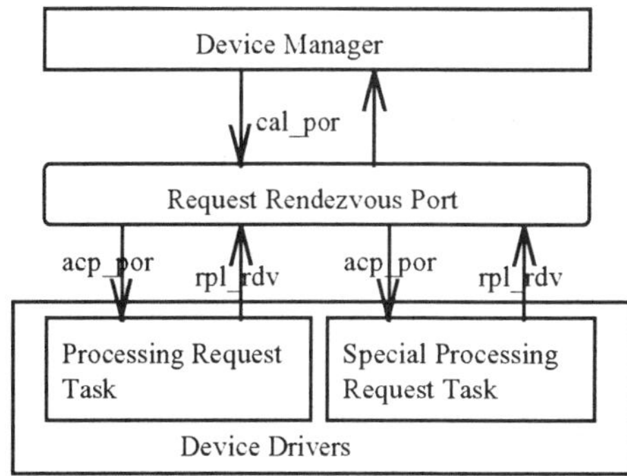

Figure 5 Interface with Device Drivers

As mentioned before, there is usually very little time for the PDA to enter "Power OFF" mode when the SUSPEND routine is triggered by an event; therefore, in order to minimize processing, we designed the BTRON-BrainPad to finish all remaining processing during the RESUME routine. When, all processing of the SUSPEND routine's requests is completed, the OS shifts to STANDBY mode and power consumption is reduced to a few μW.

4.5 RESUME

Important characteristics of a battery are voltage and internal resistance. Whether or not a battery is still usable is usually judged by the voltage, but the internal resistance is also an important element. The characteristics of a battery differ by manufacturer, and change with age and the environment under which they are stored. Many times a battery stored for a long time may still have a normal voltage, but the internal resistance is very high. Although these batteries appear normal with a voltage of about 1.5 V, there times when the voltage drops in half when a current of about 100 mA is taken from them. If you try to use these batteries in a device, it causes a quick drop in voltage and can no longer supply power to the surrounding circuitry. If one of these batteries were placed in a PDA during "Power OFF" mode, the voltage would suddenly drop when the power switch is turned on causing a loss of important data. Even if this drop in voltage is detected during the RESUME routine, the SUSPEND routine will not be executed in time to save the data.

Therefore, to avoid this problem, the BTRON-BrainPad always tests the batteries with a dummy load to make sure they have enough power to support it. If the dummy load causes a fast drop in voltage, then the hardware immediately breaks the contact and remains in SUSPEND mode. The test is carried out while the CPU is still at 32 KHz so the current consumption is low enough to ignore a sudden drop even if the internal resistance of the battery is around 10 Ω. Figure 6 shows a comparison of the waveforms of a RESUME routine testing the battery with a dummy load. Figure 6a shows the waveform of a normal battery and Figure 6b shows the waveform of a battery where the RESUME routine cannot execute. In the figures, the upper waveform represents the voltage of the battery and the lower waveform represents the duration of the dummy load.

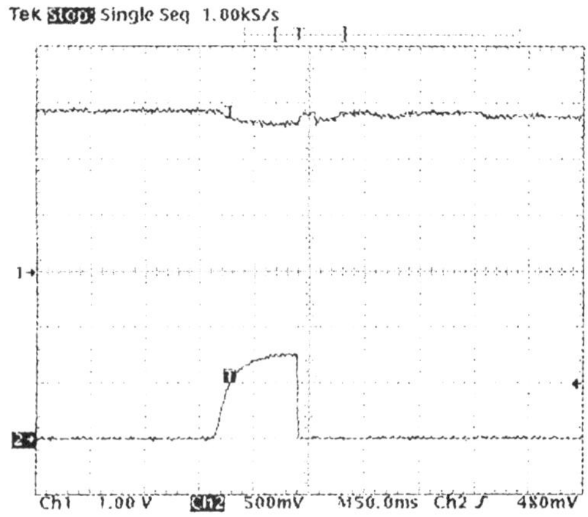

Figure 6a Normal Battery

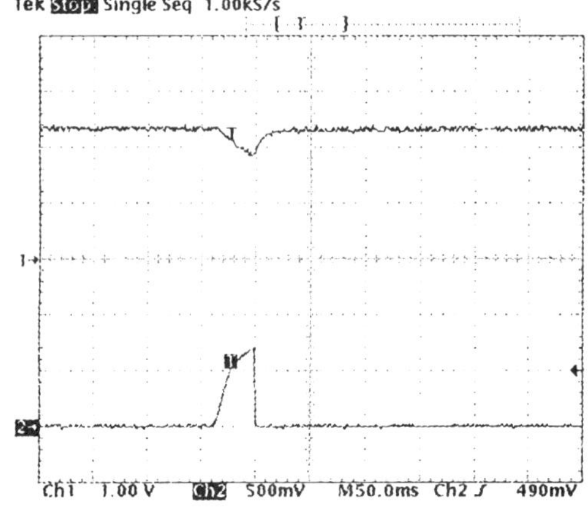

Figure 6b Abnormal Battery

Once the test detects a situation where RESUME would be dangerous, it puts up a flag in the gate array called an internal BLDL. The internal BLDL ignores any other RESUME triggers and is not cleared until the batteries are replaced.

All of this handling is done without leaving STANDBY mode. When a battery passes the dummy load test, it enters RUN mode and returns control to the OS. The OS then sends a RESUME request to the device drivers. Upon receiving the RESUME request, the drivers begin normal operation and begin recovery operations on any processing stopped when the SUSPEND request was received.

4.6 Battery Life

Table 3 shows a comparison of the current consumption of SII's current PDAs with that of a prototype of the BTRON-BrainPad. The values of operating time and battery life were calculated based on the following assumptions with the PDA in RUN mode 10% of the time and in IDLE the remaining 90%:

Assuming that the average user uses his PDA about 2 hours a day with the CPU running 10% of the time for 22 days out of a month of 30 days leads to the following equation:

Battery Life (days) =
Capacity (mWH) / Daily Current Consumption (mWH)

Daily Current Consumption (mWH) =
RUN mode Power (mW) * 0.2 (H) * 22 / 30
+ IDLE mode Power (mW) * 1.8 (H) * 22 / 30
+ STOP mode Power (mW) * (22 (H) * 22 / 30 + 24 (H) * 8 / 30)

Two Sanyo Electric AA batteries were used with a combined capacity of about 6000 mWH. This value represents the discharge characteristics of the battery which we ship in our current PDAs.

As seen in the table the battery life in the BTRON-BrainPad far exceeds that of our current model because of the better power management during IDLE mode. If you compare the scan rate of the RAM in regards to the 4-level gray scale of the BTRON-BrainPad and our current model it is almost double, which would usually mean it would consume more current. The fact that it is actually lower shows exactly how much current is saved through the gate array and IDLE mode.

The current used in STOP mode is slightly higher, but this is because the prototype contains 6 MB of DRAM, which is 3 times that of the current model.

Table 3 Battery Life

Model	CPU	RUN*	IDLE*	STOP*	Operating Time	Battery Life
BrainPad	7 MHz	70 mA	38 mA	0.25mA	48 hrs.	30 days
BTRON-BrainPad	18 MHz	120 mA	25 mA	0.57mA	57 hrs.	31 days

* The power modes in our current model are ON, DOZE and SUSPEND.

5. Conclusions

Compared to our current PDAs, with the BTRON-

BrainPad, we increased the capacity, added network capability, and changed the CPU from one based on the 8086 specifications to the V810 RISC CPU. We have also changed the OS to the multi-tasking, HMI equipped, low resource B-right, which is based on the specifications of the BTRON3 OS. B-right has microscripting for easy application development and it can operate in ROM, which makes it perfect for PDAs. With the inclusion of the B-right and its very few resources and ability to run in ROM and the creation of an exclusive gate array, we were able to develop a small (170 mm x 100 mm x 20 mm), light-weight (approx. 300 g), low-energy PDA.

After porting the B-right to the PDA we added power management tools to realize low power consumption. These power management tools include IDLE, SUSPEND and RESUME, and Auto-Power OFF. Through the combination of these tools with hardware that allows precise control of the clock speed and power supply, satisfied our original goals of creating a PDA that was 10 times faster than our current models and could run for 44 hours on two AA Sanyo Alkaline batteries.

In the future, we are aiming to increase the processing speed without increasing the current consumption in order to meet the demands of the ever expanding applications. We believe this is possible because CPUs with an even lower current consumption have been developed since we selected the V810. We will also look into adding a color LCD, built-in PHS capabilities, and an even smaller case in order to meet the demands of the marketplace. The BTRON-BrainPad is only our first attempt at a PDA with a BTRON OS. From now on we will keep improving it to make the most easy to use PDA available.

Acknowledgments

I would like to thank the people at Personal Media because it would not have been possible without their support and guidance in porting the 3B to the BTRON-BrainPad. I would also like to thank every member of the BTRON-BrainPad development team at SII. Finally, I want to give thanks to Mr. M. Hatano for his input in writing this report and to Mr. N. Plett for translating it into English.

References

[1] Akiyama Tomoko, "Reengineering of Sales Mehtods SFA", *Nikkei Business Strategies*, Feb. 1996.

[2] Y. Kushiki, M. Andoh, M. Kobayashi, Y. Imai, and K. Sakamura, "An Implementation Based upon the BTRON Specification", *TRON Project*, 1987, Springer-Verlag, pp. 113-126.

[3] *The TRON Project 1995.*

[4] A. Matsui, Implementation of a BTRON3-Specification OS,. VOL. NO.39, June-July 1995, *TRON PROJECT BIMONTHLY.*

[5] "Brief description of BTRON3-specifications OS",. TRONWARE Vol. 32.

[6] K. Sakamura, Ed. *BTRON1 Specification Software Specifications - Ver. 0.1.* Sakamura Laboratory, Faculty of Science, University of Tokyo, 1990. (Japanese).

[7] K. Sakamura, Ed. *BTRON2 Kernel Standard Handbook.* Personal Media Corporation, 1992. (Japanese).

[8] NEC UPD70732 Data Sheet.

[9] K. Fukui, Y. Ishiguro, M. Inoue, K. Ishino, A. Tsuge. An Implementation of Resume System On BTRON1 Specification Operating System, *Proceedings of TRON Technical Workshop*, Vol. 5 No. 1 (Oct. 1992) pp. 19-28 (Japanese).

Design of VACL: A Visual Script Language System which Controls and Extends Applications on a Graphical User Interface Environment

Yukihiko Shigesada
Graduate School of Science
The University of Tokyo
sigesada@um.u-tokyo.ac.jp

Noboru Koshizuka
Division of Humanities and Sociology
The University of Tokyo
koshi@l.u-tokyo.ac.jp

Ken Sakamura
The University Museum
The University of Tokyo
sakamura@um.u-tokyo.ac.jp

Abstract

We are constructing a new visual script language system called VACL. The purpose of this script language system is to perform batch operation efficiently on the graphical user interface(GUI) environment and to extend GUI applications. This system represents a script program as a 'post-it(fusen)' on a display. A user can launch the script program by attaching the fusen onto the window of the appropriate application. We call this kind of execution mechanism 'fusen metaphor'. This script language system has four major benefits. First, the script program to control application can be written transparently from the application and in a highly abstract manner. Second, a script program that extends an application can be written transparently from the application. Third, the fusen metaphor enhances the reusability of the script program and provides the hyper text programming environment. Fourth, by describing the script program in visual, the programmer can describe the two dimensional GUI application object in natural and in easy form.

1. Introduction

Recently, with the spread of graphical user interfaces(GUI), interactive computing environments have become more user-friendly. Nevertheless, there are requirements for end user programming languages. The main two applications of the end-user programming languages are 1) *batch type operation* and 2) *enhancement (customization/extension) of GUI applications*.

Batch operation is more suitable than interactive GUI operations to specify fixed type operations repeatedly. For example, to print data file made by graphical editor on the GUI environment, a user must select several items from menus and panels for every file to print. However, these operations can be specified by a very simple script program.

Another important application of the end-user programming is customization or extension of GUI applications, which we call "*application enhancement*".

In present, various users are using GUI applications. Each user has his/her own requirements for functions or user interfaces. However, each application vendor cannot support built-in customization for all these requirements, because current GUI applications are very *fat*, and even a little modification to them is very hard [10].

To overcome this problem, end-user programming with script languages is a promising approach. Conventionally, Emacs Lisp[5], AppleScript[2] and Tcl/Tk[7] are the most popular languages for the application enhancement.

However, the existing script languages on the GUI environment such as Tcl/Tk, AppleScript holds several problems.

Difficulty of programming: Most of the existing script languages are too difficult for end users because of two reasons. The first reason is that the conventional script language is difficult for end users. The second reason is the large gap of the conceptual model of computer systems between using computers with GUI and using computers with script languages.

No general purpose end-user language: Another problem making end-user programming difficult is that there are many end-user programming languages for each purpose or function. Few of today's end user script languages can describe both the batch program and the application

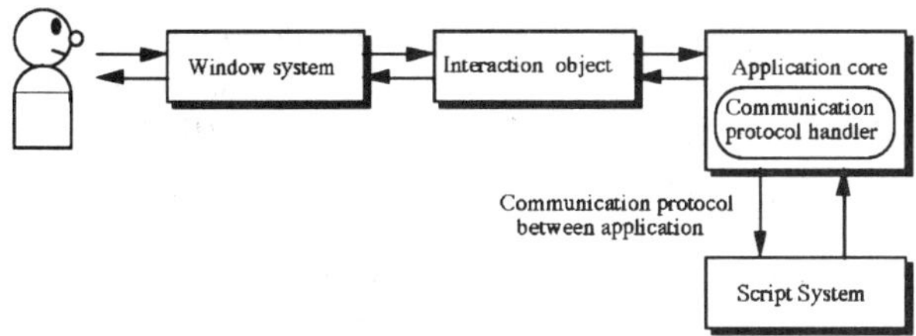

Figure 1. Application control model.

enhancement program.

Additional code for scripting protocols: Conventionally, most of the existing application control script systems control the application by invoking the semantics of the application directly(Figure1), and the application programmers must write extra codes for making the application compatible to the script system.

Application coorperation is another approach for application enhancement. In OpenDoc, several small applications are created instead of one large application to create a software. However, it is very difficult for end users to create an application enhancement program.

In this paper, we propose and implement a visual programming language and its execution environment to overcome the above problems. We call this language *Visual Application Control Language (VACL)*.

The novel design concepts of VACL are as follows:

- Visual programming

  The programmer can describe GUI application by VACL.

- Program Visualization

  The programmer can describe VACL program in visual. In VACL both the data structure and the program itself are described in visual. We also proposed "fusen metaphor" for programming.

- Application independent scripting protocol

  The script programmer can describe VACL application enhancement script transparently from the application.

- Application coorperation

  The user can combine several VACL script programs to perform a big operation.

The rest of this paper is divided into several sections. Section 2 describes the overview of the VACL. We describe how VACL is implemented in Section 3. Section 4 gives the related works. Finally, we state our conclusion in Section 5.

2. Visual Application Control Language (VACL)

2.1. The concepts of VACL

First, we describe the major concepts of VACL.

- Program Visualization

  It is commonly acknowledged that the human mind is strongly visually oriented and the people can acquire information at a higher rate from picture than from text [8]. We propose the VACL as a visual language to make the program easy to create and understand. In VACL, both the data structure and the program itself are described in visual. By constructing VACL as a visual programming language, we aimed at describing the two dimensional GUI application object in natural and easy form. In concrete, the programmer can use the two dimensional object itself to control and describe the GUI object in VACL.

- Programming in "fusen" metaphor

  In VACL, we have proposed *fusen*[1] metaphor as a metaphor of batch processing in the GUI environments[9]. In the fusen metaphor, users see target data of the script program as a document, and a script program as a fusen that contains instruction applied onto the document. To invoke the script program, a user attaches a small fusen window on a target window.

  The programming style of VACL is also based on the fusen metaphor. In VACL every unit of the program such as variable, function, control statements such as "if" and "while" are provided as fusen. Each fusen has some arguments, and the programmer fills these arguments of the fusen with another fusen or object to determine the fusen what to do. In this way, VACL provides hyper-text programming environment, and this makes the programmer easy to refer the structure of the program.

- Application independent scripting protocol

  VACL is constructed on the Shared Interaction Object Architecture [4]. The Shared Interaction Object architecture is a GUI architecture that has been researched in the Sakamura laboratory. By constructing VACL on this architecture, the VACL programmer can describe both batch operation and application enhancement program. The script programmer can also describe application transparently from the application and there is no need for the application

[1] "Fusen" is a Japanese word that means "tag", "small memo label", or "post-it".

programmer to describe extra codes to make the application program compatibly to the VACL.

2.2. Sample Session

To make the VACL more understandable we describe two sample VACL programs in this subsection.

We show the example of batch type operation and enhancement of GUI application. In the rest of this paper, we use these examples for explanation of VACL.

2.2.1. Batch type operation

When the hard disk becomes full, the user must delete or move some files from the hard disk. In such case, the user may want to delete from older file. Here, we show the example of deleting old files using VACL(Figure 2).

1. Execute three VACL script named *print selected file size*, *select file by age* and *delete selected file*. When executed, each script creates a window. The print selected file size window shows the amount of the selected file size. The select file by age window has a volume bar. The volume bar represents the time and this script selects every file created before that time. The delete selected file window has a button to delete every selected file. The target file of the VACL script is the files in the window under the lefttop position of the VACL window.

2. Move print selected file size fusen window over the *My file* window to determine the files to delete. The My file window contains five files and they are arranged in order of the age of the file. Because there are no selected files, the print selected file size window displays “000000000 bytes”.

3. Move select file by age window over the My file window. By this operation, the select file by age script selects the oldest file *File A* according to the location of its volume bar. The print selected file size window displays the size of the file File A.

4. Move the volume bar of the select file by age window to select the required amount of files. As the user move the volume bar to the right, the select file by age script selects files one after another from old file. The print selected file size window calculates and displays the total size of selected files.

5. Move delete selected file window over the My file window.

6. Push the *delete file* button to delete the selected files.

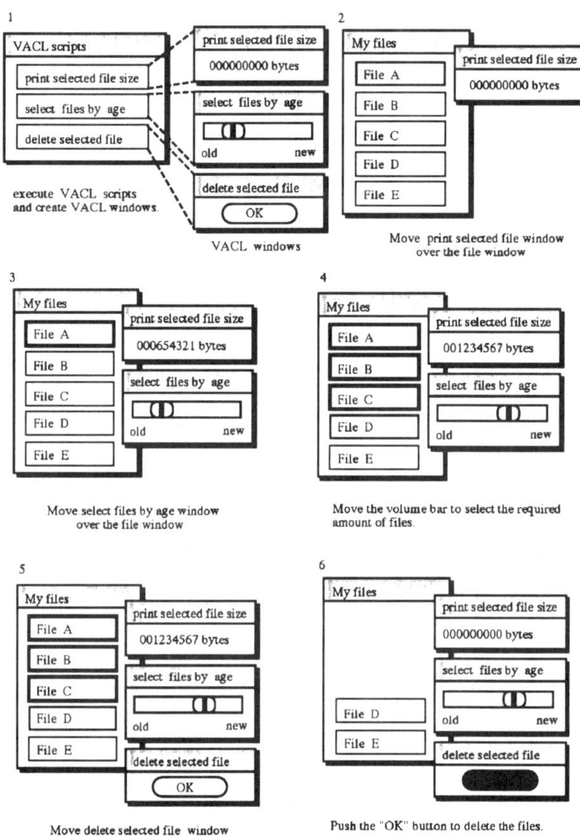

Figure 2. Example of the batch type operation.

This example shows the following two VACL features. First, the user can perform batch type operation using VACL script in GUI form. Second, the VACL programmer can combinate severarl small VACL script to perform an operation, and this feature increases the reusability of the VACL script program.

2.2.2. Enhancement of GUI application

When using graphic editor application, the user may want to tie two objects by an arrow. When the user moves one object tied by an arrow, the user must update the position of the arrow too. In this example, we show the VACL script that updates the position of the arrow automatically when the tied object is moved(Figure 3).

1. Execute *connect objects* VACL script. When executed, the VACL script creates a window. This window has three buttons to specify two objects and an arrow to connect.

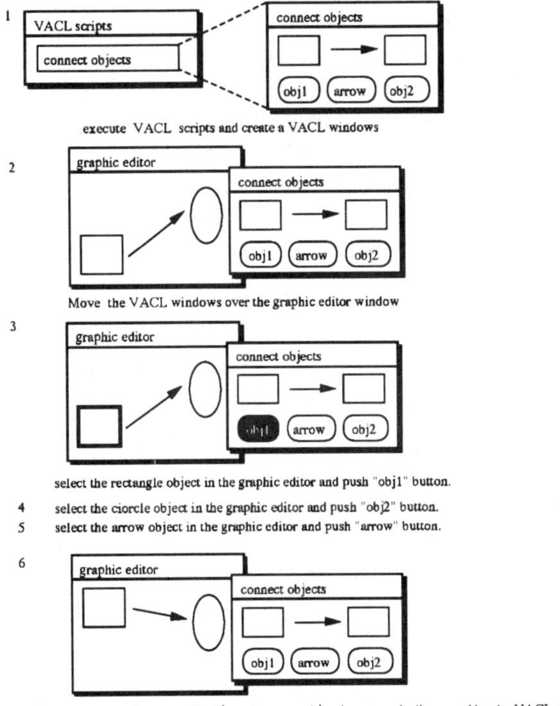

Figure 3. Example of enhancement of GUI application.

2. Move the VACL window over the graphic editor application.

3. Select the left(or top) object on the graphic editor and push the *obj1* button on the VACL window.

4. Select the right(or bottom) object on the graphic editor and push the *obj2* button on the VACL window.

5. Select the arrow on the graphic editor and push the *arrow* button on the VACL window.

After operating the above operation, the VACL script automatically updates the position of the arrow whenever the user moves the connected object.

In this example, the VACL programer does not write extra codes for the graphic editor application program to enhance the application. This example shows that the programmer can describe the application enhancement program tranceparently from the application.

2.3. The VACL programming

In this subsection, we describe the overview of the VACL programming.

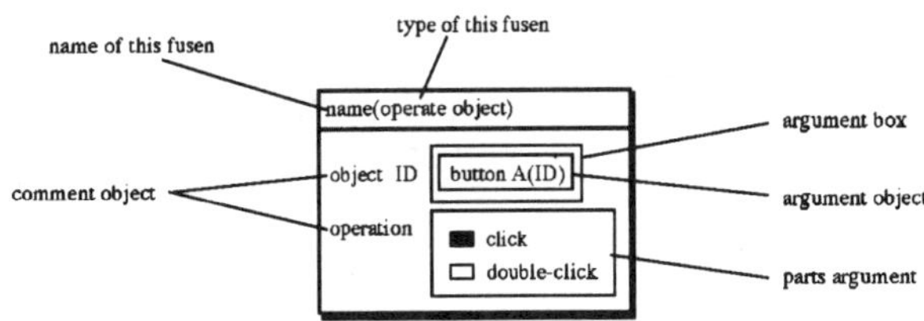

Figure 4. Example of fusen programming window.

2.3.1. Fusen

The basic programming unit of VACL is called fusen. Fusen is as a rectangle with a name(The word in the bracket represents the type of fusen) in the window. VACL provides several types of fusens such as variable fusen, comparison fusen, if fusen, repeat fusen, display fusen, function fusen, etc. A window called *fusen collection window* collects these fusens and the script programmer creates a new fusen from that window. Every fusen operates like a function, and holds some arguments. The script programmer creates a program by creating a fusen and filling the arguments of the fusen.

2.3.2. Fusen programming window

The programming interface of the VACL is called *fusen programming window*(Figure 4). The fusen programming window is a window that shows the arguments of the fusen. The contents of the fusen programming window are different by the type of fusen. There are several types of contents in fusen programming window.

Argument Box: The argument box is a rectangle that determines the place to set the argument object. To set an object in an argument box, the programmer creates or moves the lefttop position of the object over the empty argument box. When an object is set, the size of the argument box is automatically set according to the size of the argument object. No argument box can contain more than one object.

Argument Object: The argument object is the argument of the fusen. Every argument object is contained in an argument box. When the script programmer moves the lefttop position of the argument object out of the argument box, the argument object becomes a comment object(described below), and the argument box becomes empty.

Parts Argument: The parts argument is also the argument of the fusen. The difference between the argument object

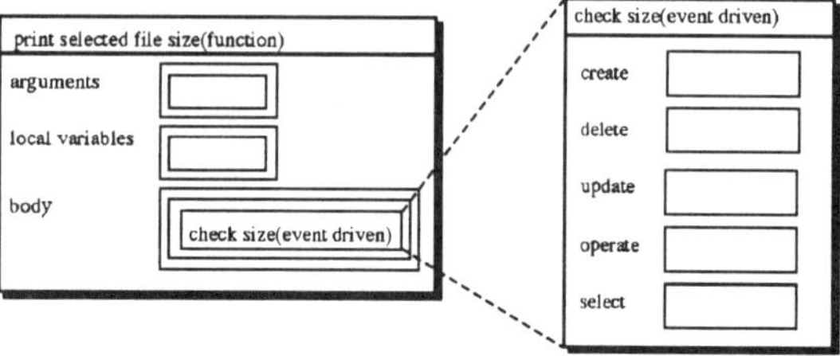

Figure 5. Programming style of the VACL.

and the parts argument is that the script programmer creates the argument object, and the fusen programming window application creates the parts argument. A parts argument is one of the control parts (switch selector,volume, etc.).

Group Box: The group box is a rectangle that groups the objects.

Comment Object: The comment object is an object that comments the program. The script programmer can set any object at any place as a comment object on the fusen programming window, except over the empty argument box. A comment object never influences the function of the fusen.

2.3.3. Programming style of the VACL

The standard programming process in VACL is as follows (Figure 5).

1. Create a new fusen. There are two ways to create a new fusen.
   - Create a new fusen from the fusen collection window: Fusen collection window is a special window that collects fusens of VACL. To create a new fusen from the fusen collection window, the script programmer finds the required type of fusen from the fusen collection window, drags the fusen by the PD and pastes it on the window where to create a new fusen, and name the new fusen by filling the panel window.
   - Create a new fusen by duplicating the other fusen. This method also duplicates the arguments of the fusen.
2. Open the fusen programming window of the new fusen.
3. Fill the arguments of the fusen programming window. If there are some new fusens in the arguments, go to phase 1.
4. Repeat above phases to fill every required argument.
5. After filling all the arguments of the fusen, save the argument of the fusen by selecting the save menu.

2.4. The overview of VACL language

2.4.1. Task

In GUI application, several things are going on parallel. Because it is difficult to write a program that does several things in parallel in single task language, it is natural to write the GUI application in multitask language[6]. Therefore, we designed the VACL as a multitask language. There are two ways to create a new task in VACL.

- Use *create task* fusen. This fusen creates a new task.
- Use *event driven* fusen. This fusen creates a new task when the specified event is happened. The most general usage of this fusen is to create a task when a button object is pressed.

When the VACL system creates a task, the VACL system creates the unique number called task ID. The script program can control the other task by using the ID number of the task.

2.4.2. Function

A function is a small program unit of the VACL. A function is a collection of fusens to perform a set of operations. The feature of the function in VACL is almost the same as the feature of the function in the C programming language. In VACL, *function* fusen declares the function and the *function call* fusen calls the function.

2.4.3. Data types

There are several data types available in VACL.

- integer value: The value of a number parts object represents the integer data type.
- graphic object: Graphic objects such as rectangle, bitmap data, etc.
- parts object: Control parts consisting of 10 kinds such as number parts, selector parts, volume parts.
- fusen object
- object identifier(ID): Every object in the application of the shared interaction object architecture holds a unique ID number. This data type holds the ID number of objects and is used to indicate an object.

2.4.4. Variables

In VACL, several type of fusens represent variables. We call these fusen variable fusen in general. Each variable fusen holds different data types.

- number fusen: This fusen holds integer data type.
- object fusen: This fusen holds graphic object data type, parts object data type, and fusen object data type.
- ID fusen: This fusen holds object ID data type.

There are two types of variable according to the scope of the variable.

- local variable: A variable declared as a local variable in function fusen is local variable. The value of the local variable is effective in only that function. If there is a global value whose name is the same as a local value, the value of local variable is used.
- global variable: The variable that is not local variable is global variable. Any task can refer global variable in any function.

2.4.5. The method to specify the application objects

We implemented the VACL system on the *shared interaction object architecture*(described in the next section). In this architecture, the programer can determine every object by ID number. In VACL script, the script programmer uses this ID number to determine the object. There are several addressing modes to determine and get the ID number of objects.

- Name. Every object has four words data field called name field. The application that creates the object usually names the name field of the object. This addressing mode uses this name field to determine an object.
- Contain Region. This addressing mode gets an object ID of the object that is in a rectangle region.
- Overlap Region. This addressing mode gets an object ID of the object that overlaps a rectangle region.
- Under fusen window Region: This addressing mode gets an object ID of the object that is under the fusen window.
- Type and attribute. This addressing mode gets an object ID of the object whose type and the attributes of the object are the same as the specified object. For example, if there is one blue rectangle in an application window, the script programmer can determine that object by duplicating the rectangle object in the argument box in the get object ID fusen.
- Selected. This addressing mode gets the selected objects.
- Menu. This addressing mode gets a menu object by the name of the menu item.

VACL provides *get ID fusen* to get the ID of an object. Figure 6 is the fusen programming window of the get ID fusen. There are three arguments in get ID fusen. The argument right to the comment object "window" determines the window that contains the object. The argument right to the "addressing mode" is a switch selector control parts to determine the addressing mode. The argument right to the "parameter" is the object that is used as a parameter for searching the object in the specified addressing mode. The return value of this fusen holds the ID of the object.

2.4.6. Change the attributes of the object in VACL

To change the attributes of an object in VACL, the programmer does not need to use a special data structure to determine the attribute of the object. For example, to set the background color of an object black in VACL, the programmer creates an object whose background color is black and use it in the script program.

2.4.7. Operate an operation to the object in VACL

In VACL, "operate object fusen" describes an operation such as "click the momentary switch object" to an object(Figure 4).

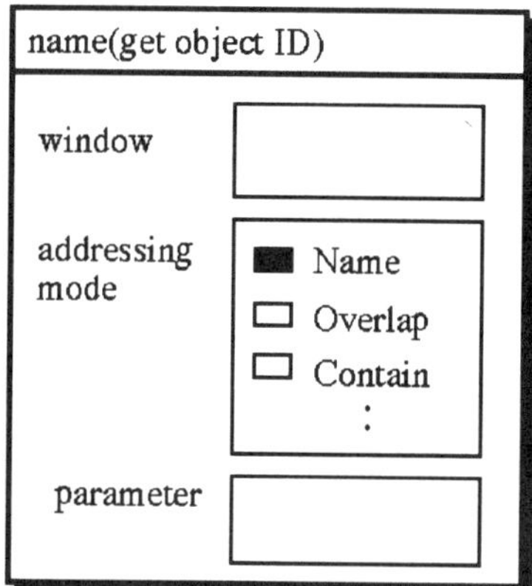

Figure 6. Get object ID fusen.

2.4.8. Create an object in VACL

The programmer can use the graphical editor directly to create an object in VACL. The "set object fusen" creates an object in VACL.

2.5. Sample program of VACL

Here we show the source program of the script "print selected file size"(Figure 7).

- print selected file size: This is a function fusen. When this fusen is executed, the VACL system executes fusens in the body argument(in this case, "display" fusen and "check size" fusen) successively.
- display: This fusen is a *create window* fusen. When this fusen is executed, the VACL system creates a VACL window whose contents are the same as this "display" fusen programming window.
- check size: This fusen is an event driven fusen. After this fusen is executed, the VACL system executes the "print size fusen" when a select object event happens.
- print size: This fusen is an *update object* fusen. This fusen updates the value of the object "000000000" in the VACL window to the return value of "get size" fusen. The script programmer duplicates the object "000000000" from the "display" fusen programming window.
- get size: This fusen is *get file data* fuesn. This fusen gets the size of the file. Because the "file" argument box is empty, this fusen gets the size of default files that are the files the window under the VACL window is selecting.

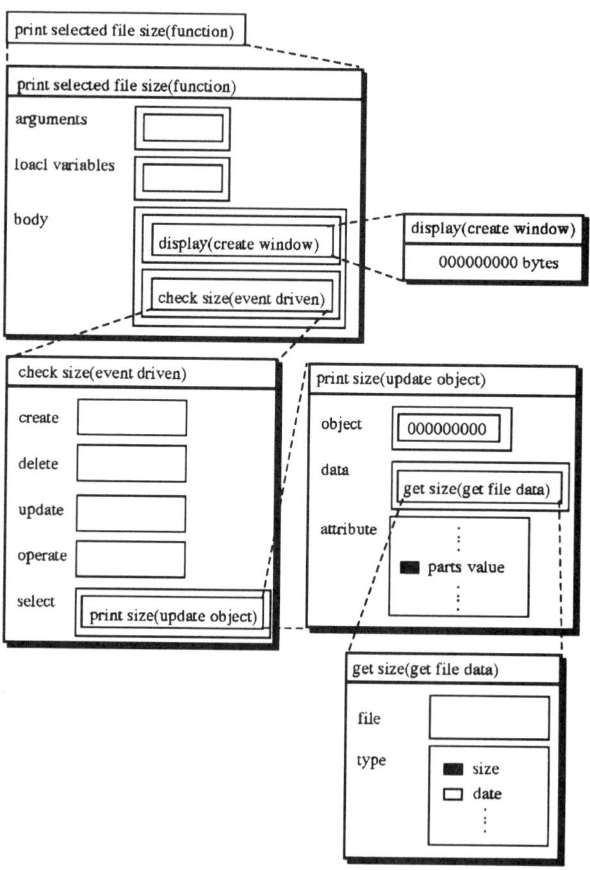

Figure 7. Source of the "print selected file size" fusen.

3. Implementation of VACL

3.1. Shared interaction object architecture

We implemented the VACL system on the shared interaction object architecture [4, 3]. In this subsection, we describe the overview and implementation of the shared interaction object architecture. The shared interaction object architecture is a GUI architecture that has been researched in the Sakamura laboratory. In this architecture, an interactive GUI application, such as graphic editors and word processors, consists of Window Real-Objects(WRO) which are storages for interaction objects, and several processes that share WRO equally. Generally, these processes are consisted of user-agent process and application core process (Figure 8).

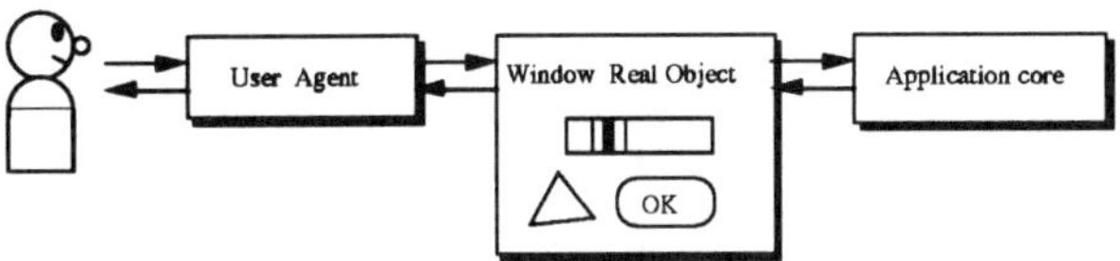

Figure 8. Shared interaction object architecture.

3.1.1. User Agent

A *user agent* provides user interfaces common to every GUI software application. There are as many user-agents as the number of users. The user-agent visualizes interaction objects in WROs. Conversely, it also applies operation to them according to user's inputs.

3.1.2. Application Core

An *application core* implements semantic actions of the GUI software. The application core interacts with users via WROs. It can output information by storing or updating interaction objects in WROs. Conversely, it can get user's actions by retrieving data from WROs or by receiving events from them.

3.1.3. Window Real-Objects

A WRO is a storage for interaction objects. There are as many WROs as windows on a screen. Interaction objects are graphical objects on a window such as segmented graphic objects, texts, bitmap data displayed on a window and can be operated by users. They include control parts, menus, virtual objects, etc.

The user-agent and WRO are provided as a part of the window system, and most GUI application developers are required to program only application core portions.

3.1.4. Window Calls

In this architecture, application developer does not use drawing function directly, but set objects in the WRO and control these data. The private functions called *window calls* are used to control the interaction objects in the WRO.

In window calls, a programmer specifies interaction objects using addressing, which is a mapping from a query key onto interaction objects to be operated.

There are two advantages of window calls. 1)application programmers do not need to manage and redraw the data on the screen. 2)application programmers do not need to handle the PD.

3.1.5. Abstract Event

A WRO provides an asynchronous message mechanism called *abstract events* to transfer controls among modules sharing the WRO. The WRO generates some abstract events when a window call modifies an interaction object, and sends them to modules that express interests in the event. When a process receives the abstract event, it executes any necessary calculation and returns feedback to users.

3.2. Implementation of VACL

We implemented VACL over the shared interaction object architecture on BTRON. The shared interaction object architecture window system is consisted of three processes, *WRO manager* process, *User Agent process* and *application core process*. The VACL system is consisted of two processes, *fusen programming window* process and *VACL interpreter* process. Here, we describe these processes.

3.2.1. WRO Manager Process

The action of the WRO manager process is as follows.

- Receive a window call from the user agent process or application core process.
- Do an operation to the WRO data (create a new WRO, create an object in a WRO, update an object in a WRO, etc.) according to the type of window call.
- Generate and send abstract events notifying the result of the operation both the user agent and the application core.

We realized the communication between the WRO manager process and the other process(user agent process and application core process) by using TCP/IP protocol. The WRO manager process is a multitask process and each communication between WRO manager process and the other process is managed by a task.

3.2.2. The User Agent process

The user agent process provides the user interface of a window and manages every window in the display. The user agent process is a multtask process and there are two tasks running concurrently.

Window Event Handling Task: This task handles the window event that holds the user action performed on the window. When the event handling task receives a window event, this task creates a window call and send it to the WRO manager process.

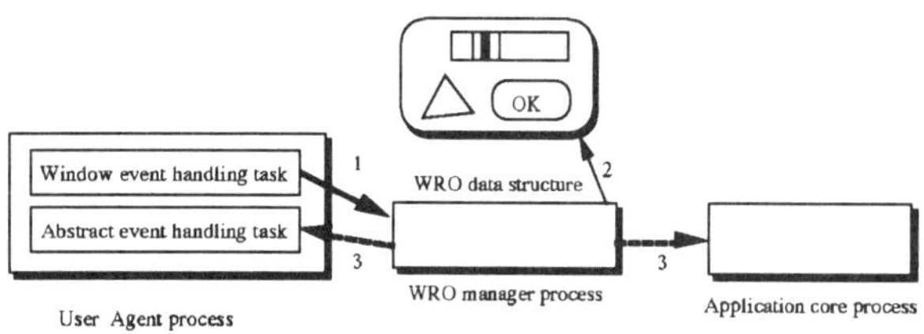

Figure 9. Example of the behavior of the shared interaction object architecture.

Abstract Event Handling Task: This task handles the abstract event. When the abstract event handling task receives an abstract event from the WRO manager process, this task redraws the window according to the contents of the abstract event.

The user agent process provides a simple graphic editor function. The user agent task comprehends the following user operations and translates them to a window call. 1)Create an object, 2)Delete an object, 3)Move an object, 4)Copy an object in that window, 5)Copy an object from another window, 6)Change an attribute of an object, 7)Operate an object.

3.2.3. Application Core process

The application core process operates the semantic action of the GUI application. The application core process has an abstract event handling task that operates a specific semantic action of the GUI application according to the abstract event from the WRO manager process. Usually, an application core process is a collection of semantic procedure invoked by abstract events.

3.2.4. Example of the behavior of the Shared Interaction Object Architecture

We show how the shared interaction object architecture behaves when the user operates an interaction object (Figure 9)

1. When the user operates an interaction object, a user agent issues a window call corresponding with the operation.

2. A WRO manager process handles the window call and change the WRO data if needed.

3. The WRO manager process generates and sends abstract events notifying both the user agent and application core process.

4. The user agent process redraw the display of the window if needed. The application core process invokes a semantic procedure if needed.

5. If necessary, the application core process applies operations to interaction objects in the WRO.

3.2.5. Fusen programming window application

Fusen programming window application creates a window that describes the argument of the fusen. Each type of fusen has a different fusen programming window application. The script programmer set the arguments of the fusen in this window.

The function of the fusen programming window is as follows.

- Read the argument data from the file and display objects (argument objects, argument boxes, etc.) in the window.

- Manage the location of the objects in the window.

- Set an object as an argument object when the script programer moves to create an object over the empty argument box. Set an argument object as a comment object when the script programer creates an object or moves an argument object out of the argument box.

- Save the contents of the fusen programming window when the user invokes the save menu. When the user invokes the save menu, the fusen programming window application translates the arguments of the fusen in a special code called *VACL code*. The VACL interpreter application uses this code to interpret the script program.

3.2.6. VACL interpreter application

When the VACL interpreter application is executed, it loads the object data and VACL code from the file that the fusen points. If there is another fusen data in the VACL code, the VACL interpreter loads the data from the file that fusen points. The VACL interpreter performs these operations recursively until every VACL data that can be traced from the original fusen.

After loading the script program, the VACL interpreter start interpreting the VACL code.

Here we describe the scripting architecture of VACL(Figure 10) by example. We use the *connect object* script as an example.

1. The user does an operation to move one of the connected object.

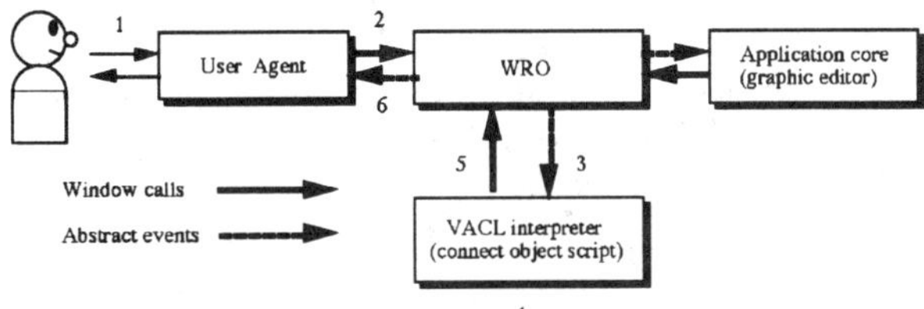

Figure 10. Scripting architecture of VACL.

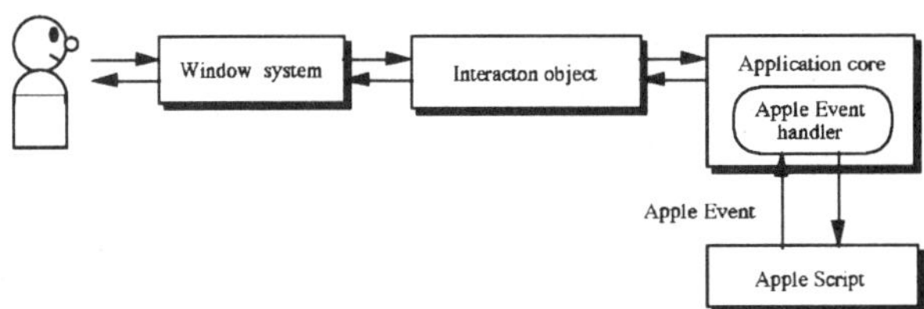

Figure 11. Scripting architecture of Apple-script.

2. The user agent interprets the operation and issues a window call to the WRO to move the object.

3. The WRO updates the object and sends an update object abstract event to the VACL interpreter(the WRO also sends the abstract event to the user agent and the application core). The update object abstract event holds the ID number of the updated objects and how the user updated that object.

4. The VACL interpreter gets the abstract event and calculates how the arrow object should be moved.

5. The VACL interpreter issues a window call to update the arrow object according to the calculation.

6. The WRO updates the arrow object and sends an update object abstract event to the user agent. When the user agent receives that abstract event, the user agent redraws the display acoording to the abstract event.

3.3. Pilot System

We are building a pilot system of the VACL system on the basis of the shared interaction object architecture. The target machine of the pilot system is the MCUBE workstation. It contains a GMICRO/300 based on the TRON VLSI CPU specification. Its kernel is based on the micro ITRON3 specification. Upon the kernel, a file system based on BTRON/FILE specification and graphic primitives based on the BTRON specification are equipped. As for its network system, we use TCP/IP protocol.

Our pilot system of the shared interaction object architecture and the VACL system is built on this environment and written in C language.

4. Related Works

In this section, we describe related works.

4.1. GUI script languages

Apple Script and Tcl/Tk are major GUI script languages.

Apple Script is a script language that can control the applications in the Apple Macintosh operation system. Apple Script uses the Apple Event [1] which is the inter-application communication mechanism of the Macintosh to control applications (Figure 11). The Apple Event provides the client-server type application collaboration mechanism. The client application such as Apple Script uses the Apple Event to request services to the server applications. These services are standardized in the document "Apple Event Registry" and the applications using this mechanism have to provide the services specified in it.

While the Apple Script has the flexibility to control every application that provides the Apple Event mechanism, there are several drawbacks.

- Since the model of the application and the Apple Script language is different, the programmer must learn the application documents describing the terms of the application to describe the script program to control the application.
- The application programmer must write the extra codes to make the application compatible to the Apple Script.
- Apple Script does not have the mechanism to enhance or configure functions of an application.

Tcl is a script language that can process data and control applications. Tcl is an application independent extensible command language and it can be embedded in the application program. Tk is a toolkit that provides an environment to create a GUI based program easily. Tcl/Tk provides a RPC-like mechanism to send a Tcl/Tk script to a Tcl/Tk embedded application. Tcl/Tk can control every application linked with the Tcl/Tk library by invoking a Tcl/Tk script in the application (Figure 12).

Tcl/Tk can be used as a general-purpose mechanism for programming the GUI of application and provides a uniform

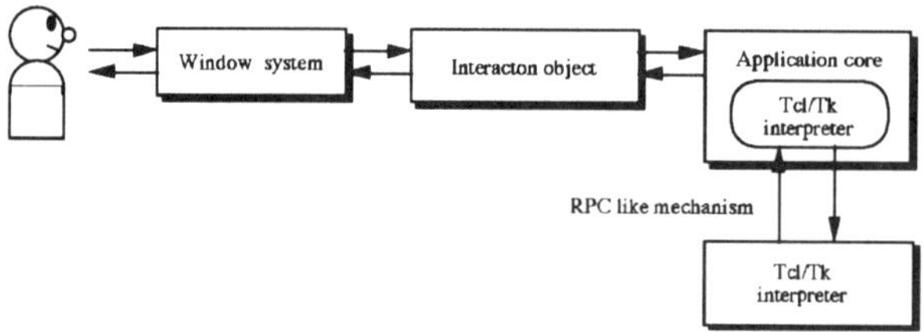

Figure 12. Scripting architecture of Tcl/Tk.

framework for communication between applications. The drawbacks of Tcl/Tk are almost the same as the drawbacks of the Apple Script.

4.2. Application Coorperation

OpenDoc is a multiplatform software architecture. In OpenDoc, instead of creating a large application, several small applications called component software are created to solve problems. For example, text editor, spreadsheets, 3-D graphs are made of component software and can run together. In this mechanism it is easy to enhance a software by creating a new component software. Because component softwares are small, the maintenance of the program is easier than that of a large application. The drawback of OpenDoc is that, the programmer must write extra codes to make the component software compatible to the OpenDoc, and this makes very difficult for end users to create a new component software.

5. Conclusion

In this paper, we described the script language VACL which control and enhance functions of GUI applications. The main VACL features are divided in three.

First, to overcome the difficulty of programming we proposed the VACL as a visual language. Instead of describing a GUI application object in a text form, the programmer can use the application object directly in the description of the script program.

Second, we proposed fusen metaphor as a metaphor of batch processing in GUI environment. In fusen metaphor, the script program is represented as a fusen. Users see the target object of the script program as a document, and users invoke the script program by attaching the fusen on the target object. In this way, the fusen metaphor fills the gap between the system model of the GUI environment and the script language. The programming style of VACL is also based on fusen metaphor and this provides a hyper text programming environment to the VACL.

Third, we implemented VACL on the shared interaction object architecture. In shared interaction object architecture, the VACL shares the interaction objects of applications and controls the application by controlling the interaction objects. This can be done because most semantics of the application can be invoked by the interaction objects. In this way, the VACL can control the application without adding extra codes to the application, and can control every application that is based on the shared interaction object architecture.

References

[1] I. Apple Computer. Apple event manager. In *Inside Macintosh, Volume VI*. Addison-Wesley, 1991.

[2] S. D. *The TAO of AppleScript*. Hayden Books, 1993.

[3] N. Koshizuka. *BTRON2 Window System: A Window System Facilitating Cooperation among GUI Applications in Distributed Environments*. PhD thesis, Univ. of Tokyo, 1994.

[4] N. Koshizuka and K. Sakamura. Window real-objects: a distributed shared memory for the distributed implementation of gui applications. In *Proceedings of the ACM Symposium on User Interface Software and Technology*, Nov. 1993. in appear.

[5] J. Levine. Why a lisp-based command language ? *ACM SIGPLAN Notice*, 15(5), May 1980.

[6] B. A. Myers. Why are human-computer interfaces difficult to design and implement? Technical Report CMU-CS-93-183, School of Computer Science Carnegie Mellon University, Pittsburgh, PA 15213, July 1993.

[7] J. K. Ousterhout. Tcl: An embeddable command language. In *Proceedings of the Winter 1990 USENIX Conference*, pages 133 – 146, 1990.

[8] G. Raeder. A survey of current graphical programming techniques. *IEEE Computer*, 18(8):11–25, Aug. 1985.

[9] K. Sakamura. TULS : TRON Universal Language System. In K. Sakamura, editor, *TRON Project 1988*. Springer-Verlag, 1988.

[10] D. C. Smith and J. Susser. A component architecture for personal computer software. In B. A. Myers, editor, *Languages for Developing User Interfaces*, pages 31–56. Jones and Bartlett, 1992.

Panel Session

Technologies for Network Computing

Organizer
Ken Sakamura and Hiroaki Takada
University of Tokyo

Abstract

Network computing is a new computing paradigm; in which all computer software is obtained from computer networks and works in cooperation with various services on the networks. Though the paradigm has the possibility to resolve many problems of current personal computer environments, there are some key technologies to be exploited.

In this panel session, what are the advantages and the problems of network computing, what are the key technologies to its realization, what are achieved so far, and what are remaining to be tackled are discussed.

0-8186-7658-2/96 $05.00 © 1996 IEEE

Enableware (TEPS)

Programs of the Center on Disabilities at California State University, Northridge

Harry J. Murphy, Ed. D.
Founder and Director
Center on Disabilities
California State University, Northridge
18111 Nordhoff Street
Northridge, California 91330-8340
(818) 677 2578
(818) 677 4929 Fax
Harry.Murphy@csun.edu

Presented at the
TEPS '96 Conference
Tokyo, Japan
December 7, 1996

1. Introduction

In forming the Center on Disabilities on May 7, 1993, the president of California State University, Northridge, Dr. Blenda J. Wilson, said: "The Center on Disabilities will conduct research and demonstration projects into new technologies and new service models. It will develop and publish materials of interest to the field of disability, assess and train persons with disabilities, and those who serve them, and continue to conduct conferences, seminars, and workshops, both in the United States and abroad." The common denominator in all of our work is technology and our mission is to place more assistive technologies in the hands of more people with disabilities.

To carry out these mandates, the Center on Disabilities has created three major program areas: (1) Students with Disabilities Resources (SDR), where more than 1,000 students with disabilities are provided with educational support services which are designed to make them successful university students, and to prepare them for employment upon graduation; (2) "Technology and Persons with Disabilities," the largest conference of its kind in the world on assistive technologies, with more than 2,600 in attendance each year. The conference has 130 exhibitors and 300 speakers. Attendees from 20 foreign countries attend this conference each year.; (3) "Leadership and Technology Management" (LTM) training program which prepares professionals in the field of disabilities to exercise leadership in the area of assistive technologies by creating new programs such as Computer Access Laboratories.

2. Students with Disabilities Resources Unit of the Center on Disabilities

For more than 30 years, California State University, Northridge (CSUN) has welcomed students with disabilities and has created an innovative student support model which has become the model that is most widely used throughout America's 3,500 colleges and universities. The model of support services, which originally provided Sign Language interpreters to deaf students, has been expanded to provide support to students with a variety of disabilities, including those who are blind, communication impaired, learning disabled, or with mobility limitations.

Support services include the following:

- Access to adaptive educational equipment, materials, and supplies, including wheelchair loan, adapted personal computers, braillers, and portable lab stations.
- Referral to appropriate campus and community agencies whose services can benefit persons with disabilities.
- On and off campus registration assistance, including priority enrollment, assistance with applications for financial aid, and related college services.
- Special parking, including on-campus parking registration and temporary parking permit arrangements.
- Specialized orientation to acquaint students with the campus environment.
- Diagnostic assessment to verify specific disabilities, such as learning disability.
- On-campus mobility assistance.
- Disability related counseling and advising.
- Reader service.

CSUN has 25,000 students on campus. Of these, 1,100 are students with disabilities. There are 350 students with learning disabilities (dyslexia and similar functional limitations) and 250 deaf students on campus. Students study in all curriculum areas of this large, liberal arts university, which offers degrees at both the bachelor's, and master's levels.

3. Computer Access Lab

In 1988, with equipment grants from Apple, IBM, Hewlett-Packard, Everex, and other computer and software companies, a "Computer Access Lab" for students with disabilities was initiated within the Students with Disabilities Resources unit of the Center. The purpose of this Lab is to provide computer access in unique ways for this population of students.

We assess and train students to be able to use assistive technology. The assessment process includes evaluating functional ability of an individual student in relationship to educational and/or employment task(s) required of him/her. We then build a bridge between these two variables with appropriate assistive technologies that permit a student to access a computer according to individual needs.

For example, a blind person may have a screen reader and speech synthesizer. These confirm the placement of the cursor on the screen and read back (through synthetic speech) what is on the screen. A person with poor fine motor movements may use an alternative keyboard, with extra large keys. A double amputee may use voice recognition and speak to the computer.

This Lab is seen as an assessment and training vehicle. Students are encouraged to use other computer labs across campus wherever they can. Each school has its own Lab: School of Education, School of the Arts, School of Computer Science and Engineering, etc. have Labs that are open very late into the evening.

4. "Technology and Persons with Disabilities" Conference

This is the largest conference of its kind in the world, with more than 2,600 people from all over the world in attendance. About 50 people from universities and/or private companies in Japan have attended one or more of our conferences over the years. The conference is actually three conferences in one: it is a conference dealing with assistive technologies which enable people with disabilities to access computers; it is an Internet and World Wide Web conference, and it is a conference which shows how assistive technologies may be used to access the Internet and the WWW.

5. "Leadership and Technology Management" (LTM) Training Program

The Leadership and Technology Management training program was developed in 1993 to prepare leaders and prospective leaders to insure that people with disabilities are full participants in the technological revolution and The Information Age. More than 50% of the 142 graduates of this one-week long program are people with disabilities or parents of persons with disabilities. Within a period of 9 to 18 months after completing this training, graduates have obtained more than $2 million dollars in new funding for technology programs for people with disabilities at all age and educational levels, from early childhood to adult training programs, and across all disabilities. The Center on Disabilities also offers an Advanced LTM course, and a Train-the-Trainer course, to graduates of this program. In addition to being offered in California, this course has also been conducted in Hawaii and Guam.

6. Impact of the Internet and the World Wide Web

Assistive technologies may be used on a closed platform. A student with a disability may work on word processing, for example, using voice recognition. More and more, however, the assistive technology becomes a means to an end. Students with disabilities at CSUN, like students with or without disabilities anywhere in the world, are seeking information from the Internet and the World Wide Web. This has created an interface challenge for the field of assistive technologies that has been successfully met.

The Center on Disabilities models use of the Internet and WWW in its three programs: Students with Disabilities Resources (Computer Access Lab), the conference, "Technology and Persons with Disabilities," where a large number of sessions deal with these topics, and the "Leadership and Technology Management" training program.

7. New, Community Computer Access Lab

Since 1988, students who enrolled at the university have been supported by technological services in the Computer Access Lab of the Students with Disabilities Resources unit of the Center. Over the years we have faced a growing request for assessment and training from community members with disabilities, people who are not enrolled as students at CSUN.

In the San Fernando Valley, where CSUN is located, 25 miles north of Los Angeles International Airport, there are 1.3 million people. One community agency, the California State Department of Rehabilitation, serves more than 4,000 adults with disabilities. Their mission is to prepare people with disabilities for employment. They have asked us to establish a second Lab, this one for community members with disabilities, to conduct assessment on their potential to use technology, and then to train them on appropriate technologies. There would also be follow-up services on-the-job for those persons who find employment. In January of 1997, we will initiate a new Lab, with the latest computers and assistive technologies, in order to meet this community need.

8. The Impact of the Center on Disabilities

The model of educational support services for students with disabilities which originated at California State University, Northridge is widely used in the United States and elsewhere.

The conference, "Technology and Persons with Disabilities," is the largest of its kind in the world. It is a conference that has merged assistive technologies with the Internet and the World Wide Web. In addition to conducting this conference, the Center on Disabilities has also conducted conferences on other new technologies: In 1991, there was a conference on "Voice Input/Output and People with Disabilities." This resulted in a national set of priorities in the voice input/output field. From 1993-95 the Center conducted conferences on "Virtual Reality and Persons with Disabilities." As a result of our work in this area, I have keynoted and spoken at conferences in Asia, Australia, New Zealand, Europe, and South America.

A comprehensive evaluation of The "Leadership and Technology Management" training program demonstrates that graduates of this one-week program are creating new programs, making significant changes in educational and rehabilitation systems.

In summary we have been true to our mission of placing more technology in the hands of more people with disabilities.

Supports for Students with Disability through Technology
– Challenge at California State University, Northridge –

Akihisa KOHAMA

Department of Physics,
Faculty of Science, University of Tokyo
7-3-1, Hongo, Bunkyo-ku, Tokyo 113, JAPAN

I am a quadriplegic and use a wheelchair in my daily life due to the spinal code injury. I am working on theoretical nuclear physics at Department of Physics, University of Tokyo.

I visited California, U.S.A. with my wife, in the summer 1991 (from July 14 to September 12) and stayed there for 2 months when I was a graduate student of the doctor course studying nuclear physics, because a professor of California State University, Northridge (CSUN) invited me to collaborate with him. He is a professor of Department of Physics & Astronomy of CSUN, and I had been working with him since I was in the master course of the Graduate School of Science.

This visit happened to have given me a precious opportunity to see a very unique facility of CSUN, the Computer Access Lab. (CAL), where they support for students with disabilities, taking advantage of technology including computers and other various equipments. I had a chance to see the activities of CAL during the stay.

Computers are indispensable for our research activity on physics. For example, numerical calculations on computer have a significant role in the research of nuclear physics, and we should express our findings by writing articles which are usually written by a word processor on computer. Therefore, it is important for us to use computers efficiently. Due to my physical handicap, it is a big issue whether I can physically manipulate computers with ease. Actually some computers do not support the function of the sticky-key. I cannot use such computers. Hence it is crucial for me to get information on technology supporting for people with disabilities to continue and enhance my career on physics,

Thus the main purpose of this visit was of course the collaboration on nuclear physics, but another important purpose was to get information on assistive technology, and to seek a good usage of computers suited for me [1].

1 Computer Access Lab.

The Computer Access Lab. (CAL) is indeed a very unique facility. They support for students with disabilities, taking advantage of technology including computers and other various equipments. The directing manager is Dr. Harry Murphy. Staffs of CAL comes from a variety of fields. I knew the one who is a computer engineer, and the other who formerly worked in the field of Rehabilitation. I heard that many students with disabilities all over the states come to enter CSUN, because CSUN provided several educational support services for students with disabilities.

During the stay I often visited CAL about once or twice a week, and look into mainly the Human Machine Interface (HMI), *i.e.*, special peripherals and special software for inputs. There were many personal computers at CAL. I was very impressed by the fact that those computers were mostly donated by Apple Computer, IBM, and other manufacturers.

Some of the staffs of CAL, Ms. Gail Pickering and Mr. Neil Scott, gave me lots of useful information on computers, and I tried many softwares at CAL, *eg.*, a screen keyboard, and an input-system by voice. I studied what method is convenient for me to input, while I used a computer for actual research on physics.

They do not develop or research any devices, though they have lots of information on various products, instead. In CAL they make use of many products available in the markets. This means, students easily get those products by themselves.

0-8186-7658-2/96 $05.00 © 1996 IEEE

2 Needs of Computer Access Lab.

Any information does not have its implication until it reaches persons who need the information. Students with disabilities of CSUN could get information on assistive technology suited for them whenever they come to CAL. Each staff helps students with disabilities to take advantage of assistive technology for their academic and career success, and provides equipments which are appropriate for them. It is very useful and convenient for them. One of such students, for example, took examinations by using computers for writings. This helped him to reduce time to fill all the questions. CAL plays such important roles at CSUN.

Recently in Japan the number of student with physical disabilities is increasing. Some universities will support those students in several aspects.

The staffs in charge might face with difficulty: One reason why I think this way is that the information on assistive technology is lacking in Japan. The other reason is that we have very short history for accepting students with disabilities. Such experiences are lacking. Such valuable experiences will disappear with high probability, when those students graduate unless staffs of the universities keep the memories. Saving memories of such experiences will be sure to make a big power.

I think that those problems could be solved if we establish facilities like CAL.

3 Summary

I have briefly reviewed my experiences at CAL of CSUN. They support students with disabilities and reduce their handicap coming from their physical disabilities, by using assistive technology. This may tell us an relevance of such technology.

After returning to Japan, I got Ph. D. on nuclear physics from University of Tokyo in 1993. Now I am working on theoretical nuclear physics, but also engaged in the TRON Project. I belong to a working group, Enableware Research Group. This group works on HMI, which *enables* anyone including persons with disabilities to use computers.

Through this activity I have confirmed that facilities like CAL are really needed in Japan. Unfortunately in Japanese universities we have no such facilities as CAL at the moment.

We indeed need such facilitiess in Japan at any school, especially at universities, because they should provide equal opportunities to every students, even if they have physical disabilities. I hope that persons associated with education or the research actively struggle with the problems including acceptance of students with disabilities.

Last but not least, I have to express my sincerest gratitude to all the staffs of CAL, especially to Ms. G. Pickering and to Dr. H. Murphy, together with Mr. N. Scott.

References

[1] A. Kohama: Usage of Computers for Quadriplegics – Present Status and Outlook –, Pages for Enableware, *TRONWARE*, **VOL.28**, Aug.10 (1994) p. 85-88, Personal Media Corp., (in Japanese).

The 26 Year History of The Tokyo Metropolitan Prosthetic and Orthotic Research Institute

Hiroshi Kawamura
Tokyo Metropolitan prosthetic
and Orthotic Research Institute
3-17-3 Toyama ,Sinjuku-ku,Tokyo,162,Japan
NCC02640@niftyserve.or.jp

Abstract

The 26 year history of the Tokyo Metropolitan Prosthetic and Orthotic Research Institute will come to an end on March 1997. The research and development and achievements of this institute up to now will be incorporated into the Welfare Device Center (tentative name) scheduled to open on June 1997. With the abolishment of the Tokyo Metropolitan Prosthetic and Orthotic Research Institute, I would like to take this opportunity to present the history of this institute thus far, as well as the achievements of our research and development.

1.Preface

The Tokyo Metropolitan Prosthetic and Orthotic Research Institute, where research and development is carried out on prosthetics and orthotics for the disabled, particularly the physically disabled, and on welfare devices for the disabled, is Japan's sole national and public experimental research institute. At the time of the founding of the institute in 1971, apparatuses that were substituted for limb function for the disabled were limited to artificial limbs and orthotic, hence the naming of this institute as the Prosthetic and Orthotic Research Institute.

Recently, however, appeals have been made calling for the necessity of having many types of welfare device, due to the severity of the disability and the promotion of rehabilitation at home, to substitute for a variety of physical functions that have been lost. A law to promote research and development and the diffusion of devices for the disabled what is known as the Law on Devices for the Disabled was passed in Japan in 1993. The necessity for developing devices for the disabled has been more and more a policy that is being carried out on the national level. In response to these needs, the research topics of this institute has focused on many areas that began with research and development of prosthetics and orthotics, method of appraising the tests, analysis of movement of the upper and lower limbs; to that of movement, transfer, communication, discharge of bodily wastes, educational devices and clothing of the physically disabled. Lately, the focus has also been on how home-care support should be ideally carried out for the seriously disabled, types of apparatuses that provide assistance, transportation accessibility, etc.

2. Details Concerning the Establishment of this Institute

Japan's standard of living improved remarkably due to industrialization and urbanization brought on by the high economic growth from the 1960s on. However, harmful effects increased in proportion with the modernization of the functions of the city and economic growth. This induced impairments such as work accidents, traffic accidents, various kinds of pollution, congenital abnormalities and losses brought on by drugs such as thalidomide, diseases from old age, etc.

A decisive difference in technical level arises when compared to the European countries and the United States in dealing with the rehabilitation of the disabled especially in prosthetics and orthotics used as a substitute for limbs lost through amputation, loss or paralysis. The level of Japan's prosthetics and orthotics is not only considerably behind these countries, but also behind domestically when compared to the level of its general industrial apparatus technology. In order to apply Japan's advanced engineering technology that has sustained its high economic growth to the area of prosthetics and orthotics to raise the level of rehabilitation technology, the Ministry of Labor established the Prosthetics Center of the Labor Welfare Projects Corporation (now called the Rehabilitation Engineering Center of the Labor Welfare Projects Corporation) in 1969 and the Ministry of Health and Welfare established the National Prosthetic and Orthotic Research Center (now called the Laboratory, National Rehabilitation Center for the Disabled) in 1960. In 1971, Tokyo established the Tokyo Metropolitan Prosthetic and Orthotic Research Institute under the jurisdiction of the Tokyo Metropolitan Public Welfare

0-8186-7658-2/96 $05.00

Bureau (now called the Bureau of Social Welfare) based on the "Tokyo Metropolitan Medium-Range Plan-1968-" .

Marking a shift from a focus on a medical standpoint in prescribing and producing prosthetic devices, this institute now focuses on engineering in systematic cooperation with the fields of medicine, psychiatry and sociology in research and development and adaptation of prosthetic gear for devices for the disabled. This institute began as a small-scale institute with a staff comprised of 1 doctor, 5 engineers (now 8), 5 in prosthetic device production (now 4), 1 in charge of clothing, 1 case worker, 1 psychologist, 1 physical therapist, and 1 occupational therapist (now 0).

3. Transformation and Results of Research Themes

The Tokyo Metropolitan Prosthetic and Orthotic Research Institute has undergone subtle changes in its research themes in dealing with the needs of the disabled and of the administration in its 26 year history. This report is divided into four sections recounting research theme trends and on our major research outcomes.

3.1 Research Concerning Devices for the Disabled

This institute has continued with its theme of research and development of devices for the disabled that aid in the mobility, transfer and communication of the disabled. In 1970, we developed the first genuine electric wheelchair in Japan. Through the adoption of environmental control devices utilizing electronic technology and communication aids, the possibility of those with paralysis of all four limbs due to spinal cord injury of the neck becoming independent by means of these devices has been an aim of this institute.

In 1980, research proceeded on an input unit on equipment for those with severe involuntary movements stemming from neural paralysis. Particularly an independent-run electric wheelchair was developed for the disabled who had difficulty handling the input method that has been used in the past. Also, this institute has sought to uncover research and development themes by promoting engineering consultation and by carrying out research concerning technical support in order to clarify problems that accompany the diffusion of these devices that were developed and to be aware of cases that are difficult to deal with technically.

In anticipation of the graying of society, this institute developed an electric wheelchair and lift suspensions in the 1980s. In view of the importance of technology that can be adapted in welfare devices that have come into common use, the know-how adaptability of these apparatuses was systematized, an appropriate manual was prepared, and lectures were held on technological transfer.

3.2 Research Concerning Artificial Limbs and Gear

At the onset of the founding of this institute, the main research theme was the development of mio-electronic hand. This research, considered ultramodern at that time, prompted the growth of rehabilitation engineering in Japan. The development of the mio-electronic hand prototype ended in the mid 1970s and was succeeded by clinical application. On the other hand, research on the lower limbs began with a functional evaluation of the existing type of artificial leg through a gait analysis. Gait analysis technology was subsequently established as a gait appraisal technology for people with disabilities in the lower limbs. A new type of gear was developed from analytical data derived from walking with the aid of gear.

To ensure the safety of artificial limb gear, importance was placed on tests to determine the strength and durability of the parts, and appraisal of tests on parts for artificial limb gear was quickly set up as a research theme. As there was a virtual lack of knowledge concerning tests on artificial limb gear at that time, the entire process was carried out from the method of testing, the development and production of test equipment and to the actual testing itself. This greatly contributed not only for JIS (Japanese Industrial Standards) but also for ISO (International Organization for Standardization) to ascertain a standard for artificial limb gear parts.

3.3 Research on Clothing for the Disabled

Research concerning clothing for the disabled has been a continuing research theme since the opening of this institute, a trailblazer in Japan in its genuine and full-scale research undertaken. This research began as an analysis of the movements of the disabled when changing clothes and in the development of women's underwear. This was followed by devising rain countermeasures for the disabled who have to use a wheelchair or for those who have to use a cane when going out and also research and development on equipment dealing with bodily wastes, which are indispensable for the disabled to take part in society. Items developed by this institute such as middle sized diaper covers, boots for use with artificial leg gear and sneakers for artificial gear have been marketed. The research theme currently being undertaken is an area where engineering technology cooperation is necessary such as in the development of a women's urine collection device and in patternization for making rainwear patterns.

3.4 Investigative Research/Clinical Research

In setting up a research theme at this institute, it is indispensable to be in tune to the needs of the disabled. In order to accomplish this, it was necessary to thoroughly investigate the disabled from the actual state of their everyday life from the facets of prosthesis/orthotics and other welfare devices and to evaluate and implement them on the basis of investigative research/clinical research.

Because prescription and treatment of amputees who are children differs from amputees who are adults, this institute has implemented a child amputee project (later changed to the Child Amputee Clinic) from the onset of its establishment. This project sees to the improvement and development of method of assembly and adaptability of artificial limb gear parts. This institute has also developed educational related equipment such as a one-hand recorder and various types of playground equipment and is striving to systematize and diffuse this technology for practical use.

4. Conclusion

With the graying of society all the more progressing into the 21st century, the Law on Welfare Device was implemented in 1993. This writer, who has been with this institute for 26 years since its inception from the planning stages, feels a great sense of regret. Although this institute will be incorporated into the Welfare Device Center (tentative name), it is considered that it will be harder to do basic research and to experiment on devices out of one's own pocket. On the other hand, it probably will become easier to ascertain the needs of the disabled and to acquire feedback on ways of improving equipment through practical application on devices for the disabled. Basic research will have to be conducted in cooperation with universities and trial production of apparatuses will have to be undertaken in cooperation with private enterprises. We will continue to strive to create equipment necessary for the disabled and the elderly that are more convenient, safer, and easier to use.

In closing, I would like to thank Dr. Ken Sakamura for giving me this opportunity to present this report upon the closure of the Tokyo Metropolitan Prosthetic and Orthotic Research Institute.

Tutorial Session

The $500 Internet Computer

Henry Neugass
Microsystems Consultant
3352 Bryant Street
Palo Alto, CA 94306 USA
henry.neugass@spacebbs.com

Abstract

The Internet Computer is one of the most important new technologies today. This tutorial describes the history of computers designed specifically for Internet/World Wide Web access, the design approaches, component technologies, and likely near-term trends.

1. Introduction

The Internet Computer is one of the most important new technologies today. Large numbers of technology companies in the U.S., and many world-wide, are participating in some area related to the Internet Computer.

1.1. What is an Internet Computer?

Definition: A network computer is a device designed for accessing networks, most generally, the Internet /World Wide Web (WWW).

Synonyms: Information Appliance, Thin Client, Network Computer, NC, Internet Appliance, $500 Internet Computer, Internet Toaster.

Note: Network Computer *and* NC *are registered trademarks of Oracle Corporation. All Product or Company names mentioned here are for identification only and may be trademarks of their owners.*

The mainstream Internet Computer has the following characteristics:

- Provides access to the World Wide Web with a browser interface
- Downloads applications from Web servers
- Simple to operate and maintain; requires minimal technical skills
- A special purpose device; not a general-purpose Personal Computer
- Costs $500 or less

1.2. What determines these characteristics?

Four main factors have determined the mainstream Internet Computer characteristics:

The first factor is the explosive growth of information, products, and services available via the World Wide Web. It is necessary to make Web access more available to more people.

The second factor is the relative saturation of the Personal Computer (PC) market. It might be said that there is no way to sell significantly more PC's in the industrialized world because virtually everyone who now has the skills to operate a PC already is operating one. The obvious solution is to develop a device applicable to a new user base, that is, everyone else.

Moving current PC users to a different technology is not desirable for PC vendors, so the third factor is maintaining the existing PC market.

The final factor is achieving a price point consistent with "appliance" status, and $500 is most often estimated to be that point.

Beyond this logic, there is an underlying driving force based on the ambition to develop a device as useful and widely used as, say, the telephone–and to reap the benefits.

1.3. Why are Internet Computers important?

Supporters of the Internet Computer claim a huge potential market for a simple network access device in two markets:

For businesses, the Internet Computer promises to supplement conventional computers, providing improved information access and exchange to a very broad range of workers with initial and maintenance costs significantly below those of current personal computers. In the business context, "network" may mean an internal network ("Intranet") or the Internet, or both.

For the home market, Internet Computers promise to provide net access to people who resist current PC technology because of complexity and cost.

0-8186-7658-2/96 $05.00

For hardware and software vendors, network service providers, and net-based businesses, the Internet Computer promises new customers virtually without limit.

1.4. Why $500?

The price of $500 is arbitrary. It is widely thought to be the price point at which consumers in larger numbers will be willing to buy an Internet Computer.

1.5. What is the history of the Internet Computer?

Much of the product definition and the specific term "Network Computer" were originated by Larry Ellison, CEO of Oracle Corporation in 1995.

The underlying motivation is the common sense observation of anyone using a fully-equipped PC –complete with large, expensive software packages– to access the WWW.

1.6. Do Internet Computers exist?

As of this writing (September, 1996) no mainstream Internet Computers are available to the U.S. public in significant quantities.

2. The Internet Computer Technology Basis

The following technological factors form the basis of the Internet Computers:

- Success of the personal computer market in general
- Extremely rapid growth of public Internet technology infrastructure
- Success of browser technology as a human interface to information on the World Wide Web
- Advances in incremental application programs ("componentware")
- Wide use of intranet technologies in businesses
- Availability of high-performance, inexpensive microprocessors
- Advances in integrated circuit design, promising "total system integration"

The success of the personal computer and the explosive growth of the Internet are well-known and need no further discussion.

A key to the success of the Internet outside technical communities are browsers, Graphic User Interface (GUI) programs used for accessing the World Wide Web. The most well-known of these is NetScape Navigator.

Sun Microsystems has recently pioneered a new programming technology supporting "componentware" application programs with limited function called "applets." Programmed in a language called Java, applets are platform-independent and can be dynamically and incrementally combined as required to provide customized functionality at the time of use. This application environment is designed to support distribution of application functionality to individual computers over networks.

Meanwhile, U.S. businesses have widely embraced internal networks ("intranets") in some form or another. This technology has matured and become standardized. Wiring for networks is done routinely. Trained network administrators are available. Users are familiar with basic network concepts and operating characteristics.

Advances in microprocessor technology have produced a broad selection of high-performance RISC and CISC microcontrollers from U.S., Japanese, and European vendors. These devices are cheaper and faster than ever before. Widely-developed product lines offer many choices of price/performance.

Techniques of integrated circuit large-scale integration have also advanced, and the ability to put most of an Internet Computer on a single chip seems to be within reach. Current technology is sufficient to integrate to integrate a CPU core, a geometry processing engine, a graphics processor, a sound processor, a JPEG decoder, and other functions on a single LSI device. Even higher-level integration is likely in the future.

2.1. The Network Computer Reference Profiles

Apple Computer, Inc., International Business Machines Corporation Inc., Netscape Communications Corporation, Oracle Corp., and Sun Microsystems, Inc. are jointly issuing a series of successive Reference Profiles for Network Computers that have already been endorsed by over 70 international companies. The profiles are based on the following goals:

Architectural neutrality. Internet Computers don't favor any particular architecture and may be built with any microprocessor.

Reduced initial costs. Many business and home users don't need the full function of a modern personal computer. By focusing on the functions these users really require, between two to four Internet Computers can take the place of one PC on the basis of initial price differentials alone. Internet Computers are expected to be a key factor in interrupting the "upgrade spiral" that now dominates the personal computer market: more and more comprehensive (larger) applications lead to higher performance requirements; a new computer meeting these requirements is equipped with even larger applications, and so on.

Reduced total cost of ownership. Business users, in particular, have begun accounting for the total cost of owning and maintaining a standard PC and found the amount to be unacceptably high. Internet Computers are expected to have greatly reduced total costs.

Making use and administration significantly easier. Internet Computers will have a simplified operator interface –the standard interface is simply a browser– that should result in easier use by people with less training. At the same time, Internet Computers are designed to be administered from a central point, so upgrades and other maintenance should be much more convenient. Preliminary estimates show significantly lower administration costs for Internet Computers.

Security-enabling. The Reference Profile allows for security and user identification/profiling through optional use of ISO 7816 Smart Cards.

The profile includes guidelines for hardware resources (screen resolution, i/o devices, etc.), Internet protocols, hypertext and application language, mail protocols, multimedia formats, security, and printing.

In general, these guidelines endorse existing or currently emerging standards as defined by participants, for example, Java as the application language. The most notable feature is that hardware resources need not include local persistent storage. That is, disk drives or the equivalent need not be present.

2.2. The Internet Appliance Model

The word "appliance" is used very frequently in descriptions of Internet Computers. This term brings to mind the vision of a device that has a specific function –in this case, access to the Internet.

The following factors describe the "appliance" concept as it applies to Internet Computers:

Utility. The Internet Computer fills a significant and practical need. It is not a luxury.

Availability. The Internet Computer is always available for use. Start-up, warm-up, and maintenance don't significantly affect its availability.

Functionality. The Internet Computer does what it perceived to do, does it very well, and can't easily be modified to do anything else.

Longevity. The Internet Computer is continuously useful over a relatively long term.

Compatibility. The Internet Computer is physically compatible with the environment in which it is to be used, and doesn't require rebuilding or rewiring.

Usability. The Internet Computer is usable to its full functionality, without significant training, by its intended users.

Supportability. Supplies and maintenance required for the Internet Computer will be readily available.

Reliability. Internet Computers don't break in normal operation.

Modernity. The Internet Computer is a modern solution to a modern problem.

Democracy. The Internet Computer is available to everyone; there are no inherent exclusions.

3. The Internet Computer Vision

What does an Internet Computer look like?

There is no single answer to this question. In the idealized view, an Internet Computer is an appliance like any other in a home or office. It doesn't look like a computer and doesn't operate like a computer. In practice, so far, no one has achieved this ideal, and Internet Computers generally look like familiar personal computers, television set-top boxes, or other computer-based equipment.

Here are the main Internet Computer architectures:

3.1. Appliance

Pure "appliance" Internet Computers have so far been produced only in design sketch form by a few Internet Computer designers.

Probably the most important problem facing designers of appliance Internet Computers is information display. There is currently no economically feasible alternative to CRT displays, and any device using a CRT is limited to some very specific form factors due to the tube geometry. Unfortunately, none of these form factors is particularly convenient for a household appliance. Even when dependence on CRT's is overcome –LCD's are the likely candidate– some fundamental design innovations will be required to display large amounts of graphical information in a convenient package.

The next most important factor is information input. Pointing devices are sufficient for many aspects of browser operation, but not all of them. So far, no practical alternatives to a keyboard have been found.

3.2. Cut-down PC

Some vendors view an Internet Computer as simply a cost-reduced general-purpose computer and are endeavoring to product an approximately standard PC at or around the $500 price point. This approach attempts no fundamental technology change besides re-examining each PC component to see if it is really necessary and exploring innovative low-cost manufacturing techniques.

3.3. Improved Terminal

There are three types of remote terminals still widely in use in various service industries: "Dumb" or ASCII terminals, "X-terminals" for UNIX X-Windows operation, and "Win-terminals" for Windows operation. Computation and data storage are performed at a central computer.

Some view the Internet Computer as an ideal replacement for terminals of each of these type. It may be possible for one generic Internet Computer model to serve in each of these roles, though not –of course– at the same time.

This solution is applicable mainly to business applications.

3.4. Set-top box

Set-top boxes are currently in service in the U.S. for decoding and selecting cable video services in homes. These boxes are nearly always operated by a simple remote control unit. There is currently a good deal of attention toward extending this model to Internet Computers. In this view, the set-top box would be internally enhanced, and the World Wide Web would simply appear to subscribers as another video channel.

Major difficulties with this approach are textual data entry and information display. Some vendors are providing cordless remote keyboards. Ultimately, users may not find keyboard use convenient in home TV viewing locations. Testimonials by some vendors to the contrary, observers have noted that U.S. television resolution is currently insufficient for display of the large amount of textual information commonly present within the graphical WWW--browser environment.

3.5. Improved Video Game

A number of industry observers have pointed out that many existing video games fulfill many of the design parameters of an Internet Computers. While there are some predictions that game manufacturers are poised to adapt video games into Internet Computers –a very attractive possibility, if video game pricing can be maintained– there is no direct evidence of efforts do so.

4. Component Technologies

From an implementation point of view, the ideal Internet Computer is an embedded system: a "box" that operates without any user knowledge of its internal structure. Many forthcoming Internet computers follow this model and little detailed implementation information is available.

More information is available about the parts being used in Internet Computer designs. A rich variety of component choices are available. If marketing efforts are to be believed, component vendors are beginning to tailor products for the Internet Computer market. (For example, some vendors of personal computer power supplies are marketing new variants of their products adapted to the requirements of Internet Computers.)

4.1. CPU Technologies

The Network Computer Reference Profiles have so far been completely successful in this one area: no single CPU has dominated Internet Computer technologies. Internet Computer vendors are choosing from virtually every product family, ranging from the '486 family to advanced RISC architectures.

4.2. Operating System

There is a clear realization that Personal Computer operating systems, which have grown to huge sizes, are inappropriate for Internet Computers. Some vendors are using proprietary or unspecified "microkernel" operating systems. Real-Time Operating System (RTOS) technology from the embedded systems market place is being proposed for Internet Computers.

4.3. User Interface

The clear winner in Internet Computer user interface technology is Netscape Navigator.

4.4. Application environment

The clear winner is the interpreted Java application environment, which is yet unproven. Observers are predicting a competing product from Microsoft.

4.5. Memory

As with personal computers, Internet Computers use DRAM technology for volatile storage. Internet Computers are commonly equipped with 1 to 8 MB.

4.6. Display

Only two display technologies are considered for Internet Computers, standard CRT's and standard televisions.

4.7. Text Entry

The issue of text entry is not given much attention. No significant alternatives to standard keyboards for text entry have been proposed. Some vendors, particularly those following the set-top box model, are describing wireless keyboards. In a few cases, requirements for text entry are predicted to be limited to user-specific information.

4.8. Pointing Device

A pointing device is integral to the browser human interface. Because desk space may not be available, mouse technology is avoided, but other familiar technologies – joystick and trackballs– are common. For television-linked Internet Computers, a remote controller similar to those already in use for TV's and VCR's will be supplied.

5. Analysis and Conclusion

Can the Internet Computer become a true information appliance?

Does the Internet Computer meet the test of *utility*, in other words, do large number of people have daily need for large amounts of information? This is the trend for business and technical workers, but there is no proof that home users are ready or eager for what amounts to unlimited information; indeed some people may regard the home as the last refuge in an increasingly complex and noisy world.

Based on current trends, consistent *availability* is probably assured; most implementations will have a very short start-up time. Some are design to be powered on all the time.

There is little doubt about Internet Computer *functionality*, at least in the narrow sense. It is a matter of transferring existing Personal Computer technology to Internet Computers.

The overall worldwide trend is clear: access to information will increasingly be considered a basic human right, so –in some form or another– the *longevity* of some form of Internet Computer is assured.

Compatibility with business environments is probably assured, but it is unclear that Internet Computers are compatible with home environments outside of areas now dedicated to Personal Computers.

Internet Computer *usability* is a postulate of the Internet Computer revolution, implicitly depending on the explosion of browser use worldwide. The reasoning: many people use browsers; Internet Computers will have a browser operator interface, therefore Internet Computers will be usable by everyone.

Internet Computers will be *supportable* only if vendors succeed in making installation, operation, and maintenance as simple as these tasks for, say, a dishwasher.

Internet Computer *reliability* will benefit from simplification and, in particular, the potential for eliminating local mass storage. Considering improvements seen in PC's, it is possible to anticipate very high reliability in Internet Computers themselves. However, Internet Computers are wholly network-dependent and recent experience in the U.S. would indicate that a significant improvement in network and server technology will be necessary.

Modernity. The Internet Computer is self-evidently a modern solution to a modern problem.

Although Internet Computers would seem to be an obviously *democratic* technology, this issue will best be decided in retrospect.

5.1. Near-term Trends

Java. There should be a large amount of activity in the near-term to prove Java, the practicality of downloading applets, and distribution mechanisms. Java development environments, technical books, and training are already widely available in the U.S. It will be very important to determine if the target execution environments are likely to reach performance limits, triggering a new round of upgrade spirals.

Country-of-origin. Although much of the publicity and the initial standards have come from the U.S., implementation will likely be entirely international.

Vendor Specialization. Companies attempting to develop and produce a complete Internet Computer will continue, in the near-term, to be forced to specialize. It appears to be very difficult for a single company to track the necessary technology alone.

Strategic Alliances, sometimes of unexpected partners, will continue to be a feature of the Internet Computer industry until the concept is finally proven or disproving.

Memory. Browser memory requirements are probably higher than Internet Computer vendors admit, and there is an evident trade-off for browsers between performance and memory. If memory prices stabilize at moderate levels or continue to drop, there will be increased pressure to equip Internet Computers with larger amounts of RAM memory, reducing the distinction between Internet Computers and PC in this respect.

Displays. The price of the display is often omitted from the $500 Internet Computer price, which is possibly justified in the case of devices intended for use with home televisions, but is otherwise somewhat misleading. As all other costs decrease, there will be increasing pressure on display technology and price.

PC -- Internet Computer distinction. Unless a breakthrough technology is discovered, it is likely that the stated object of keeping a distinction between the Internet Computer and a PC will not be achieved, but rather there will be a continuum between the two.

5.2. Final Comments

The Internet Computer is both a product of global, technical, and social forces and is evolving with these forces in real time.

By most appearances, the most important factor in the Internet Computer market is bringing a product to market as soon as possible. There are few signs of planning for future product generations. It is likely that many of the initial products will fail. Given the large body of experience in component technologies, innovators should be able to produce a second- or third-generation technology right away.

One key factor required for producing a fully functional Internet Computer is the Java model, in which application modules are downloaded as required by users. Industry observers have noted that no significant applets yet exist and there is little evidence that this technology has been proven in any environment.

On the promise of a virtually unlimited market, Internet Computer designers in many cases appear to be victims of their own wishful thinking. One manifestation of this is reliance on very small sources of experience, for example, focus groups.

A key factor in the Internet Computer market is the search for a counterforce to Microsoft Windows -- Intel ("Wintel") market dominance in PC's, which is often hidden just beneath the surface and fairly often explicitly stated by observers. While a possibly worthy cause, this goal cannot substitute for strong, consistent Internet Computer product design and execution.

So far, CPU architectural dependence appears extremely low in Internet Computers. This trend is seen in other computer-based technologies –for example, embedded systems– and is likely to continue.

It is clear that the success of the Internet Computer will make strong demands on the technical infrastructure, for example, having the potential to overwhelm existing telecommunications bandwidth. The social and political implications are also significant and will need to be addressed.

Smartcards Become an International Technology

James J. Farrell III, Motorola

Abstract

Smartcards were first introduced nearly 20 years ago in France to reduce credit card fraud. This new technology grew slowly but steadily for several years. It is now making a leap into new application areas and international markets. Smartcards are now used in many countries and acceptance is expected to grow dramatically.

Magnetic Stripe Cards

The standard magnetic stripe card certainly has been a booming success. Today there are several hundred million magnetic stripe cards in circulation worldwide. The largest application is by far credit cards. Worldwide, there are over 375,000 ATM machines and over 12 million POS (point of sale) readers that will accept them.

However more intelligence, functionality, capacity and security are being required by existing and new card applications than magnetic stripe cards can provide. "Smartcards" are becoming more attractive as the price of microcomputing power and storage continues to decline. Smartcards have two main advantages over magnetic stripe cards. First, they can carry up to 100 times as much information, and hold it much more reliably. Second, they can independently perform complex computations in conjunction with a terminal. A Smartcard and a card reader can engage in a sequence of interaction that validates the card reader as well as the Smartcard. This provides a form of mutual authentication. Using advanced algorithms, a credit card holder will be able to use a local terminal without revealing his or her identity.

In May 1995 an industry magazine [2] published an estimate of the 1994 market volume for microcontroller Smartcards as being 45 million units, based on its own research. These Smartcards, made by companies including Orga, Gemplus, Schlumberger, Giesecke and Devrient (G+D) among others, range in price from less than ¥110 to about ¥2200. A magnetic stripe card may cost from less than ¥100 to ¥300 depending on whether it is bare or incorporates a photograph or a holographic image. The silicon used in Smartcards range normally in price from around ¥60 to ¥2,000, and is provided by a number of companies including Motorola, Siemens, SGS Thomson, and Hitachi.

Smartcard Genesis

Twenty years ago, Motorola started working with Bull, the French computer company, on a project initiated by the French banking association, Cartes Bancaires. Cartes Bancaires, who at the time were issuing credit cards based on magnetic-stripe technology, were growing very concerned about fraudulent credit card incidents, and its costs to its member banks. Together, Bull and Motorola designed and developed the world's first Smartcard in 1977 for Cartes Bancaires. Today, because of Smartcards, French merchants rely on personal identification numbers (PINs) to verify the ownership of a card simply by checking the PIN typed in by a customer against the record on the card itself. They did not have to go on-line (usually by telephone) to centralized databases. There are more than 20 million of these cards in use now in France.

Smartcards Defined

A Smartcard is usually the same size as a conventional credit card but incorporates a small gold-colored metal "button", or module, on the front side of the card. This contains a specially designed silicon chip called a Smartcard microcontroller. When the card is inserted into a reader, the embedded chip is powered up by means of six electrical contacts. The five active contacts are:

1. Power
2. Ground
3. Reset
4. System clock
5. A single Input/Output (I/O) position for the bidirectional transfer of information.

The six contact is not yet defined.

The Smartcard incorporates a central processing unit (CPU), memory, and Input/Output (I/O) capability. Because the cards are dependent on an outside power source provided by the reader interface, any information held in conventional random-access memory (RAM) will be lost every time it is removed from a reader. Hence they use only a few hundred bytes of RAM as a scratchpad for working on transactions in progress. The software that controls the card's operations must used frequently, and so it occupies between three and 20 kilobytes (KB) of permanent nonvolatile read-only memory (ROM). This software in ROM is permanently "masked" into the device at the time of fabrication. The personal, financial or medical data that give each card value to its owner reside in an alterable nonvolatile memory of between one and eight kilobytes. This EEPROM (Electrically Erasable Programmable ROM) provides the flexibility required to personalize the card to the individual card carrier.

Memory Cards

However, not all credit sized plastic cards with an embedded module are Smartcards. In fact, today, the majority are not. For example the French government public telephone card looks like a "Smartcard" but it is not. It is a memory card. The integrated circuit on the card is just a memory chip with security features. The user buys the card, usually from a local tobacco shop, or news stand, and uses it until its "calling units" are depleted. The card is then discarded and a new one purchased. This card can not be "recharged" and it has no owner protection features. If you lose a card before it is depleted, anyone can use the card.

For an IC card to be a "Smartcard" it must be "smart". "Smart" implies that it has intelligence and processing capability to be able to interpret the data it receives. Microcontroller cards, are true Smartcards. They contain a microcontroller chip and offer full information storage, security features and manipulation facilities.

Applications

The smartcard's ability to store and manipulate information means that it can be used in a wide variety of applications, which provide the key to the industry's growth. A Smartcard can be thought of as a rechargeable electronic purse with a computer inside: a single Smartcard could act as a debit card, credit card, driving license, car-park pass, corporate security card, health card, product loyalty card (gasoline, fast food, video rental), transport pass (airlines, mass transit, road tolls), passport and ID card, for example. Using a biometric PIN system, such as a fingerprint, currently being promoted by a major international credit card provider. Other biometric identifiers include: voice prints, fingerprints, retina scans, iris scans, and dynamic signature patterns. Presented with a card holding the reference pattern, the reading terminal can now determine with great accuracy how well the bearer matches the smartcard's pattern

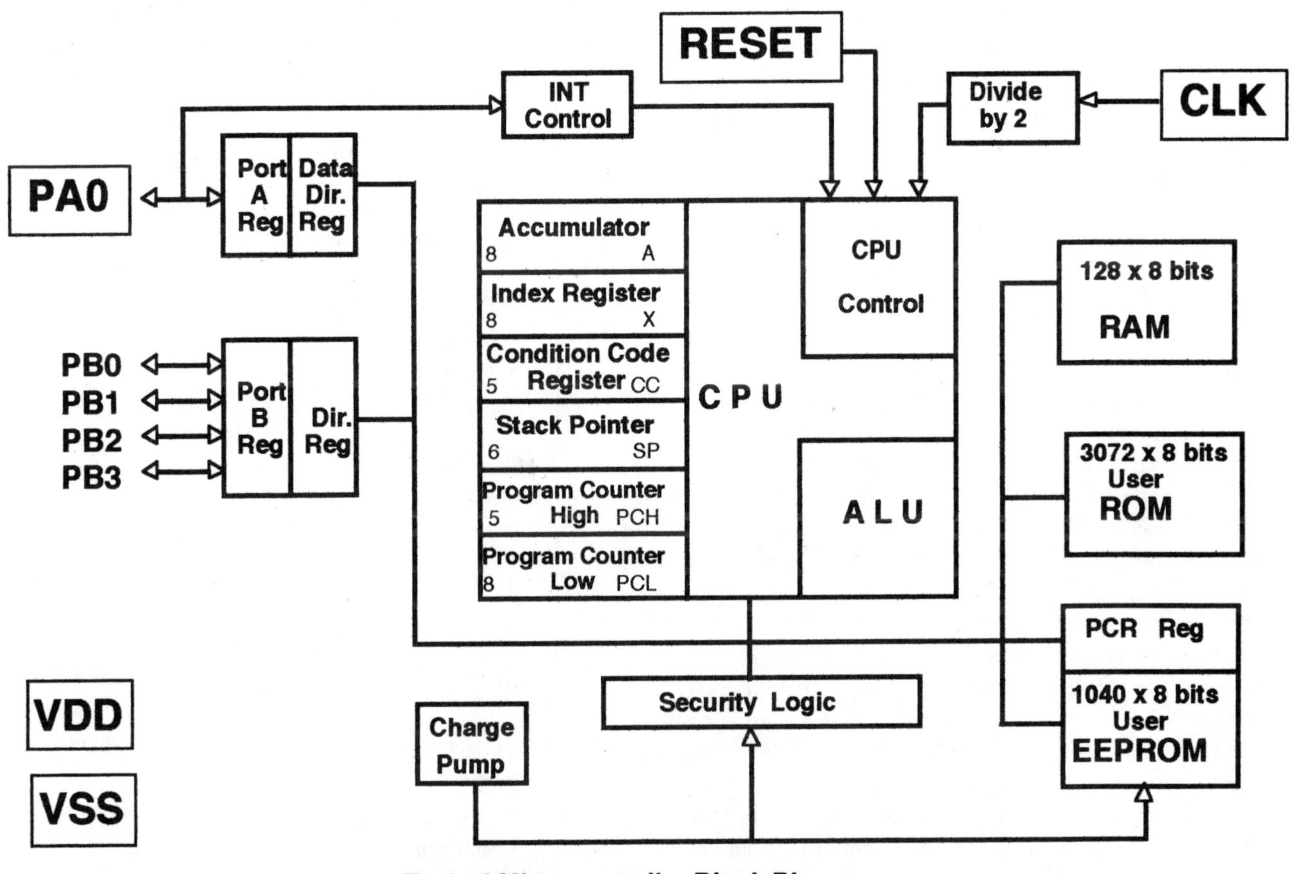

Typical Microcontroller Block Diagram

for identification.

Governments and other authorities throughout the world are investigating the use of Smartcards for many applications in fields such as social security and health. In Spain, for example, the government will issue around 35 million Smartcards to residents who claim social security. The Czech Republic and Taiwanese governments are both planning to implement Smartcards for their health services, as is the French health consortium, which plans to issue all French citizens with Smartcards starting in 1998. In Japan, Sony is researching a contactless Smartcard for use by commuters and travelers on the Japanese rail systems. The contactless system will allow extremely fast "turnstile" verification of the paid fare, greatly reducing the "people jam" bottlenecks which are currently a major problem at many urban train stations. The time-consuming and annoying "Fare Adjustment" machine or window will become history.

Smartcards are also being proposed and investigated for uses such as diverse as road tolls, bus tickets, retailer loyalty cards, Internet-access cards and electronic purses. Contactless toll road Smartcards allow the drivers to pay the toll while traveling at highway speeds, without having to be distracted from their driving. In addition to the obvious safety benefits of not having to make a stop on a high-speed road, the drivers are spared the frequent long waits and wasted gas gasoline spent in long toll booth queues.

However, perhaps the most interesting development is the use of Smartcards which perform more than one function, called multifunction cards. In the USA, for example, a number of universities now issue multipurpose 'campus' cards where students have their library ticket, car-park details and an electronic purse on one card. NTT in Japan has upgraded its corporate security cards so that they can be used as electronic purses for the staff cafeteria as well as allowing access to restricted parts of the building, and to restricted computer systems. In Denmark, residents can buy multifunction "city cards" which act as a library ticket, parking pass and transport ticket, among other services.

Health applications provide an extremely important applications area for Smartcards, that also may make the most important implementation of this technology, by improving health and saving lives. In France and Japan, kidney patients can carry cards that hold their dialysis records and treatment prescriptions. Dialysis patients often need dialysis two or three times a week. Each dialysis session involves a unique set of machine parameters and a special combination of drugs as well as time attached to a kidney dialysis machine. Prior to the introduction of the Smartcards, patients could only go to the local dialysis center where their records were kept. Now, they have the geographic mobility most of us take for granted. Security checks built into the cards ensure that only doctors and other authorized persons can read or update treatment information. France and Sweden are conducting pilot programs in which current records of prescription drug use will be maintained on Smartcards. Many people take multiple prescription drugs, for different conditions, possibly prescribed by different doctors and filled by different pharmacies at different times. Smartcard records can alert the pharmacist, doctor or user of adverse drug interactions.

General purpose health Smartcards can carry and individual's vital medical information, provide basic medical information such as lists of unique individual drug sensitivities, current conditions being treated, the name and phone number of a patient's doctor and other information vital in an emergency.

Below is a consolidation of current and future Smartcard applications are being developed or evaluated in the following areas:

- Transport
  - City Projects
  - Public Transport Payment
  - Contactless Technology
- Phone Cards
  - Migration from Memory and Magnetic to Smartcard
- Banking (see detailed breakdown in "International Financial Applications")
  - French Banks
  - German EC Card
  - Russian Banks
  - Electronic Purse
  - International Credit Cards
- National Health
  - France (GIP)
  - Germany
  - Many Other Countries Evaluating
- Identification Cards
  - South America
  - Egypt
  - China/Hong Kong
  - UK
  - Passports
- Pay TV
  - Sky
  - DirecTV
  - PC2E
  - STAR
  - Canal Plus

Cellular Telephone
- GSM
- NADC
- PCN
- Other Mobile Communications

Road Tolls
- Singapore
- Germany
- Italy
- UK
- Others Also in Evaluation

International Financial Applications

Financial applications will become and remain the largest application area for Smartcards for the foreseeable future. Below is an overview of current financial Smartcard electronic purse activities around the world [1]:

Australia:

MasterCard Cash® started its pilot this year in Canberra. Up to $500 (Australian Dollars) may be loaded on the card at a time, and the card can be debited at a large number of different consumer stores and vendors. Future cards will handle up to ten different currencies.

Quicklink SVC started in 1995. Up to $500 (Australian Dollars) may be loaded on the card at a time, and the card can be debited at a large number of different consumer stores and vendors.

Transcard started in Sydney in 1995. It is used for charge accounts. Tickets, incentives and memberships.

VISA Cash® started in 1995 north of Brisbane, this trial uses both disposable and reloadable cards.

Austria:

QUICK is a Europay® project that became countrywide in late 1995. They are used in restaurants, taxis, vending machines, parking meters, shops and public transport.

Belgium:

Clip is a Europay® pilot started in 1996. It is used for low-value purchases, video rentals, pay-per-view TV and Internet purchases.

PROTON is another 1996 national start by Banksys of Belgium. This card is used for vending machines, car parking, telephone calls, public transit, newspapers, groceries and fast food restaurants.

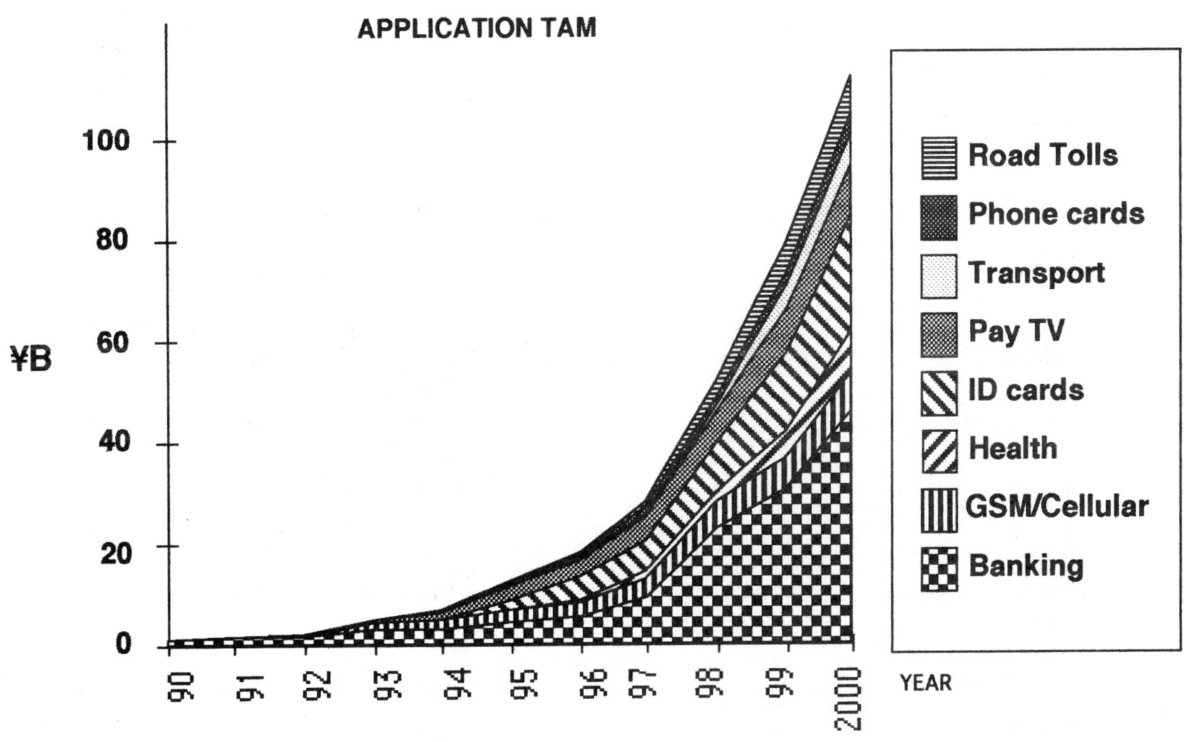

Canada:

Mondex plans an electronic cash pilot late in 1996.

China:

The Great Wall Card is a multi-application banking card, started in 1995 by the Bank of China.

CIS (Former USSR):

Zolotaya Korona is a multi-application card launched in 1994 by the Center Financial Technologies.

Denmark:

DANMØNT is a rechargeable multi-application card since 1995.

Finland:

AVANT is issued by Automatia Rahakorit Oy since early 1994. It is used for fast food, postage, municipal services and other consumer expenditures.

Aspects of Various Card Technologies

Type of Card	Cost	Capacity	Versatility	Security
Embossed Plastic	Low	None	None	None
Hologram Card	Low	None	None	Low
Magnetic Stripe	Low	Low	Low	Low
Magnetic Stripe with Hole Punch	Low	Medium	Low	Low-Medium
with Non-Volatile Memory	Medium	Medium	Low	Low
with Battery-Backed RAM	High	Medium	Medium	Low
with MCU	**Medium**	**Medium**	**High**	**High**
with Multi-Chip Solution	High	Medium	High	High
Optical Storage	Medium	High	Medium	Medium
with Mechanical Storage	Low	Low	None	None

Germany:

Geld Karte is issued by ZKA in cooperation with Systemhans. The six-month pilot started in March 1996, and is an electronic purse for retail outlets, public transit and telephones.

P-CARD is owned by EBS GmbH, and is licensed to various banks and other institutions. It is used for multi-function credit, debit, electronic entrance key, pocket money and other applications.

Indonesia:

SMARTBRI EP and Passbook are issued by Bank Rakyat Indonesia, and are used for off-line banking.

Italy:

Cassamat was developed by VERON SpA since 1994, and is used as an electronic purse.

MINI PAY was developed by SSB SpA and launched in 1996. It is used for electronic payments and telephone calls.

Japan:

Smart Commerce Japan was developed jointly by Toshiba Corporation and VISA®. Planned for a pilot launch in early 1997, this Smartcard will be an electronic purse used at kiosks, Internet and other applications.

Latvia:

LATkarte was developed by SWH Informatívás sistémas and launched in 1993. It is used for cashless payments for goods and services.

Lebanon:

LINC EP was developed by LINC Lebanese Interbank Card and launched in 1993. It is used for electronic purse and credit applications.

Netherlands:

Chip Knip was developed by Interpay BV, and launched nationally in 1996. It is an electronic purse for small payments.

Portugal:

PMB was developed by SIBS and rolled out in 1995. This card is used for small purchases to replace cash.

Singapore:

CashCard EP was developed by Singapore Computer Systems and Tandem Computers International, Inc. This credit card uses the magnetic stripe as well as a microcontroller.

South Africa:

Interbank EP was developed by Gemplus and Net I and rolled out nationally in 1996. It is used as a debit card or PIN purse card.

Spain:

SEMP Spanish EP was developed by SEMP and launched in 1995. It is a multipurpose Smart Card.

Switzerland:

CASH is underdevelopment by Banksys and Telekurs Payserv AG, and will be used as an electronic purse.

POSTCARD is a reloadable electronic purse, that is debited from the users postal account.

Taiwan:

The FISC system is used to settle interbank transactions.

Thailand:

(TFP) EP was developed by LOXBIT in 1995 and is used for small transactions.

USA:

MasterCash® was developed by MasterCard® and several banks and other organizations. It is currently being used is several USA locations for retail purchases, gasoline, and similar applications.

VISA Cash® was developed by VISA®, and has both disposable and reloadable cards for low-value purchases.

The above listing is a sample of electronic purse applications, and is not comprehensive. There are a number of international trials in addition to those listed above.

Contactless Cards

Most Smartcards require physical contact between the card and pins in the reader, but some can operate by electrical induction with the reader and card a millimeter or so apart.

Contactless Smartcards are frequently used in situations where cards must be processed very fast, as in mass transit turnstiles, or as noted earlier, on toll roads. Some vendors have produced "radio frequency tags," which can function effectively at ranges of from a few centimeters to a meter. The tags come in a variety of shapes and usually do not necessarily have to conform to the same mechanical standards as Smartcards with contacts. There will also be a big growth in the use of contactless Smartcards, because they can be read remotely without having to be inserted in a reader.

Security

Smartcards are usually produced for applications which have some need for security. Either the card is going to have some monetary value stored or accessible, or the card contains some information that is proprietary in nature. This need for security influences every aspect of the application and specifically the handling of the card and the microcontroller. The microcontrollers used in Smartcards are specifically designed to restrict access to information stored on the device and prevent the card device from coming under the control of unauthorized parties.

The microcontroller and the specialized software stored in it provide the first of many barriers against fraud, as well as many other user benefits. The microcontroller, like the magnetic stripe, stores information but, because it has the capability to encrypt this data and store it in areas that are designated to be unreadable, it helps prevent the unauthorized reading and subsequent cloning which is problematic with some magnetic stripe card systems.

Various security mechanisms keep the device working in only a well-characterized operating environment, provide special areas of memory that can only be accessed under control of the code in ROM, provide other "lockout" modes which restrict the unauthorized alteration of any data in the device, or utilize special tamper-resistant layers or layout techniques that would prevent a determined thief from getting to the microscopic circuitry directly. Depending on the importance of the information involved, application system security might rely on a personal identification number like those used with automated teller machines, biometrics that uniquely connect the card to the card-carrier, a mid-range encryption systems such as the Data Encryption Standard (DES), or a highly secure public key scheme.

Standards

Mechanical and electrical standards have been established by the International Organization for Standardization (ISO) to govern the placement of contacts on the face of a Smartcard so that any card and reader will be able to communicate with each other. (The standards also specify the flexibility of the plastic to make sure that both chips and card can survive in a wallet.) Beyond the card, standards are being developed to use the card in applications as diverse as digital cellular phones, satellite and cable television and of course many financial areas. Recently Visa, MasterCard, and Europay (called the EMV consortium) have agreed on a common specification for Smartcards that can supplement the magnetic stripe currently used for credit and debit cards. This agreement could bring the convenience of a single card for purchases, automated teller machine access, frequent flyer bonuses and even Internet access all over the world.

Future Developments

Magnetic stripe cards are not going to suddenly disappear off the face of the earth. The overwhelming majority of bank credit Smartcards now being issued will be "Smartcard-Magnetic stripe" hybrid cards, that will operate in both environments. This will continue for several years into the future to accommodate the transition of the 12 million reading terminals to Smartcard capability. By the same token, in those geographical areas with poor telephone service, the Smartcard usage should grow quickly, because the Smartcard does not require the telephone verification that magnetic stripe cards frequently do.

Semiconductor technology advancements in the manufacturing process mean that the Smartcard microcontroller chip will continue to get smaller, cheaper and more versatile, offering a wider range of features. At the same time, however, there will be a trend towards more complex cards for some applications. Dedicated hardware encryption for very high security applications is an example.

References:

[1] Smart Card News - Special Report, Summer, 1996

[2] Smart Card Monthly - May, 1995

[3] IEEE MICRO, Spring, 1996

[4] Smartcard Technology International - MasterCard®- Spring, 1996

[5] ***Smart Cards*** by Carol Hovenga, **Scientific American** August, 1996, Vol. 275, No. 2

Appendices

Overview of the TRON Project

TRON (The Real-time Operating system Nucleus) is a project aimed at creating an ideal computer architecture for the future computerized society. The project was started by Dr. Ken Sakamura of the University of Tokyo in 1984. Private industry is cooperating with academia to bring a whole new computer order into reality.

The TRON Project is being carried out viewing the future computerized society. In the computerized society, most kind of equipment, appliances, tools, and other objects making up our living environments will be augmented with embedded computers, be connected with networks, and co-operate each other to provide better living environments for human beings. In other words, these *intelligent objects* and networks constitute a large distributed computing system and support human activities on many aspects. This kind of system is called a *highly functionally distributed system (HFDS)* and its realization is the most important goal of the TRON Project.

Work is now going ahead on various subprojects, including six fundamental subprojects and some application subprojects. The fundamental subprojects study each component of the computer systems to construct an HFDS. They include ITRON (real-time multitasking OS specifications for embedded systems), BTRON (an architecture centering on OS specifications for personal computers and workstations), CTRON (OS interface specifications for communication and information processing), the TRON-specification CHIP (VLSI microprocessor architecture), MTRON (an attached operating system architecture to link systems based on the TRON architecture), and TRON Electronic Equipment HMI (standard guidelines for human-machine interface in electronic equipment of various kinds).

The application subprojects test out actual applications in HFDS, find problems in them, break the problems down into more concrete sub-problems, and solve each of them. They simulate the future computerized society on a relatively small scale, and evaluate the architecture being developed in the fundamental subprojects. The application subprojects use the results of the fundamental subprojects to solve the problems, and the fundamental subprojects receive vital feedback from the application subprojects.

For the 1990's and on to the 21st century

The TRON Project aims at an ideal computer architecture targeted at the technological levels of the 1990's and into the 21st century. This ideal is premised on advanced VLSI technology and, emphasizes real-time processing and cost-performance.

The TRON Project is applying consistent and brand new design principles to architectures spanning the whole range of computer applications, from consumer electronics and personal computers to industrial robots, large-scale computers, and telephone switching systems.

Open architecture

A fundamental policy of the TRON Project is that the results of the project, in the form of published specifications and guidelines, are made available to the public. Anyone throughout the world is free to develop and market products implementing the specifications. This is considered essential from the standpoint of realizing the HFDS concept.

The TRON Association has been established as the core organization for the purpose of preparing the TRON specification references and conducting conformance testing. Membership in the TRON Association is open to anyone in the world who shares in the objectives of the TRON Project.

Loose standardization

TRON specifications set rules for computer interfaces, but do not presuppose any particular hardware or software implementation. They do not specify the operating systems themselves, but only their interfaces. The aims are to achieve program and data compatibility, to reduce development costs, and to facilitate the training of users and application programmers.

The TRON Project adopts *loose standardization*, which stipulates only the design concepts. The actual systems are built by implementors freely along with the standardized design concepts. The loose standardization is a reasonable compromise to have both the adoption of emerging technologies and the compatibility of various components of HFDS.

Fundamental Concepts Governing the TRON Project

1. The computer architecture TRON originated by Dr. Ken Sakamura is an open computer architecture. The TRON Specifications are made publicly available to anyone in the world.
2. Copyrights to the TRON Specifications belong to the TRON Association. Anyone is entitled to utilize the TRON Specifications in developing and merchandising products conforming to the TRON Specifications.
3. The TRON Association has been established as the core organization for the purpose of preparing the TRON Specifications, conducting conformance testing, and otherwise promoting the TRON Project. Membership in the TRON Association is open to anyone in the world who shares in the objectives of the TRON Project and agrees to observe the TRON Association's rules.

Interface functions are specified hierarchically; they consist of the microprocessor instruction set, operating system nucleus (kernel), operating system outer nucleus (middleware), and application programs. Hierarchical specification makes it possible to implement each layer separately by different companies. Even if the implementations below a given layer are different, the upper layers can still be used as is. Moreover, because of the consistent architecture throughout, standardization is achieved while allowing numerous companies to participate in free competition.

Compatibility with the future

The TRON Project is freeing the computer world from the fetters of compatibility with the past, for the sake of compatibility with the future. Many computer systems of today are extensions of early architectures. They are like houses that have been enlarged many times. The TRON Project, on the other hand, is building a brand new architecture on the basis of the VLSI technology of the future.

TRON specifies a standard data format called TAD (TRON Application Databus) guaranteeing data interchange across applications. The TAD format also offers a way of achieving coexistence with the world of existing operating systems.

Drive computers like a car – standard operation –

Another goal of the TRON Project is to allow anyone to use computers. Something like this already exists with automobiles, all of which are driven in basically the same way regardless of manufacture or model. Similar standardization of human-machine interface is needed especially for personal computers, allowing hardware and applications to be upgraded or changed without any extra load for re-learning.

For further information on the TRON Project, refer to the TRON Project Home Page at the following URL.

http://tron.um.u-tokyo.ac.jp/TRON/

Bibliography of the TRON Project (1984 – 1996)

Preface

Activities of the TRON Project in these past twelve years have produced a large amount of technical results which are published as papers, books, and reports. Because such publications of TRON are scattered among diverse journals, proceedings, technical reports, etc., it is difficult for the new TRON researchers and developers to discover relevant documents. The primary objective of this bibliography is to eliminate this difficulty, and to improve the accessibility of technical information of the TRON Project. Its contents are restricted to publications on technical issues; non-technical publications are out of its scope.

At present, the bibliography contains more than 600 entries. Entries in this bibliography are classified into ten sections by their interests: books on the TRON Projects, Specifications, and technical papers on general issues, on TRON Specification CHIP, on ITRON, on CTRON, on BTRON, on HMI, on Enableware, and on MTRON/HFDS. In each section, entries are first sorted in the order of publishing year. Next, entries with the same publishing year are sorted in the alphabetical order of their authors' names.

In closing, we would be very glad if many researchers and developers interested in the TRON Project would make use of this bibliography for their activities.

Ken Sakamura

TRON Project Leader
The University of Tokyo

1 Introduction – General Sources of the TRON Project–

Many books or journals featuring the TRON Project have been published up to now. This section describes useful reference sources for readers interested in the special issues on TRON.

On-line Information

Sakamura Laboratory is operating three kinds of information servers that provide information on the TRON Project. These servers give overall information on the TRON Project, and also the original bibliography database of this article. All entries in the bibliography database are in the BibTeX format. Their addresses in the URL format are as follows:

- World Wide Web Server:
  `http://tron.is.s.u-tokyo.ac.jp/`
  (133.11.14.100).
- Gopher Server:
  `gopher://tron.is.s.u-tokyo.ac.jp/`
  (133.11.14.100).
- Anonymous Ftp Server:
  `ftp://tron.is.s.u-tokyo.ac.jp/`
  (133.11.14.100).

Regular Publications

- *TRONWARE* Vol. 1–42 (in Japanese)

  TRONWARE is published bimonthly from Personal Media Co. This journal targets computer engineers and researchers who want technical information on TRON.

- *TRON Project Journal* (in both English and Japanese)

  TRON Project Journal reports news and information in the TRON Association as well as new results of the TRON Project. However, its distribution is limited to the members of the TRON Association.

Proceedings of Annual Symposiums

- *TRON Project 1987–1990*
- *Proceedings of the TRON Project International Symposium, 1991–1995*

  "TRON Project 1987, 1988, 1989, and 1990" and "Proceedings of the TRON Project International Symposium, 1991, 1992, 1993, 1994 and 1995" are the proceedings of the TRON Project International Symposium, which is a conference on purely technical/scientific content. The symposium is annually held. The proceedings of the TRON Symposium were published by Springer-Verlag. Since 1991, the symposium has been held in cooperation with IEEE Computer Society and the proceedings have been published from the IEEE Computer Society Press.

Proceedings of Workshops

- *Proceedings of the Realtime-OS-TRON Technical Workshop* (First—Fourth)
- *Proceedings of the TRON Technical Workshop* (Fifth—Sixteenth)
- *Proceedings of the TRON EnableWare Symposium '88, '90, '92, '93, '94 and '95*

  Proceedings of '90, '92, '93 '94 and '95 are available in both printed form and braille form.

TRON Technical Workshops are regularly held from once to three times a year. Originally, the workshop was named "the Realtime-Architecture-TRON Technical Workshop" and was held by the Institute of Electronics, Information, and Communication Engineers (IEICE). Ever since TRON Association was established, the name of the workshops has been "TRON Technical Workshop", which have been held by TRON Association. In both workshops and proceedings have been published.

In the TRON EnableWare Symposium, technical issues for the realization of a computer for handicapped people are discussed. The discussions are mainly devoted to human machine interface and social problems. This symposium has been held five times (1988, 1990, 1992, 1993, and 1994). The result of discussions in the symposium is available as Proceedings of the EnableWare Symposium and BTRON Enableware Specification.

TRON Specification Books

Many specification books have been published from TRON Association, Personal Media Corporation, and Ohmsha Ltd.

Journals Featuring TRON

Some journals have special issues featuring articles on the TRON Project. The representative ones are as follows:

- IEEE Micro (April 1987, April 1988, June 1989, April 1990, August 1991)

  Volume 7, Number 2 of IEEE Micro (April 1987) has bee translated into Japanese and is published from Kyoritsu Publishing (Introduction to TRON).
- Microprocessors and Microsystems (October 1989)
- Journal of Information Processing Society of Japan (May 1989, October 1994, in Japanese)

However, many other references are scattered among many journals, proceedings of conferences and workshops, and technical reports. We are very glad if this bibliography helps you access such literature.

2 Specification Books

[1] K. Sakamura, Ed. *ITRON Specification.* TRON Association, 1987.

[2] K. Sakamura, Ed. *BTRON: TRON Keyboard Operation Summary.* TRON Association, 1988.

[3] K. Sakamura, Ed. *BTRON/286 Specification Summary.* TRON Association, 1988.

[4] K. Sakamura, Ed. *Enableware Specification – Extracts from BTRON MMI External Specification.* TRON Association, 1988. in Japanese.

[5] K. Sakamura, Ed. *BTRON1 Specification Software Specification.* TRON Association, 1989.

[6] K. Sakamura, Ed. *BTRON2 Specifications Software Specifications – ver 0.1.* Sakamura Laboratory, Faculty of Science, University of Tokyo, 1990. in Japanese.

[7] K. Sakamura, Ed. *ITRON Specification ITRON2.* TRON Association, 1990.

[8] K. Sakamura, Ed. *μITRON Specification.* TRON Association, 1990.

[9] K. Sakamura, Ed. *Specification of the Chip Based on the TRON Architecture.* TRON Association, 1990.

[10] K. Sakamura, Ed. *TRON Specification Chip: Guide Book for the Construction of Evaluation Systems.* TRON Association, 1990.

[11] K. Sakamura, Ed. *TRON Specification Chip Standard Assembler Specifications.* TRON Association, 1990.

[12] K. Sakamura, Ed. *BTRON1 Specification AV Manager Specification.* TRON Association, 1991.

[13] K. Sakamura, Ed. *TRON Specification Chip Architecture Overview.* TRON Association, 1991.

[14] K. Sakamura, Ed. *TRON-specification VLSI CPU Standard Handbook.* Personal Media Corporation, 1991. in Japanese.

[15] CTRON Technical Committee of TRON Association. *Outline of CTRON*, Vol. 1 of *New Edition of CTRON Interface Specification.* Ohmsha, Ltd., Nov. 1992. in Japanese.

[16] K. Sakamura, Ed. *BTRON1 Programing Standard Handbook.* Personal Media Corporation, 1992. in Japanese.

[17] K. Sakamura, Ed. *BTRON2 Kernel Standard Handbook.* Personal Media Corporation, 1992. in Japanese.

[18] K. Sakamura, Ed. *ITRON Standard Guidebook '92-'93.* Personal Media Corporation, 1992. in Japanese.

[19] K. Sakamura, Ed. *ITRON/FILE Standard Handbook.* Personal Media Corporation, 1992. in Japanese.

[20] K. Sakamura, Ed. *TRON-specification CHIP Standard Guidebook.* Personal Media Corporation, 1992. in Japanese.

[21] K. Sakamura, Ed. *TRON-specification FPU Standard Handbook.* Personal Media Corporation, 1992. in Japanese.

[22] K. Sakamura, Ed. *TRON Standard System Bus TOBUS.* TRON Association, 1992.

[23] K. Sakamura, Ed. *TRON Standard System Bus TOXBUS.* TRON Association, 1992.

[24] CTRON Technical Committee of TRON Association. *Communication Control Interface(CASE/P, FTAM, Syntax Conversion Utilities)*, Vol. 7 of *New Edition of CTRON Interface Specification.* Ohmsha, Ltd., Feb. 1993. in Japanese.

[25] CTRON Technical Committee of TRON Association. *Communication Control Interface(CMISE)*, Vol. 9 of *New Edition of CTRON Interface Specification.* Ohmsha, Ltd., Sep. 1993. in Japanese.

[26] CTRON Technical Committee of TRON Association. *Communication Control Interface(ISDN User Control), Speech Path Control Interface*, Vol. 10 of *New Edition of CTRON Interface Specification.* Ohmsha, Ltd., Jan. 1993. in Japanese.

[27] CTRON Technical Committee of TRON Association. *Communication Control Interface(Layer Common, Basic Communication Control)*, Vol. 6 of *New Edition of CTRON Interface Specification.* Ohmsha, Ltd., Feb. 1993. in Japanese.

[28] CTRON Technical Committee of TRON Association. *Communication Control Interface(MHS/MTA, MHS/MS, OSI/TP)*, Vol. 8 of *New Edition of CTRON Interface Specification.* Ohmsha, Ltd., Mar. 1993. in Japanese.

[29] CTRON Technical Committee of TRON Association. *Data Storage Control Interface(General File Management, Database Management)*, Vol. 4 of *New Edition of CTRON Interface Specification.* Ohmsha, Ltd., Sep. 1993. in Japanese.

[30] CTRON Technical Committee of TRON Association. *Design Guidance :Fault Tolerance*, Vol. Appendix 1 of *New Edition of CTRON Interface Specification.* Ohmsha, Ltd., Sep. 1993. in Japanese.

[31] CTRON Technical Committee of TRON Association. *Design Guidance :Software Portability*, Vol. Appendix 2 of *New Edition of CTRON Interface Specification.* Ohmsha, Ltd., Aug. 1993. in Japanese.

[32] CTRON Technical Committee of TRON Association. *Execution Control Interface, Operation Administration and Maintenance Management Interface*, Vol. 5 of *New Edition of CTRON Interface Specification.* Ohmsha, Ltd., Sep. 1993. in Japanese.

[33] CTRON Technical Committee of TRON Association. *I/O Control Interface*, Vol. 3 of *New Edition of CTRON Interface Specification.* Ohmsha, Ltd., Aug. 1993. in Japanese.

[34] CTRON Technical Committee of TRON Association. *Kernel Interface*, Vol. 2 of *New Edition of CTRON Interface Specification.* Ohmsha, Ltd., Aug. 1993. in Japanese.

[35] K. Sakamura, Ed. *μITRON 3.0 Standard Handbook.* Personal Media Corporation, 1993. in Japanese.

[36] K. Sakamura, Ed. *TRON Human Interface Specifications.* TRON Association, 1993. English Version of "TRON Human Interface Specifications for Computers in Everyday Life".

[37] K. Sakamura, Ed. *TRON Human Interface Specifications for Computers in Everyday Life.* Personal Media Corporation, 1993. in Japanese.

[38] K. Sakamura, Ed. *ITRON Standard Guidebook 2.* Personal Media Co., Dec. 1994. in Japanese.

[39] K. Sakamura, Ed. *TRON Human Interface Specifications.* Personal Media Co., Mar. 1996. (in Japanese).

3 Books

[1] Hitachi, Ltd., Ed. *Realtime Operating System HI68K.* Personal Media Corporation, 1987. in Japanese.

[2] K. Sakamura. *Computer City.* Iwanami Shoten, Nov. 1987. in Japanese.

[3] K. Sakamura. *The Making of TRON.* Kyoritsu Publishing, 1987. in Japanese.

[4] K. Sakamura. *New Concepts From TRON Project.* Iwanami Shoten, 1987. in Japanese.

[5] K. Sakamura. *TRON Will Change Computers.* Nihon Jitsugyo Publishing, 1987. in Japanese.

[6] Y. Saeki, K. Sakamura, and A. Akagi. *Future of Computer and Children.* Iwanami Booklet No. 109. Iwanami Shoten, 1988. in Japanese.

[7] K. Sakamura, Ed. *Introduction to ITRON: Concepts and Implementations.* Iwanami Shoten, 1988. in Japanese.

[8] K. Sakamura. *Introduction to TRON.* Kyoritsu Publishing, 1988. in Japanese.

[9] K. Sakamura. *The TRON Declaration.* Walkman Books. Epic/SONY Records, 1988. in Japanese.

[10] K. Sakamura, Ed. *The Computers in the Future.* Kadokawa Shoten, 1989. in Japanese.

[11] T. Ohkubo. *Introduction to CTRON.* com series. Ohmsha Ltd., 1990. in Japanese.

[12] K. Sakamura, Ed. *Computer Augmented Environments – Technologies and Perspectives of Everywhere Computing.* Personal Media Co., 1994. (Translation of CACM vol. 36, no. 7, Special Issue on "Computer Augmented Environments: Back to the Real World").

4 Technical Papers

4.1 General Issues

[1] K. Sakamura. TRON – Total Architecture. In *Proceedings of Architecture Workshop in Japan '84* (Aug. 1984), IPSJ, pp. 41–50. in Japanese.

[2] M. Hatayama, and K. Sakamura. Intelligent Technology and Computer Science. In *Thinking about Science and Technology.* Shobunsha, 1985, pp. 61–89. in Japanese.

[3] K. Sakamura. Future of the Computer. In *Challenging the Frontiers of Technology.* Nikkei Science, 1985, pp. 179–210. in Japanese.

[4] K. Sakamura. The Objectives of the TRON Project. In *TRON Project 1987* (1987), Springer-Verlag, pp. 3–16.

[5] K. Sakamura. The TRON Project. *IEEE Micro*, Vol. 7, No. 2 (Apr. 1987), pp. 8–14.

[6] K. Sakamura. What Does TRON Mean? Where is TRON Now? *Transactions of JSPE*, Vol. 53, No. 10 (Oct. 1987), pp. 44–47. in Japanese.

[7] K. Sakamura. TRON Project – in Search of Better Interaction Between the Computer and the Individual. *The University of Tokyo Library Bulletin*, Vol. 27, No. 7/8 (Oct. 1988), pp. 59–70. in Japanese.

[8] K. Sakamura. TULS: TRON Universal Language System. In *TRON Project 1988* (1988), Springer-Verlag, pp. 3–19.

[9] J. Farrell. TRON A Lack of Technical Understanding Outside Japan. *Microprocessors and Microsystems*, Vol. 13, No. 8 (Oct. 1989), pp. 555.

[10] J. D. Mooney. TRON: A View from the U.S.A. *Microprocessors and Microsystems*, Vol. 13, No. 8 (Oct. 1989), pp. 550–553.

[11] J. Ready. TRON Architecture Faces a Challenging U.S. Market. *Microprocessors and Microsystems*, Vol. 13, No. 8 (Oct. 1989), pp. 554.

[12] K. Sakamura. The Computerized Society. In *TRON Project 1989* (1989), Springer-Verlag, pp. 3–14.

[13] K. Sakamura. The Concepts Behind the TRON Project and Development. *Journal of Information Processing Society of Japan*, Vol. 30, No. 5 (May 1989), pp. 522–531. in Japanese.

[14] K. Sakamura. Ken Sakamura answers key questions about TRON. *Microprocessors and Microsystems*, Vol. 13, No. 8 (Oct. 1989), pp. 548–549.

[15] K. Sakamura. The TRON Project. *Microprocessors and Microsystems*, Vol. 13, No. 8 (Oct. 1989), pp. 493–502.

[16] K. Sakamura. TRON Project and Its Background. In *Proceedings of Microcomputer Conference in Japan '89* (May 1989), JEIDA, pp. 25–33. in Japanese.

[17] K. Sakamura. The Current Japanese Computer Scene. *IEEE Micro*, Vol. 10, No. 2 (Apr. 1990), pp. 12–13.

[18] K. Sakamura. TRON and the Standardization of Software. *Computer Software*, Vol. 7, No. 3 (1990), pp. 83–89. in Japanese.

[19] K. Sakamura. TRON-concept Intelligent House. *The Japan Architect* (Apr. 1990), pp. 35–40. in Japanese.

[20] K. Sakamura. TRON-concept Intelligent House. *Living Life*, No. 192 (1990), pp. 6–10.

[21] K. Sakamura. TRON in the Future. In *The Planning of the Future*, K. Takeuchi, Ed. University of Tokyo Press, 1990. in Japanese.

[22] K. Sakamura. The TRON Intelligent House. *IEEE Micro*, Vol. 10, No. 2 (Apr. 1990), pp. 6–7.

[23] K. Sakamura. Computerized Living Environment. *Transactions of IEICE*, Vol. 111–D, No. 5 (1991), pp. 347–348. in Japanese.

[24] K. Sakamura. Media and Computerized Living. *IPSJ SIG Notes on Information Media*, 1-1 (May 1991), IPSJ, pp. 1–6. in Japanese.

[25] K. Sakamura. TRON Application Projects: Gearing Up for HFDS. In *Proceedings of the Eighth TRON Project Symposium* (Nov. 1991), IEEE Computer Society Press, pp. 2–14.

[26] H. Hayashi. Defining a Numerical Phonetic Code Set. *Proceedings of TRON Technical Workshop*, Vol. 5, No. 1 (Oct. 1992), pp. 29–46.

[27] K. Saito. TGHC: Time Guarded Horn Clauses. In *Proceedings of the Ninth TRON Project Symposium* (Dec. 1992), IEEE Computer Society Press, pp. 122–135.

[28] A. Watanabe, H. Takada, and K. Sakamura. The Multi-Layered Design Diversity Architecture: Application of the Design Diversity Approach to Multiple System Layers. In *Proceedings of the Ninth TRON Project Symposium* (Dec. 1992), IEEE Computer Society Press, pp. 116–121.

[29] T. Hardjono, T. Chikaraishi, and T. Ohta. Secure Delegation of Tasks in Distributed Systems. In *Proceedings of the Tenth TRON Project Symposium* (Dec. 1993), IEEE Computer Society Press, pp. 98–112.

[30] H. Mori, and K. Sakamura. Complexity Optimization Technique for Sound Synthesis on Digital Sound Processing Architecture. In *Proceedings of the Tenth TRON Project Symposium* (Dec. 1993), IEEE Computer Society Press, pp. 113–125.

[31] K. Sakamura. Infrastructures for an Age of Computerized Environments. In *Proceedings of the Tenth TRON Project Symposium* (Dec. 1993), IEEE Computer Society Press, pp. 2–14.

[32] K. Sakamura. TRON Hyper-Intelligent Building. In *Proceedings of IQ93 Conference* (Jul. 1993), Real Estate Developers' Association of Singapore and Asia-Pacific Exhibitions, pp. 1–11.

[33] K. Sakamura, and H. Takada. Real-Time Processings in TRON Project. In *Proceedings of the RTP '93* (Mar. 1993), IPSJ and IEICE, pp. 1–8. IPSJ SIG Notes on Computer Architectures, Vol. 93, No. 20, in Japanese.

[34] A. Watanabe. A Proposal of the Multi-layered Design Diversity Architecture. Master's thesis, Graduate School of University of Tokyo, Division of Science, Feb. 1993.

[35] A. Watanabe, H. Takada, and K. Sakamura. An Application of the MLDD (Multi-layered Design Diversity) Architecture Reliability Model. *Proceedings of TRON Technical Workshop*, Vol. 5, No. 2 (Mar. 1993), pp. 75–82. in Japanese.

[36] H. Mori. Complexity Optimization Technique for Sound Synthesis on Digital Sound Processing Architectures. Master's thesis, Graduate School of University of Tokyo, Division of Science, Feb. 1994.

[37] K. Sakamura. After a Decade of TRON, What Comes Next. In *Proceedings of the Eleventh TRON Project Symposium* (Dec. 1994), IEEE Computer Society Press, pp. 2–16.

[38] K. Sakamura. Computer City. In *ARS ELECTRONICA 94 Intelligent Environment Band 1* (Jun. 1994), PVS Verleger, pp. 131–137.

[39] K. Sakamura. Computers as Infrastructure in the Future Society and the TRON Project. *Journal of Information Processing Society of Japan*, Vol. 35, No. 10 (Oct. 1994), pp. 895–902. in Japanese.

[40] K. Sakamura. The Prospects Plan for Information Super Highway – TRON Project 10 Years! –. In *Proceedings of the Korea-Japan Joint Workshop on Electronics Technology '94* (Oct. 1994), Korea Electronics Technology Institute, pp. 15–67.

[41] A. Watanabe, and K. Sakamura. Implementation of Backward Error Recovery Mechanism through Exchanging Diverse Operating Systems. *IEICE SIG Report*, FTS 94-402 (Dec. 1994), IEICE, pp. 1–6. in Japanese.

[42] A. Watanabe, and K. Sakamura. MLDD(Multi-Layered Design Diversity) Architecture for Achieving High Design Fault Tolerance Capabilities. In *Proceedings of the First European Dependable Computing Conference (EDCC)* (Oct. 1994), Springer-Verlag (LNCS 854), pp. 336–349.

[43] A. Watanabe, and K. Sakamura. An Operating System Design Fault-Tolerance Scheme by Switching Between Diverse Implementations. *IEICE SIG Report*, FTS 94-31 (Jun. 1994), IEICE, pp. 29–36. in Japanese.

[44] A. Nakajima. Evolution Toward Mobile Multimedia Communication Network. In *Proceedings of the Twelfth TRON Project International Symposium* (Nov.-Dec. 1995), IEEE Computer Society Press, p. 20.

[45] K. Sakamura. Panel Session: The Future of Mobile Computing. In *Proceedings of the Twelfth TRON Project International Symposium* (Nov.-Dec. 1995), IEEE Computer Society Press, p. 22.

[46] M. Shima. Microprocessors Past and Future. In *Proceedings of the Twelfth TRON Project International Symposium* (Nov.-Dec. 1995), IEEE Computer Society Press, pp. 16–18.

[47] H. Takada. Panel Session: TAD: The Data Exchange Format for HFDS. In *Proceedings of the Twelfth TRON Project International Symposium* (Nov.-Dec. 1995), IEEE Computer Society Press, p. 54.

[48] H. Takada, and K. Sakamura. Compact, Low-Cost, but Real-Time Distributed Computing for Computer Augmented Environments. In *Proceedings of the 5th IEEE CS Workshop on Future Trends of Distributed Computing Systems (FTDCS)* (Aug. 1995), IEEE Computer Society, pp. 56–63.

[49] A. Watanabe, and K. Sakamura. Design Fault Tolerance in Operating Systems Based on a Standardization Project. In *Proceedings of 25th International Symposium on Fault Tolerant Computing (FTCS-25)* (Jun. 1995), IEEE Computer Society Press, pp. 372–380.

[50] A. Watanabe, and K. Sakamura. Improving Design Dependability Based on the TRON Loose Standardization Approach. In *Proceedings of the Twelfth TRON Project International Symposium* (Nov.-Dec. 1995), IEEE Computer Society Press, pp. 43–52.

[51] T. Yamane. An Application Adaptive Compression System For Multimedia Data. Master's thesis, Graduate School of University of Tokyo, Division of Science, Feb. 1995.

[52] A. Watanabe. *A Study of Design Fault Tolerance Based on Natural Design Diversity.* PhD thesis, School of Science, University of Tokyo, Feb. 1996.

[53] A. Watanabe, and K. Sakamura. Implementation of Design Fault Tolerance Based on a Standardization Project for Operating Systems. *Transactions of IEICE (D-I)*, Vol. J79-D-I, No. 7 (Jul. 1996), pp. 468–474. (in Japanese).

[54] A. Watanabe, and K. Sakamura. A Specification-Based Adaptive Test Case Generation Strategy for Open Operating System Standards. In *Proceedings of the 18th International Conference on Software Engineering (ICSE-18)* (Mar. 1996), IEEE Computer Society Press, pp. 81–89.

4.2 TRONCHIP

[1] K. Sakamura. Development of TRON Chip: a Single Chip VLSI Computer Architecture in the 1990's. In *Proceedings of IFIP TC 10/WG 10.5 International Conference on Very Large Scale Integration* (1985), IFIP, pp. 115–124.

[2] T. Enomoto. M32: Mitsubishi 32-bit Microprocessor Based on TRON CPU Specification. In *Proceedings of the Second TRON Project Symposium* (Mar. 1987), TRON Association, pp. 40–47. in Japanese.

[3] J. J. Farrell III. The CPU to System Connection. In *TRON Project 1987* (1987), Springer-Verlag, pp. 18–25.

[4] H. Inayoshi, and M. Itoh. Development of HF32 Family VLSI Processor. In *Proceedings of the Second TRON Project Symposium* (Mar. 1987), TRON Association, pp. 56–70. in Japanese.

[5] M. Itoh. Architecture Characteristics of GMICRO/300. In *TRON Project 1987* (1987), Springer-Verlag, pp. 273–280.

[6] M. Kainaga, T. Nojiri, and T. Kawasaki. A Study of High Level Language Based Machine Description Language. In *Proceedings of the Second Realtime-OS-TRON Technical Workshop* (Jul. 1987), IEICE, pp. 2–12. in Japanese.

[7] S. Kamiya. Toshiba VLSI CPU Based on TRON CPU Specification. In *Proceedings of the Second TRON Project Symposium* (Mar. 1987), TRON Association, pp. 48–55. in Japanese.

[8] T. Kiyohara, M. Deguchi, and T. Sakao. Implementation Methods of CPU's Based on TRON CPU Specification. In *Proceedings of the Second TRON Project Symposium* (Mar. 1987), TRON Association, pp. 34–39. in Japanese.

[9] T. Kiyohara, M. Deguchi, and T. Sakao. Pipeline Structure of Matsushita 32-bit Microprocessor. In *TRON Project 1987* (1987), Springer-Verlag, pp. 281–289.

[10] M. Miyata, Y. Masubuchi, and H. Kishigami. Design of TX1 Pipeline Structure. In *Proceedings of the Second Realtime-OS-TRON Technical Workshop* (Jul. 1987), IEICE, pp. 13–22. in Japanese.

[11] K. Namimoto, T. Satoh, and A. Kanuma. TX Series Based on TRONCHIP Architecture. In *TRON Project 1987* (1987), Springer-Verlag, pp. 291–308.

[12] Y. Nozuyama, A. Nishimura, and J. Iwamura. Testability Design of High-Performance 32bit-Microprocessor TX1. In *Proceedings of the National Convention of IEICE: Semiconductor and Device* (1987), pp. 1–124. in Japanese.

[13] K. Sakamura. Architecture of the TRON VLSI CPU. *IEEE Micro*, Vol. 7, No. 2 (Apr. 1987), pp. 17–31.

[14] K. Sakamura. Architecture of VLSI CPU in the TRON Project. In *Proceedings of the Second TRON Project Symposium* (Mar. 1987), TRON Association, pp. 1–33.

[15] K. Sakamura. Instruction Format of TRON VLSI CPU. In *Proceedings of the Third Realtime-Architecture-TRON Technical Workshop* (Oct. 1987), IEICE, pp. 8–39. in Japanese.

[16] K. Sakamura. TRON VLSI CPU: Concepts and Architecture. In *TRON Project 1987* (1987), Springer-Verlag, pp. 199–238.

[17] A. J. Smith. Design Considerations for TRON Cache Memories. In *TRON Project 1987* (1987), Springer-Verlag, pp. 239–247.

[18] K. Takagi, T. Nishimukai, K. Iwasaki, I. Kawasaki, and H. Inayoshi. Outline of GMICRO/200 and Memory Management Mechanism. In *TRON Project 1987* (1987), Springer-Verlag, pp. 259–272.

[19] O. Tomisawa, T. Yoshida, M. Matsuo, T. Shimizu, and T. Enomoto. Design Considerations of the GMICRO/100. In *TRON Project 1987* (1987), Springer-Verlag, pp. 249–258.

[20] T. Yoshida, M. Matsuo, T. Ueda, and T. Shimizu. Branch Prediction in a Pipelined Microprocessor. *IPSJ SIG Notes on Microcomputer*, 44-1 (Mar. 1987), IPSJ. in Japanese.

[21] A. Bigazzi, J. E. Lillge, and D. E. Jaskolski. An Integrated Software Development Toolkit for the GMICRO/200. In *TRON Project 1988* (1988), Springer-Verlag, pp. 363–380.

[22] C. Hori, J. Iwamura, and M. Miyata. Design Methodology of TX1 Based on the TRON Architecture. *IEICE SIG Reports*, CPSY 88–58 (Dec. 1988), IEICE, pp. 9–13. in Japanese.

[23] H. Inayoshi, I. Kawasaki, T. Nishimukai, and K. Sakamura. Realization of GMICRO/200. *IEEE Micro*, Vol. 8, No. 2 (Apr. 1988), pp. 12–21.

[24] S. Ishimaru, and K. Tamaru. Development Support System for TX Series. In *TRON Project 1988* (1988), Springer-Verlag, pp. 351–361.

[25] N. Itoh, H. Nojima, and Y. Mori. Architectural Features of OKI 32-Bit Microprocessor. In *TRON Project 1988* (1988), Springer-Verlag, pp. 247–262.

[26] J. Iwamura, H. Kishigami, A. Ishii, and K. Usami. Implementation and Evaluation of the TRONCHIP Specification for the TX1. In *TRON Project 1988* (1988), Springer-Verlag, pp. 285–300.

[27] J. Iwamura, T. Tokumura, and K. Okamoto. 32-bit Microprocessor Family Based on TRON Architecture, TX Series. *TOSHIBA Review*, Vol. 43, No. 11 (1988), pp. 1–4. in Japanese.

[28] K. Iwasaki, H. Aoki, M. Hanawa, I. Kawasaki, T. Nakazawa, and H. Inayoshi. A Consideration of 2-clock Bus Cycle Access for GMICRO/200 Microprocessor. In *Proceedings of the Fall National Convention of IEICE* (1988), pp. c–2–92. in Japanese.

[29] Y. Kashiwagi, H. Chaki, and M. Narushima. Development of a C Compiler for GMICRO Microprocessor Based on TRON Architecture. In *TRON Project 1988* (1988), Springer-Verlag, pp. 341–350.

[30] H. Kida, M. Watabe, T. Nakamikawa, S. Morinaga, S. Kawasaki, and H. Inayoshi. A Floating Point Processing Unit for the GMICRO CPU. In *TRON Project 1988* (1988), Springer-Verlag, pp. 301–316.

[31] M. Kimura, T. Iwasaki, S. Mori, K. Fujita, and S. Hazama. A 40 MB/s 32 Bit DMA Controller with 3411 Product Terms PLA. In *TRON Project 1988* (1988), Springer-Verlag, pp. 332–339.

[32] H. Kishigami, Y. Masubuchi, T. Utsumi, T. Miyamori, and M. Miyata. CPU Architecture of 32bit Microprocessor TX1 Based on TRONCHIP Specification. *IPSJ SIG Notes on Microcomputer*, 48-9 (Jan. 1988), IPSJ, pp. 65–72. in Japanese.

[33] T. Kitahara, M. Yuhara, A. Fujihira, M. Mitsuhashi, and M. Itoh. High Performance Bus Interface of GMICRO/300. In *TRON Project 1988* (1988), Springer-Verlag, pp. 317–329.

[34] T. Kiyohara, T. Sakao, K. Adachi, and O. Nishijima. Design Considerations of the Matsushita 32-Bit Microprocessor for Real-Memory Systems. In *TRON Project 1988* (1988), Springer-Verlag, pp. 263–273.

[35] E. Masuda, and K. Okamoto. Design Methodology of the TRONCHIP TX1. *Proceedings of TRON Technical Workshop*, Vol. 1, No. 2 (Oct. 1988), pp. 49–58. in Japanese.

[36] T. Matsuzaki, M. Deguchi, and T. Sakao. Parallel Variable-Length Instruction Decoding. *Proceedings of TRON Technical Workshop*, Vol. 1, No. 2 (Oct. 1988), pp. 33–36. in Japanese.

[37] T. Miyamori, H. Kishigami, and M. Miyata. The Characteristic of TRONCHIP Instruction Set in the 32bit MPU TX1 System. *IEICE SIG Reports*, CPSY 88–57 (Dec. 1988), IEICE, pp. 1–8. in Japanese.

[38] T. Miyamori, H. Kishigami, and M. Miyata. Considerations for CPU Architecture of 32bit Microprocessor TX3 Based on TRONCHIP Specification. *IEICE SIG Reports*, CPSY 87–53 (Mar. 1988), IEICE, pp. 31–36. in Japanese.

[39] M. Miyata, H. Kishigami, K. Okamoto, and S. Kamiya. The TX1 32-Bit Microprocessor: Performance Analysis and Debugging Support. *IEEE Micro*, Vol. 8, No. 2 (Apr. 1988), pp. 37–46.

[40] S. Narita, T. Okada, M. Hanawa, and T. Nishimukai. High-Speed Branch Control Scheme for Microprogram-Controlled Microprocessor. *Proceedings of TRON Technical Workshop*, Vol. 1, No. 2 (Oct. 1988), pp. 37–48. in Japanese.

[41] Y. Nishikawa, M. Deguchi, and T. Sakao. An Examination of the Fundamental Configuration of the Microprocessor for Virtual Memory Systems. In *TRON Project 1988* (1988), Springer-Verlag, pp. 275–283.

[42] T. Nishimukai, H. Inayoshi, K. Takagi, K. Iwasaki, I. Kawasaki, M. Hanayama, and T. Okada. Cache-based Pipeline Architecture in the Hitachi H32/200 32-bit Microprocessor. In *Proceedings of the International Conference on Computer Design* (Rye Brook, NY, Oct. 1988), pp. 102–105.

[43] A. Nishimura, Y. Nozuyama, and J. Iwamura. Testability Design of a 32bit Microprocessor TX1. *IEICE SIG Reports*, ICD 88–28 (Jun. 1988), IEICE, pp. 9–15. in Japanese.

[44] Y. Nozuyama, A. Nishimura, and J. Iwamura. Design for Testability of a 32-bit Microprocessor, the TX1. In *Proceedings of the International Test Conference 1988* (Washington D. C., Sep. 1988), pp. 172–182.

[45] T. Okada, F. Arakawa, S. Narita, K. Iwasaki, K. Takagi, T. Nishimukai, T. Kawasaki, and H. Inayoshi. Some Techniques to Improve GMICRO/200 Performance Utilizing Pipeline Processing. In *Proceedings of the Fourth Realtime-Architecture-TRON Technical Workshop* (Feb. 1988), IEICE, pp. 4–13. in Japanese.

[46] K. Okamoto, M. Miyata, H. Kishigami, T. Miyamori, and T. Sato. Design Considerations for 32bit Microprocessor TX3. In *Proceedings of the 33rd IEEE Computer Society International Conference* (1988), IEEE Computer Society Press, pp. 25–29.

[47] Y. Saitoh, T. Yoshida, M. Matsuo, Y. Watanabe, and T. Shimizu. Design of Pipeline Structure in a TRON Based Microprocessor GMICRO/100. *IEICE SIG Reports*, CPSY 88–59 (Mar. 1988), IEICE. in Japanese.

[48] K. Sakamura, K. Kinbara, and Y. Tominaga. The TRON Project and Development of a TRON-Spec 32-Bit Microprocessor. In *Proceedings of 1988 Symposium on VLSI Circuits* (Tokyo, 1988), The Japan Society of Applied Physics and the IEEE Solid-State Circuits Council in Cooperation with the IEICE.

[49] K. Sakamura, R. Sano, and K. Honma. Introducing Tobus, the System Bus in the TRON Architecture. *IEEE Micro*, Vol. 8, No. 2 (Apr. 1988), pp. 47–59.

[50] T. Shimizu, T. Yoshida, Y. Saito, M. Matsuo, and T. Enomoto. A 32bit Microprocessor Based

on the TRON Architecture: Design of the GMICRO/100. In *Proceedings of the 33rd IEEE Computer Society International Conference* (1988), IEEE Computer Society Press, pp. 30–33.

[51] K. Tamaru, S. Kamiya, and M. Miyata. Development Support System for TRON TX Series. *TOSHIBA Review*, Vol. 43, No. 11 (1988), pp. 905–908. in Japanese.

[52] O. Tomisawa, N. Yamada, K. Saito, and S. Ishiyama. VLSI Microprocessor. *Technical Reviews of Mitsubishi Electric*, Vol. 62, No. 8 (1988), pp. 657–660.

[53] M. Tonomura, I. Kawasaki, H. Inayoshi, and K. Hashimoto. Common Controlling Method for Microprogram. In *Proceedings of the Fall National Convention of IEICE* (1988), pp. C-2-92. in Japanese.

[54] T. Yaguchi, K. Tanaka, K. Tamaru, and A. Kanuma. Performance Analysis of Token Ring LAN Processor TRL1 Which Super-integrates the 32bit TRONCHIP TX1. In *Proceedings of the Fourth Realtime-Architecture-TRON Technical Workshop* (Feb. 1988), IEICE, pp. 14–25. in Japanese.

[55] T. Yoshida, Y. Saitoh, M. Matsuo, and T. Shimizu. The Pipelining Mechanism of a TRON Based Microprocessor GMICRO/100. *IEICE SIG Reports*, CPSY 87-52 (Mar. 1988), IEICE. in Japanese.

[56] D. Agarwal, F. Wang, and M. Ghiassi. Generation and Debugging of Optimized Code for the TRON Architecture. In *TRON Project 1989* (1989), Springer-Verlag, pp. 297–320.

[57] F. Arakawa, K. Iwasaki, N. Yamaguchi, and M. Hanawa. Proposal of Design for Testability of VLSI Processors and Its Application to GMICRO/200. *Proceedings of TRON Technical Workshop*, Vol. 2, No. 2 (Jul. 1989), pp. 27–38. in Japanese.

[58] Y. Asao, T. Yoshida, and K. Tamaru. Designs for a Single Board Computer with the TRON Specification Microprocessor TX1. *Proceedings of TRON Technical Workshop*, Vol. 2, No. 2 (Jul. 1989), pp. 1–9. in Japanese.

[59] C. Franklin, and M. Haden. Advanced Optimizing Compilers Boost Performance on TRON Specification Chip Pipelined CISC Architectures. In *TRON Project 1989* (1989), Springer-Verlag, pp. 253–270.

[60] K. Hashimoto, M. Kubo, A. Hasegawa, S. Yoshioka, S. Matsui, and M. Tonomura. Microprogram Evaluation Scheme for GMICRO/200. *Proceedings of TRON Technical Workshop*, Vol. 2, No. 1 (Apr. 1989), pp. 1–10. in Japanese.

[61] J. Hinata, T. Yoshida, Y. Saito, A. Ohtsuka, T. Shimizu, and O. Tomisawa. Implementation and Performance Evaluation of the M32/100. In *TRON Project 1989* (1989), Springer-Verlag, pp. 285–295.

[62] J. Hinata, S. Ishiyama, T. Yoshida, O. Tomisawa, and J. Korematsu. TRON Specification 32-bit Microprocessor M32/100. *Technical Reviews of Mitsubishi Electric*, Vol. 63, No. 11 (1989), pp. 921–924.

[63] A. Ishii, H. Kishigami, K. Usami, and J. Iwamura. Implementation and Evaluation of the TRON Specification for the TX1. *IEICE SIG Reports*, ICD 89-13 (Apr. 1989), IEICE, pp. 37–42. in Japanese.

[64] J. Iwamura, C. Hori, and M. Miyata. Design Methodology of a VLSI Processor Based on the TRON Architecture. In *Design Methodologies for VLSI and Computer Architecture* (1989), pp. 341–345.

[65] S. Iwata, T. Shimizu, M. Matsuo, T. Yoshida, J. Hinata, and O. Tomisawa. Implementation of a 32-bit Microprocessor GMICRO/100 Based on TRON Specification: (1) Implementation and Evaluation of Microprogram. In *Proceedings of the 38 th National Convention IPSJ* (1989), IPSJ. in Japanese.

[66] R. Kato, T. Miyamori, S. Hayashida, and M. Miyata. Performance Evaluation of 32-bit Microprocessor TX1. In *Proceedings of the 39th National Convention IPSJ* (1989), IPSJ, pp. 1816–1817. in Japanese.

[67] S. Katsunori, T. Shimizu, S. Iwata, T. Yoshida, J. Hinata, and O. Tomisawa. Implementation of a 32-bit Microprocessor GMICRO/100 Based on TRON Specification: (3) Microprogramming Support System on the Relational Database. In *Proceedings of the 38 th National Convention IPSJ* (1989), IPSJ. in Japanese.

[68] S. Kawasaki, M. Watabe, and S. Morinaga. A Floating Point VLSI Chip for the TRON Architecture: An Architecture for Reliable Numerical Programming. *IEEE Micro*, Vol. 9, No. 3 (Jun. 1989), pp. 26–44.

[69] K. Kimura, T. Kiyohara, M. Deguchi, and T. Sakao. Instruction Decoding Method for a 32-Bit Microprocessor Based on TRON Specification. *Proceedings of TRON Technical Workshop*, Vol. 2, No. 3 (Oct. 1989), pp. 11–18. in Japanese.

[70] H. Kishigami, and T. Miyamori. Performance Analysis of TRON 32-bit TX1 Microprocessor. *TOSHIBA Review*, Vol. 44, No. 7 (1989), pp. 566–569. in Japanese.

[71] H. Kishigami, T. Miyamori, and M. Miyata. The Effectiveness of TRONCHIP Instructions in the TX1 System. In *Proceedings of the 34th IEEE Computer Society International Conference — COMPCON Spring 1989* (1989), IEEE Computer Society Press, pp. 43–47.

[72] T. Kitahara, T. Satoh, T. Ohshima, and A. Yoshitake. Pipeline Structure of GMICRO/300 32bit Microprocessor. *Proceedings of TRON Technical Workshop*, Vol. 2, No. 3 (Oct. 1989), pp. 1–10. in Japanese.

[73] M. Matsuo, T. Ueda, T. Yoshida, and Y. Saitoh. The Instruction Pipeline Used for the TRON Based 32-bit Microprocessor M32/100 and Its Performance Evaluation. *IEICE SIG Reports*, ICD 89–161 (Nov. 1989), IEICE. in Japanese.

[74] T. Miyamori, T. Yoshida, and H. Kishigami. Design of Microcomputer Systems Using the TX1 Family LSIs. In *TRON Project 1989* (1989), Springer-Verlag, pp. 271–284.

[75] T. Nakano, Y. Saitoh, M. Matsuo, T. Ueda, Y. Watanabe, T. Yoshida, S. Iwata, S. Kobayashi, T. Shimizu, and J. Hinata. The Logic Verification Method Applied to a TRON Based Microprocessor GMICRO/100. *IEICE SIG Reports*, CAS 89–8 (Jun. 1989), IEICE. in Japanese.

[76] A. Nishimura, Y. Nozuyama, and J. Iwamura. Design for Testability of a 32Bit Microprocessor TX1 and Its Application to the Evaluation and Debugging. *Transactions of IEICE*, Vol. J72–C–II, No. 5 (May 1989), pp. 449–455. in Japanese.

[77] Y. Nozuyama, A. Nishimura, and J. Iwamura. Implementation and Evaluation of Microinstruction Controlled Self Test Using a Masked Microinstruction Scheme. In *Proceedings of the International Test Conference 1989* (Washington D. C., Aug. 1989), pp. 624–632.

[78] A. Ohtsuka, S. Kobayashi, F. Kitamura, Y. Kittaka, T. Yoshida, and J. Hinata. The Bus-Interface in M32/100. *Proceedings of TRON Technical Workshop*, Vol. 2, No. 2 (Jul. 1989), pp. 11–25. in Japanese.

[79] K. Okamoto, H. Kishigami, and T. Miyamori. The Characteristic and Effectiveness of TX1 Instructions Based on TRON Specification. *Proceedings of TRON Technical Workshop*, Vol. 2, No. 1 (Apr. 1989), pp. 53–64. in Japanese.

[80] K. Sakamura, and T. Enomoto. 32-bit Microprocessors Based on the TRON Specification. *Microprocessors and Microsystems*, Vol. 13, No. 8 (Oct. 1989), pp. 503–513.

[81] K. Sakamura, and T. Enomoto. 32-bit Microprocessors Based on the TRON Specification. *Journal of Information Processing Society of Japan*, Vol. 30, No. 5 (May 1989), pp. 565–573. in Japanese.

[82] T. Shimizu, S. Iwata, Y. Saito, T. Yoshida, M. Matsuo, J. Hinata, and K. Saito. A 32-bit Microprocessor with High Performance Bit-map Manipulation Instructions. In *Proceedings of the 1989 International Conference on Computer Design: VLSI in Computers and Processors* (Cambridge, MA, Oct. 1989), pp. 406–409.

[83] M. Suzuki, Y. Nishikawa, M. Deguchi, and T. Sakao. The Microprogram Verification of a 32-Bit Microprocessor MN10400 Based on TRON Specification. *IEICE SIG Reports*, ICD 89–162 (Nov. 1989), IEICE. in Japanese.

[84] T. Takahashi, N. Ito, T. Hoshino, Y. Watanabe, K. Sakamura, H. Takada, H. Nakamura, and N. Nishio. Development of a Parallel Computer System Using TRON Chip and Its Application to Physics. *Proceedings of TRON Technical Workshop*, Vol. 2, No. 1 (Apr. 1989), pp. 21–30. in Japanese.

[85] T. Tokumura, E. Masuda, C. Hori, K. Usami, M. Miyata, and J. Iwamura. Design of a 32-bit Microprocessor, TX1. *IEEE Journal of Solid-State Circuits*, Vol. 24, No. 4 (Aug. 1989), pp. 938–944.

[86] Y. Toshiya, Y. Asao, K. Chiba, and N. Handa. TRON 32-bit TX1 Single-board Computer. *TOSHIBA Review*, Vol. 44, No. 7 (1989), pp. 570–573. in Japanese.

[87] K. Usami, and J. Iwamura. Optimized Design Method for Full-Custom Microprocessors. In *Proceedings of the IEEE 1989 Custom Integrated Circuits Conference* (San Diego, CA, May 1989), pp. 19.5.1–19.5.5.

[88] K. Usami, and J. Iwamura. Optimized Design Method for Full-Custom Microprocessors. *IPSJ SIG Notes on Design Automation*, 47-1 (May 1989), IPSJ. in Japanese.

[89] Y. Watanabe, T. Shimizu, S. Iwata, Y. Saito, T. Yoshida, and O. Tomisawa. Implementation of a 32-bit Microprocessor GMICRO/100 Based on TRON Specification: (2) Management of Microprogram and Design of Microdecoder by Relational Database. In *Proceedings of the 38 th National Convention IPSJ* (1989), IPSJ. in Japanese.

[90] C. Franklin, and C. Rosenberg. Inline Procedures Boost Performance on TRON Architecture. In *TRON Project 1990* (1990), Springer-Verlag, pp. 275–292.

[91] S. Fukuda, and M. Itoh. Introduction and Features of TOXBUS (TRON-Specification Bus). *Proceedings of TRON Technical Workshop*, Vol. 3, No. 1 (Jun. 1990), pp. 65–78. in Japanese.

[92] K. Kimura, T. Kiyohara, and M. Deguchi. Instruction Decoder Applied to Variable-Length Instruction. *IEICE SIG Report*, CPSY 90–86 (Nov. 1990), IEICE. in Japanese.

[93] Y. Kimura, H. Shida, S. Sasaki, and H. Ito. SRM32: Implementation of Symbolic ROM Monitor on GMICRO F32 Series. In *TRON Project 1990* (1990), Springer-Verlag, pp. 325–345.

[94] T. Kitahara, and T. Satoh. The GMICRO/300 32-bit Microprocessor. *IEEE Micro*, Vol. 10, No. 3 (Jun. 1990), pp. 68–75.

[95] T. Kitahara, T. Satoh, T. Ohshima, and A. Fujihira. Performance Evaluations of TRON Based 32-bit Microprocessor GMICRO/300. *IEICE SIG Report*, ICD 90-5 (1990), IEICE.

[96] T. Kiyohara, M. Deguchi, T. Sakao, K. Adachi, O. Nishijima, S. Araki, E. Tadamatsu, H. Miyazaki, and T. Sakurai. 32-Bit Microprocessor MN10400. *National Technical Report*, Vol. 36, No. 3 (Jun. 1990), pp. 63–70.

[97] T. Kiyohara, and K. Adachi. 32 Bit Microprocessor MN10400. *Proceedings of TRON Technical Workshop*, Vol. 2, No. 4 (Feb. 1990), pp. 57–63. in Japanese.

[98] M. Miyazaki, T. Kiyohara, T. Watanabe, M. Deguchi, and T. Sakao. The Pipleline Control System and Verification Method of a 32-bit Microprocessor MN10400 Based on TRON Specification. *IEICE SIG Reports*, ICD 90–3 (Apr. 1990), IEICE. in Japanese.

[99] M. Miyazaki, T. Kiyohara, T. Watanabe, M. Deguchi, and T. Sakao. The Pipeline Control System and Verification Method of a 32-bit Microprocessor MN10400 Based on TRON Specification. *IEICE SIG Report*, ICD 90-3 (1990), IEICE.

[100] Y. Mori, Y. Haneda, Y. Arakawa, T. Mori, and M. Kumazawa. Implementation and Evaluation of Oki 32-bit Microprocessor O32. In *TRON Project 1990* (1990), Springer-Verlag, pp. 221–234.

[101] H. Nakagawa, A. Yamada, M. Hata, T. Hiraki, K. Nishida, J. Korematsu, K. Sawai, I. Ishida, T. Watanabe, and A. Ohsaki. The Configuration of Cache Controller/Memory (CCM) for the GMICRO Family Microprocessors. *Proceedings of TRON Technical Workshop*, Vol. 3, No. 1 (Jun. 1990), pp. 29–38. in Japanese.

[102] Y. Nakao, M. Ohki, and N. Kitakami. A Development of ASSP with M32/100 MPU Core Based on TRON Specifications. *IPSJ SIG Notes on Microcomputer and Workstation*, 62-4 (Jun. 1990). in Japanese,MIC 62-4.

[103] S. Narita, F. Arakawa, T. Okada, and K. Uchiyama. Parallel Instruction Decoding for Variable Length Instruction Set. In *Proceedings of the Fall National Convention of IEICE* (1990), pp. 6–78. in Japanese.

[104] H. Neugass. A Forth Kernel for GMICRO. In *TRON Project 1990* (1990), Springer-Verlag, pp. 293–310.

[105] Y. Nozuyama. Realization of an Efficient Design Verification Test Based on a Microinstruction Controlled Self Test. In *Proceedings of the International Test Conference 1990* (Washington D. C., Sep. 1990), pp. 327–336.

[106] A. Ohtsuka, Y. Saitoh, F. Itomitsu, , S. Iwata, and T. Yoshida. Testability Features of the 32-bit Microprocessor M32/10. *IEICE SIG Reports*, ICD 90–4 (Apr. 1990), IEICE. in Japanese.

[107] K. Okada, M. Itoh, S. Fukuda, T. Hirosawa, T. Utsumi, K. Yoshioka, Y. Tanigawa, and K. Hirano. Performance Evaluation of TOXBUS. In *TRON Project 1990* (1990), Springer-Verlag, pp. 347–374.

[108] C. Reiher, and W. P. Taylor. The GMICRO Microprocessor and the AT&T UNIX Operating System. In *TRON Project 1990* (1990), Springer-Verlag, pp. 311–324.

[109] M. Sakamoto, T. Shimizu, and K. Saitoh. The Design of M32/100's Bitmap Instructions Used

in the Graphic Primitive. In *TRON Project 1990* (1990), Springer-Verlag, pp. 261–271.

[110] K. Sakamura, and T. Enomoto. 32-Bit Microprocessors Based on the TRON Architecture Specification. *Transactions of Information Processing Society of Japan*, Vol. 30, No. 5 (Feb. 1990), pp. 565–573. in Japanese.

[111] M. Suzuki, T. Kiyohara, and M. Deguchi. Design Considerations of On-Chip-Type Floating-Point Units. In *TRON Project 1990* (1990), Springer-Verlag, pp. 235–248.

[112] T. Ueda, M. Matsuo, S. Iwata, and T. Yoshida. The Functional Simulator of the TRON Based 32-bit Microprocessor M32/100. *IEICE SIG Report*, VLD 89-111,ICD 89-199 (1990), IEICE.

[113] T. Ueda, M. Matsuo, S. Iwata, and T. Yoshida. The Functional Simulator of the TRON Based 32-bit Microprocessor M32/100. *IEICE SIG Reports*, VLD 89–111 (Mar. 1990), IEICE. in Japanese.

[114] T. Watanabe, M. Tazumi, T. Kiyohara, and M. Deguchi. Logic Verification of High Performance Processor MN10400 Based on TRON Specification for Real Memory System. *IEICE SIG Report*, FTS 90–3 (Apr. 1990), IEICE. in Japanese.

[115] T. Watanabe, M. Tazumi, T. Kiyohara, and M. Deguchi. Logic Verification of High Performance Processor MN10400 Based on TRON Specification for Real Memory System. *IEICE SIG Report*, FTS 90-3, VLD 90-3 (1990), IEICE.

[116] A. Yamada, H. Nakagawa, M. Hata, M. Satoh, K. Nishida, and T. Hiraki. The Design Method of High Speed Cache Controller/Memory(CCM) for the GMICRO Family Microprocessors. In *TRON Project 1990* (1990), Springer-Verlag, pp. 249–260.

[117] T. Yoshida, M. Matsuo, T. Ueda, and Y. Saito. A Strategy for Avoiding Pipeline Interlock Delays in a Microprocessor. In *Proceedings of the 1990 International Conference on Computer Design: VLSI in Computers and Processors (ICCD '90)* (Cambridge, Massachusetts, Sep. 1990), pp. 14–19.

[118] K. Yoshioka. TOBUS Outline and Its Feature. *Proceedings of TRON Technical Workshop*, Vol. 3, No. 1 (Jun. 1990), pp. 47–64. in Japanese.

[119] A. Kabemoto, and H. Yoshida. The Architecture of the Sure System 2000 Communications Processor. *IEEE Micro*, Vol. 11, No. 4 (Aug. 1991), pp. 28–31, 73–78.

[120] M. Kainaga, K. Yamada, and H. Inayoshi. Analysis of SPEC Benchmark Programs. In *Proceedings of the Eighth TRON Project Symposium* (Nov. 1991), IEEE Computer Society Press, pp. 208–215.

[121] M. Kainaga, K. Yamada, and H. Chaki. CISC, Optimizing Compiler and Super Scalar. *Proceedings of TRON Technical Workshop*, Vol. 3, No. 3 (1991), pp. 55–73. in Japanese.

[122] S. Kinoshita, and Y. Mori. Development of a Single-board Computer System with TRON Specification Chip O32. *Proceedings of TRON Technical Workshop*, Vol. 4, No. 1 (Jul. 1991), pp. 53–62. in Japanese.

[123] Y. Kittaka, T. Nasu, N. Kobayashi, and K. Saitoh. Development of M32/100 Application System. *Proceedings of TRON Technical Workshop*, Vol. 3, No. 3 (1991), pp. 43–54. in Japanese.

[124] H. Neugass, G. Espin, H. Nunoe, R. Thomas, and D. Wilner. VxWorks: An Interactive Development Environment and Real-Time Kernel for GMICRO. In *Proceedings of the Eighth TRON Project Symposium* (Nov. 1991), IEEE Computer Society Press, pp. 196–207.

[125] Y. Saito, H. Yoshida, H. Takada, and K. Sakamura. Godzilla's Guide to Developing a Programming Environment for a New CPU. In *Proceedings of the 32th Programming Symposium* (Tokyo, Jan. 1991), IPSJ, pp. 131–142. in Japanese.

[126] Y. Shibata, M. Okazaki, M. Asai, and N. Kanazawa. Development of TOXBUS-Based BUS Interface LSI. In *Proceedings of the Spring National Convention of IEICE* (Mar. 1991), IEICE.

[127] M. Tazumi. The Method for Implementing the Microprogram-Simulator. *IPSJ SIG Notes on Computer Architecture*, 87-6 (Mar. 1991), IPSJ. in Japanese.

[128] O. Tomisawa. Recent Advances in TRON-Spec. Chips. In *Proceedings of the Eighth TRON Project Symposium* (Nov. 1991), IEEE Computer Society Press, pp. 178–184.

[129] K. Yamada, M. Kainaga, H. Yajima, Y. Tawara, and S. Kawanoue. C Compiler Optimization for GMICRO. In *Proceedings of the 43rd National Convention of IPSJ* (Oct. 1991), IPSJ, pp. 5.203–5.204.

[130] T. Yoshiba, T. Shimizu, S. Mizugaki, and J. Hinata. The GMICRO/100 32-bit Microprocessor. *IEEE Micro*, Vol. 11, No. 4 (Aug. 1991), pp. 20–23, 62–72.

[131] H. Yoshida, Y. Saitoh, H. Takada, and K. Sakamura. A Study on the Register Passing of Parameters on the TRON Specification Chip. *Proceedings of TRON Technical Workshop*, Vol. 3, No. 3 (1991), pp. 29–42. in Japanese.

[132] T. Yoshida, M. Matsuo, and S. Iwata. The Approach to Multiple Instruction Execution in the GMICRO/400 Processor. In *Proceedings of the Eighth TRON Project Symposium* (Nov. 1991), IEEE Computer Society Press, pp. 185–195.

[133] S. Hayashida, and K. Tamaru. Optimizing Method of C Compiler for TRON Architecture. In *Proceedings of the Ninth TRON Project Symposium* (Dec. 1992), IEEE Computer Society Press, pp. 70–76.

[134] K. Hirano. A M32/100 Application to the X-Terminal. *Proceedings of TRON Technical Workshop*, Vol. 4, No. 3 (Mar. 1992), pp. 13–23. in Japanese.

[135] H. Iino, H. Takahashi, T. Sukemura, M. Kimura, K. Fujita, and S. Mori. A 289MFLOPS Single-Chip Supercomputer. In *1992 IEEE International Solid-State Circuits Conference Digest of Technical Papers* (Feb. 1992), IEEE Computer Society Press, pp. 112–113.

[136] S. Inoue, S. Matsui, and M. Suzuki. TRON-specification CHIP Compatibility Validation. In *Proceedings of the Ninth TRON Project Symposium* (Dec. 1992), IEEE Computer Society Press, pp. 47–55.

[137] Y. Kashiwagi, Y. Tawara, H. Chaki, K. Yamada, Y. Kainaga, and T. Isobe. An Optimizing C Compiler for the GMICRO/500 Microprocessor. In *Proceedings of the Ninth TRON Project Symposium* (Dec. 1992), IEEE Computer Society Press, pp. 63–69.

[138] S. Matsui, M. Yamamoto, I. Kawasaki, S. Narita, F. Arakawa, K. Uchiyama, and K. Hashimoto. GMICRO/500 Microprocessor: Pipeline Structure of Superscalar Architecture. In *Proceedings of the Ninth TRON Project Symposium* (Dec. 1992), IEEE Computer Society Press, pp. 56–62.

[139] K. Matsunami, T. Yamana, and H. Ito. Optimizing C Compiler for the TRON Architecture. In *Proceedings of the Ninth TRON Project Symposium* (Dec. 1992), IEEE Computer Society Press, pp. 77–87.

[140] K. Okada, and T. Komachiya. TRON-Specification Serial Bus. *Proceedings of TRON Technical Workshop*, Vol. 4, No. 3 (Mar. 1992), pp. 1–11. in Japanese.

[141] T. Ueda, H. Kondo, T. Yoshida, and T. Miyake. Evaluation of the Microprocessor M32/100-boosted Performance by Onchip Cache in Xbench Program. In *Proceedings of the Workshop on Computer Systems; Integrated Circuits and Devices* (Oct. 1992), Vol. 92, IPSJ, pp. 9–16. in Japanese.

[142] H. Yoshida. Data Profiler for Code Optimizations. Master's thesis, Graduate School of University of Tokyo, Division of Science, Feb. 1992.

[143] M. Awaga, and H. Takahashi. The microVP 64-Bit Vector Coprocessor: A New Implementation of High-Performance Numerical Computation. *IEEE Micro*, Vol. 13, No. 5 (Oct. 1993), pp. 24–36.

[144] H. Goto, and Y. Nozuyama. Design of 32-bit TX2 Microprocessor Based on TRON Specification. In *Proceedings of the Tenth TRON Project Symposium* (Dec. 1993), IEEE Computer Society Press, pp. 68–77.

[145] T. Inoue. TRON-specification Chip Compatibility Validation of TX1. *Proceedings of TRON Technical Workshop*, Vol. 5, No. 2 (Mar. 1993), pp. 67–73. in Japanese.

[146] A. Matsui. GMICRO/500 Microprocessor Application System: Performance Evaluation of Graphic Primitives. In *Proceedings of the Tenth TRON Project Symposium* (Dec. 1993), IEEE Computer Society Press, pp. 61–67.

[147] S. Mori, H. Kishigami, I. Kawasaki, and Y. Saitoh. Future Technology Directions in TRON-Specification Chips. In *Proceedings of the Tenth TRON Project Symposium* (Dec. 1993), IEEE Computer Society Press, p. 79.

[148] M. Yamamoto, and I. Kawasaki. Performance Evaluation of GMICRO/500 Microprocessor for CTRON based kernel. In *Proceedings of the Tenth TRON Project Symposium* (Dec. 1993), IEEE Computer Society Press, pp. 52–60.

[149] H. Hayashi, and E. Masuda. Accelerating Multiplication and Division in High-Speed Microprocessor Systems. *Proceedings of TRON Technical Workshop*, Vol. 6, No. 1 (Mar. 1994), pp. 37–45. in Japanese.

[150] J. Korematsu, T. Ueda, M. Matsuo, K. Tani, N. Okumura, K. Ishimi, T. Yoshida, Y. Saito,

and J. Hinata. A 32-bit Superscalar Microprocessor Gmicro/400 for Embedded Systems. In *Proceedings of the Eleventh TRON Project Symposium* (Dec. 1994), IEEE Computer Society Press, pp. 115–121.

[151] S. Mori. The Present and Future of the TRON-specification CHIP – Promoting Open Architecture and Standardization –. *Journal of Information Processing Society of Japan*, Vol. 35, No. 10 (Oct. 1994). in Japanese.

[152] Y. Nozuyama, H. Mitani, T. Fukumoto, T. Utsumi, and K. Hashimoto. A 32-bit Microprocessor with Efficient Testable Designs, the TX2. In *Proceedings of the Eleventh TRON Project Symposium* (Dec. 1994), IEEE Computer Society Press, pp. 122–130.

[153] H. Shimbo, E. Masuda, and K. Okada. Quantitative Evaluation of the Reliability Benefits of Maintenance Bus Implementation. In *Proceedings of the Eleventh TRON Project Symposium* (Dec. 1994), IEEE Computer Society Press, pp. 131–139.

[154] K. Tani, S. Kobayashi, M. Matsuo, Y. Saito, and J. Hinata. Hardware Structure of 32-bit Microprocessor GMICRO/400. *Proceedings of TRON Technical Workshop*, Vol. 6, No. 1 (Mar. 1994), pp. 37–45. in Japanese.

[155] T. Usaka, Y. Sasaki, H. Takada, and K. Sakamura. A Software Development Environment for TRON-Specification Chips. In *Poster Session Material of the Eleventh TRON Project Symposium* (Dec. 1994), TRON Association.

4.3 ITRON

[1] A. Matsui, and K. Sakamura. A Draft Plan of Standard Realtime Operating System for Microprocessors: TRON – 3. Kernel (2). In *Proceedings of the 28th National Convention IPSJ* (1984), IPSJ, pp. 277–278. in Japanese.

[2] A. Matsui, and K. Sakamura. I-TRON/86. In *Proceedings of the 29th National Convention IPSJ* (1984), IPSJ, pp. 1559–1560. in Japanese.

[3] K. Sakamura. A Draft Plan of Standard Realtime Operating System for Microprocessors: TRON – 1. Architecture. In *Proceedings of the 28th National Convention IPSJ* (1984), IPSJ, pp. 273–274. in Japanese.

[4] K. Sakamura. I-TRON Architecture. In *Proceedings of the 29th National Convention IPSJ* (1984), IPSJ, pp. 1555–1556. in Japanese.

[5] K. Sakamura. Real-Time Operating System - ITRON. *IPSJ SIG Notes on Operating System*, 24-10 (1984), IPSJ, pp. 59–64. in Japanese.

[6] T. Shimizu, and K. Sakamura. A Draft Plan of Standard Realtime Operating System for Microprocessors: TRON – 4. Development Environment. In *Proceedings of the 28th National Convention IPSJ* (1984), IPSJ, pp. 279–280. in Japanese.

[7] M. Umeda, and K. Sakamura. A Draft Plan of Standard Realtime Operating System for Microprocessors: TRON – 2. Kernel (1). In *Proceedings of the 28th National Convention IPSJ* (1984), IPSJ, pp. 275–276. in Japanese.

[8] M. Umeda, and K. Sakamura. I-TRON/68K. In *Proceedings of the 29th National Convention IPSJ* (1984), IPSJ, pp. 1557–1558. in Japanese.

[9] K. Sakamura. Realtime Operating System: ITRON. *Journal of Robotics Society of Japan*, Vol. 3, No. 5 (Oct. 1985), pp. 459–466. in Japanese.

[10] K. Sakamura. ITRON - Real-Time Operating System: Architecture and Future Perspective. *IPSJ SIG Notes on Computer Architecture*, 61-1 (1986), IPSJ, pp. 1–12.

[11] H. Horita, K. Nakada, T. Shimizu, and K. Saito. The Structure and Performance of ITRON for NS32000. In *Proceedings of the First Realtime-OS-TRON Technical Workshop* (Apr. 1987), IEICE, pp. 40–51. in Japanese.

[12] H. Monden. Introduction to ITRON, the Industry-oriented Operating System. *IEEE Micro*, Vol. 7, No. 2 (Apr. 1987), pp. 45–52.

[13] H. Monden, and T. Iwasaki. An Proposal to Performance Evaluation for the ITRON. In *Proceedings of the Third Realtime-Architecture-TRON Technical Workshop* (Oct. 1987), IEICE, pp. 2–5. in Japanese.

[14] H. Monden, T. Iwasaki, and N. S. Fukui. The Implementation and Evaluation of the RX116 Version 2.0. In *TRON Project 1987* (1987), Springer-Verlag, pp. 35–43.

[15] K. Sakamura. ITRON: An Overview. In *TRON Project 1987* (1987), Springer-Verlag, pp. 29–34.

[16] K. Sakamura. The Present and Future of the ITRON Real-Time Operating Architecture. *IPSJ SIG Notes on Computer Architecture*, 61-1 (1987), IPSJ, pp. 11. In Japanese.

[17] A. Shimohara. REALOS/286: An Implementation of ITRON/MMU on 80286. In *TRON Project 1987* (1987), Springer-Verlag, pp. 45–56.

[18] H. Takeyama, T. Shimizu, and K. Horikoshi. The HI Series of Operating Systems with the ITRON Architecture. In *TRON Project 1987* (1987), Springer-Verlag, pp. 57–71.

[19] K. Kudo, and A. Honda. An Implementation of Micro-ITRON on the F^2M-8. *Proceedings of TRON Technical Workshop*, Vol. 1, No. 2 (Oct. 1988), pp. 59–68. in Japanese.

[20] K. Nakata, H. Tsubota, T. Shimizu, K. Saitoh, and T. Enomoto. MR7700: Implementation of μ-ITRON Specification on 16-Bit Single-Chip Microcontroller. In *TRON Project 1988* (1988), Springer-Verlag, pp. 55–66.

[21] J. Ready, and D. Kalinsky. An Integrated Embedded Systems Software Development Environment for ITRON. In *TRON Project 1988* (1988), Springer-Verlag, pp. 67–76.

[22] K. Sakamura. Design Concepts of Micro-ITRON. *Proceedings of TRON Technical Workshop*, Vol. 1, No. 1 (Jun. 1988), pp. 1–17. in Japanese.

[23] H. Takeyama, T. Shimizu, and M. Kobayakawa. HI8: A Realtime Operating System with μITRON Specifications for the H8/500. In *TRON Project 1988* (1988), Springer-Verlag, pp. 35–54.

[24] S. Hirao. Static Implementation of a Real-time Operating System. *Proceedings of TRON Technical Workshop*, Vol. 2, No. 3 (Oct. 1989), pp. 63–78. in Japanese.

[25] Y. Kisuki, H. Tsubota, and K. Saitoh. MR3200F: File System Based on the ITRON/FILE Specification. *Proceedings of TRON Technical Workshop*, Vol. 2, No. 3 (Oct. 1989), pp. 43–51. in Japanese.

[26] N. Morita, S. Kitajima, H. Saitoh, K. Kuwazura, and J. Sugano. Application of ITRON Specification Based OS in the Mobile Radio Communication System. In *TRON Project 1989* (1989), Springer-Verlag, pp. 59–68.

[27] S. Nakano, A. Ikeda, and O. Miyagishi. Design and Evaluation of Modular Programs Operating under ITRON for ISDN Terminals. In *Transactions of IEICE* (1989), Vol. J73-B-I, IEICE, pp. 44–52. in Japanese.

[28] K. Nakata, H. Tsubota, T. Shimizu, and K. Saito. Performance Evaluation of MR7700: A Realtime Operating System Based on the μ-ITRON Specification. *Proceedings of TRON Technical Workshop*, Vol. 2, No. 1 (Apr. 1989), pp. 31–40. in Japanese.

[29] N. Nishio, and K. Sakamura. Considerations on Designing the ITRON Specification for a Tightly-Coupled Multiprocessor Environment – Real-Time Scheduling of the ITRON External Kernel –. *Proceedings of TRON Technical Workshop*, Vol. 2, No. 3 (Oct. 1989), pp. 53–62. in Japanese.

[30] T. Nissim, and J. Ready. The Design of a Real-time Operating Sysem Kernel for the GMICRO Family of Processors. In *TRON Project 1989* (1989), Springer-Verlag, pp. 69–75.

[31] A. Shimohara, T. Minohara, K. Kudoh, and H. Itoh. REALOS/F32: Implementation of ITRON2 Specification on GMICRO F32. In *TRON Project 1989* (1989), Springer-Verlag, pp. 33–43.

[32] H. Takeyama, and K. Sakamura. Design and Implementation of the ITRON Specification — An Embedded Industrial Real-time OS. *Microprocessors and Microsystems*, Vol. 13, No. 8 (Oct. 1989), pp. 514–524.

[33] H. Takeyama, and K. Sakamura. Design Concept and Implementation of the ITRON Specification Embedded Real-time Operating System. *Journal of Information Processing Society of Japan*, Vol. 30, No. 5 (May 1989), pp. 532–543. in Japanese.

[34] H. Takeyama, T. Shimizu, and M. Kobayakawa. Design Concept and Implementation of μITRON Specification for the H8/500 Series. In *Proceedings of the 34th IEEE Computer Society International Conference — COMPCON Spring 1989* (1989), IEEE Computer Society Press, pp. 48–53.

[35] H. Takeyama, T. Shimizu, and M. Kobayakawa. Design Concept and Implementation of μITRON Specification for the Single Chip Microcomputer H8/500 Series. *Proceedings of TRON Technical Workshop*, Vol. 2, No. 1 (Apr. 1989), pp. 65–72. in Japanese.

[36] H. Tsubota, O. Yamamoto, T. Shimizu, and K. Saitoh. MR3210 Based on ITRON2 Specification Realtime OS. In *TRON Project 1989* (1989), Springer-Verlag, pp. 17–31.

[37] D. Wallace. An Integrated Approach to HI8 System Development. In *TRON Project 1989* (1989), Springer-Verlag, pp. 45–58.

[38] S. Yamada, K. Horikoshi, T. Shimizu, and H. Takeyama. HI32: An ITRON-specification Operating System for the H32/200. In *TRON Project 1989* (1989), Springer-Verlag, pp. 77–97.

[39] O. Yamamoto, K. Nakata, H. Tsubota, and K. Saitoh. Performance Evaluation of MR3200: A Realtime Operating System Based on the MICRO-ITRON Specification. *Proceedings of TRON Technical Workshop*, Vol. 2, No. 2 (Jul. 1989), pp. 39–50. in Japanese.

[40] A. Yokozawa, K. Fukuoka, and K. Tamaru. Real-Time OS Nucleus for TX1 TRON-Architecture 32-bit Microprocessor. *TOSHIBA Review*, Vol. 44, No. 7 (1989), pp. 574–577. in Japanese.

[41] N. Honda, N. Ogata, K. Sakai, and A. Kanomata. Implementation of the ITRON for Z80 Microprosessors. In *Proceedings of the Spring National Convention of IEICE* (Mar. 1990), IEICE, pp. 144–144.

[42] N. Kanekawa, H. Ihara, and H. Katoh. Operating System for Fault-Tolerant Onboard Space Computers. *IPSJ SIG Notes on Microcomputer and Workstation* (Nov. 1990), pp. 64–2.

[43] M. Kobayakawa, T. Nagasawa, T. Shimizu, and H. Takeyama. HI8-3X: A μITRON-Specification Realtime Operating System for H8/300 Series Microcontrollers. In *TRON Project 1990* (1990), Springer-Verlag, pp. 85–99.

[44] N. Nishio, H. Takada, and K. Sakamura. Dynamic Stepwise Task Scheduling Algorithm for a Tightly-Coupled Multiprocessor ITRON. In *TRON Project 1990* (1990), Springer-Verlag, pp. 43–62.

[45] T. Shimizu, M. Kobayashi, and H. Takeyama. HI32A: The File Management System with ITRON/FILE Specification for H32. *Proceedings of TRON Technical Workshop*, Vol. 2, No. 4 (Feb. 1990), pp. 65–73. in Japanese.

[46] D. Wallace. A Graphical Debugger for HI8. In *TRON Project 1990* (1990), Springer-Verlag, pp. 63–84.

[47] K. Yamada, Y. Okada, M. Tamura, and S. Takanashi. An Implementation of Micro-ITRON Specification on the Single Chip Microcontroller TLCS-90 Series. *Proceedings of TRON Technical Workshop*, Vol. 3, No. 1 (Jun. 1990), pp. 39–46. in Japanese.

[48] K. Yamada, S. Takanashi, Y. Okada, and M. Tamura. Realtime OS TR90 Based on Micro-ITRON Specification. In *TRON Project 1990* (1990), Springer-Verlag, pp. 377–390.

[49] A. Yokozawa, K. Fukuoka, and K. Tamaru. Considerations of the Performance of a Real-time OS. In *TRON Project 1990* (1990), Springer-Verlag, pp. 25–42.

[50] K. Fukuoka, A. Yokozawa, and K. Tamaru. Hierarchical Design of a μITRON Specification Kernel: TR2. In *Proceedings of the Eighth TRON Project Symposium* (Nov. 1991), IEEE Computer Society Press, pp. 69–76.

[51] H. Hayashi. A Study of Scheduling Algorithm for Multi Processor Environment. Master's thesis, Graduate School of Musashi Institution of Technology, Mar. 1991. in Japanese.

[52] S. Itoh, and T. Ishikawa. Consideration of Performance Evaluation Method of Realtime Operating System and Its Application to a micro-ITRON OS: HI8. *Proceedings of TRON Technical Workshop*, Vol. 3, No. 3 (1991), pp. 1–14. in Japanese.

[53] T. K. Johnson, and C.-L. Dai. Extending the ITRON2 Specification for MMU Equipped Processors. In *Proceedings of the Eighth TRON Project Symposium* (Nov. 1991), IEEE Computer Society Press, pp. 25–37.

[54] A. Miyatomi, T. Fujimoto, and I. Nakamura. αWIT On-Line Debugger for Application Systems Using a μITRON-Specification Operating System. In *Proceedings of the Eighth TRON Project Symposium* (Nov. 1991), IEEE Computer Society Press, pp. 38–42.

[55] T. Ogasawara. Half-fit: Real-time Dynamic Storage Allocation Technique. Master's thesis, Graduate School of University of Tokyo, Division of Science, Feb. 1991.

[56] K. Saitoh. ITRON Standards. In *Proceedings of the Eighth TRON Project Symposium* (Nov. 1991), IEEE Computer Society Press, pp. 16–24.

[57] K. Sato, H. Tsubota, O. Yamamoto, and K. Saitoh. An Experimental Implementation of Unified Real-Time Operating System. In *Proceedings of the Eighth TRON Project Symposium* (Nov. 1991), IEEE Computer Society Press, pp. 57–68.

[58] H. Takada, and K. Sakamura. Implementation of Inter-processor

Synchronization/Communication and Design Issues of ITRON-MP. In *Proceedings of the Eighth TRON Project Symposium* (Nov. 1991), IEEE Computer Society Press, pp. 44–56.

[59] H. Takada, and K. Sakamura. ITRON-MP: An Adaptive Real-time Kernel Specification for Shared-Memory Multiprocessor Systems. *IEEE Micro*, Vol. 11, No. 4 (Aug. 1991), pp. 24–27, 78–85.

[60] M. Fukuda, and H. Nokubi. An RTOS Allowing Gradual Migration. In *Proceedings of the Ninth TRON Project Symposium* (Dec. 1992), IEEE Computer Society Press, pp. 107–114.

[61] K. Fukuoka, A. Yokozawa, K. Tamaru, and K. Yamada. Universal Real-time Kernel Based on the ITRON Specification. In *Proceedings of the Ninth TRON Project Symposium* (Dec. 1992), IEEE Computer Society Press, pp. 96–106.

[62] T. Matsuyama, Y. Matsui, and D. Fujii. Development of Digital Protection Relay Using Operating System. In *Proceedings of the 44th National Convention of Electric Society* (Mar. 1992), Electric Society. in Japanese.

[63] Y. Saito. Specifying and Testing Operating System Kernel Using Formal Specification Language. Master's thesis, Graduate School of University of Tokyo, Division of Science, Feb. 1992.

[64] Y. Saito, H. Takada, and K. Sakamura. Specifying and Testing ITRON Using A Formal Specification Description Language. *Proceedings of TRON Technical Workshop*, Vol. 4, No. 3 (Mar. 1992), pp. 63–74. in Japanese.

[65] H. Takada, and K. Sakamura. Advances in the ITRON Specifications – Supporting Multiprocessor and Distributed Systems. In *Proceedings of the Ninth TRON Project Symposium* (Dec. 1992), IEEE Computer Society Press, pp. 89–95.

[66] N. Kishi, and T. Ishikawa. Making of ITRON Real-Time OS Simulator. In *Proceedings of the 47th National Convention of IPSJ* (Oct. 1993), IPSJ, pp. 4.55–4.56. in Japanese.

[67] H. Maezawa. CTC-RPC/NIEP: Consistent Time Constrained Remote Procedure Call on Network ITRON Efficient Protocol. Master's thesis, Graduate School of University of Tokyo, Division of Science, Feb. 1993.

[68] H. Maezawa, H. Takada, and K. Sakamura. Design and Implementation of NIEP: Lightweight Protocol for Efficient Realtime Communications. *Proceedings of TRON Technical Workshop*, Vol. 5, No. 2 (Mar. 1993), pp. 51–65. in Japanese.

[69] H. Takada. To Be Standardized or Not To Be Standardized? In *Proceedings of the Tenth TRON Project Symposium* (Dec. 1993), IEEE Computer Society Press, pp. 48–49.

[70] H. Takada, and K. Sakamura. Bounded Spin Lock Algorithm with Preemption. Tech. Rep. 93-2, Department of Information Science, Faculty of Science, University of Tokyo, Jul. 1993.

[71] H. Takada, and K. Sakamura. Intra-Processor and Inter-Processor Synchronizations in Real-Time Multiprocessor Systems. In *Proceedings of the RTP '93* (Mar. 1993), IPSJ and IEICE, pp. 41–48. IPSJ SIG Notes on Computer Architectures, Vol. 93, No. 20, in Japanese.

[72] Y. Kawata, H. Kobayashi, A. Yabu, K. Onogawa, A. Kawasaki, and M. Maekawa. Eunice/ITRON: A Control System Development Environment for ITRON Machine. In *Proceedings of the Eleventh TRON Project Symposium* (Dec. 1994), IEEE Computer Society Press, pp. 91–105.

[73] N. Kishi, K. Matsuura, and T. Ishikawa. Development of ITRON Specification Real-Time Operating System Simulator on MS-DOS. *Proceedings of TRON Technical Workshop*, Vol. 6, No. 1 (Mar. 1994), pp. 11–26. in Japanese.

[74] H. Kobayashi. A Platform for Real-Time Software Development: Full-Lifecycle-Support Language Nike. Master's thesis, Graduate School of University of Tokyo, Division of Science, Feb. 1994.

[75] K. Matsuura, N. Kishi, and T. Ishikawa. Making of ITRON Real-Time OS Simulator. In *Proceedings of the 48th National Convention of IPSJ* (Mar. 1994), IPSJ, pp. 1.71–1.72. in Japanese.

[76] T. Nakano, M. Itabashi, U. Andy, A. Shiomi, and M. Imai. The Evaluation of Silicon TRON Design. *Proceedings of the RTP '94* (Mar. 1994), pp. 79–86. IEICE SIG Notes, CPSY 93-62, in Japanese.

[77] H. Takada, and K. Sakamura. Adaptability and Standardization in the μITRON Specification. *Proceedings of the RTP '94* (Mar. 1994), pp. 71–78. IEICE SIG Notes, CPSY 93-61, in Japanese.

[78] H. Takada, and K. Sakamura. Experimental Implementations of Priority Inheritance

Semaphore on ITRON-specific Kernel. In *Proceedings of the Eleventh TRON Project Symposium* (Dec. 1994), IEEE Computer Society Press, pp. 106–113.

[79] H. Takada, and K. Sakamura. Predictable Spin Lock Algorithms with Preemption. In *Proceedings of the 11th IEEE Workshop on Real-Time Operating Systems and Software (RTOSS)* (May 1994), IEEE Computer Society Press, pp. 2–6.

[80] H. Takada, and K. Sakamura. Real-Time Synchronization Protocols with Abortable Critical Sections. In *Proceedings of the 1st International Workshop on Real-Time Computing Systems and Applications (RTCSA)* (Seoul, Korea, Dec. 1994), pp. 48–52.

[81] H. Takada, K. Tamaru, K. Kudou, T. Shimizu, and H. Tsubota. The Present and Future of the ITRON Subproject – Kernel Specifications and their Implementation –. *Journal of Information Processing Society of Japan*, Vol. 35, No. 10 (Oct. 1994), pp. 903–909. in Japanese.

[82] T. Takeuchi. The Implementation of a Test Data Generator for Automated Testing of ITRON OS. Master's thesis, Graduate School of University of Tokyo, Division of Science, Feb. 1994.

[83] T. Takeuchi, H. Takada, and K. Sakamura. An Implementation of a Test Data Generator for an OS Based on the ITRON specification. *Proceedings of TRON Technical Workshop*, Vol. 6, No. 1 (Mar. 1994), pp. 1–10. in Japanese.

[84] N. Iga, Y. Nakamoto, and H. Monden. Real-Time Software Development System RTplus. In *Proceedings of the Twelfth TRON Project International Symposium* (Nov.-Dec. 1995), IEEE Computer Society Press, pp. 24–33.

[85] T. Nakano, A. Utama, M. Itabashi, A. Shiomi, and M. Imai. Hardware Implementation of a Real-Time Operating System. In *Proceedings of the Twelfth TRON Project International Symposium* (Nov.-Dec. 1995), IEEE Computer Society Press, pp. 34–42.

[86] T. Nakano, A. Utama, M. Itabashi, A. Shiomi, and M. Imai. VLSI Implementation and Evaluation of a Real-Time Operating System. *Transactions of IEICE*, Vol. J78–D-I, No. 8 (Aug. 1995), pp. 679–685. in Japanese.

[87] N. Sakiyama, H. Takada, and K. Sakamura. Bubble Lock: Another Priority-orderd Spin Lock Algorithm. In *Collection of Position Papers for the 2nd Youth Forum in Computer Science and Engineering (YUFORIC)* (Oct. 1995).

[88] H. Takada, and K. Sakamura. Controlling Priority Inversion using Abortions. Tech. Rep. 95-02, Department of Information Science, Faculty of Science, University of Tokyo, Jan. 1995.

[89] H. Takada, and K. Sakamura. μITRON for Small-Scale Embedded Systems. *IEEE MICRO*, Vol. 15, No. 6 (Dec. 1995), pp. 46–54.

[90] H. Takada, and K. Sakamura. Queueing Spin Lock Algorithms with Preemption. *Transactions of IEICE*, Vol. J78–D-I, No. 8 (Aug. 1995), pp. 661–669. in Japanese.

[91] H. Takada, and K. Sakamura. Real-Time Scalability of Nested Spin Locks. In *Proceedings of the 2nd International Workshop on Real-Time Computing Systems and Applications (RTCSA)* (Oct. 1995), IEEE Computer Society Press, pp. 160–167.

[92] H. Takada, and K. Sakamura. Towards a Scalable Real-Time Kernel for Asymmetric Multiprocessor Systems. *IEICE SIG Report (Proceedings of RTP'95)*, RT 94-573 (Mar. 1995), IEICE, pp. 1–8. in Japanese.

[93] H. Takada, and K. Sakamura. Towards a Scalable Real-Time Kernel for Function-Distributed Multiprocessors. In *Proceedings of the IFAC/IFIP 20th Workshop on Real-Time Programming (WRTP)* (Nov. 1995).

[94] H. Mori, Y. Mano, H. Takada, and K. Sakamura. μITRON bus: A Real-Time Control LAN for Open Network Environment. In *Proceedings of the 3rd International Workshop on Real-Time Computing Systems and Applications (RTCSA)* (Oct. 1996), IEEE CS Press. (to appear).

[95] M. Suzuki, K. Okabe, R. Tokita, and T. Ishikawa. Development of ITRON simulator MITOS. In *IEICE Technical Report (Proceedings of RTP'96)* (Mar. 1996), Vol. 95, Institute of Electronics, Information and Communication Engineers, pp. 7–14. in Japanese.

[96] H. Takada. *Studies on Scalable Real-Time Kernels for Function-Distributed Multiprocessors.* PhD thesis, School of Science, University of Tokyo, Jul. 1996.

[97] H. Takada, and K. Sakamura. Inter- and Intra-Processor Synchronizations in Multiprocessor Real-Time Kernel. In *Proceedings of the 4th International Workshop on Parallel and Distributed Real-Time Systems (WPDRTS)* (Apr. 1996), IEEE CS Press, pp. 69–74.

[98] H. Takada, and K. Sakamura. Scalable Implementations of Multiprocessor Real-Time Kernels. In *IEICE Technical Report (Proceedings of RTP'96)* (Mar. 1996), Vol. 95, Institute of Electronics, Information and Communication Engineers, pp. 1–6. (in Japanese).

[99] C.-D. Wang, H. Takada, and K. Sakamura. Performance Evaluation of Priority Inheritance Spin Locks. In *IEICE Technical Report (Proceedings of RTP'96)* (Mar. 1996), Vol. 95, Institute of Electronics, Information and Communication Engineers, pp. 47–54. (in Japanese).

[100] C.-D. Wang, H. Takada, and K. Sakamura. Priority Inheritance Spin Locks for Multiprocessor Real-Time Systems. In *Proceedings of the International Symposium on Parallel Architectures, Algorithms, and Networks (I-SPAN)* (Jun. 1996), IEEE CS Press, pp. 70–76.

4.4 CTRON

[1] K. Kumazaki. Design of the CTRON File Management. In *TRON Project 1987* (1987), Springer-Verlag, pp. 173–182.

[2] S. Narimatsu. Design of CTRON Input-Output Control Interface. In *TRON Project 1987* (1987), Springer-Verlag, pp. 183–196.

[3] T. Ohkubo, T. Wasano, and I. Kogiku. Configuration of the CTRON Kernel. *IEEE Micro*, Vol. 7, No. 2 (Apr. 1987), pp. 33–44.

[4] K. Sakamura. CTRON: An Overview. In *TRON Project 1987* (1987), Springer-Verlag, pp. 154–156.

[5] T. Wasano, M. Ohminami, Y. Kobayashi, T. Ohkubo, and K. Sakamura. Design Principles and Configuration of CTRON. In *Proceedings of the Second Realtime-OS-TRON Technical Workshop* (Jul. 1987), IEICE, pp. 25–39. in Japanese.

[6] T. Wasano, M. Ohminami, Y. Kobayashi, T. Ohkubo, and K. Sakamura. Design Principle and Configuration of CTRON. In *Proceedings of FJCC '87 – 1987 Fall Joint Computer Conference* (Dallas, Texas, 1987).

[7] T. Wasano, M. Ohminami, Y. Kobayashi, T. Ohkubo, and K. Sakamura. Design of CTRON. In *TRON Project 1987* (1987), Springer-Verlag, pp. 157–172.

[8] Y. Baba, M. Ohminami, H. Kusumoto, and H. Kosugi. Design of CTRON Execution Control Interface. In *TRON Project 1988* (1988), Springer-Verlag, pp. 167–187.

[9] Y. Baba, M. Ohminami, H. Kusumoto, and H. Kosugi. Design of CTRON Execution Control Interface. *Proceedings of TRON Technical Workshop*, Vol. 1, No. 1 (Jun. 1988), pp. 35–46. in Japanese.

[10] M. Ishizuka, Y. Ikeda, M. Fukuyoshi, T. Ogawa, T. Sakuma, and M. Matsushita. An Implementation of the CTRON Basic OS. In *TRON Project 1988* (1988), Springer-Verlag, pp. 213–234.

[11] M. Ishizuka, T. Noda, H. Konishi, M. Fukuyoshi, T. Ogawa, and M. Matsushita. An Implementation of CTRON Basic OS. *Proceedings of TRON Technical Workshop*, Vol. 1, No. 1 (Jun. 1988), pp. 81–104. in Japanese.

[12] I. Kogiku, T. Ohkubo, and M. Matsushita. Enhancement of the CTRON Kernel Interface. In *TRON Project 1988* (1988), Springer-Verlag, pp. 189–211.

[13] I. Kogiku, T. Ohkubo, and M. Matsushita. Enhancement of the CTRON Kernel Interface. *Proceedings of TRON Technical Workshop*, Vol. 1, No. 2 (Oct. 1988), pp. 69–86. in Japanese.

[14] J. D. Mooney. Perspectives on CTRON. In *TRON Project 1988* (1988), Springer-Verlag, pp. 135–144.

[15] K. Oda, N. Shimizu, N. Inoue, and Y. Iba. An Implementation of CTRON Basic OS on a Lap-Top Workstation. In *TRON Project 1988* (1988), Springer-Verlag, pp. 235–243.

[16] K. Oda, N. Shimizu, N. Inoue, and Y. Iba. Implementation of CTRON Basic OS on a Lap-top Workstation. *Proceedings of TRON Technical Workshop*, Vol. 1, No. 1 (Jun. 1988), pp. 65–71. in Japanese.

[17] T. Ohrui, K. Suda, and R. Ohkubo. A CTRON Operating System Applicable to Switching Systems. *Proceedings of TRON Technical Workshop*, Vol. 1, No. 1 (Jun. 1988), pp. 73–79. in Japanese.

[18] Y. Shimizu. Design of CTRON Communication Control Interface. In *TRON Project 1988* (1988), Springer-Verlag, pp. 157–166.

[19] M. Tabe. Design of the CTRON Communication Control Interface. *Proceedings of TRON Technical Workshop*, Vol. 1, No. 1 (Jun. 1988), pp. 47–64. in Japanese.

[20] T. Wasano, Y. Kobayashi, and K. Sakamura. CTRON Reference Model. In *TRON Project 1988* (1988), Springer-Verlag, pp. 145–155.

[21] A. Clements. Creating the Universal Computer. *Microprocessors and Microsystems*, Vol. 13, No. 8 (Oct. 1989), pp. 553–554.

[22] M. Fukuyoshi, N. Furuya, M. Ishizuka, and T. Ohta. Design of CTRON Fault Tolerance Functions. In *TRON Project 1989* (1989), Springer-Verlag, pp. 183–208.

[23] M. Ishizuka, N. Furuya, M. Fukuyoshi, and T. Ohta. Design of CTRON Fault Tolerance Functions. *Proceedings of TRON Technical Workshop*, Vol. 2, No. 2 (Jul. 1989), pp. 81–99. in Japanese.

[24] T. Nakamura, and T. Ohrui. A Study of the Support Environment for CTRON-based Operating System. *IEICE SIG Report*, SSE 89-131 (1989), IEICE.

[25] T. Nitta. Design of the CTRON Application Oriented Communication Control Interface. In *TRON Project 1989* (1989), Springer-Verlag, pp. 225–250.

[26] T. Nitta. Design of the CTRON Application Oriented Communication Control Interface. *Proceedings of TRON Technical Workshop*, Vol. 2, No. 2 (Jul. 1989), pp. 61–79. in Japanese.

[27] K. Oda, N. Inoue, T. Murooka, and M. Nakata. An Experiment Implementation for One Level Storage on CTRON Kernel. In *TRON Project 1989* (1989), Springer-Verlag, pp. 209–224.

[28] I. Takenaka, and H. Oda. The CTRON Interface Validation System. In *TRON Project 1989* (1989), Springer-Verlag, pp. 171–181.

[29] T. Wasano, and Y. Kobayashi. Application of CTRON to Communication Networks. *Microprocessors and Microsystems*, Vol. 13, No. 8 (Oct. 1989), pp. 537–547.

[30] T. Wasano, and Y. Kobayashi. Operating System Interface CTRON Applicable to Information Communication Networks. *Journal of Information Processing Society of Japan*, Vol. 30, No. 5 (May 1989), pp. 553–564. in Japanese.

[31] T. Wasano, Y. Kobayashi, T. Terazaki, and K. Sakamura. Design of General Rules in CTRON Interfaces. In *TRON Project 1989* (1989), Springer-Verlag, pp. 135–154.

[32] K. Watanabe, H. Sunaga, and D. Zingale. The Basic Concept of CTRON Switching Control. In *TRON Project 1989* (1989), Springer-Verlag, pp. 155–170.

[33] Y. Adachi, N. Shigeta, and M. Hatanaka. Development of CTRON Operating System for Communication Processing. *Proceedings of TRON Technical Workshop*, Vol. 3, No. 1 (Jun. 1990), pp. 79–89. in Japanese.

[34] A. Chao. Realization on the Micro-CTRON Kernel under pSOS+. In *TRON Project 1990* (1990), Springer-Verlag, pp. 427–432.

[35] T. Fujii, S. Kasuga, and A. Takura. Applying Systems Design Environment "SDE" to CTRON. In *Proceedings of the Spring National Convention of IEICE* (Mar. 1990), IEICE, pp. 408–408.

[36] Y. Fujino, A. Yamakami, Y. Ishitani, and S. Yamashita. Software Construction Method of Operating System Based on CTRON Specification. *IEICE SIG Report*, SSE 90-26 (1990), IEICE.

[37] R. Hama, M. Sawada, T. Ogawa, T. Fukuchi, and M. Komiya. An Implementation of CTRON Specification Based I/O Control on Tightly Coupled Multi-processor System. In *Proceedings of the Autumn National Convention of IEICE* (Oct. 1990), IEICE, pp. 6–91.

[38] T. Hashizume, K. Satoh, T. Hirosawa, K. Miyake, and S. Tatsuzawa. Hardware Organization of the Tightly Coupled Multi-processor System with CTRON. In *Proceedings of the Autumn National Convention of IEICE* (Oct. 1990), IEICE, pp. 6–89.

[39] M. Hatanaka, Y. Adachi, N. Shigeta, Y. Ohmachi, and M. Ohminami. Development of CTRON Operating System for Communication Processing. In *TRON Project 1990* (1990), Springer-Verlag, pp. 201–217.

[40] Y. Igarashi, M. Joh, T. Hirai, K. Kawai, and K. Kawanishi. An Imprementation of CTRON Specipication Based Kernel on Tightly Coupled Multi-processor System. In *Proceedings of the Autumn National Convention of IEICE* (Oct. 1990), IEICE, pp. 6–90.

[41] M. Ishizuka, M. Fukuyoshi, K. Yabe, T. Fukuchi, and T. Onozawa. A Study of Multiple Disk Control on CTRON. In *Proceedings of the Spring National Convention of IEICE* (Mar. 1990), IEICE, pp. 143–143.

[42] M. Joh, Y. Igarashi, T. Hirai, K. Kawai, and K. Kawanishi. A Study of CTRON Specification Kernel to Multi Processer System. *IEICE SIG Report*, SSE 90-65 (1990), IEICE.

[43] S. Kasuga, T. Tokoyoda, T. Itoh, and N. Suzuki. Applying SDE for Switching Program. In *Proceedings of the Autumn National Convention of IEICE* (Oct. 1990), IEICE, pp. 3-63.

[44] H. Kurosawa. On a Method for Performance Evaluation of CTRON Basic OS. In *Proceedings of the First Software Portability Symposium* (Sep. 1990), TRON Association, pp. 115–124. (*TRON Technical Workshop*, Vol. 3, No. 2).

[45] H. Kurosawa, H. Itoh, and O. Watanabe. A Performance Evaluation Method for CTRON Operating System. *Proceedings of TRON Technical Workshop*, Vol. 2, No. 4 (Feb. 1990), pp. 75–83. in Japanese.

[46] H. Kurosawa, O. Watanabe, and Y. Kobayashi. An Evaluation Method of Kernel Products Based on CTRON. In *TRON Project 1990* (1990), Springer-Verlag, pp. 191–200.

[47] M. Matsushita, T. Ebisu, T. Ozeki, and T. Sakuma. Architecture of Tightly Coupled Multiprocessor System with CTRON. In *Proceedings of the Autumn National Convention of IEICE* (Oct. 1990), IEICE, pp. 6–88.

[48] Y. Minowa, T. Furuya, J. Watanabe, K. Morioka, K. Suzuki, and T. Yamada. A Study of Depelopment Support Environment on CTRON Specification OS. *IEICE SIG Report*, SSE 90-66 (1990), IEICE.

[49] J. D. Mooney. Pitfalls on the Road to Portability. In *TRON Project 1990* (1990), Springer-Verlag, pp. 409–426.

[50] J. D. Mooney. Pitfalls on the Road to Portability. In *Proceedings of the First Software Portability Symposium* (Sep. 1990), TRON Association, pp. 17–32. (*TRON Technical Workshop*, Vol. 3, No. 2).

[51] I. A. Newman. Portability in Europe. In *Proceedings of the First Software Portability Symposium* (Sep. 1990), TRON Association, pp. 1–15. (*TRON Technical Workshop*, Vol. 3, No. 2).

[52] C. Nishimura, S. Wada, A. Takei, M. Nakazawa, A. Yamamoto, and K. Nakayama. Methods of Developing Portable Extended Operating Systems. In *Proceedings of the First Software Portability Symposium* (Sep. 1990), TRON Association, pp. 87–96. (*TRON Technical Workshop*, Vol. 3, No. 2).

[53] Y. Nosaka, A. Ishii, and H. Kusumoto. Porting the Extended OS to the Basic System Based on GMICRO. In *Proceedings of the First Software Portability Symposium* (Sep. 1990), TRON Association, pp. 55–73. (*TRON Technical Workshop*, Vol. 3, No. 2).

[54] H. Oda, T. Suga, and M. Nakamura. The CTRON Interface Validation Trials. In *Proceedings of the First Software Portability Symposium* (Sep. 1990), TRON Association, pp. 75–86. (*TRON Technical Workshop*, Vol. 3, No. 2).

[55] K. Oda, Y. Izumi, H. Ohta, N. Shimizu, and N. Yoshida. Porting to i386-based Basic OS (OS/CT). In *Proceedings of the First Software Portability Symposium* (Sep. 1990), TRON Association, pp. 31–54. (*TRON Technical Workshop*, Vol. 3, No. 2).

[56] K. Oda, Y. Izumi, H. Ohta, N. Shimizu, and N. Yoshida. Portability Consideration of i386-Based Basic OS (OS/CT). In *TRON Project 1990* (1990), Springer-Verlag, pp. 149–172.

[57] T. Ohta, T. Terazaki, T. Ohkubo, and M. Hanazawa. CTRON Software Portability Experiment. In *Proceedings of the First Software Portability Symposium* (Sep. 1990), TRON Association, pp. 1–16. (*TRON Technical Workshop*, Vol. 3, No. 2).

[58] T. Ohta, T. Terasaki, T. Ohkubo, M. Hanasawa, and M. Ohtaka. CTRON Software Portability Evaluation. In *TRON Project 1990* (1990), Springer-Verlag, pp. 133–148.

[59] R. Saitoh, Y. Kanada, and M. Matsumoto. Control Methods for Picture Signal Storage on CTRON Interface. In *Proceedings of the Autumn National Convention of IEICE* (Oct. 1990), IEICE, pp. 6–128.

[60] T. Sakano, T. Noda, M. Matsushita, and M. Ohtaka. Portability Evaluation Test on MC68020 Based Basic System. In *Proceedings of the First Software Portability Symposium* (Sep. 1990), TRON Association, pp. 17–29. (*TRON Technical Workshop*, Vol. 3, No. 2).

[61] H. Shibagaki, and T. Wasano. OS Interface Subsetting. *IPSJ SIG Notes on Operating System*, 48-1 (Sep. 1990).

[62] H. Shibagaki, and T. Wasano. OS Interface Subsetting. In *Proceedings of the First Software Portability Symposium* (Sep. 1990), TRON Association, pp. 97–113. (*TRON Technical Workshop*, Vol. 3, No. 2).

[63] H. Shibagaki, and T. Wasano. OS Subset Structure Achieving AP Portability. In *TRON Project 1990* (1990), Springer-Verlag, pp. 173–189.

[64] H. Shibagaki, and T. Wasano. Subsetting of OS Interfaces and AP Portability. In *Proceedings of the 41st National Convention of IPSJ* (Sep. 1990), IPSJ, pp. 4.59–4.60.

[65] J. Watanabe, Y. Minowa, K. Morioka, T. Yamada, and H. Ishihara. A Study of Development Support System on Tightly Coupled Multi-processor System with CTRON. In *Proceedings of the Autumn National Convention of IEICE* (Oct. 1990), IEICE, pp. 6–92.

[66] Y. Igarashi, M. Joh, T. Hirai, K. Kawai, and K. Kawanishi. Realization of CTRON Based Kernel for Tightly Coupled Multi-processor System. *Proceedings of TRON Technical Workshop*, Vol. 3, No. 3 (1991), pp. 15–27. in Japanese.

[67] M. Joh, Y. Igarashi, and T. Ozeki. CTRON-Specification Kernel Implementation for a Tightly Coupled Multiprocessor System. In *Proceedings of the Eighth TRON Project Symposium* (Nov. 1991), IEEE Computer Society Press, pp. 118–129.

[68] Y. Kaneda, and R. Saitoh. Fault Tolerance Function on CTRON General File Management. In *Proceedings of Autumn National Convention of IEICE* (Sep. 1991), IEICE, pp. 6–106. in Japanese.

[69] H. Kise, H. Ikuta, S. Fushimi, A. Takei, and A. Yamamoto. Realization of Real-time System Based on CTRON Interface Communication Control. In *Proceedings of the 42nd National Convention of IPSJ* (Mar. 1991), IPSJ, pp. 4.31–4.32.

[70] T. Koizumi. Topics of CTRON Sub-project in 1991. In *Proceedings of the Eighth TRON Project Symposium* (Nov. 1991), IEEE Computer Society Press, pp. 78–85.

[71] K. Marubayashi, A. Settsu, and H. Itoh. A Development Environment for CTRON Spec.OS(1) – System Components –. In *Proceedings of the 43rd National Convention of IPSJ* (Oct. 1991), IPSJ, pp. 4.39–4.40.

[72] H. Matsuzawa. A Consideration of Naming Rule for Functions. In *Proceedings of the Spring National Convention of IEICE* (Mar. 1991), IEICE.

[73] Y. Nosaka, K. Shigeno, T. Takahashi, T. Okada, and K. Shibuya. An Implementation of Basic OS Based on CTRON Specification. In *Proceedings of the Spring National Convention of IEICE* (Mar. 1991), IEICE.

[74] Y. Nosaka, K. Shigeno, and K. Takayama. A Study on Implementation of Realtime Operating Syste m. *IEICE SIG Report*, SSE 90-113,CMN 91-9 (1991), IEICE.

[75] T. Ohta, T. Terazaki, T. Wasano, and M. Hanazawa. Software Portability in CTRON. In *Proceedings of the Eighth TRON Project Symposium* (Nov. 1991), IEEE Computer Society Press, pp. 86–92.

[76] M. Ohtaka, M. Hanazawa, N. Iwata, T. Sakano, and K. Sudoh. Portability Evaluation of CTRON General File Management. In *Proceedings of the Eighth TRON Project Symposium* (Nov. 1991), IEEE Computer Society Press, pp. 93–102.

[77] K. Saitoh, M. Tabata, and Y. Satoh. Applying Object Oriented Programming to Developing Programs on CTRON Interfaces. In *Proceedings of the Eighth TRON Project Symposium* (Nov. 1991), IEEE Computer Society Press, pp. 103–117.

[78] R. Saitoh, and Y. Kanada. System Initiate and Restart Methods on CTRON Interface. In *Proceedings of the Autumn National Convention of IEICE* (Sep. 1991), IEICE, pp. 6–67.

[79] Y. Saitoh, A. Sekine, K. Saitoh, and K. Naiki. Realization of Highly Real-time System Based on CTRON Interface Specifications. In *Proceedings of the 42nd National Convention of IPSJ* (Mar. 1991), IPSJ, pp. 4.33–4.34.

[80] Y. Sato, Y. Watanabe, and N. Nishimoto. A Study on Switch Fabric Control Software of Broadband ISDN Switching System. In *Proceedings of the 42nd National Convention of IPSJ* (Mar. 1991), IPSJ, pp. 1.263–1.264.

[81] K. Sawada, and K. Noguchi. A Study of Constructing Communication Control Functions. In *Proceedings of the Autumn National Convention of IEICE* (Sep. 1991), IEICE, pp. 3–65.

[82] K. Sekino. A Study on Software Porting from UNIX to CTRON. In *Proceedings of the 43rd National Convention of IPSJ* (Oct. 1991), IPSJ, pp. 5.501–5.502.

[83] A. Settsu, K. Marubayashi, and H. Itoh. A Development Environment for CTRON Spec.OS(2) – Implementation Method –. In *Proceedings of the 43rd National Convention of IPSJ* (Oct. 1991), IPSJ, pp. 4.41–4.42.

[84] N. Shigeta, S. Tomita, and S. Miyata. The Implementation of OSI Protocols in Conformity to

Standardized Interface Specifications. In *Proceedings of the 42nd National Convention of IPSJ* (Mar. 1991), IPSJ, pp. 1.253–1.254.

[85] Y. Terashima, H. Matsuyama, A. Ohtsuka, M. Akihara, and S. Itoh. A Study of Test Environment for CTRON Extension OS. In *Proceedings of the Spring National Convention of IEICE* (Mar. 1991), IEICE.

[86] J. Yamazaki, Y. Watabe, and M. Baba. Object-oriented Call Processing Programs Based on CTRON. *IEICE SIG Report*, SSE 91-79 (1991), IEICE. in Japanese.

[87] H. Yoshise, H. Ikuta, and A. Takei. Realization of Real-Time System Based on CTRON Interface Communication Control. In *Proceedings of the 42nd National Convention of IPSJ* (Mar. 1991), IPSJ, pp. 4.31–4.32. in Japanese.

[88] M. Fukazawa, Y. Watanabe, M. Kakemizu, and M. W. Kim. An ATM Switching Software Using CTRON with Distributed Support Function. In *Proceedings of the Ninth TRON Project Symposium* (Dec. 1992), IEEE Computer Society Press, pp. 194–202.

[89] K. Fukuma, and T. Hasumi. Development of Small Medium Capacity PBX with CTRON Specification OS. *IEICE SIG Report*, SSE 92-52,IN 92-43 (1992), IEICE. in Japanese.

[90] A. Hirata, and T. Ishikawa. A Proposal of Real-time Operating System in Multiprocessor Environment. In *Proceedings of the 44th National Convention of IPSJ* (Mar. 1992), IPSJ, pp. 4.29–4.30. in Japanese.

[91] Y. Kanada, and M. Matsumoto. Realtime Operating System for Storage Communication Processing Systems. In *Proceedings of the Fall National Convention of IEICE* (Sep. 1992), IEICE. in Japanese.

[92] H. Kise, and H. Ikuta. Portability of Real-time System Based on CTRON Interface Communication Control. In *Proceedings of the 45th National Convention of IPSJ* (Oct. 1992), IPSJ, pp. 5.309–5.310. in Japanese.

[93] Y. Mochida, H. Matsuda, H. Ikuta, and T. Ohno. Portability Experiment for CTRON Communication Control (Transport Layer and Session Layer). In *Proceedings of the Ninth TRON Project Symposium* (Dec. 1992), IEEE Computer Society Press, pp. 146–153.

[94] H. Nakajima, Y. Fujino, and H. Hakamada. Study of CTRON Specification OS Simulator. In *Proceedings of the Spring National Convention of IEICE* (Mar. 1992), IEICE, pp. 3–102. in Japanese.

[95] T. Nishihara, J. Kikuchi, and T. Takehisa. A DB/DC Platform for Real-time Operating Systems Based on CTRON Specifications. In *Proceedings of the Ninth TRON Project Symposium* (Dec. 1992), IEEE Computer Society Press, pp. 163–171.

[96] N. Nishimoto, H. Ochiai, Y. Watanabe, and J. Yamazaki. An Experimental Inter-module Distributed Processing Function of ATM Switching Software. In *Proceedings of the Spring National Convention of IEICE* (Mar. 1992), IEICE, pp. 3–76. in Japanese.

[97] C. Nishimura, T. Hayashi, H. Tominaga, and R. Kawai. Portability Experiment for CTRON General Program Management. In *Proceedings of the Second Software Portability Symposium* (Jan. 1992), TRON Association, pp. 19–31. (*TRON Technical Workshop*, Vol. 4, No. 2).

[98] C. Nishimura, N. Iwata, T. Tanaka, and K. Nakayama. Portability Experiment for CTRON General Program Management. In *Proceedings of the Ninth TRON Project Symposium* (Dec. 1992), IEEE Computer Society Press, pp. 137–145.

[99] K. Noguchi, H. Araki, and T. Ohrui. A Study of Communication Software Techniques Aiming at Improving Reusability. In *Proceedings of the Fall National Convention of IEICE* (Sep. 1992), IEICE. in Japanese.

[100] K. Noguchi, T. Ohrui, and I. Kogiku. Modeling of Communication Control Software for Advanced Switching Systems. In *IEEE Region 10 Conference, Tencon 92* (Nov. 1992), IEEE Computer Society Press, pp. 654 – 658.

[101] T. Ohta, T. Terazaki, and T. Wasano. Software Portability Evaluation Experiment in CTRON. In *Proceedings of the Second Software Portability Symposium* (Jan. 1992), TRON Association, pp. 1–17. (*TRON Technical Workshop*, Vol. 4, No. 2).

[102] S. Ohtsuka, M. Kanda, and Y. Nakamoto. A Method to Support to Develop Very Large Software in an Embedded System. In *IPSJ SIG Notes on Software Engineering* (Mar. 1992), IPSJ, pp. 92–84. in Japanese.

[103] T. Ozeki, T. Ogawa, T. Noda, and M. Matsushita. Development of a CTRON-conformant

Operating System on the OKITRON-SV Processor System. In *Proceedings of the Ninth TRON Project Symposium* (Dec. 1992), IEEE Computer Society Press, pp. 172–184.

[104] T. Sakano, H. Matsuda, H. Ikuta, H. Shimojo, and N. Ohtoshi. CTRON Portability Experiment Step 2 (Communication Control). In *Proceedings of the Second Software Portability Symposium* (Jan. 1992), TRON Association, pp. 61–79. (*TRON Technical Workshop*, Vol. 4, No. 2).

[105] O. Sasaki, M. Tsuda, K. Tanaka, K. Suzuki, H. Hatakeyama, and J. Watanabe. A Development Processor System with CTRON Specificati on OS. *IEICE SIG Report*, SSE 91-126,IN 91-129,OS 91-36 (1992), IEICE. in Japanese.

[106] K. Sekino, N. Iwata, T. Hayashi, and T. Tanaka. Measures for Enhacing Portability of Extended OS Program. In *Proceedings of the Second Software Portability Symposium* (Jan. 1992), TRON Association, pp. 47–60. (*TRON Technical Workshop*, Vol. 4, No. 2).

[107] M. Tabata, K. Saito, T. Hayashi, and Y. Satou. Applying Object Oriented Programming to Develop of System Based on the CTRON Interfaces. In *Proceedings of the 44th National Convention of IPSJ* (Mar. 1992), IPSJ, pp. 5.35–5.36. in Japanese.

[108] Y. Terashima, T. Iwahashi, and T. Mizuno. A Development Environment of Scenario Programs for CTRON Communication Control Part. In *Proceedings of the Spring National Convention of IEICE* (Mar. 1992), IEICE. in Japanese.

[109] Y. Terashima, T. Iwahashi, and T. Mizuno. A Study of Conformance Testing CTRON Extended OS. In *Proceedings of the 44th National Convention of IPSJ* (Mar. 1992), IPSJ, pp. 5.251–5.252. in Japanese.

[110] T. Tokuyama, N. Ohtoshi, and Y. Suzuki. A Basic OS Developed for Software Portability. In *Proceedings of the Second Software Portability Symposium* (Jan. 1992), TRON Association, pp. 33–45. (*TRON Technical Workshop*, Vol. 4, No. 2).

[111] M. Uraguchi, and T. Ishikawa. Consideration of Performance Evaluation Method of Realtime Operating System. In *Proceedings of the 45th National Convention of IPSJ* (Oct. 1992), IPSJ, pp. 4.11–4.12. in Japanese.

[112] M. Wakano, and N. Sugiyama. A Study on the Portability of CTRON FTAM-CCL and CMISE-CCL Interfaces. In *Proceedings of the Ninth TRON Project Symposium* (Dec. 1992), IEEE Computer Society Press, pp. 154–161.

[113] K. Yamamoto, S. Futagami, T. Ohkubo, and H. Kurosawa. A CTRON Kernel Benchmark Program. In *Proceedings of the Ninth TRON Project Symposium* (Dec. 1992), IEEE Computer Society Press, pp. 185–193.

[114] K. Yamamoto, T. Takahashi, S. Futagami, and T. Ohkubo. A Study on Performance Evaluation Methods for CTRON Using Benchmark Program. In *Proceedings of the Fall National Convention of IEICE* (Sep. 1992), IEICE. in Japanese.

[115] Y. Fujino, K. Ohtani, A. Yamakami, K. Watanabe, and T. Kan. Applying HC68K, an Operating System Based on CTRON Specifications for a Duplicated Telecommunication System. In *Proceedings of the Tenth TRON Project Symposium* (Dec. 1993), IEEE Computer Society Press, pp. 128–135.

[116] T. Furutono, and M. Fukazawa. An Evaluation of Object-oriented Call Processing Program Based on CTRON. In *Proceedings of the Spring National Convention of IEICE* (Mar. 1993), IEICE, pp. 3–99. in Japanese.

[117] S. Futagami, I. Kogiku, and T. Ohkubo. A Conformance Testing Method for Telecommunication Realtime Platforms. In *IEEE Workshop on Parallel and Distributed Real-Time Systems* (Apr. 1993), IEEE Computer Society Press.

[118] N. Iwata, and M. Hanazawa. Porting Classes and Coding Rules for C Program on CTRON. In *Proceedings of the Tenth TRON Project Symposium* (Dec. 1993), IEEE Computer Society Press, pp. 144–155.

[119] T. Kunieda, S. Sugimoto, and N. Sasaki. A Synchronous Digital Hierarchy Network Management System. *IEEE Communications*, Vol. 31, No. 11 (Nov. 1993), pp. 84–90.

[120] K. Sawada, H. Araki, and T. Ohrui. Implementation and Evaluation of Logical Communication Device Interfaces. In *Proceedings of the Tenth TRON Project Symposium* (Dec. 1993), IEEE Computer Society Press, pp. 136–143.

[121] A. Settsu. The Design of the MP-CTRON for Communications Equipment. In *Proceedings of the 46th National Convention of IPSJ* (Mar. 1993), IPSJ, pp. 4.63–4.64. in Japanese.

[122] T. Soneoka, A. Oizumi, and K. Suda. Highly Multi-Tasking Real-Time Systems and Their Evaluation. In *Proceedings of the Real-Time Systems Symposium* (Dec. 1993), IEEE Computer Society Press, pp. 249–252.

[123] System Interface Conformance Testing Study Group. Present Status of System Interface Conformance Testing and Accrediation. *Journal of Information Processing Society of Japan*, Vol. 34, No. 3 (Mar. 1993), pp. 324–335. in Japanese.

[124] T. Takahashi, K. Yamamoto, T. Futagami, and T. Soneoka. Performance Evaluation by CTRON Kernel Benchmark. In *Proceedings of the Tenth TRON Project Symposium* (Dec. 1993), IEEE Computer Society Press, pp. 156–164.

[125] B. Benton, H. Kobado, and H. Yamada. A Fault-Tolerant Implementation of the CTRON Basic Operating System. In *Proceedings of the Eleventh TRON Project Symposium* (Dec. 1994), IEEE Computer Society Press, pp. 65–74.

[126] Y. Fujino, H. Aoe, and I. Minamikawa. Implementation of a Fault Tolerant Communication Platform, the HPT500. In *Proceedings of the Eleventh TRON Project Symposium* (Dec. 1994), IEEE Computer Society Press, pp. 75–80.

[127] S. Miyata, T. Ozawa, Y. Sadakane, and M. Ohminami. Performance Analysis of Communication Control Programs Based on CTRON Interface. In *Proceedings of the Eleventh TRON Project Symposium* (Dec. 1994), IEEE Computer Society Press, pp. 43–50.

[128] S. Nakahara, J. Gohhara, H. Kohama, and M. Nakao. Expansion of CTRON Interface for Fault-Tolerant System. In *Proceedings of the Eleventh TRON Project Symposium* (Dec. 1994), IEEE Computer Society Press, pp. 81–89.

[129] H. Nakamura, and S. Kosai. A Study of OS Kernel Functions for Debugging. *IEICE SIG Report*, SSE 94-21 (1994), IEICE, pp. 123–128.

[130] T. Ohkubo, T. Soneoka, and M. Hanazawa. The Present and Future of the CTRON Subproject – Real-time Performance and Portability –. *Journal of Information Processing Society of Japan*, Vol. 35, No. 10 (Oct. 1994), pp. 918-925. in Japanese.

[131] T. Tanaka, K. Sekino, Y. Sadakane, and M. Ohminami. CTRON Extended OS Application to a Gateway System. In *Proceedings of the Eleventh TRON Project Symposium* (Dec. 1994), IEEE Computer Society Press, pp. 31–42.

[132] T. Yamamoto, T. Takahashi, S. Futagami, and K. Yamamoto. A Benchmark Program and Normalization Method for Evaluating Communication Systems-Oriented Realtime OS Performance. In *Proceedings of the Eleventh TRON Project Symposium* (Dec. 1994), IEEE Computer Society Press, pp. 20–30.

[133] T. Hayashi, K. Yamagishi, N. Shigeta, and M. Ohminami. Applying a Real-time OS to Transmission Equipment Management. In *Proceedings of the Twelfth TRON Project International Symposium* (Nov.-Dec. 1995), IEEE Computer Society Press, pp. 56–63.

[134] T. Ohkubo. A Multimedia Networking OS: Requirements and Research Issues. In *Proceedings of the Twelfth TRON Project International Symposium* (Nov.-Dec. 1995), IEEE Computer Society Press, pp. 64–72.

[135] T. Ohkubo, S. Kosai, S. Futagami, and M. Ohminami. Design and Evaluation of Realtime Operating System Interfaces for Telecommunication Systems. *Transactions of IEICE*, Vol. J78-D-I, No. 8 (Aug. 1995), pp. 687–698. in Japanese.

[136] T. Tanaka, M. Hakuta, N. Iwata, and M. Ohminami. Approaches to Making Software Porting More Productive. In *Proceedings of the Twelfth TRON Project International Symposium* (Nov.-Dec. 1995), IEEE Computer Society Press, pp. 73–85.

4.5 BTRON

[1] K. Sakamura. BTRON Super Personal Computer. *IPSJ SIG Notes on Computer Architecture*, 57-4 (1985), IPSJ, pp. 59–64. in Japanese.

[2] K. Sakamura. Computer Architecture As a Thought-Support System — the TRON Project. *Science*, Vol. 55, No. 9 (Sep. 1985), pp. 530–531. in Japanese.

[3] K. Sakamura. A Proposal of New Unified Model of Man-Machine Interaction in the BTRON Environment. *Journal of Information Processing Society of Japan*, Vol. 26, No. 11 (Nov. 1985), pp. 1321–1328. in Japanese.

[4] K. Sakamura. Method of Input Japanese Characters in the BTRON Environment. *IPSJ SIG Notes on Japanese Input*, 7-2 (1986), IPSJ, pp. 1–8. in Japanese.

[5] M. Andoh, Y. Imai, and Y. Kushiki. An Implementation of Nucleus Based upon BTRON Specification on an 80286. In *Proceedings of the First Realtime-OS-TRON Technical Workshop* (Apr. 1987), IEICE, pp. 22–30. in Japanese.

[6] J. Iwamura, T. Ishida, Y. Imai, and Y. Kushiki. An Implementation of the Real/Virtual Object Model. In *Proceedings of the Third Realtime-Architecture-TRON Technical Workshop* (Oct. 1987), IEICE, pp. 42–55. in Japanese.

[7] M. Kobayashi, S. Takenouchi, and Y. Kushiki. The Software Structure of Extended Nucleus Based on BTRON Specification. In *Proceedings of the First Realtime-OS-TRON Technical Workshop* (Apr. 1987), IEICE, pp. 31–38. in Japanese.

[8] M. Kobayashi, S. Takenouchi, Y. Kushiki, and K. Sakamura. The Software Structure of Extended Nucleus Based on BTRON Specification. In *Proceedings of FJCC '87 – 1987 Fall Joint Computer Conference* (Dallas, Texas, 1987), pp. 153–158.

[9] Y. Kushiki. A Study on Implementation of Multilingual-processing on BTRON Specification. In *Proceedings of the Third Realtime-Architecture-TRON Technical Workshop* (Oct. 1987), IEICE, pp. 79–80. in Japanese.

[10] Y. Kushiki, M. Andoh, M. Kobayashi, Y. Imai, and K. Sakamura. An Implementation Based upon the BTRON Specification. In *TRON Project 1987* (1987), Springer-Verlag, pp. 113–126.

[11] Y. Kushiki, and K. Sakamura. The Operating System Based upon BTRON Specification on an 80286. *IPSJ SIG Notes on Microcomputer*, 45-4 (Jun. 1987), IPSJ. in Japanese.

[12] Y. Murata. Some Problems for the Input of Chinese Characters in BTRON Environment. In *Proceedings of the Third Realtime-Architecture-TRON Technical Workshop* (Oct. 1987), IEICE, pp. 72–74. in Japanese.

[13] R. T. Myers. Desirable Features for Multilingual Processing. In *Proceedings of the Third Realtime-Architecture-TRON Technical Workshop* (Oct. 1987), IEICE, pp. 75–78.

[14] K. Sakamura. BTRON: An Overview. In *TRON Project 1987* (1987), Springer-Verlag, pp. 75–82.

[15] K. Sakamura. BTRON: Business-oriented Operating System in the TRON Project. In *Proceedings of the Second TRON Project Symposium* (Mar. 1987), TRON Association, pp. 71–95.

[16] K. Sakamura. BTRON: Human-Machine Interface. In *TRON Project 1987* (1987), Springer-Verlag, pp. 83–96.

[17] K. Sakamura. BTRON: The Business-oriented Operating System. *IEEE Micro*, Vol. 7, No. 2 (Apr. 1987), pp. 53–65.

[18] K. Sakamura. The Design Approach of BTRON Human Interface. *Transactions of IEICE*, Vol. J70–D, No. 11 (Nov. 1987), pp. 2039–2046. in Japanese.

[19] K. Sakamura. File Management System in BTRON. In *Proceedings of the First Realtime-OS-TRON Technical Workshop* (Apr. 1987), IEICE, pp. 2–21. in Japanese.

[20] K. Sakamura. Keyboard Unit in the TRON Project. In *Proceedings of the Second TRON Project Symposium* (Mar. 1987), TRON Association, pp. 96–99.

[21] K. Sakamura. Multi-language Character Sets Handling in TAD. In *TRON Project 1987* (1987), Springer-Verlag, pp. 97–111.

[22] K. Sakamura. Multi-language Character Sets Handling in TAD. In *Proceedings of the Third Realtime-Architecture-TRON Technical Workshop* (Oct. 1987), IEICE, pp. 56–69. in Japanese.

[23] K. Sakamura, T. Ohnishi, E. Tange, Y. Kushiki, and K. Oda. BTRON MMI Standardization Project. In *Proceedings of the Second TRON Project Symposium* (Mar. 1987), TRON Association, pp. 100–138. in Japanese.

[24] K. Sakamura, K. Tsurumi, and H. Kato. μBTRON Bus: Design and Evaluation of Musical Data Transfer. In *TRON Project 1987* (1987), Springer-Verlag, pp. 127–138.

[25] S. Tachibana, and K. Sakamura. An Implementation of the TRON Keyboard. In *TRON Project 1987* (1987), Springer-Verlag, pp. 139–150.

[26] Y. Imai, M. Ando, M. Kobayashi, Y. Kushiki, and K. Sakamura. An Implementation Based on the BTRON Specification. In *Proceedings of the 33rd IEEE Computer Society International Conference* (San Francisco, 1988), IEEE, pp. 22–24.

[27] K. Kajimoto, M. Shimizu, and Y. Kushiki. A Study on Video Manager of the BTRON Specification. In *TRON Project 1988* (1988), Springer-Verlag, pp. 109–118.

[28] J. Kubota, S. Kabasawa, and Y. Kushiki. An Implementation of Japanese Language Processing in the Multilingual Environment. *IPSJ SIG Notes on Microcomputer*, 49-3 (Feb. 1988), IPSJ. in Japanese.

[29] T. Matsuse, and K. Sakamura. Features of the Standard TAD for Interchanging the Data of Application Programs. *Proceedings of TRON Technical Workshop*, Vol. 1, No. 2 (Oct. 1988), pp. 1–9. in Japanese.

[30] Y. Mimura, and K. Masuda. Design of Application Programs Based on the Real/Virtual Object Model. *Proceedings of TRON Technical Workshop*, Vol. 1, No. 2 (Oct. 1988), pp. 11–19. in Japanese.

[31] R. T. Myers, and K. Sakamura. Natural Language Translation Services in BTRON. In *TRON Project 1988* (1988), Springer-Verlag, pp. 93–108.

[32] K. Sakamura. Design Approach of BTRON Human Interface. *Systems and Computers in Japan*, Vol. 19, No. 12 (Dec. 1988), pp. 35–44.

[33] K. Sakamura. TACL: TRON Application Control-flow Language. In *TRON Project 1988* (1988), Springer-Verlag, pp. 79–92.

[34] K. Sakamura, K. Tsurumi, and H. Kato. Applying the μBTRON Bus to a Music LAN. *IEEE Micro*, Vol. 8, No. 2 (Apr. 1988), pp. 60–66.

[35] H. Takada, and K. Sakamura. Configuration Management and Version Control in TIPE System. *Proceedings of TRON Technical Workshop*, Vol. 1, No. 2 (Oct. 1988), pp. 21–31. in Japanese.

[36] H. Takada, and K. Sakamura. The Type Mechanism of the TIPE/L Programming Language. In *TRON Project 1988* (1988), Springer-Verlag, pp. 119–132.

[37] K. Toriya. A Proposal of Integrated Software Development Environment for BTRON Operating System. *Proceedings of TRON Technical Workshop*, Vol. 1, No. 1 (Jun. 1988), pp. 19–33. in Japanese.

[38] K. Tsurumi, A. Kanuma, and K. Sakamura. Applying of μBTRON Bus to Music LAN. In *Proceedings of the Fourth Realtime-Architecture-TRON Technical Workshop* (Feb. 1988), IEICE, pp. 28–32. in Japanese.

[39] K. Kajimoto, F. Nakayama, T. Nonomura, Y. Imai, S. Isoda, and Y. Kushiki. New-Media Document (NewDoc) and Dynamic Navigation on the BTRON Specification. In *Proceedings of the 34th IEEE Computer Society International Conference — COMPCON Spring 1989* (1989), IEEE Computer Society Press, pp. 40–42.

[40] K. Kajimoto, T. Nonomura, Y. Imai, and Y. Kushiki. Dynamic Navigation and New-Media Document Its Concept and an Implementation on the BTRON Specification. *Proceedings of TRON Technical Workshop*, Vol. 2, No. 1 (Apr. 1989), pp. 41–52. in Japanese.

[41] N. Koshizuka, H. Takada, M. Saito, Y. Saito, and K. Sakamura. Implementation Issues of the TACL/TULS Language System on BTRON. In *TRON Project 1989* (1989), Springer-Verlag, pp. 113–132.

[42] Y. Kushiki, and M. Shimizu. The Realization and the Evaluation of an Operating System Based on the BTRON Specification Offering the Unified Human Interface. *Journal of Information Processing Society of Japan*, Vol. 30, No. 5 (May 1989), pp. 544–552. in Japanese.

[43] T. Matsumoto. BTRON Mail System Design. *Proceedings of TRON Technical Workshop*, Vol. 2, No. 1 (Apr. 1989), pp. 11–19. in Japanese.

[44] Y. Mimura, and M. Ando. Design of Flexible Hypermedia System Based on BTRON. *Proceedings of TRON Technical Workshop*, Vol. 2, No. 2 (Jul. 1989), pp. 51–60. in Japanese.

[45] Y. Mimura, and M. Ando. An Object-oriented Extension of the Real-Object/Virtual-Object Model. *Proceedings of TRON Technical Workshop*, Vol. 2, No. 3 (Oct. 1989), pp. 31–42. in Japanese.

[46] K. Oda, and K. Sakamura. Educational Aspects of BTRON. In *Proceedings of the IFIP TC 3/WG 3.1 Working Conference* (Raykjavik, Iceland, Jun. 1989), IFIP, pp. 65–72.

[47] K. Sakamura, Y. Kushiki, and K. Oda. An Overview of the BTRON/286 Specification. *IEEE Micro*, Vol. 9, No. 3 (Jun. 1989), pp. 14–25.

[48] K. Sakamura, K. Tamai, K. Tanaka, S. Tsunoda, K. Tsurumi, and M. Kaneko. The μBTRON Bus: Function and Applications. In *TRON Project 1989* (1989), Springer-Verlag, pp. 101–112.

[49] M. Shimizu, Y. Kushiki, and K. Sakamura. Operating System Based on the BTRON Specifications. *Microprocessors and Microsystems*, Vol. 13, No. 8 (Oct. 1989), pp. 525–535.

[50] K. Sugisita, T. Tsubosaki, M. Ito, and M. Shimizu. BTRON Communication Facility and Dialogue Monitoring. *Proceedings of TRON Technical Workshop*, Vol. 2, No. 3 (Oct. 1989), pp. 19–29. in Japanese.

[51] H. Takada, and K. Sakamura. The Data Portability and the TULS/TACL Environment in TRON. *The Theory of Numerical Information Environment and Its Development* (Jun. 1989). in Japanese.

[52] N. Enoki, H. Oka, A. Yoneda, and M. Ando. Communication Terminal for Heterogeneous Network Based on BTRON HMI. In *TRON Project 1990* (1990), Springer-Verlag, pp. 391–408.

[53] T. Inada. BTRON Applied to JAL Computer Reservation System. *Proceedings of TRON Technical Workshop*, Vol. 2, No. 4 (Feb. 1990), pp. 47–55. in Japanese.

[54] T. Ishida, T. Nakatsuka, M. Morita, and M. Andoh. The Construction of the Supporting Environment for BTRON Application Development. *Proceedings of TRON Technical Workshop*, Vol. 2, No. 4 (Feb. 1990), pp. 35–46. in Japanese.

[55] K. Kajimoto, and T. Nonomura. A Study on a Hypermedia Editor on BTRON1 Specification Operating System. In *TRON Project 1990* (1990), Springer-Verlag, pp. 119–130.

[56] N. Koshizuka, N. Inoue, H. Takada, N. Nishio, and K. Sakamura. Interface Manager Based on Abstract Event for BTRON. *Proceedings of TRON Technical Workshop*, Vol. 2, No. 4 (Feb. 1990), pp. 1–21. in Japanese.

[57] K. Masuda, M. Ando, Y. Mimura, and T. Hashizume. Auto-operation Capability on BTRON Specification. In *Proceedings of the 40th National Convention of IPSJ* (Mar. 1990), IPSJ, pp. 769–770.

[58] K. Masuda, and M. Andoh. Auto-operation Capability on BTRON1 Specification. *Proceedings of TRON Technical Workshop*, Vol. 2, No. 4 (Feb. 1990), pp. 23–34. in Japanese.

[59] T. Matsuse, and C.-C. Ku. A Study for Implementation of the Multi-language Processing Based on the BTRON Specification OS. *Proceedings of TRON Technical Workshop*, Vol. 3, No. 1 (Jun. 1990), pp. 17–27. in Japanese.

[60] M. Morita, T. Ishida, Y. Nakatsuka, and M. Ando. Development Support Tools for Applications Which Have Graphical User Interface. In *Proceedings of the 40th National Convention of IPSJ* (Mar. 1990), IPSJ, pp. 927–928.

[61] M. Saitoh. Mail Flow and Processing Time Model in Office Environment Using BTRON. Master's thesis, Graduate School of University of Tokyo, Division of Science, Jan. 1990.

[62] K. Sakamura. Design Policy of the Operating System Based on the BTRON2 Specification. In *TRON Project 1990* (1990), Springer-Verlag, pp. 103–118.

[63] M. Kobayashi, and Y. Kushiki. An Update on BTRON-Specification OS Development. In *Proceedings of the Eighth TRON Project Symposium* (Nov. 1991), IEEE Computer Society Press, pp. 132–140.

[64] N. Koshizuka. A Distributed Shared Memory Model for Window System Construction and Its Extension to a General Shared Memory Framework. Master's thesis, Graduate School of University of Tokyo, Division of Science, Feb. 1991.

[65] N. Koshizuka, H. Takada, and K. Sakamura. Window Shared Data Pool. *IPSJ SIG Notes on Operating System*, 52-2 (Sep. 1991), IPSJ. in Japanese.

[66] N. Koshizuka, H. Takada, and K. Sakamura. Window Shared Data Pool: A New Window System for BTRON2. In *Proceedings of the Eighth TRON Project Symposium* (Nov. 1991), IEEE Computer Society Press, pp. 151–168.

[67] T. Miyake, N. Sakamoto, and K. Saitoh. A Consideration for Compiler System Using BTRON Object Format. *Proceedings of TRON Technical Workshop*, Vol. 4, No. 1 (Jul. 1991), pp. 27–38. in Japanese.

[68] N. Osawa. 2B: An Operating System Based on BTRON2 Specification. In *Proceedings of the Eighth TRON Project Symposium* (Nov. 1991), IEEE Computer Society Press, pp. 141–150.

[69] N. Osawa. The Design and Implementation of 2B – An Operating System Based on BTRON2 Specification. *Proceedings of TRON Technical Workshop*, Vol. 4, No. 1 (Jul. 1991), pp. 39–52. in Japanese.

[70] A. Tsuge, and Y. Mimura. An Implementation of Window Auto-redrawing System on BTRON1 Specification Operating System. *Proceedings of TRON Technical Workshop*, Vol. 4, No. 1 (Jul. 1991), pp. 17–26. in Japanese.

[71] M. Uematsu, N. Koshizuka, H. Takada, and K. Sakamura. BTRON Multilingual Panel Manager. *Proceedings of TRON Technical Workshop*, Vol. 4, No. 1 (Jul. 1991), pp. 1–15. in Japanese.

[72] Y. Ueshima, M. Zeze, Y. Yamamoto, and K. Sakamura. A Fundamental Study on Picture Motion TAD on BTRON Specification Operating System. In *Proceedings of the Eighth TRON Project Symposium* (Nov. 1991), IEEE Computer Society Press, pp. 169–176.

[73] K. Hukui, Y. Ishiguro, M. Inoue, K. Ishino, and A. Tsuge. An Implementation of Resume System on BTRON1 Specification Operating System. *Proceedings of TRON Technical Workshop*, Vol. 5, No. 1 (Oct. 1992), pp. 19–28. in Japanese.

[74] T. Kawashima, K. Oohara, K. Tanaka, K. Tamai, and Y. Yamada. LSI for Local Area Network Controller. In *Proceedings of the Fall National Convention of IEICE* (Sep. 1992), IEICE. in Japanese.

[75] N. Koshizuka, and K. Sakamura. Software Architecture and Application Program Interface Model for the BTRON GUI Shell. Tech. Rep. 92-4, Department of Information Science, Faculty of Science, University of Tokyo, Jun. 1992.

[76] K. Ohhara, Y. Shimizu, and K. Tamai. A Consideration of Repeater. In *Proceedings of the Fall National Convention of IEICE* (Sep. 1992), IEICE. in Japanese.

[77] K. Sato, and S. Itou. A Classroom Network on a BTRON1-Specification OS. *Proceedings of TRON Technical Workshop*, Vol. 5, No. 1 (Oct. 1992), pp. 9–18. in Japanese.

[78] K. Tanaka, Y. Shimizu, K. Tamai, S. Tsunoda, and H. Kato. Performance Evaluation of the μ-BTRON Bus. In *Proceedings of the Ninth TRON Project Symposium* (Dec. 1992), IEEE Computer Society Press, pp. 40–45.

[79] Y. Yamada, K. Masuda, T. Nonomura, and K. Yamanaka. Hypermedia Using Public Transmission Line – Facsimile Function on BTRON1 Specification Operating System –. *Proceedings of TRON Technical Workshop*, Vol. 4, No. 3 (Mar. 1992), pp. 25–34. in Japanese.

[80] N. Kimura. A Study of a Scripting Language and Application Program Collaboration in Graphical User Interface Environment. Master's thesis, Graduate School of University of Tokyo, Division of Science, Feb. 1993.

[81] R. Kondo. The Design of BTRON Human Machine Interface for Groupware Systems. Master's thesis, Graduate School of University of Tokyo, Division of Science, Feb. 1993.

[82] R. Kondo, N. Koshizuka, H. Takada, and K. Sakamura. An Extension of BTRON HMI Specification for Multi-user Applications. *Proceedings of TRON Technical Workshop*, Vol. 5, No. 2 (Mar. 1993), pp. 31–37. in Japanese.

[83] N. Koshizuka. *BTRON2 Window System: A Window System Facilitating Cooperation among GUI Applications in Distributed Environments.* PhD thesis, Graduate School of University of Tokyo, Division of Science, Dec. 1993.

[84] N. Koshizuka, and K. Sakamura. Highly Responsive Implementation of the BTRON2 Window System. In *Proceedings of the Tenth TRON Project Symposium* (Dec. 1993), IEEE Computer Society Press, pp. 78–93.

[85] N. Koshizuka, and K. Sakamura. Window Real-Objects: a Distributed Shared Memory for the Distributed Implementation of GUI Applications. In *Proceedings of the ACM Symposium on User Interface Software and Technology* (Nov. 1993). 237–247.

[86] A. Matsui, N. Koshizuka, and M. Kobayashi. How to Educate a True Beginner about Computers. In *Proceedings of the Tenth TRON Project Symposium* (Dec. 1993), IEEE Computer Society Press, p. 95.

[87] N. Osawa, and N. Kimura. A Programming Language: Kinari. *Proceedings of TRON Technical Workshop*, Vol. 5, No. 2 (Mar. 1993), pp. 39–50. in Japanese.

[88] H. Takahashi, K. Yamamura, and K. Sato. Sound Environment on BTRON1 Specification OS. *Proceedings of TRON Technical Workshop*, Vol. 5, No. 2 (Mar. 1993), pp. 19–30. in Japanese.

[89] K. Tamai, K. Tanaka, and K. Ohhara. An Implementation of Communication Software for a Real-Time LAN and Its Performance Evaluation. In *Proceedings of the Spring National Convention of IEICE* (Mar. 1993), IEICE, pp. 3–240. in Japanese.

[90] M. Uematsu. A Study on Generic Writing System of Multilingual Computer. Master's thesis, Graduate School of University of Tokyo, Division of Science, Feb. 1993.

[91] M. Uematsu, N. Koshizuka, and K. Sakamura. A Proposal of Multilingual Representaion Mechanism on BTRON. *Proceedings of TRON Technical Workshop*, Vol. 5, No. 2 (Mar. 1993), pp. 1–18. in Japanese.

[92] N. Koshizuka, and K. Sakamura. Design and Implementation of Multiuser Interface System Based on the Shared Interaction Object Model. *Transactions of Information Processing Society of Japan*, Vol. 35, No. 9 (Sep. 1994), pp. 1779–1793. in Japanese.

[93] N. Koshizuka, and K. Sakamura. Flexible User Interface Independence Functions in Shared Interaction Object Architecture. In *Proceedings of Groupware '94* (Nov. 1994), IPSJ, pp. 37–42.

[94] N. Koshizuka, and K. Sakamura. Implementation of Label Metaphor Using Shared Interaction Object Architecture. In *Proceedings of the Eleventh TRON Project Symposium* (Dec. 1994), IEEE Computer Society Press, pp. 52–62.

[95] N. Koshizuka, and K. Sakamura. Shared Interaction Object Architecture: A GUI Architecture Facilitating Cooperation among GUI Applications in Distributed Environments. In *Proceedings of Workshop on Interactive Systems and Software (WISS'94)* (Dec. 1994), Japan Society for Software Science and Technology, Kindaikagaku-Sha, pp. 65–74. in Japanese.

[96] A. Matsui. The Current Status of the BTRON Subprojects and their Future. *Journal of Information Processing Society of Japan*, Vol. 35, No. 10 (Oct. 1994), pp. 910–917. in Japanese.

[97] T. Tanuma. A Study on a Visual Shell to Handle OS Resources by Direct Manipulation. Master's thesis, Graduate School of University of Tokyo, Division of Science, Feb. 1994.

[98] T. Tanuma, N. Koshizuka, and K. Sakamura. Design and Implementations of Tools for Manipulating OS Resources on BTRON. *Proceedings of TRON Technical Workshop*, Vol. 6, No. 1 (Mar. 1994), pp. 27–36. in Japanese.

[99] N. Koshizuka, and K. Sakamura. Multiuser Interface Architecture Using Structured Distributed Shared Memories. In *Proceedings of the IFIP TC2/WG2.7 Working Conference on Engineering for Human-Computer Interaction (EHCI '95)* (Aug. 1995), IFIP, Chapman & Hall, pp. 271–290.

[100] N. Koshizuka, and K. Sakamura. The Shared Interaction Object Architeture: Integration of Advanced GUI Techniques in Distributed Environments. In *Proceedings of the 1995 East-West International Conference on Human-Computer Interaction (EWHCI)* (Jul. 1995), International Centre for Scientific and Technical Information, pp. II–143–159. (also appeared on *Human-Computer Interaction (5th International Conference, EWHCI '95, Selected Papers)*, pp. 149–165, Springer Verlag (LNCS 1015)).

[101] K. Sakamura. Multilingual Computing as a Global Communications Infrastracture. In *Proceedings of the Twelfth TRON Project International Symposium* (Nov.-Dec. 1995), IEEE Computer Society Press, pp. 2–14.

[102] K. Sakamura, T. Tamura, H. Katayama, and A. Yamaguchi. Panel Session: Multilingual Computing Project ata the University of Tokyo. In *Proceedings of the Twelfth TRON Project International Symposium* (Nov.-Dec. 1995), IEEE Computer Society Press, p. 98.

[103] Y. Sasaki. Data Fornat Extension Based on Programmable Interface. Master's thesis, Graduate School of University of Tokyo, Division of Science, Feb. 1995.

[104] N. Koshizuka, and K. Sakamura. A GUI Architecture Facilitating Cooperation among Software Components in Distributed Environments. *Computer Software*, Vol. 13, No. 3 (May 1996), pp. 49–64. (in Japanese).

[105] Y. Shigesada. Research of VACL: A visual script language system which controls and extends applications on a graphical user interface environment. Master's thesis, Graduate School of University of Tokyo, Division of Science, Feb. 1996.

[106] T. Usaka. A Large Scaled Multi-User Virtual Environment System for Digital Museums. Master's thesis, Graduate School of University of Tokyo, Division of Science, Feb. 1996.

[107] S. Yura. Real Time Client for Digital Museum. Master's thesis, Graduate School of University of Tokyo, Division of Science, Feb. 1996.

4.6 HMI

[1] N. Koshizuka, R. Kondo, and K. Sakamura. A Proposal of Special User Interface Parts Model. *Proceedings of TRON Technical Workshop*, Vol. 4, No. 3 (Mar. 1992), pp. 35–62. in Japanese.

[2] A. Marcus. The Future of Advanced User Interface in Product Design. In *Proceedings of the Ninth TRON Project Symposium* (Dec. 1992), IEEE Computer Society Press, pp. 14–21.

[3] K. Sakamura. Human Interface with Computers in Everyday Life. In *Proceedings of the Ninth TRON Project Symposium* (Dec. 1992), IEEE Computer Society Press, pp. 2–12.

[4] T. Fujii. Problems of HMI Design Analysis by the Semiotic Approach. In *Proceedings of the Tenth TRON Project Symposium* (Dec. 1993), IEEE Computer Society Press, pp. 29–36.

[5] T. Muto. How Design guidelines Should Evolve? - Methodology to Update the Guidelines in the TRON project -. In *Proceedings of the Tenth TRON Project Symposium* (Dec. 1993), IEEE Computer Society Press, pp. 37–40.

[6] K. Sakamura. Building Human Interface for Computerized Environments. In *Proceedings of the Tenth TRON Project Symposium* (Dec. 1993), IEEE Computer Society Press, pp. 21–28.

[7] T. Yamada. Human-Machine Interface for Electronic Equipment. In *Proceedings of the Tenth TRON Project Symposium* (Dec. 1993), IEEE Computer Society Press, pp. 45–46.

[8] T. Yamaoka, and H. Tamura. Information Display Method and Process Considerations in the TRON/GUI. In *Proceedings of the Tenth TRON Project Symposium* (Dec. 1993), IEEE Computer Society Press, pp. 41–44.

[9] N. Koshizuka, T. Mutoh, and K. Sakamura. TRON Human-Machine Interface Specifications for Everyday Life. *Journal of Information Processing Society of Japan*, Vol. 35, No. 10 (Oct. 1994), pp. 934–939. in Japanese.

[10] N. Koshizuka, T. Muto, and K. Sakamura. Human-Machine Interface Specifications in the "Computer Everywhere" Age. In *Proceedings of the Twelfth TRON Project International Symposium* (Nov.-Dec. 1995), IEEE Computer Society Press, pp. 87–96.

4.7 EnableWare

[1] K. Sakamura. Concept of TRON Enableware. In *Proceedings of the TRON Enableware Symposium '88* (Jul. 1988), pp. 1–3. in Japanese.

[2] N. Kimura, and K. Sakamura. Design and Implementation of Enableware Specification for BTRON. *Proceedings of TRON Technical Workshop*, Vol. 3, No. 1 (Jun. 1990), pp. 1–15. in Japanese.

[3] K. Sakamura. Coming Computer Society and the Support for the Handicapped. *Shitai Fujiyuu Kyouiku*, No. 98 (1990), pp. 4–23. in Japanese.

[4] K. Sakamura, and N. Kimura. Functions of BTRON Enableware. In *Proceedings of the TRON Enableware Symposium '90* (Mar. 1990), pp. 1–16. in Japanese.

[5] S. Hasegawa, and Y. Tsukuda. Braille Computer with Integrated Display and Keyboard Unit — Display Frames on Top of Keys —. In *Proceedings of the TRON Enableware Symposium '92* (Dec. 1992), pp. 27–34.

[6] S. Hasegawa, and Y. Tsukuda. Braille Computer with Integrated Display and Keyboard Unit (Display Frames on Top of Keys). *Proceedings of TRON Technical Workshop*, Vol. 5, No. 1 (Oct. 1992), pp. 1–9. in Japanese.

[7] H. Kawamura. Devises for the Motory Disabled in Using Word Processors. In *Proceedings of the TRON Enableware Symposium '92* (Dec. 1992), pp. 2–9. in Japanese.

[8] H. Kawamura. Information Offering to the Visually Disabled — From the Investigation of the Next Generation System of IFLA —. In *Proceedings of the TRON Enableware Symposium '92* (Dec. 1992), pp. 35–36. in Japanese.

[9] N. Koshizuka, M. Uematsu, N. Kimura, and K. Sakamura. Design and Implementation of the Enableware Specification – A Human-Machine Interface for Physically Challenged People. In *Proceedings of the Ninth TRON Project Symposium* (Dec. 1992), IEEE Computer Society Press, pp. 23–39.

[10] N. Koshizuka, and K. Sakamura. An Overview of the BTRON Enableware. In *Proceedings of the TRON Enableware Symposium '92* (Dec. 1992), pp. 12–21. in Japanese.

[11] A. Takamura. Devices Required for the Visually Disabled. In *Proceedings of the TRON Enableware Symposium '92* (Dec. 1992), pp. 37–40. in Japanese.

[12] T. Yamada. Applications of Personal Computers in the Education of the Auditory Disabled. In *Proceedings of the TRON Enableware Symposium '92* (Dec. 1992), pp. 10–11. in Japanese.

[13] T. Yoshiizumi. A Problem on Information Processing for the Visually Disabled. In *Proceedings of the TRON Enableware Symposium '92* (Dec. 1992), pp. 24–26. in Japanese.

[14] S. Fukushima. View Ahead: The Technology for Deaf-Blind Individuals. In *Proceedings of the TRON Enableware Symposium '93* (Dec. 1993), pp. 24–28. in Japanese.

[15] S. Fukushima. View Ahead: The Technology for Deaf-Blind Individuals. In *Proceedings of the Tenth TRON Project Symposium* (Dec. 1993), IEEE Computer Society Press, pp. 169–172.

[16] H. Kawamura. Copyright Issues and the Development of Information Access Devices for the Visually Handicapped. In *Proceedings of the TRON Enableware Symposium '93* (Dec. 1993), pp. 49–51. in Japanese.

[17] K. Kawamura, and K. Sakamura. BTRON Speech Sound User Interface. In *Proceedings of the TRON Enableware Symposium '93* (Dec. 1993), pp. 14–22. in Japanese.

[18] A. Kohama. The Current State and a Prospect of the Use of Computers for the Limbs-Paralyzed. In *Proceedings of the TRON Enableware Symposium '93* (Dec. 1993), pp. 8–13. in Japanese.

[19] K. Sakamura. Enableware: Adaptive Technologies for Disabled People on the TRON Architecture. In *Proceedings of the Tenth TRON Project Symposium* (Dec. 1993), IEEE Computer Society Press, pp. 166–168.

[20] K. Sakamura. Enableware and Ubiquitous Computing Environments. In *Proceedings of the TRON Enableware Symposium '93* (Dec. 1993), pp. 2–5. in Japanese.

[21] T. Takaoka. Issues of Communication and Broadcasting for the Auditory Disabled. In *Proceedings of the TRON Enableware Symposium '93* (Dec. 1993), pp. 43–48. in Japanese.

[22] E. Tatematsu. How Do We Understand Mentally Handicapped Children. In *Proceedings of the TRON Enableware Symposium '93* (Dec. 1993), pp. 30–42. in Japanese.

[23] Y. Eda. What Does a Information Communications Network Bring Physically Handicapped People. In *Proceedings of the TRON Enableware Symposium '94* (Dec. 1994), pp. 8–12. in Japanese.

[24] H. Mori. Another Network: Control of Domestic Electrical Products by the Use of BTRON and Network. In *Proceedings of the TRON Enableware Symposium '94* (Dec. 1994), pp. 2–7. in Japanese.

[25] H. Shima. Physically Handicapped People and Nifty-serve. In *Proceedings of the TRON Enableware Symposium '94* (Dec. 1994), pp. 13–18. in Japanese.

[26] T. Takizawa. Participation in Computer Network and Cooperation. In *Proceedings of the TRON Enableware Symposium '94* (Dec. 1994), pp. 22–26. in Japanese.

[27] The TRON Enableware Working Group. BTRON Enableware. In *Proceedings of the TRON Enableware Symposium '94* (Dec. 1994), pp. 27–34. in Japanese.

[28] T. Yoshiizumi. Visually Handicapped People's Practical Use of a Communications Network with Personal Computer. In *Proceedings of the TRON Enableware Symposium '94* (Dec. 1994), pp. 19–21. in Japanese.

[29] Sakamura Laboratory. BTRON with Multi-interfaces. In *Proceedings of the TRON Enableware Symposium '95* (Dec. 1995), pp. 1–5. in Japanese.

[30] Y. Takamine. A Decade of the Handicapped and Its Evaluation. In *Proceedings of the TRON Enableware Symposium '95* (Dec. 1995), pp. 6–11. in Japanese.

4.8 MTRON/HFDS

[1] K. Sakamura. Design of MTRON: Construction of the HFDS. In *TRON Project 1988* (1988), Springer-Verlag, pp. 21–32.

[2] K. Sakamura. TRON As a Highly Functional Distributed System. *Systems, Control and Information*, Vol. 33, No. 1 (Jan. 1989), pp. 8–14. in Japanese.

[3] K. Sakamura. Programmable Interface Design in HFDS. In *TRON Project 1990* (1990), Springer-Verlag, pp. 3–22.

[4] E. E. Bowles. A Routing Update Mechanism for Networks with Highly Mobile Hosts. Master's thesis, Graduate School of University of Tokyo, Division of Science, Feb. 1991.

Author Index

Notes

http://www.computer.org

IEEE Computer Society Press Publications

The world-renowned Computer Society Press publishes, promotes, and distributes a wide variety of authoritative computer science and engineering texts. These books are available in two formats: 100 percent original material by authors preeminent in their field who focus on relevant topics and cutting-edge research, and reprint collections consisting of carefully selected groups of previously published papers with accompanying original introductory and explanatory text.

Submission of proposals: For guidelines and information on CS Press books, send e-mail to cs.books@computer.org or write to the Acquisitions Editor, IEEE Computer Society Press, P.O. Box 3014, 10662 Los Vaqueros Circle, Los Alamitos, CA 90720-1314. Telephone +1 714-821-8380. FAX +1 714-761-1784.

IEEE Computer Society Press Proceedings

The Computer Society Press also produces and actively promotes the proceedings of more than 130 acclaimed international conferences each year in multimedia formats that include hard and softcover books, CD-ROMs, videos, and on-line publications.

For information on CS Press proceedings, send e-mail to cs.books@computer.org or write to Proceedings, IEEE Computer Society Press, P.O. Box 3014, 10662 Los Vaqueros Circle, Los Alamitos, CA 90720-1314. Telephone +1 714-821-8380. FAX +1 714-761-1784.

Additional information regarding the Computer Society, conferences and proceedings, CD-ROMs, videos, and books can also be accessed from our web site at www.computer.org.